In the Name of Social Democracy

In the Name of
Social Democracy

The Great Transformation,
1945 to the Present

———————◆———————

GERASSIMOS MOSCHONAS

Translated by Gregory Elliott

VERSO
London • New York

This book is supported by the French Ministry for Foreign Affairs as part of the Burgess Programme, headed for the French Embassy in London by the Institut Français du Royaume Uni

ǁ institut français

This edition (revised and updated from the French original)
first published by Verso 2002
© Verso 2002
Translation © Gregory Elliott 2001
First published as *La social-démocratie de 1945 à nos jours*
© Montchrestien, E.J.A. 1994

1 3 5 7 9 10 8 6 4 2

Verso
UK: 6 Meard Street, London W1F 0EG
USA: 180 Varick Street, New York, NY 10014–4606
www.versobooks.com

Verso is the imprint of New Left Books

ISBN 1–85984–639–4
ISBN 1–85984–346–8 (pbk)

British Library Cataloguing in Publication Data
A catalogue record for this book is available from the British Library

Library of Congress Cataloging-in-Publication Data
A catalog record for this book is available from the Library of Congress

Typeset by SetSystems Ltd, Saffron Walden, Essex
Printed by Biddles Ltd, Guildford and King's Lynn

Society must be understood starting from its weakest link.

> (Jean-Paul Fitoussi and Pierre Rosanvallon,
> *Le nouvel âge des inégalités*)

Reform can best be made effective and durable when tactics are able to link the interests and fate of the poor with the fortunes of the better-off . . . not ethics, but politics explains it.

> (Peter Baldwin, *The Politics of Social Solidarity*)

Contents

14 The Unions and Left Oppositions   251

15 The European Union, Globalization and 'No Alternative'   261

16 The Party of European Socialists and Socialist Co-operation
    in Europe   269

Part V: Social Democracy in Historical Perspective   287

17 On the Verge of an Identity Change   289

18 A Moment of Strategic Pessimism?   305

    Conclusions   313

    Epilogue   327

    Select Bibliography   331

    Postscript   351

    Index   361

Tables

Principal Abbreviations

CDU	Christlich Demokratische Union (German Christian Democratic Party)
CPS	Confederation of Socialist Parties of the European Community
DC	Democrazia Christiana (Italian Christian Democratic Party)
DNA	Det Norske Arbeiderparti (Norwegian Labour Party)
EPP	European People's Party
FDP	Freie Demokratische Partei (German Free Democratic Party)
FN	Front National (France)
FPÖ	Freiheitliche Partei Österreichs (Austrian Freedom Party)
IU	Izquierda Unida (United Left, Spain)
KKE	Kommounistiko Komma Elladas (Greek Communist Party)
ÖVP	Österreichs Volkspartei (Austrian People's Party)
PASOK	Panellinio Sosialistiko Kinima (Pan-Hellenic Socialist Movement)
PCF	Parti Communiste Français (French Communist Party)
PCI	Partito Comunista Italiano (Italian Communist Party)
PDS	Partei des Demokratischen Socialismus (Democratic Socialist Party, Germany)
PDS	Partito Democratico della Sinistra (Democratic Party of the Left, Italy)
PES	Party of European Socialists
PS	Parti Socialiste (Socialist Party, France)
PSB	Parti Socialiste Belge (Belgian Socialist Party)
PSI	Partito Socialista Italiano (Italian Socialist Party)
PSOE	Partido Socialista Obrero Español (Spanish Socialist Workers Party)

PSP   Partido Socialista Português (Portuguese Socialist Party)

PvdA   Partij van de Arbeid (Labour Party, Holland)

SAP   Social demokratiska Arbetarepartiet (Swedish Social-Democratic Party)

SD   Social demokratiet (Danish Social-Democratic Party)

SF   Socialistik Folkeparti (Socialist People's Party, Denmark)

SFIO   Section Française de l'Internationale Ouvrière (France)

SPD   Sozialdemokratische Partei Deutschlands (German Social-Democratic Party)

SPÖ   Sozialistische Partei Österreichs (Austrian Socialist Party, Austrian Social-Democratic Party since 1991)

Preface

A first version of this book was published in France in 1994 by Montchrestien as *La Social-démocratie de 1945 à nos jours*. The original ambition of the
English edition was to offer an updated translation of it. But as work
progressed, that objective underwent significant alteration, and I have
expanded my horizons considerably. It is always in the act of writing that a
book is produced and, at the same time, transformed and unveiled. In
truth, the present work is *new* and different, but the themes and problematic it develops are very closely related to those presented more succinctly
in the French. While there is no need for the reader to refer to it, it is
worth indicating that the French text is not simply a shorter version of the
current work, although it is that too.

Six years later, the 'change' in social democracy has become the focal
point of our analysis. The present study does still seek to provide an
overview of the evolution of social democracy, particularly since the Second
World War, but the main emphasis is on social democracy today – on what
(to adopt Karl Polanyi's well-known phrase) we regard as a 'great transformation'. Although the foundations and reference points on which the
historical social-democratic movement was constructed are neither totally
shaken nor eroded, social democracy is living through a change of epoch.
This explains the book's subtitle.

The constraints inherent in any publication have obliged me to disaggre-
gate certain aspects of the social-democratic phenomenon for the purposes
of examining them more closely. I have therefore set aside a detailed study
of socialism in southern Europe – something undertaken, in succinct but
incomplete fashion, in the French edition (a very detailed examination of
the French case was the subject of my doctoral thesis in 1990). This basic
choice derived from a concern not to exceed the stipulated word length.
But another reason informed my decision and explains this lacuna, which
is unquestionably a major one. Although they belong to the same great
European socialist/social-democratic family, the parties of southern Europe
are less and less strictly tied as political forms to the binary opposition
between the 'social-democratic' and the 'non-social-democratic'. In and
through a dual dynamic of convergence, the socialisms of the south are
converging with the more classical social democracies, which are themselves
undergoing 'de-social-democratization'. The effect is to reduce the old
contrasts and narrow the gaps characteristic of a still recent past. Thus,
the 'opposition' between southern socialism and more classical social

democracy (conceived as an opposition between 'logical types') is in part –
but only in part – diluted. Apart from the space constraints on an already
long book, this is the main reason for not examining southern European
socialism in detail.

Obviously, perception of social democracy in terms of a 'model' – hence
in opposition to that which is not social-democratic (*omnis determinatio est
negatio*) – is central in what follows; and this only serves to underline the
lacuna in question. But such a perception serves as an instrument to guide
the analysis, and is not to be taken for the analysis itself. In any event some
'harmonics' are missing in the score of this book, and they are not
insignificant. Even so, the analysis that follows, however partial, cannot but
engage with some of the more general meanings of social democracy, and
cannot avoid providing an overview and suggesting a global logic. That is
certainly its ambition, possibly its strength, and definitely its weakness. And
that is what renders it anxious about its own certainties.

A book is never a personal matter. I wish to thank a number of colleagues
who provided valuable comments on drafts of various chapters of the work:
Eustache Kouvélakis, University of Wolverhampton, Chapters 14–18; Gérard Grunberg, Institut d'Études Politiques (Paris), Chapter 7; Sia Anagnos-
topoulou, Cyprus University, Chapters 17–18 and Introduction.

I wish also to thank Pierre Avril, University of Paris-II, who directed my
attention to the PES. Research on the PES (Chapter 16) would not have
been possible without the financial support of the University of Paris-II and
the French Ministry of Foreign Affairs.

I owe a particular debt to Dominique Vivien-Zamboulis, who has proof-
read the French manuscript.

Gregory Elliott translated this book with deep knowledge and great
finesse. Not only has he produced an impeccable translation, he has also
devoted an extraordinary amount of time and effort to editing footnote
references and quoting available English editions of the works I refer to. I
thank him very much.

Last but not least, I would like to thank the people at Verso. Their
goodwill, immense understanding, and patience in the face of significant
delays, alone made production of this book possible. I am very indebted to
Sebastian Budgen, who provided his constant support in the realisation of
this project.

The people closest to me already know how grateful I am to them.

Introduction

That admirable Revolution, to which we owe our being, is not
over . . . we remain actors in it . . . the same men are still doing
battle with the same enemies. . . . You have stayed the same. We
have not changed.

(Georges Clémenceau, speech given in 1891)[1]

'Political choice usually takes the form of a choice between two alternatives,' wrote Maurice Duverger in his classic work on *Political Parties*: 'A
duality of parties does not always exist, but almost always there is a duality
of tendencies. Every policy implies a choice between *two kinds of solution*.'[2]
The notion that political competition inevitably tends to a duality of
tendencies is not new. 'In truth,' wrote Thomas Jefferson in 1823, 'the
parties of Whig and Tory are those of nature. They exist in all countries,
whether called by those names, or by those of Aristocrats and Democrats,
Côte Droite and Côte Gauche, Ultras and Radicals, Serviles and Liberals.'[3]

Obviously, far from being permanent, the identity of any political current
and cleavage – in other words, the identity of any duality of tendencies – is
changing. Political identities are simply the invariably uncertain and contested result of 'multiple struggles' over positioning – ideological, institutional or class positioning.[4] Identities are *events*, major events of a certain
duration, not 'essences'. Once constituted and consolidated, the political
and electoral market likewise possesses a certain duration. As a result, it
tends to stabilize, at least for a period of time.

In fact, for a long period the European party systems – and hence the
main political alternatives available to voters – were remarkably persistent,
stable structures. Initially formulated by Seymour Martin Lipset and Stein
Rokkan,[5] and then adopted and adapted by others, this perspective reckoned European party systems, from the time of their original crystallization
during the 1920s, to be strongly consolidated and to have remained
essentially 'frozen' for half a century.

Now, especially during the last quarter of the twentieth century, party
systems have entered into a phase of turbulence and increased instability.
The relatively stable patterns of political polarization represented by the
inherited cleavages, together with their sociological, ideological and
political content, have been subject to challenge. New actors have sprung
up (Greens, extreme right); others have undergone a profound crisis

(communists); and yet others have recast themselves and hit upon a new identity (centre-left, centre-right). The question of a major electoral dealignment or realignment is on the agenda, and has been for a long time.

Also on the agenda is the issue of a major *ideological realignment*. Today, the great left-wing themes of a still recent past – the centrality of the working class and the state, nationalization, collective and solidaristic mass action, and above all anti-capitalism, whether real or rhetorical – 'fall outside the parameter of significant debate'.[6] And while the familiar 'duality of tendencies' and the binary logic of political competition survive, the idea, so dear to Duverger, that 'every policy implies a choice between two kinds of solution', is challenged. The 'unbearable weight' of a trend towards programmatic and ideological convergence seems to mark the competition between the great left- and right-wing parties. The parties that 'haunt the house of power' (in Max Weber's memorable phrase) have become more interchangeable than they were in the past.

At the heart of these political and ideological reclassifications, and of the renewed interest in the development of party systems and 'old' polarities, in the 'decline' of the left/right divide, in the fate of the class model of politics, in the future of working-class politics and institutions of working-class origin, in the future of capitalism and globalization, in the future of the party form itself – in the future, even, of European civilization – lies a very old political family: social democracy.

Semper vetus, semper novus?

In the eye of the storm since the second half of the 1970s, and racked by the abandonment of Keynesian solutions, the transformation of the traditional working class, and the renewed influence of enterprise culture, the social democracy of the new millennium has reacted very effectively to the dynamism of the right and the centre-right. Having been prepared to envisage a genuine problematization of its political and economic strategies, it was clearly the victorious camp at the dawn of the twenty-first century. Instead of being severely weakened and thwarted, social democracy was the great victor at the *fin-de-siècle* elections.

Semper novus? In and through the changes prompted by social evolution, social democracy emerges and re-emerges as an enduring historical current, invariably capable of bouncing back. This venerable political family, which has participated in great collective projects that have been denatured, deconstructed or shattered, is still with us.

The historical trajectory of social democracy is made up of renunciations and betrayed loyalties, of successful ideological/programmatic 'overhauls', and a demonstrable ability to modernize itself. No doubt capitalism has transformed social democracy more than social democracy has transformed capitalism. From a revolutionary force, spokesman for the masses, and tribunitian party, social democacy, abandoning its founding project of socialism, has become an essential component of the capitalist universe. Moreover, the golden age of social democracy – a peaceful, prosperous society with a clearly delineated social state, site, perhaps, of the realization of that 'mediocre happiness' to which Tocqueville referred – is probably, at least in large part, simply a retrospective rationalization sustained 'by the misty nostalgia for better days bygone'.[7] Social democracy has abandoned its anti-capitalist vocation, and did so long ago; this represents the *great break* and *great event* in its political trajectory. Nevertheless, if we consider the longer history, the conclusion is unequivocal: the working-class movement has profoundly marked the experience, representations, and social and institutional 'texture' of European civilization; and *with* social democracy, *because* of social democracy, *despite* the shattered dreams of social democracy, something incontestably changed in our societies.

The idea that 'social democracy means something completely different before the first war, after the second, and again after the present economic crisis' is not, as such, unfounded.[8] Change has unquestionably been a constant in the long history of social democracy. It is not at all surprising, therefore, that in this period of great transformations, contemporary social democracy has changed once again. Yet its actions today, like its victories and defeats, unfold under the shadow of a historically novel 'threat': the threat of a radical loss of identity.

Even the most superficial examination reveals that social democracy today is exploring new ideological and electoral territory, 'testing' novel organizational forms and disciplines, proposing and implementing unprecedented solutions in government. Having made its majority vocation – one might say its 'majority impatience'[9] – second nature after a long apprenticeship, social democracy is in the process of changing its horizons. The social-democratic past, which was not always glorious, seems to be absorbed into an inordinately cramped and conservative present. Decidedly open to the fascination exercised by the 'iron law' of capital, divided between 'catch-all' roaming, popular implantation and neoliberal logic, contemporary social democracy has – at least according to many observers – fully entered the magnetic field of its opponents. The philosopher Jean Vogel has written:

> The gravity of the current crisis of the left's reference points unquestionably lies ... in the fact that it is not confined to the sphere of politics in the narrow sense, but affects the imaginary hearth thanks to which the left was a warm current in history for two centuries. ... If this mutation in the imaginary persists, *there will come a time when the notion of the left will denote no more than the void.*[10]

The social-democratic 'snail' – to borrow the image used by Günter Grass and Olaf Palme[11] – has lost its bearings according to some, and is enjoying a new youth according to others. In its obsession with adapting to the most difficult and harsh terrain, has this habitual gradualist lost its sense of direction and its reference points? Has the 'snail' committed the brazen indiscretion of crossing the 'boundary', the imaginary red line that imparts significance to the famous 'duality of tendencies', the distinction between dominant and dominated, and the left/right divide? In other words, has the time come when the notion of social democracy denotes no more than the void?

The Purpose of this Study

Supposedly in a state of gradual decline, social democracy has reasserted its powers. Supposedly ageing intellectually, it has also reasserted its capacity for renewing both its ideas and itself. Social democracy has changed. That much is 'obvious'.

But there are very different ways of talking about the same 'obvious' thing, without being able to agree on the content, the significance, or the extent of the 'change'. The purpose of the present work, in general terms, is to identify the character of the change in social democracy. However, the current reality of formations as old as the social-democratic parties cannot be grasped in an instant. To employ an established formula: 'The past is not another country'. The objective of this book is thus twofold: on the one hand, to examine the various (and sometime disparate) 'minor' and 'major' changes that are affecting the contemporary social democracies, while integrating them into an overall logic; on the other hand, to apprehend the *dynamic* of social-democratic recomposition in the light of both a still recent, and an already far distant, past. The study that follows aims to render the logic of the constitution and action of postwar social democracy intelligible, but will devote more space to the present period, that of social-democratic crisis and mutation. It begins with the present and ends in the present. The present, as A.N. Whitehead would say, is 'a holy land'.

Following the fall of the communist regimes in eastern Europe, however, social-democracy-in-the-present has acquired a new historical dimension, with its division – by enlargement – into western and eastern parts. The social democracy that forms our subject matter is neither that of the east nor that of the developing countries. It comprises western and Nordic Europe, and also southern Europe – the half of the European continent that represents the Europe of the affluent countries.

How are we to explain the 'magical return' and *fin-de-siècle* victories of a political force that seemed, not so very long ago, to be in the vice-like grip of 'historical decline'? What does social democracy represent in an epoch when 'farewells to the proletariat' are expressed with all the confidence of self-evidence?[12] What has happened to the unique 'features' (which I am not going to enumerate here) that historically defined social democracy, which were interdependent, and constituted the support and vital base that made social democracy 'social-democratic'? Does social democracy still represent a specific and original way of structuring the left,[13] a complex – and hence *rare* – political species? Or has it been stripped of its originality, to the point of becoming a political force and form like all the others?

Today, how does the group that was designated in the past by different names (manual workers, fourth estate, poor classes, dangerous classes, inferior classes, labouring classes, proletariat, working classes) – the group that finally became '*the working class*,'[14] and (until recently) formed the veritable backbone of social-democratic influence and stability – behave? What role has the social democracy of the 'third way' or the 'plural left' assigned the figure of the working class – a central social figure, and the founding myth of social-democratic history and passions?

Does contemporary social democracy contribute to the establishment of a new compromise and a new generation of social pacts, or not? Is there still a specifically social-democratic political *logic* and project (whether reformist or not)? Similarly, does the new profile of social democracy, lost amid a plethora of national particularities, possess a certain coherence and robustness? Or is it fragile and ephemeral, a sort of interregnum destined rapidly to disappear? What is the specific contribution and influence of the British 'third way' in the emergence and consolidation of the 'new' social democracy? Is there a different approach to modernization in social-democratic ranks from that of identifying it with a race to the centre and a 'managerial contest between two teams of administrators'? What of '*la gauche plurielle*', the latest version of what George Ross calls 'popular power in France'?[15] How does social democracy seek to respond today to the two major challenges confronting any left-wing force: Europe and globalization? Does it propose – or will it be in a position to propose in the foreseeable future – an alternative to the dominant neoliberalism, whether on its own or in conjunction with the trade unions or political poles to its left (communists, post-communists, Greens)? Finally, is there a *potential coherence* between the new ideological/programmatic profile of contemporary social democracy and the historical identity of social democracy? What is the 'hard core' – if there is one – ensuring continuity within a long tradition that is marked by more breaks than continuities? Has the link with the past – or rather, with the different social-democratic pasts – been definitively snapped, making the modernization in progress one that is *external to social-democratic tradition*? Does current social-democratic moderation, based on ideological and programmatic 'minimalism' (a postmodern moderation, as it were), signal the end of the long reformist social-democratic tradition, however resolutely and incorrigibly moderate it may have been? Finally, *semper novus*? In all likelihood, yes. But how? To what extent, with what consequences, and at what cost to its identity?

In the Name of Social Democracy will attempt an answer to all these questions. But they can basically all be summed up in one question, which Georges Clémenceau, quoted above, formulated emphatically: that of the singular bond, both rare and mysterious, which links – and sometimes ceases to link – the *present* and *past being* of a political current and, by extension, the *present* and *past being* of a political-ideological divide. To pose this question is to pose the simple and crucial question of identity – a very complex question, which in a sense there is no need to pose. For social democracy has performed different functions at different moments of its history, and has changed its objectives on several occasions;[16] social democracy is 'inconsistent and its historic path ruptural'.[17] In the Europe of the twenty-first century, the question of the identity of this 'inconsistent' force is the motor behind renewed intellectual and political debate on this venerable political family. The 'eternal' question of identity – which, if we look at history, follows social democracy like its shadow – is at the heart of this work. It is to be found at the beginning, at the end, and at the intersections and crossroads of all the chapters (that is, of all the debates conducted separately) that structure the present study.

The Scope of the Book

If we study the numerous occurrences of the term 'social democracy', we can see that it covers a very wide semantic field.[18] Let us stick with the basic, uncontested usage. The usual employment of the term 'social democracy' refers either to a particular social group – the party – or to its objectives and achievements. By virtue of the decisive role of social-democratic parties in defining the basic consensus after the Second World War – some have spoken in this context of a 'social-democratic consensus', others of a 'social-democratic civilization' – this second use of the term 'social democracy' has acquired legitimacy. It specified a *way of seeing* the *social and the economic*, a *model of problems and solutions*, which furnished the outline and prototype of 'normal politics', particularly during the *trente glorieuses*.

In this study, the main emphasis will be on the party and its 'identity' traits. Because of social democracy's particular historical trajectory, however, it acquired its full specificity only through its achievements, through a socioeconomic model peculiar to itself. A knowledge of how the junction between the identity traits of the social-democratic party and its governmental performance operated in the postwar period is a nodal point that will permit us to establish a better connection between the partisan force and its historical achievements.

If – according to the central hypothesis of this book – we are witnessing a *recasting* of the European social democracies, the *end of a political and social cycle*, it is impossible to grasp this process without some provisional definition of the specificity of the 'typical' social democracy of the 1950s and 1960s. Foregrounding the social-democratic *differentia specifica* of the 1950s and 1960s, a period that marks the high point of governmental social democracy, will provide us with the requisite interpretative grid to cover contemporary social democracy. This line of approach must thus be regarded as a central organizing principle that implicitly runs through the analysis, and structures it in its entirety.

Establishing the specificity of social democracy consists essentially in describing its general features, enumerating a certain number of distinctive characteristics. The initial impression conveyed by observation of this political force is, however, one of diversity: a variety of historical destinies, organizational structures, and political achievements. In the face of this diversity, what gives it its unity is open to question. In this respect, the first aim of the present work is to demonstrate that social democracy is a *specific* mode of constitution of the left, and that parties of a social-democratic *type*, although perceived, conceived or named in different ways, share – despite their great diversity – a number of general common features.

In effect, what is involved is an operation of *conceptual homogenization* to extract the general characteristics of the political type 'social democracy' from the *multitudo dissoluta* of real, historical social democracies. If this operation is successful, it will facilitate transition from intuitive, observational reconnaissance of the object to its *conceptual reconnaissance*. Accordingly, in some respects this study is intended to account for the logic and action of social democracy *in its entirety*, not of 'individual' social-democratic parties. Here, on the basis of dissimilar experiences and actors, it aims to determine the physiognomy of a unique, abstract, coherent, and hence somewhat unreal actor. In other respects, however, emphasis will be put on *national specificities*, the better to account for the richness of a complex, ambivalent, multiple reality. Here also, on the basis of dissimilar experiences and actors, it is a question of signalling the *distinctions* – which, I hope, are pertinent – in order to illuminate original party trajectories that are not reducible to a common model.

This work thus contains two complementary aspects. On the one hand – and primarily – it seeks to understand social democracy and its *political capacity* by asking on what structure and coherence – a coherence that is political, and not necessarily logical – it is based. On the other hand, it tries to understand the *plurality* and *ambiguity* of social democracy, which in and through the complexities of its national versions – seems to partake of different, partly contradictory 'natures', and to call for qualified and partly contradictory judgements. The proliferation of national forms scarcely fit for insertion into an economic, 'geometrical' composition dictates an incessant toing-and-froing between the 'general' and the 'national', in order to deal with disproportions, ruptures and transitions. This labour of conceptual homogenization will be undertaken in the introductory part of the book, and resumed in Part III and the Conclusions.

As for the structure of the argument (and the book), I have deliberately opted for a step-by-step, sectoral analysis of social-democratic-type parties (generally, but not always, adopting the following order: party-organization, party-in-the-electorate, party-in-competition, party-in-government). We shall consider these 'sectors' or dimensions not only in their static structure, from the standpoint of what Auguste Comte called 'social statics', but in their evolution and development, from the standpoint of their 'social dynamics'. This division into domains or 'spaces' – which, when all is said and done, is rather commonplace – will first of all allow us to establish inventories and propose reference points. Next, it will enable us to tackle the different aspects and dimensions of the great transformation of social democracy, whose cumulative effects lead to a dilution of the specificity (the 'banalization') of this great political family. Basically, the division into spheres or 'spaces' accords with the central hypothesis of this book. According to this hypothesis, the social-democratic 'great transformation' *is not only ideological/programmatic* (for all that public debate often focuses on this aspect), but encompasses *all* the spaces of the 'system' of social democracy. It is the product of several 'little great transformations'. It is to be understood as a change that involves *every* dimension of the social-democratic universe (ideology and programmes, organizational structures, leadership, link with the trade unions, sociology of the organization and electorate, governmental policies). This division, then, will determine and punctuate the steps of the reconnaissance and deeper knowledge of the phenomenon; it will offer nothing more than 'some reference points, some indices of weighting'.[19]

The Plan of the Book

The book is divided into five parts.

The introductory part (Chapters 1–5) offers an account of the social-democratic *differentia specifica* of the 1950s and 1960s, draws up an inventory, and proposes some reference points. Intent on clarification, it aims to render the logic of the constitution and action of postwar social democracy intelligible.

Part II endeavours to furnish a concrete, 'sectoral' view of the social-democratic mutation. On the one hand, the erosion or progressive altera-tion of the 'supporting institutions' and 'supporting social base', as well as the gradual disappearance of the old ideological reference points, make social democracy a decreasingly 'distinctive set of institutions and policies' (Karl Ove Moene and Michael Wallerstein). On the other hand, the new aspects of social democracy are outlined sector by sector. Chapter 6 sets out the electoral record of the social-democratic parties from 1960 to 2000; this is somewhat surprising, and does not support the thesis of a new electoral 'golden age'. Chapter 7 treats the issue of class voting at length. The architecture of the electoral space of the *vieille maison*, divided between working-class erosion and defection and the *deus ex machina* of the middle classes, is in the process of being renewed and revitalized. Next, I examine the new sociology of the organizations: an evident waning of the popular presence, a displacement in the centre of gravity towards leader and experts, the major 'paradox' of leadership, the end of strong integrating bonds and a new 'utilitarian' ethos among activists, the decline in trade-union influence – all these are analysed. The internal social-democratic space – the party *intra-muros* – appears genuinely, profoundly and irrevo-cably altered (Chapter 8). Chapter 9 examines the programmatic/ideologi-cal response of social democrats to the dual challenge represented by the strong rise of neoliberalism and the 'new politics'. Emphasis is placed on the content of the current strategy of a 'natural party of government', and on what distinguishes it from the 'semi-working-class/semi-catch-all' strategy of the 1950s and 1960s. Is there really a left variant of this strategy?

What of the 'project of rectification' that defines the left, and the 'regulative ideal' of equality?[20] Chapter 10 queries socialists' ability to renew the redistributive agenda. Two pairs of governmental experiences are analysed: first, Sweden and Austria (countries with 'labour dominant corporatism'), where the initial outline of a specifically social-democratic response to the economic crisis (formulated in the 1980s) came to grief on the reef of expanding neoliberalism, capping the decline of Keynesian social democracy; second, France and Great Britain, two cases considered representative – in their rivalry, whether alleged or real – of contemporary socialism. The crisis of corporatist co-ordination and the relative decentralization of systems of national collective bargaining will likewise be at the centre of our analysis.

In Part III (Chapters 11–12), the main lines and *decisive form* of the social-democratic 'great transformation' will be delineated. The innovation made by supporters of the 'third way'; the internal cohesion (and points of tension) of social democracy's new physiognomy; the entrepreneurial culture and strategic flexibility that distinguish contemporary social democracy's system of action; its ideological 'adaptability' and programmatic modesty; the solidity or fragility of its social and electoral anchorage; the 'left marketing' aspect – these are themes that our attempted synthesis cannot ignore (Chapter 13).

In Part IV, the following question is tackled: is social democracy in a position – on its own, or with the trade unions or forces to its left – to implement a modern version (national and inter- or supranational) of 'politics against markets'? What can we expect of the other left? Or of Europe and the Party of European Socialists, a Europarty summoned to assume the role of co-ordinator and engine of integration, but one which seems incapable of transcending its own 'immature', transnational make-up? The history of European socialism teaches us that it is not always the great 'ideological' paradigms that generate effective policies: effective policies can also give rise to ideological paradigms. What potential for effectiveness does social democracy harbour (Chapters 14–16)?

In the final, concluding part, I round off my analysis of the social-democratic mutation. The main issue I shall tackle is whether there is *consistency* between the new ideological/programmatic profile of contemporary social democracy and the historical social-democratic inheritance. What are the 'ultimate' reference points that guarantee continuity, and how does the modernization in progress differ from those of the past (Chapter 17)? Where does the project of the century – the 'project of politicization' derived from working-class culture – stand, following the social-democratic turn and the wreck of communism (Chapter 18)?

In conclusion, I shall take up the main themes elaborated in the book again, one by one – both to satisfy the impatient reader and to connect up the 'sectoral' analysis of the social-democratic phenomenon with the problematic of the 'great transformation', which itself developed in stages.

The '*longue durée*' of Modernity

In the Name of Social Democracy aims to recount the history – a history which is not that of the historian – of the 'great transformation' of social democracy. Its objective is to understand and assess the parameters of this great change – step by step, social-democratic space by space. Our object is the social-democratic 'structure' – or, better: the soul of a unique structure which was born, matured and consolidated with the *social question*, and which today, perhaps, is imperilled and losing its soul. Losing its soul? In questions of identity, 'loss' betokens 'gain'. The abandonment, exhaustion, or simple alteration of historical social-democratic identity allows a new identity to emerge. It permits the emergence of new ideological and programmatic reference points, a new organizational 'formula', a different electoral coalition, different sociological markers, a new effectiveness and ineffectiveness, another ambiance, a different 'style' – all of which means (to draw on Michelet) a 'new soul'. Having frequently demonstrated its capacity for self-renewal, social democracy will probably be able to escape the void. Not necessarily the 'void' indicated by Jean Vogel, but certainly the political void. Social democracy is not dead. It is with us, and will remain so for a long time yet – as will the social question. For the social question is not like other questions. To borrow Eustache Kouvélakis's fine phrase, it is inscribed 'in the *longue durée* of modernity'.[21] The same applies, we should add, to the left/right divide.

At its root, the real question addressed to this social democracy in the throes of modernization – and to the left in its entirety – is not of modernity, but of *which* modernity. In politics, as in life, there are different ways of being 'modern'. One can be 'modernist' in an economic sense, modernist 'with a heart',[22] and possibly 'modernist' in other ways as well. But how? Moreover, the modernity of the other side, the opponent, is equally modern. Operating in a period of accelerated change, where time has become 'condensed' and the terrain is mined, contemporary social democracy is in the process of defining, inventing and, finally, selecting its *own* modernity.

The subject of this work is a force that is at once old and admirably youthful, which in its frantic pursuit of modernization (so that it remains a 'warm current' in history) is prey to a strange difficulty. It is succeeding in its modernization, yet at the same time (precisely because of this successful modernization!) it appears profoundly incapable of dealing with a formidable challenge, perhaps the greatest challenge of the new century: the '*longue durée* of modernity'.

Notes

1. Quoted in Pierre Dauzier and Paul Lombard, *Anthologie de l'éloquence française*, Éditions Table Ronde, Paris 1995, p. 304.

2. Maurice Duverger, *Political Parties*, trans. Barbara and Robert North, Methuen, London 1964, p. 215; emphasis added.

3. Quoted in Jeff Faux, 'Lost on the Third Way', *Dissent*, Spring 1999, p. 76.

4. See Michel Offerlé, *Les Partis politiques*, Presses Universitaires de France, Paris 1987, p. 40.

5. See Seymour Martin Lipset and Stein Rokkan, *Party Systems and Voter Alignments: Cross-National Perspectives*, Free Press, New York and Collier-Macmillan, London 1967.

6. Perry Anderson, 'Renewals', *New Left Review* (second series), no. 1, 2000, p. 13.

7. Peter Beilharz, 'The Life and Times of Social Democracy', *Thesis Eleven*, no. 26, 1990, p. 91.

8. Ibid., p. 79.

9. The term is Daniel Bensaïd's, from *Lionel, qu'as-tu fait de notre victoire?*, Albin Michel, Paris 1998, p. 273.

10. Jean Vogel, 'De la gauche imaginée à l'imaginaire de gauche', *Politique*, nos 9–10, 1999, pp. 100, 103; emphasis added.

11. See Klaus Misgeld, Karl Molin and Klas Amark, *Creating Social Democracy: A Century of the Social Democratic Labor Party in Sweden*, Pennsylvania University Press, Pittsburgh 1992, p. xi.

12. René Mouriaux, quoted in Jacques Capdevielle, *Les opinions et les comportements politiques des ouvriers: une évolution inévitable? Irréversible?*, Les Cahiers du CEVI-POF, Presses de la Fondation Nationale des Sciences Politiques/CEVIPOF, Paris 1999, p. 127.

13. See Gerassimos Moschonas, *La Social-démocratie de 1945 à nos jours*, Montchrestien, Paris 1994.

14. Offerlé, *Les Partis politiques*, p. 41.

15. George Ross, 'The Changing Face of Popular Power in France', in Frances Fox Piven, ed., *Labor Parties in Postindustrial Societies*, Oxford University Press, New York 1992.

16. Gérard Grunberg, *Vers un socialisme européen?*, Hachette, Paris 1997, p. 8.

17. Beilharz, 'The Life and Times of Social Democracy', p. 79.

18. 'In all these writings I never describe myself as a social-democrat, but as a communist,' wrote Engels: 'For Marx, as for me, it is absolutely impossible to use such an elastic term to denote our own conception' (quoted in Roger Dangeville, trans., *La Social-démocratie allemande par Engels et Marx*, Union Générale d'Éditions, Paris 1975, p. 7).

19. Pierre Avril, *Essai sur les partis*, Payot, Paris 1990, p. 92.

20. See, respectively, Steven Lukes, 'What is Left? Essential Socialism and the Urge to Rectify', *Times Literary Supplement*, 27 March 1992, and Vogel, 'De la gauche imaginée à l'imaginaire de gauche', p. 101.

21. Eustache Kouvélakis, *Philosophie et révolution de Kant à Marx*, doctoral thesis, University of Paris VIII, 1998, p. 1; Presses Universitaires de France, Paris 2001.

22. George Ross, 'Saying No to Capitalism at the Millennium', in Leo Panitch *et al.*, eds, *Socialist Register 1995*, Merlin Press, London 1995, p. 59.

Part I

Introduction:
Social Democracy, 1945–73

The past is a bottomless abyss that engulfs everything ephemeral.

(Pascal Quignard)

1

Which Social Democracy?

Two Approaches to Social Democracy

Any political current we glance at becomes, by definition, an object of ambiguity and controversy, creating some perplexity. This is also true of social democracy – possibly rather more so than of other political currents.

Indeed, in so far as the notion of social democracy was constituted as a practical, all-encompassing notion, and in so far as it has become an object of theoretical, ideological and political struggle since Marx, Engels and Lenin, it was destined to be polysemic. Today, depending on the country and tradition concerned, it still arouses multiple echoes. For this reason – and without taking stock of the literature devoted to it – we can say that its various uses are not distinguished by any high degree of consistency and precision. This inevitably limits the *heuristic* potential of the notion. Moreover, the 'steady crisis' and transformation of the various social democracies over the last two decades have called into question the content and coherence of the social-democratic model of the 1950s and 1960s. This crisis, and the ensuing transformation, have made a further dent in the coherent perception of this 'coherence'.

There are two main approaches to the phenomenon of social democracy, representing different problematics. The first emphasizes the 'gradualist' character of the social democratic approach, underscoring its effective accommodation to the capitalist socioeconomic system. The social-democratic party was an 'outsider' that managed to instal itself at the centre of the system, without thereby becoming a centrist party. Located in a temperate zone, it is a force situated between the political extremes. In a sense, social democracy becomes synonymous with 'reformism' – that 'old word saturated with meaning' – and their relationship would appear to be tautological. This is the crucial distinguishing characteristic, the *unum necessarium*, the essential ingredient, of the notion.[1] Anthony Crosland's conception – social democracy = political liberalism + mixed economy + welfare state + Keynesian economic policy + commitment to equality – may be regarded as the classical version of this approach. Here the category of social democracy is basically a *generic* one, referring to *all parties of electoral socialism*, whether social-democratic or not.

Social democracy is certainly profoundly reformist. However anti-capitalist it may originally have been, it yielded a social and political regime that is generally regarded as a 'reformed' capitalism, both in the methods employed and in the results obtained. But other political currents have been (or are) 'reformist', whether out of conviction or necessity (and sometimes in a similar direction to that taken by social democracy), without thereby being (or becoming) 'social-democratic'. In truth, the real question is not whether social democracy is reformist, but whether there is such a thing as a social-democratic reformism – a *specifically* social-democratic reformist *savoir-faire*. That said, this first way of defining social democracy, schematically set out here – the *broad definition* – results, in my view, in an unduly 'extensive' concept of it, one that is not discriminating enough to be operational. Furthermore, because it is so widely applicable, the 'commitment to reformist measures' seems to me to mask, in the name of a general and 'generalized' reformism, some substantial differences between the concrete parties that have historically belonged to the great European social-democratic/socialist family. The universality of the experience of reformism in Europe, particularly after the Second World War, reduces, without wholly cancelling, the descriptive and explanatory reach of this approach, in which the term 'social democracy', extended indefinitely and used in numerous ways, subsumes the specificity of the political forces to which it refers. Thus gains in 'extension' are accompanied by a 'loss in specificity', if not (to borrow a phrase from Giovanni Sartori) a very significant 'increase in confusion'.

A contrasting approach, advanced in sophisticated academic versions, understands social democracy as a specific partisan and trade-union structuration of the working-class movement. According to Michel Winock:

> Historically, the label [of social democracy] applies to mass working-class parties that achieve a threefold, necessary integration in and through these organizations:
> 1. the integration or interpenetration of socialism and trade-unionism;
> 2. the integration of the working class into a complex system constituting a counter-society, which is organized in a network of co-operatives, training schools, youth associations, cultural groups, sports clubs . . . ;
> 3. the *de facto* integration of the socialist movement into parliamentary democracy.[2]

Specialists are agreed on these three historical features of the European social-democratic and labour parties. They add two further characteristics: the great strength of the social-democratic organization in terms of activists and finances; and its ability, as the undisputed representative of the world of labour, to impose 'a long-term compromise on the ruling classes, embodied in the Welfare State'.

This second approach to defining social democracy – the *narrow definition* – possesses greater power of discrimination, and I think it is better equipped to account, through the range and variety of its implications, for the reality of European socialism. If ideological coherence and a specific operational logic distinguish the social-democratic parties, as Alain

Bergounioux and Bernard Manin have aptly demonstrated,[3] these basically depend upon the *structural specificity* of the social democracies. Thus, for example, achievement of the social-democratic compromise, which is in a sense the 'natural' vocation of every party of a social-democratic type, does not stem exclusively from it, is not principally bound up with a reformist ideology and 'spirit'. It forms part of a whole, an organism whose axis, frame, nervous system, was constituted by the connection between mass party, labour union and popular electorate, which was achieved early on and proved remarkably resilient. Emphasis is thus put on the *more or less structured and distinctive* character of the social-democratic edifice, and the unity and 'complicity' connecting its component parts. More than ideology and programmes, it is this unity that is at the base of the destiny of social democracy, an actor that has been in place for at least a century, proving its powers of endurance. 'Social democracy', Karl Ove Moene and Michael Wallerstein have written, 'is a distinctive set of institutions and policies that fit together and worked relatively efficiently to reduce both the insecurity and the inequality of income without large sacrifices in terms of economic growth or macroeconomic instability.'[4]

While I obviously do not imagine that such a definition – or any definition – could encompass the essence of social democracy and its historical variants, I think that it permits a better grasp of the true dimensions of the phenomenon. Accordingly, I shall construct my own analysis of social-democratic reality in accordance with it. I shall seek to delineate the components of this 'distinctive set of institutions and policies', to extract the skeletal structure and establish how these components function when they are integrated into a political whole possessed of *coherence* – a coherence that is practical, and not necessarily logical. At the risk of being too neatly diagrammatic, exaggerating the lines and over-simplifying the architecture, this book will seek to describe the decisive forms and foundations of the social-democratic edifice, as well as – and especially – the transformation of this architecture that is now in progress.

The thesis that treats social democracy as a 'constellation', a *specific political structuration*, is the departure and arrival point of the present work, which will in turn, perhaps, provide some arguments for – and against – this thesis.

Word and Thing: A Rapid Historical Overview

In France, the term 'social democracy' appeared in the immediate after-math of the 1848 Revolution. Faced with the party of order, a reconciliation was effected between the democratic republicans of the Mountain (Ledru-Rollin) and the socialists, and their union, proclaimed on 27 January 1849, resulted in the birth of the 'democratic-socialist' or 'social-democratic' party that February: 'The socialist and the democratic parties,' Marx wrote, 'the party of the workers and the party of the petty bourgeoisie, united to form the *social-democratic party* – the *Red* party.'[5] This coalition – which, according to Marx, stripped the social demands of the proletariat of their 'revolutionary thrust' by giving them a 'democratic cast' – was crushed by force in June 1849.

In Saxony, Liebknecht and Bebel organized an anti-Prussian collectivist party, of Marxist allegiance, in 1869: the Social-Democratic Workers' Party, which rapidly became 'social democracy' for short. Initially critical – and always hesitant about the term, preferring the epithet 'communist' – Marx and Engels nevertheless ended up supporting its use politically, particularly after the reunification of the German socialists under Marxist auspices (1875).

The historic contribution of the First International (1864–76), the first co-ordinating body of a nascent working-class movement, consists in the fact that 'the demand by the proletariat for the conquest of political power was precisely stated for the first time'.[6] After the dispersal of this conglomerate of unions, co-operatives and embryonic parties, the working-class movement went through a process of constitution marked by the formation of great national parties and the rapid diffusion of Marxist ideas. It increasingly adopted the 'revolutionary-rational' format described by Seraphim Seferiades.[7] In the last quarter of the century, the proletariat transformed itself into a mass movement as well as a political actor. Thus, in a spectacular shift, from the 1880s onwards the term 'social-democratic' referred to parties influenced by Marxism. In this respect we must stress that during the First International three terms were used to describe the three main tendencies, their objectives and methods. The first – 'communism' – was linked with Marx (and, in part, with the Blanquists); the second – 'collectivism' – was applied to Bakunin and his tendency; and the third – 'socialism' – designated the moderate tendencies of petty-bourgeois connotation. Following the dissolution of the First International, the labels changed, and it is very interesting to note that 'social-democratic' was precisely substituted for 'communist', designating those working-class tendencies and parties that accepted the *principle of class struggle* and the *supremacy of political struggle* as a means of action. Thus, especially from the 1880s, 'social-democratic' became associated with 'Marxist', in opposition to the moderate socialists and 'possibilists'.[8] Having imposed itself as the dominant current in opposition to anarchism and 'reformism', above all in central Europe, Marxism became the official doctrine of the Second International after 1896. Emulating the German party (founded at Gotha in 1875) – which set as its objective integrating the democratic task into the social revolution, and which consequently called itself 'social-democratic' – numerous political formations throughout Europe adopted the name.

To understand the identity-formation of social democracy, it is perhaps useful to note here that, in order to achieve its political objectives, it quickly decided to make a double breach in a political system involving property qualifications. It aimed on the one hand to extend political rights to the working class (and hence expand the very restricted civil society of the era); and on the other, to equip the working class intellectually and culturally to master its own political destiny. According to Eduard Bernstein:

> A working class without political rights, steeped in superstition and with deficient education, will indeed revolt from time to time and engage in conspiracies on a small scale, but it will never develop a socialist movement. . . . So political rights and education have a prominent position in every socialist programme of action.[9]

Accordingly, these parties, with the help of their relay-organizations (trade unions and associations of every sort), tended not only to mobilize 'the people *behind* the electorate' (in the words of the Dutch Protestant party ARP),[10] but also, prior to the institutionalization of universal suffrage, to mobilize the people *before* the electorate (and, later, the *people as electorate*).

Once the incubation period was over, socialism became (as Anton Pelinka put it so eloquently) 'a political practice, a party, a social democracy'. The third of these – which found its most illustrious expression in the German social-democratic party, and its emblem in the creation of the Second International (1889) – emerged as a 'developed political instrument' at the turn of the century, constituted around three objectives: opposition in principle to the capitalist order; extension of political democracy; and reinforcement of international solidarity. In addition, it was constituted around a fourth objective, often 'underestimated' and little mentioned by social-democratic doctrinal orthodoxy of the period, but of decisive importance for the penetration and anchorage of social democracy in working-class and popular milieux: *immediate improvement in the condition of the working class*. As August Bebel said: 'we enjoy the immense influx and confidence of the working masses only because they can see that we are acting for them in practice, and not simply referring them to some future socialist state, the date of whose arrival nobody knows'.[11]

Towards 1914, the term 'social-democratic' covered the three great tendencies – orthodox, revisionist, revolutionary (Leninist or council-communist) – which crystallized and clashed, in extremely diverse forms and variants, within the European socialist movement. Conveying a culture and an 'accent' that were in large part German, thus construed the term assumes a *generic* character. As such, it does not make it possible to grasp the differences and oppositions that ran through the socialist parties of the epoch. Like Engels before them, Kautsky, Lenin, Bernstein, Branting, Rakovsky or Luxemburg were all social democrats.

Nevertheless, some of the characteristic features long retained by the social-democratic parties were unquestionably fashioned in the period before 1914. In the first place, there was the constitution of the party as strategic locus and centre of impetus for the 'three-stage structuration' of the organized working-class movement (party + trade union + ring of specialized associations and organizations of all sorts). In its pilot version – German social democracy – this party was generally thought of as a veritable party-society, at once *sub-* and *counter-society*. Secondly, there was the constitution of the party in the form of a *class party* (based on group social solidarity) and a *mass party*, a large, robust, centralized organization with a professional apparatus and its own financial basis.

Two main facts caused the birth of the social-democratic party in the *modern* sense of the term: the contamination of the old working-class parties by nationalism, and the October Revolution. Rather than being the 'twilight of the gods for the bourgeois regime', as Bebel had hoped in 1911, the First World War smashed the Second International to pieces, even though it was at the height of its power. By voting military credits one after the other, with very few exceptions, socialists were reduced from enormous influence to virtual total ideological ruin. This remarkable defeat, this paralysis in the face of war, would leave a lasting memory. Amid the turmoil of 1914, the career of prewar social democracy came to an end in schism and extreme debility. A cycle was over. On the basis of the radical potential it liberated, the October Revolution led to an avalanche of splits and the formation of communist parties. This great historical schism, crystallized from 1919 around the creation of the Third (Communist) International, was consummated and consolidated in 1923 with the creation of the Socialist International, rallying prewar revisionist and orthodox currents. The advent of this new divide, the outcome of a differentiation between a 'reformist right' and a 'revolutionary left' already clearly visible before the war, was of decisive importance. Henceforth, socialists and communists – fraternal enemies, modern Cains and Abels – defined themselves largely in terms of this opposition. The social democrats, deprived of their left wing and hampered by the adhesion to the new communist formations of a significant section of the working class and the younger generations, emerged from the ordeal politically and intellectually impoverished. The intense confrontation between the two great tendencies identified with socialism during the 1920s marked social democracy profoundly, and prompted its identification with *reformism*. Thus, through the mechanics of this confrontation, social democracy progressed still further in its specificity. Henceforth, 'social-democratic' was conventionally attributed to the 'reformist' political component of the socialist movement, which – whether dubbed socialist, labour, workers or social-democratic party – was positioned to the 'right' of communism, and constructed in direct competition with it. The label 'social democrat' – abandoned by Lenin on the eve of the October Revolution – was disparaged and identified, in word and in deed, with effective accommodation to the capitalist socioeconomic system.

During the same period, as severe defeats multiplied for extra-parliamentary action – abortive uprisings in Germany (1919 and 1921), Hungary (1919), Bulgaria and Poland (1923); failed general strikes in France and Czechoslovakia (1920), Norway (1921), and Great Britain (1926) – and as the Soviet regime moved away from democracy, total adherence to parliamentarism and 'electoralism' became, in contrast, a central constitutive principle of social democracy's make-up. Attachment to parliamentary procedures thus became an integral part of the political culture of social democrats – all the more so since parliamentary democracy appeared historically as 'the result of their struggle'.[12]

The search for social allies inherent in 'electoralism' henceforth tended to reorientate the class character of the social-democratic parties, making them increasingly receptive to the promptings of other social milieux.

Certainly, as Stefano Bartolini has correctly emphasized, 'electoral socialism was, from the beginning, "entrapped" with large electoral allies – more or less wanted or unwanted – which surely were linked to socialism by politico-ideological motivation, but deprived of solid encapsulation into its organisational network'.[13] But 'total' acceptance of parliamentary-electoral logic intensified and, above all, imparted a *strategic* character to the opening to the middle classes. Moreover, it appears as the first stage of a *de facto* integration into the capitalist order. Marxism survived in social democratic programmes and phraseology, but not in practical activity.[14] Interwar social democracy – a *reform party with an anti-capitalist programme* – plotted its course 'with its head facing in one direction, its body in another'.

After the Second World War, the social-democratic parties successively embarked on a process of doctrinal and programmatic de-radicalization, constituting themselves as parties of 'all the people'. If the anti-capitalist ideal still haunted their internal life, this was mere nostalgia. With the Cold War, the anti-capitalist vocation of social democracy was completely blurred, and it became definitively synonymous with 'reformism'. The logic of 'small steps' and smooth change was substituted for the heroic dream of the past, and any talk of breaks. In the initial postwar period, social democracy was distinguished by the following characteristics, which were common to the majority of European socialist parties, and marked its new doctrine and practice: (a) outright abandonment of the idea of using violence as a means of achieving power; (b) definition of socialism as a social ideal inseparable from the idea of parliamentary democracy; (c) abandonment of the idea of state property in the means of production as a fundamental principle of socialism. The *mixed economy*, an 'advanced form of capitalism' combining a public and a private sector, was henceforth considered the most desirable solution; (d) total opposition to communism, which went back a long way, but now took the form of a virtually unconditional support for the Atlantic Alliance to thwart 'Soviet expansionism'.[15]

The blossoming of this social democracy, which found its symbolic reference points in the SPD's Bad Godesberg programme (1959), was inextricably linked to the expansion in the role of the state and Keynesianism. Through the techniques it offered – which social democracy had sorely lacked in the 1920s and 1930s except in Sweden and Norway – Keynesianism made possible an *electorally ideal juncture* between the sectoral interests of the working class (fairer distribution of wealth, full employment, strengthening of the role of trade-unionism) and the national interest (sustaining growth). Social democracy in its current and 'usual' sense – *mature* social democracy – was born in this era. The social-democratic synthesis (welfare state, advanced social policy, full employment), which was of central importance in the postwar formation of 'consensual pragmatism', served as a criterion and prototype for 'normal politics', particularly from 1960 to 1973. This was the era of the 'social-democratic consensus'.

Although they were perceived, conceived or named differently, in their mature 1960s form, parties of the social-democratic type shared a number of general features, which were partly the legacy of pre-1914 social democracy, and partly new:

1. They were equipped with a mass organization structured around an apparatus that possessed great strength in terms of activists and finances.
2. They retained a privileged link, whether institutionalized or not, with the collective historical force of a working-class trade-unionism that was representative, unified and invariably centralized.
3. In terms of their electoral bases, despite their interclassist ideological profile they remained *parties of the working class* (in the sense that they were supported by a clear majority – even, in some cases, an overwhelming majority – of that class), without always being *class parties*. In reality, they were *coalition parties* whose strength combined a very powerful class base with the gradual crystallization of a significant influence among certain segments of the middle classes (employees, new salaried strata).
4. Their strong domination of the left part of the electoral and political spectrum – the absence, in other words, of a significant competitor on the left – made the social-democratic parties, for all their legendary moderation, popular *left-wing* parties, not politically and socially intermediate formations, equidistant from the extremes and extremities.
5. They were, in addition, *legitimate* parties with a governmental vocation, close to 'majority conformism'. Hence they did not provoke hostility and rejection on the part of the 'average voter', as was the case with other 'reformist' parties (e.g. the 'Eurocommunist' parties), which did not enjoy the same degree of governmental legitimacy despite their often extreme programmatic moderation.
6. The product of these identity traits was the 'social-democratic compromise' which, finding its fullest expression in Sweden and Austria, involved the institutionalization of a mode of regulation of social conflicts based on the multiplication of bi- or trilateral arrangements between unions, employers and state. The specific aim of this system was the development and implementation of public policies, especially incomes policies, without major industrial conflicts. It rested on the working-class implantation of the party and the party/union axis, which was the veritable keystone of the edifice.

Thus defined, the 'social-democratic system of action'[16] did not really become established outside central and northern Europe (Scandinavia, Austria, West Germany in part, and, to a lesser extent, the Benelux countries). Labourism – in particular British Labourism, which from the outset did not develop on the basis of a socialist project – represents a borderline case, a less structured version which, at the same time, is clearly distinct and moulded. In contrast, in countries with an influential communist party, a fragmented trade-unionism, and/or significant religious divisions (France, Italy, Portugal, Greece, Spain), socialist parties deviate sharply from this model, despite sometimes possessing a common doctrinal and programmatic framework. The characteristics of this socialism (absence or weakness of the union relay, reduced working-class audience, deficiency of active members, heavy preponderance of middle classes) and its governmental practice (inability to implement enduring procedures of tripartite consultation) mean – at least *prima facie* – that it is not the equivalent of formations of a social-democratic type.[17]

The differences indicated here – which are of structural importance, since they concern the very matrix of the parties in question – definitely contribute to dividing the great European socialist/social-democratic family into subgroups with distinct contours.

Notes

1. This attitude towards the social-democratic phenomenon, very widespread in France and abroad, has a large audience – indeed, enjoys a virtual monopoly – in the media. In academic studies it is present implicitly, rather than as an explicit logical construct, adopted as such.
2. Michel Winock, 'Pour une histoire du socialisme en France', *Commentaire*, vol. 11, no. 41, Spring 1988, p. 166.
3. Alain Bergounioux and Bernard Manin, *La Social-démocratie ou le compromis*, Presses Universitaires de France, Paris 1979. This work represents one of the most lucid elaborations of what might be taken as an introduction to the phenomenon of social democracy.
4. Karl Ove Moene and Michael Wallerstein, 'How Social Democracy Worked: Labor-Market Institutions', *Politics and Society*, vol. 23, no. 2, 1995, p. 186.
5. Karl Marx, 'The Class Struggles in France: 1848 to 1850', in *Surveys from Exile*, ed. David Fernbach, Penguin/*New Left Review*, Harmondsworth 1973, p. 90.
6. Jacques Droz, *Le Socialisme démocratique (1884–1960)*, Armand Colin, Paris 1968, p. 13.
7. Seraphim Seferiades, *Working-Class Movements (1780s–1930s). A European Macro-Historical Analytical Framework and a Greek Case Study*, Ph.D. thesis, Columbia University, 1998, p. 89.
8. Georges Haupt, *Aspects of International Socialism 1871–1914*, Cambridge University Press, Cambridge 1986, pp. 6–7.
9. Eduard Bernstein, *The Preconditions of Socialism*, trans. Henry Tudor, Cambridge University Press, Cambridge 1993, p. 160.
10. Quoted in Ruud Koole, 'Cadre, Catch-all or Cartel? A Comment on the Notion of the Cartel Party', *Party Politics*, vol. 2, no. 4, 1996, p. 511.
11. Quoted in Joseph Rovan, *Histoire de la Social-démocratie allemande*, Éditions du Seuil, Paris 1978, p. 87.
12. Alain Bergounioux and Gérard Grunberg, *L'utopie à l'épreuve. Le socialisme européen au XXᵉ siècle*, Éditions de Fallois, Paris 1996, p. 34.
13. Stefano Bartolini, *Electoral, Partisan and Corporate Socialism. Organisational Consolidation and Membership Mobilisation in Early Socialist Movements*, Estudio/Working Paper 83, Juan March Institute, Madrid 1996, p. 53.

14. Mario Telo, *Le New Deal européen: la pensée et la politique sociales-démocrates face à la crise des années trente*, Université de Bruxelles, Brussels 1988.
15. Daniel Bell, 'Socialism', *International Encyclopaedia of the Social Sciences*, pp. 506–32 (523–5).
16. Marc Lazar, 'La social-démocratie européenne à l'épreuve de la réforme', *Esprit*, no. 251, 1999, p. 124.
17. To a certain extent, but a certain extent only, the parties identified here as the most typically social-democratic correspond to what Bartolini calls 'encapsulated socialism'. This socialism, characteristic of Sweden, Denmark, Austria and, to a lesser degree, Norway, is distinguished by the fact that the mobilizations of the working-class movement – partisan-organizational, electoral and trade-union – are very strong and interdependent. The British case is representative of the model designated 'union socialism', which is characterized, at least initially, by 'retarded electoral mobilisation, extremely weak partisan mobilisation in the context of early and high corporate mobilisation'. What distinguishes France and Italy and, in another context, the Netherlands, 'is simply class cleavage undermobilisation in all dimensions'. This is the model of 'undermobilised socialism' (Bartolini, *Electoral, Partisan and Corporate Socialism*, pp. 46 and 52).

2

The Party-Organization

The Origins of Social-Democratic Organization

Activist Parties: *Die Organisation ist alles*

Since they first emerged in the last quarter of the nineteenth century, socialist parties have tended to base their power on 'force of numbers', on the collective action of the labouring masses. In this they enjoyed a prerogative exclusive to the 'European case': the largely shared history of trade unions and working-class parties, and the interaction between trade-union action and political action.[1]

Indeed, in a number of European countries (e.g. Germany, Sweden, Denmark, Norway, Austria, Belgium, later the Netherlands and, in an original and belated form, Great Britain) the relationship between the working-class party and the unions was very close at the end of the nineteenth century or the beginning of the twentieth. Even in Italy and Spain, where the influence of the anarchist current remained considerable, provoking splits within the trade-union movement (in 1912 and 1910 respectively), organizational links between socialists and unions were strong.[2] With the partial but notable exception of France, the privileged link between party and union was a semi-constant. Obviously, the structure of mobilization of the working-class movement – and the organizational forms it took – varied significantly from country to country. According to Bartolini, whom we shall take the liberty of citing at length:

> in the majority of cases central co-ordination of the political organisation took place before a similar process was accomplished in the corporate channel. Denmark is the clearest case: a socialist national party was already set up in 1876–78, but it took twenty-two more years to reach a national Trade Unions confederation (1898). Also in Belgium, the Netherlands, Italy, Norway and Sweden political centralisation was reached before corporate centralisation, but with a less important delay, ranging from twelve to fourteen years. In Germany, Austria, Finland and France the national political party precedes the national corporate organisation, but the delays are so small that the process is one of almost parallel development. In contrast, Switzerland, Great Britain and Ireland are the only cases where centralisation in the Trade Unions sector preceded that in the political one.[3]

The convergence between trade-unionism and politics in a more or less hostile environment, the reinforcement and mutual support of party and union resources, was to manifest itself in striking fashion, despite tensions and conflicts, in an organization *with no real equivalent* in the known partisan universe: the socialist or social-democratic organization. This organization, which spread throughout Europe and blossomed in the quarter-century before the First World War, marked the emergence of a party of a new type in terms of size, complexity and functions, which differed sharply from the established bourgeois parties. The socialist and social-democratic parties, the most developed specimen of a new generation of parties, presented and asserted themselves legitimately as the accredited form of modernity when it came to political organization. The invention of the social-democratic organization forms a large part of the 'institutionalized-rational organizational pattern', which 'marks a qualitative break with the general organizational weakness characterizing the plebeian and plebisci-tarian patterns'.[4]

Initially extremely hostile towards capitalism, and often subject to severe repression, the workers' parties – which, as a general rule, were formed outside parliament – acquired unprecedented organizational features as a result. Only well-structured and fairly centralized organizations – very attentive to the indoctrination of their members, and based on a powerful (though often cursory) ideology and social affinities of a communitarian type – could constitute themselves as an effective means of compensation for the strength of the power elites in a hostile environment.[5]

What historically defined these parties of militants, for which members were 'the very stuff of the party, the substance of its action' (Duverger), was their capacity, with the aid of relay-organizations (unions and associations of every sort), for organizing large segments of the population. Indeed, a network of diverse organizations was constructed around the party, touching numerous spheres of life (economic struggle, social security, cultural life, education, leisure activities). The importance attributed to the function of *socializing* and *mobilizing* the world of labour, and hence to organization and ideology, enabled them to create bonds of identification, loyalty and fervour – in short, collective identities.

Parties of social protest thus assumed the appearance of a veritable political community in struggle; and in some cases – following the example of German social democracy, the guiding light at the beginning of the century – of a community *tout court*: anxious to cater for the social, cultural, educational and political expectations and needs of its members and the environment that formed its reference point. This was the party-ghetto, the party transformed into a *milieu de vie*.

The 'communitarian tradition' and 'associational independence' of the British working class – long predating the foundation of the Labour Party, as well as the pacts with the Liberals made by the unions – prevented Labour becoming the vehicle and centre of a 'labourist' counter-society. The relative 'autonomy' of British working-class networks, product of a long and gradual maturation, which had no equivalent in Germany, rendered them unreceptive to any 'total' political ascendancy. By contrast, the much later development of working-class communities and the trade-union movement in Germany – a development that occurred only *with* social democracy, and in part *because* of it – together with the hostility of the middle classes and the state, contributed to the SPD finding itself at the heart of a ghetto culture.

Obviously, the different histories of the working-class movement in western Europe resist any summary presentation. Even so, we may stress that the belatedness of German industrialization, and the 'premature' appearance of an independent working-class party in an adverse environment, encouraged the SPD to take on the character of both a 'counter-society' and a 'sub-society'. The 'precociousness' of English indus trialization, and the greater openness and 'reform potential' of the British elites, as well as the delay in the emergence of the Labour Party, were among the factors that led to a different pattern in Great Britain.[6]

The SFIO – a party on the borderline of the mass model, with a very weak capacity to organize the population – never became a genuine counter-society able to offer a 'whole way of life' to its members and the working class. The weakness and 'independence' of the French unions, the heterogeneity and relative dispersion of the working class, did not create the conditions for an evolution of this sort. France is an exemplary instance of 'electoral socialism', to employ Bartolini's typology: 'The weakness of the Socialist movement in both corporate and partisan channels is astonishing if compared with its electoral development. This was a Socialism whose source of strength certainly did not lie in organisational infrastructure.'[7] In addition, the socialists' frequent co-operation with the Radicals before 1905, the year in which the SFIO was founded, 'provided an important bridge between workers and the Republic'.[8] If the 'constitutional weakness', both electoral and organizational, of the SFIO prevented it from 'colonizing' the working-class environment, the creation of the PCF in the interwar period was to mark a new step in the constitution of the left-wing popular space in France. Gaining the adherence of revolutionary syndicalist militants from the outset, and implanting itself (especially from 1924 onwards) among the most combative working-class groups, the Communist Party became *the sole authentic representative instance of the organized working-class movement* in the 1930s. The SFIO's weakness allowed the Communists to conquer 'a position which was largely vacant' in the working-class milieu.[9] The PCF's success was based on an astonishing paradox: from 1935, it succeeded (in the words of Stéphane Courtois and Marc Lazar) in 'fusing communist universalism, which reactivated the spontaneous collectivism of traditional peasant and working-class communities, with the individualist universalism derived from 1789'. Thus the PCF was able to create – and sustain itself from – an authentic communist counter-society whose core was working-class culture, whether 'real or fantasized'.[10]

Mass Organizations and Popular Public Space

The most significant contribution of this organizational evolution (if not revolution) consisted in the major political – and cultural – fact of establishing the 'working-class people' as a central political-social actor of modernity. And this applied at the levels of social discourses and representations and strategic political action alike. Given that the majority of the working class 'did not have an interest in socialism', socialist parties of the period were first and foremost *parties of propaganda*, while in the countries where they were 'politicized', unions functioned in part as 'schools of socialism'.[11] 'The popular movement tradition', Göran Therborn has written, 'tends to give to politics a reformatory, educational orientation and a collective organizational form.'[12] In fact, social democracy exerted a considerable (but not exclusive) *formative influence* on the construction of the identity of working-class people and, at the same time, established itself as their privileged (though not sole) spokesman. The subaltern classes, the 'uneducated', the 'simple people', the 'ignorant' – in short, the 'people' – were encouraged to think of themselves as a 'subject', and to act as a historical 'subject'. So, a new popular 'imaginary' was progressively created around the idea of the social subject-actor and popular ways of life. In different ways, depending on the country, it selectively integrated cultural codes and practices (which formed part of the popular memory and 'collective unconscious') and important aspects of socialist ideology (an intentional product of the organizations), into a more or less co-ordinated corpus of representations. Before the Great War (and in the interwar period as well, especially for those countries without an influential communist party), the social-democratic constellation (party + unions + associational network) was, in a way, the political spinal column – ideological, organizational, electoral – of the urban working-class/popular environment. By making themselves the 'tribunes', educators and organizers of the workers and the 'have-nots'; by contributing to the establishment or consolidation of a vast network of working-class organizations; by radically discrediting the pretensions of the ruling classes, parties of a social-democratic type tended to constitute the working class *as a class*, and the people as the 'sovereign power'. In this sense, social democracy was constructed as a central, strategic pole, as a pole of *attraction*, among the working-class and disadvantaged sections of the population.

Social democracy and its collateral organizations thus succeeded in giving powerful voice to those excluded from economic, political and cultural capital, in a language derived from working-class and popular idioms. With radical intellectuals they contributed (to borrow a term from Habermas in a quite different context) to the establishment of a kind of *plebeian public sphere*, at once complementing and rivalling the celebrated bourgeois public sphere.[13] In fact, for the first time in history a great popular public space was constructed, just as powerfully structured and equally durable. This space, which was simultaneously popular 'movement' and popular 'public opinion', expressed and asserted itself in ways other than unco-ordinated actions, riots and 'spasms'.[14] It thus superseded its 'proto-revolutionary-plebeian' or 'reformist-plebeian' character,[15] and adopted a 'rational' organizational format (in the Weberian sense of the term) which, because of its effectiveness, later became largely 'trans-classist'.

The difference between this space and the popular movements of the past was its robust institutional and ideological framework. 'Rational' political and associational organization not only gave workers a capacity for *defining their own identity* rarely achieved among other popular groups; unlike them, it also imparted a strong *strategic capacity*.[16] Organization thus made the working class an 'inductor group' whose influence was to be progressively exercised not only over its immediate environment but also over more distant layers of the population, including even certain sections of the middle classes. This allowed the working-class movement to root itself deeply in European societies, to exert considerable influence over the political, social and economic process, and to capture the imagination and mind of the 'masses' on a long-term basis.

If social democracy played a decisive role in the formation, unification and cohesion of its immediate social milieu, it was nevertheless formed and fashioned by it in turn. Thanks to their *strategy of presence* and their 'capillary' work on the ground, parties of the social-democratic type were able to control *their* class and their reference groups. But the effect of presence on the social terrain, the effect of *proximity*, also worked in the opposite direction: this environment, which was not some mere passive milieu, was in turn a source of sensitization and change for the mass socialist parties. They thus functioned as structures for the reception and registration of social actions and reactions. At root, parties of the social-democratic type were *structures for organizing the masses*, and simultaneously – this is too often forgotten – *structures organized by the masses*. The case of the Swedish social democrats is an excellent illustration. In their constant effort to strike a balance between the ideology of socialism and 'the current interests of the people', they themselves were ideologically transformed.[17] The example of 1914 is also illuminating. The desertion of a majority of European socialists to the ideologically dominant representation of the moment – 'the tidal wave of nationalism' – was the best-known manifestation – the most discussed, and also the most controversial – of adaptation to the surrounding environment.[18] Famous for the formulation of the 'iron law of oligarchy', Robert Michels expressed this tendency in his peremptory but invariably thought-provoking fashion: 'It is a disastrous and fatal illusion to believe that the German party has hold of the masses; it is the masses who have hold of the party.'[19] In this perspective, social democracy must be regarded not only as a sociopolitical 'attractor' – as a pole of attraction among the popular classes – but also, and simultaneously, as a pole *attracted by them*.

Basically, the organizational characteristics of social democracy, which crystallized gradually, were the historical product of four major phenomena: first of all, the construction of parties of the social-democratic type as

parties of the working class (in close liaison with the trade unions); next –
and simultaneously – the working-class movement's encounter with democracy, which assumed different forms depending on the country; in the
third place, the tendency of working-class parties – whose origin as *outsiders*,
as it were, stuck to them – to let themselves be integrated into the capitalist
system; and finally, the tendency of the social-democratic parties, initially
largely restricted to the dimensions of a single social class, to become great
working-class/popular formations whose horizons were no longer limited
exclusively to the working class. Only through these four interdependent
phenomena, and their combined effects, is social-democratic organization
intelligible, and its organizational code legible.

Parties with a Strong Bureaucracy

Socialist/social-democratic organizations were not constructed out of scat-
tered pieces and elements. Equipped with a strong armature, historically
the working-class parties were vast, complex organisms whose administration required the development of a stratum of functionaries and full-
time officials responsible for *making the machine run*. The existence of a
well-formed bureaucracy, characteristic of parties with multiple structures
and an intensely active membership life, most often – but not always –
became a major feature of the organized social-democratic space. For Max
Weber, organization of a bureaucratic type constituted the 'paradigmatic
institutional expression' of the modern destiny.[20]

Is organization synonymous with oligarchy? According to Michels, the
true face of bureaucratic power is oligarchic. Conceived as a way of
operating effectively, and being inherently *inegalitarian* (since it establishes
a hierarchical ladder of responsibilities in the very name of equality),
bureaucracy allots itself a central and relatively autonomous institutional
role: 'from being a servant, it becomes a mistress'.

Nevertheless, the bureaucratic phenomenon does not lend itself to
unambiguous interpretation. And the 'demonization' of bureaucracy does
not square with the complex reality of political organizations. Moreover,
bureaucracy has profoundly ambivalent relations with democracy.[21]
Bureaucratization is a process with two sides to it, correlative and simultaneous. On the one hand, it is 'democratic', since it establishes the
primacy of abstract rule over the prerogatives of uncontrolled grandees
and leaders. The largely non-bureaucratized structure of some liberal or
conservative parties, as of various contemporary southern European socialist parties, which are largely in thrall to the power of their 'barons',
grandees and leader as a result, perfectly illustrates this thesis. On the
other hand, it is scarcely democratic, since it expands the gulf between
the mass membership, the different strata of the party elite and the
leader.

Thus, this bureaucracy, composed either of 'administrators' (executive
bureaucracy) or of 'administrators' who are simultaneously political leaders

empowered by the base (representative bureaucracy), constituted the veri-table backbone of the majority of social-democratic organizations. And it performed two functions. First, it formed the administrative element in the party, its principal task being the maintenance and smooth operation of the party machine. Next, it formed the group of militants who were supposed to ensure close liaison between the party leadership and the mass membership and, via the latter, the social base, especially the party's privileged class. In this respect, the role of the bureaucracy, particularly the representative bureaucracy, while it is administrative, is eminently political: it contributes to *fixing the party in its social space, to its 'auto-nomy', and capacity for controlling its environment better.*[22]

While it doubtless raises the issue of 'oligarchical' domination by the leadership circle over the party as a whole, the presence of a well-developed and politically coherent bureaucracy is the sign of a strong institution, one that is well entrenched and relatively stable. Viewed from a macroscopic angle, the robustness of social-democratic parties with a compact, well-delineated bureaucracy – the SPD, the SPÖ, the SAP or, in a quite different perspective, the PCI or PCF – compared with the fragility of parties with a meagre bureaucracy – the SFIO, the Italian PS, or even the British Labour Party (at once both armoured and vulnerable) – attests to the generally stabilizing role of a strong bureaucracy in the face of the turbulence of political and social life.

Moreover, the dysfunctions and *effets pervers* inherent in the bureaucratic model (ritualism and an inability to adapt to new situations, a decline in initiative, a gulf between the bureaucrats and the 'public', means that tend to 'consume the ends',[23] a dynamic of rationalization that 'bit by bit drains the sources of innovation and rarefies charisma',[24] etc.) have not stopped the mass socialist parties renewing themselves and remaining in place as central forces for at least a century. Obviously, it is impossible to say what the fate of social democracy without this bureaucratic frame, a famous 'apparatus' more decried than described, would have been. Undertaking the sociology of an absence is a perilous exercise. But the facts are stubborn, and their reality is inescapable: the social-democratic parties were constituted as great societal organizations that did not 'cut themselves off' from the 'public'; if they had, they would not have remained great organizations. Despite – or perhaps because of – their bureaucratization, as organizations they proved capable of ensuring the circulation of infor-mation and ideas – 'the circulation of meaning', as Jean Baudrillard would say, between the leadership circle and the electorate.

Organization after the War

The Decline in Membership Density and Working-Class Presence

Two major trends characterized the make-up of social-democratic organizations in the first phase of the postwar period: a decline in membership
density and working-class presence.

In the period 1945 to 1994, parties of the social-democratic type
remained mass parties, but their membership figures, as well as the extent
of their enrolment of their own electoral base or the electorate in its
entirety, were in decline.[25] During these years, socialist numbers fell overall
in both absolute and relative terms, having briefly attained a peak following
the war.

In absolute terms (i.e. number of members), the downward trend began
in the case of the Finnish SDP and SFIO at the end of the 1940s; in the case
of the DNA and Danish SD in the 1950s; and for the PvdA in the 1960s.[26]
After a recovery during the 1970s, membership trends from the 1980s
onwards exhibit the characteristics of a *fundamental and well-nigh generalized
erosion* (with the exception of certain southern parties like the PSOE, the
Portuguese PS, and PASOK, which proved rather more resilient). Compared
with the organizational density of the 1930s, in some cases (Denmark,
Norway and, to some extent, the Netherlands), this deterioration took the
form of a gradual but violent contraction.[27] In relative terms (i.e. membership as a proportion of the electorate), the trend was identical, despite the
fact that the organizational penetration of some social-democratic parties
remained comparatively sizeable: SPÖ 8.9 per cent in 1994 (against 14.3 in
1953); SAP 4.0 in 1994 (against 15.5 in 1952, indirect members included in
this figure); DNA 3.2 in 1993 (against 7.9 in 1953); Belgian PS 3.2 in 1991
(against 2.6 in 1954); Danish SD 2.3 in 1994 (against 10.8 in 1953); Finnish
SDP 2.0 in 1990 (against 2.9 in 1951). The organizational penetration of the
SPD was both weaker and more stable throughout the period in question
(1.4 in 1994, as against 1.8 in 1954). The British Labour Party – 0.7 in 1992
against 2.5 in 1951 (collectively affiliated members not included) – remains,
as ever, a separate case, since the combination of individual membership
and collective affiliations (the latter underscoring, as in the case of the SAP
and in part the DNA, the importance of the unions as recruitment channels)
relativizes this weakness significantly, but not decisively. The PvdA, 0.6 in
1994 (1.9 in 1952), was (as Ruud Koole put it) henceforth a 'modern cadre
party'.[28]

Within the rather disparate and fragmented European socialist family,
we can, at first glance, isolate two subsets distinguished by their level of
organization. The first includes the most classically social-democratic
parties (Sweden, Austria, Denmark, FRG, Norway); those that approximate
to it (Belgium, Finland); and the highly original variant of Great Britain.
During most of the postwar period, these parties were characterized by a
very or fairly high degree of organization. This subset corresponds roughly

to what is intuitively regarded as 'social democracy' in European public opinion. A second subset includes parties such as the French PS, the Portuguese PS, PSOE, PASOK – parties whose membership fabric is very thin (the French PS), or fairly thin (the Portuguese PS, PSOE and, to a lesser extent, PASOK). This group is commonly – though inaccurately, given its pronounced internal heterogeneity – referred to as 'southern European socialism'.

Some notable 'exceptions' in terms of organizational density and penetration nevertheless preclude a clear division between more or less classically social-democratic parties and the socialisms of southern Europe. The case of the SPD and the PvdA, marked throughout the postwar period by an organizational density situated at a level 'intermediate' between north and south (the PvdA having been greatly weakened recently); and the traditionally strong organization of the Italian PS during the same period (it has now disappeared from the political scene: a veritable organizational event!) – these rule out such a dichotomy.[29] Consequently, in the framework of this introductory general survey, we shall limit ourselves to stressing the 'preponderant' trend: *social democracy is no longer the formidable organization it once was*, and no longer constitutes a model or guide as far as organization is concerned. The most classically social-democratic parties, those corresponding to Bartolini's model of 'encapsulated socialism', certainly retain their historical advantage. But their extraordinary organizational density of yesteryear is in the process of losing its originality (more so in the case of the Danes and Norwegians than in that of the Swedes and Austrians). Thus, while retaining their differentiated levels of mobilization, the formerly 'organisationally over-mobilised socialism' (Austria, Denmark, Sweden, in part Norway), 'union socialism' (Great Britain), and 'electoral socialism' (Germany, Belgium and Finland) are all converging on the model of 'organisationally under-mobilised socialism' (historically represented by France, the Netherlands and Italy, and today, in addition to these countries, by Spain, Greece and Portugal).

In the postwar period, changes in social stratification, the strengthening of the tertiary sector of the economy, and the slow but continuous 'rise' of the salaried middle strata are reflected in the gradual restructuring of the organizational space of social democracy.

The data collected in Table 2.1 are merely indicative,[30] but they capture the general trend well, and permit the following conclusions:

1. The very weak representation of the urban and rural self-employed (shopkeepers, artisans, small businessmen, liberal professions, farmers) among members of socialist parties conveys the salience of the divide between employed and self-employed, pointing up the profound and persistent inability of the left to penetrate the core social fabric of its 'bourgeois' opponents. The Austrian and German social democrats are not in a position to enlarge their *organizational base* there. A persistent, invisible structural barrier seems to hold them back, allowing room only for a 'war of position' at the margins.

Table 2.1   Social composition of SPÖ and SPD memberships (1929–70)

	SPÖ 1929	SPD 1930	SPÖ 1955	SPD 1952	SPÖ 1970	SPD 1966
Workers	51.2	59.5	42.1	45	38.3	32
White-collar Workers/Managers	20.4	13.9	22.3	22	31.1	27
Self-employed/Liberal Professions	5.8	4.5	5.3	12	3.9	5
Farmers	–	–	–	2	–	0
Retired	2.2	4.6	11.4	12	16.4	18
Housewives	16.1	17.1	17.3	7	12.2	16
Students	–	0.2	–	–	0.6	–
Various	1.6	–	1.6	–	1.4	1

Sources: For the SPÖ (1929) in William Paterson and Alastair Thomas, eds, *Social-democratic Parties in Western Europe* (Croom Helm, London 1977), p. 233; for the SPD (1930) in Klaus von Beyme, *Political Parties in Western Democracies* (Gower, London 1985), p. 215; for the SPÖ (1955–70) in Paterson and Thomas, eds, *The Future of Social-Democracy* (Clarendon Press, Oxford 1986), p. 166; and for the SPD (1952–66) in Anton Pelinka, *Social Democratic Parties in Europe* (Praeger, New York 1983), p. 48.

2. In terms of their sociology the social-democratic parties remained *popular* parties during the 1950s and 1960s, their organization being focused on two social pillars: the working class and salaried middle strata.
3. However, the imposing predominance of the working-class component tended gradually to fray. In fact, we witness a progressive 'slippage' of the endo-organizational centre of gravity towards the middle classes, which deepened from one decade to the next, so that by the end of the 1960s two social bases of tendentially equal numerical importance emerged at the heart of the social-democratic organization.

Accordingly, the dominant role played by the working-class element within the party, which contributed to fashioning the texture, language and style of the social-democratic organization, was eroded. No doubt the construction of the social democracies as working-class institutions rapidly became a highly ambiguous phenomenon. But (as we shall see) this did not prevent the decline of working-class weight being markedly more pronounced among members than among social-democratic voters as a general rule. As a result, the 'internal' sociological arithmetic seems to outstrip, precede and anticipate the 'external' sociological arithmetic, rather than following or merely accompanying it. Time sapped and eroded the social specificity of the social-democratic *organizations* a good deal more quickly than it did the social-democratic *electorate*.

Organization Foreshadows the Future

A structure can survive for a very long time, well past the conflicts and imperatives that produced it. Once established and consolidated, it 'immobilizes time in its own way'. In this sense, the organizations engendered during the conjuncture of constitution of the social-democratic parties are *matrix-structures*: 'short time organizes long time'.[31] Naturally, the organizational development of the socialist parties was constantly affected by changes in their political, social and cultural environment. But certain major elements in their *genetic pattern* endured, albeit transformed, right up to the end of the 1960s and even beyond.

Nevertheless, in the postwar period, as at the beginning of the century, *no single model of social-democratic organization is open to generalization*. And it is certainly not possible in this introductory part to engage in a minute description of the whole range of socialist parties, from the SPD, model party of the beginning of the century, or the SAP, a veritable party-society, up to the PvdA, a modern cadre party, or British Labour, an 'open' party with badly defined organizational boundaries and a weak bureaucratic structure. But without searching for some organizational specificity to social democracy at any price – something it would be impossible to establish in the postwar period – we can say that in the years 1945 to 1973 parties of the social-democratic type, as a general rule, displayed a certain number of properties which, *while not being peculiar to them*, all the same pertained to the social-democratic mode of existence:

1. The constitution of the party in the form of a mass party, a great membership organization with a remarkable capacity – albeit reduced by comparison with 'times past' – for the mobilization and orientation of its social base.
2. The constitution of the party most often in the form of an organization with a strong armature, a well-formed and well-developed bureaucracy, possessing its own financial basis.
3. The constitution of the party as the strategic centre of a relatively wide spectrum of collateral organizations (unions, associations).

This structure goes back to the very origins of the social-democratic parties. Indeed, they continued to refer to a model of organization that *differs substantially from a simple electoral machine* concentrating its activity on election times. Rooted in the working-class environment, buttressed by trade-union strength and their associational implantation, they left their mark on the social fabric. In the 1950s and 1960s the foundation of the parties of a social-democratic type remained, to a considerable extent, group social solidarity.

However, social-democratic membership density, as well as working-class presence within the organization, declined. This dual decline coincided with the gradual and *partial* transformation of social-democratic-type parties from mass parties into *coalition, catch-all* parties.

Gradually relinquishing any aspiration to 'intellectual and moral *encadre-ment* of the masses',[32] more attuned to voters than to members, and tending to transcend class boundaries and address themselves to the whole popula-tion, the social-democractic parties *renounced their vocation as explicit political and ideological organizer of the working class.* Their integration, political education and mobilization activity declined. The social democrats' capacity
to stimulate a collective adhesion and dynamic, to perform the function of 'relay' between the state and their immediate social environment, decreased. In the name of a politics of openness towards the middle classes – since the 1950s there has been no social-democratic political project that does not take account of, or end up with, the middle classes – the social-democratic parties risked politically weakening and ideologically dispersing the working-class milieu from which they traditionally drew their identity, stength and energy.

Undoubtedly, in the 1950s and 1960s social democracy expanded rapidly on the basis of a carefully cultivated, *fundamental ambiguity*: the fact that it was at once – and principally – a 'party of social integration', a mass party developed in a working-class matrix; and at the same time a party which, for electoral reasons, cut free and tended to transform itself into a 'catch-all' political force.

Untroubled by the contradiction, and turning the ambiguity to its advantage, in these years social democracy managed to play its hand well, combining these two 'natures' in itself without impairing its electoral effectiveness.

Here we doubtless encounter the two faces, but also the two develop-mental rhythms – and all the ambiguity – of postwar social democracy: on the one side, an ideological and programmatic profile of a *semi-catch-all* type; on the other, an electoral make-up focused, as we shall see, on the *working class.* As for the organization, it was sociologically situated at the junction point of the faces and rhythms of the social-democratic Janus: semi-working-class, semi-interclassist, it was at the intersection. In very marked fashion from the 1960s onwards, the evolution of social-democratic membership structure signalled – or, rather, foreshadowed – the sociologi-cal trajectory of social democracy in the last quarter of the century.

Notes

1. Mario Telo, *Le New Deal européen: la pensée et la politique sociales-démocrates face à la crise des années trente,* Université de Bruxelles, Brussels 1988, p. 42.
2. See Edward Malefakis, 'A Comparative Analysis of Workers' Movements in Spain and Italy', in Richard Gunther, ed., *Politics, Society and Democracy: The Case of Spain,* Westview Press, Boulder, CO and Oxford 1993.
3. Stefano Bartolini, *Electoral, Partisan and Corporate Socialism. Organisational Consoli-dation and Membership Mobilisation in Early Socialist Movements,* Estudio/Working Paper 83, Juan March Institute, Madrid 1996, pp. 12–13.
4. Seraphim Seferiades, *Working-Class Movements (1780s–1930s). A European Macro-*

Historical Analytical Framework and a Greek Case Study, Ph.D. thesis, Columbia University, 1998, p. 65.

5. Klaus von Beyme, *Political Parties in Western Democracies*, Gower, London 1985, p. 160. It seems that the degree of hostility of the environment and the incumbent government impacted considerably on the structuration of the organization. In the so-called 'a-liberal' societies (e.g. Sweden, Germany, Norway, Belgium, and to some extent Denmark), the lack of integration of the working class into the political system favoured the establishment of highly disciplined, coherent and centralized organizations. Confronted with hostile liberal movements, hostile or indifferent states, and fairly well-organized employers, the constitution of the socialist space as a *strong system of organization* seemed the only effective option. In these countries the organizational imperative (constructing and preserving the power and identity of the organization) became central. Sometimes it even became a veritable obsession, because 'those organizations were all workers in aliberal societies had' (Gregory Luebbert, *Liberalism, Fascism or Social Democracy. Social Classes and the Political Origins of Regimes in Interwar Europe*, Oxford University Press, New York and Oxford 1991, p. 187). Moreover, was it not Machiavelli who said that 'all armed prophets have conquered, and unarmed ones have been destroyed'? By contrast, in countries like Great Britain and, to a lesser extent, France, where the state was less threatening, the working-class movement less isolated, and where experiences of the Lib–Lab type before the Great War had permitted a greater legitimation of the unions and labour leaders, the organized socialist space was less coherent, less dense and less disciplined. It was also, especially in France, less effective in attracting the working-class vote. Obviously, the matrix and organizational contours of trade-union or party 'collectives of struggle' were the product of innumerable national factors. However, the inimical or co-operative attitude of the urban middle classes, the aggressiveness or otherwise of the state towards the working class and, more generally, the 'alternative patterns of working-class entry into politics', largely account for the heavy infrastructure of socialist parties in 'a-liberal' societies, and their markedly lighter infrastructure in France and Great Britain (Luebbert, *passim*).

6. Christiane Eisenberg, 'The Comparative View in Labour History. Old and New Interpretations of the English and German Labour Movements before 1914', *International Review of Social History*, vol. XXXIV, 1989, pp. 424–9.

7. Bartolini, *Electoral, Partisan and Corporate Socialism*, p. 45.

8. Luebbert, *Liberalism, Fascism or Social Democracy*, p. 32.

9. Georges Lavau, *À quoi sert le Parti communiste français?*, Fayard, Paris 1981, pp. 66, 72.

10. Stéphane Courtois and Marc Lazar, *Histoire du Parti communiste français*, Presses Universitaires de France, Paris 1995, pp. 407–8.

11. Jae-Hung Ahn, 'Ideology and Interest: The Case of Swedish Social Democracy, 1886–1911', *Politics and Society*, vol. 24, no. 2, 1996, p. 169.

12. Göran Therborn, 'A Unique Chapter in the History of Democracy: The Social Democrats in Sweden', in Klaus Misgeld *et al.*, eds, *Creating Social Democracy: A Century of the Social Democratic Labor Party in Sweden*, Pennsylvania State University Press, Pittsburgh 1992, p. 13.

13. Jürgen Habermas, *The Structural Transformation of the Public Sphere*, trans. Thomas Burger, Polity Press, Cambridge, 1989.

14. See Arlette Farge and Eustache Kouvélakis, 'Y a-t-il un espace publique populaire?', interview in *Futur antérieur*, nos 39–40, 1997.

15. Seferiades, *Working-Class Movements*, p. 89.
16. Michel Verret, *Chevilles ouvrières*, Éditions de l'Atelier, Paris 1995, p. 189.
17. Ahn, 'Ideology and Interest', pp. 176–9.
18. In a very polemical spirit, not devoid of a certain prophetic sense, Charles Andler accused the German social democrats: 'This socialism is novel in its lack of scruple. It maintains a vigilant concern for immediate working-class interests; but it is not ashamed to reorient its principles. . . . Henceforth we know that there is a socialism ready to vote [military] credits, resolved not to harass German diplomacy, and disposed to stress solidarity with the dynasty. It is the only socialism that could ever accede to power; hence it is what will seduce the spirit of the masses' (Andler, *Le Socialisme impérialiste de l'Allemagne contemporaine. Dossier d'une polémique avec J. Jaurès 1912–1913*, Bossart, Paris 1918, quoted in Jacques Droz, *Le Socialisme démocratique*, Armand Colin, Paris 1968, pp. 144–5).
19. Robert Michels, *Critique du socialisme*, Kimé, Paris 1992, pp. 56–7.
20. Michael Reed, 'Organizations and Modernity: Continuity and Discontinuity in Organization Theory', in John Hassard and Martin Parker, *Postmodernism and Organizations*, Sage, London 1993, p. 166.
21. See Philippe Reynaud, *Max Weber et les dilemmes de la raison moderne*, Presses Universitaires de France, Paris 1987, p. 195.
22. On the distinction between executive bureaucracy and representative bureaucracy, and the importance of bureaucracy in the construction of a strong institution, see Angelo Panebianco, *Political Parties, Organization and Power*, Cambridge University Press, Cambridge 1988, especially pp. 60–64, 225, 264.
23. Reynaud, *Max Weber et les dilemmes de la raison moderne*, pp. 199–200.
24. P. Cours-Salies and Jean-Marie Vincent, 'Présentation', in Michels, *Critique du socialisme*, p. 27.
25. See, respectively, Gerassimos Moschonas, *La Social-démocratie de 1945 à nos jours*, Montchrestien, Paris 1994, Table 1; Gerrit Voerman, 'Le paradis perdu. Les adhérents des partis sociaux-démocrates d'Europe occidentale, 1945–1995', in Marc Lazar, ed., *La Gauche en Europe depuis 1945*, Presses Universitaires de France, Paris 1996, Table 2.
26. Voerman, 'Le paradis perdu', pp. 565–8.
27. Moschonas, *La Social-démocratie de 1945 à nos jours*, Table 1.
28. Ruud Koole, 'The Dutch Labour Party: Towards a Modern Cadre Party', in Wolfgang Merkel *et al.*, *Socialist Parties in Europe II: Class, Popular, Catch-all?*, ICPS, Barcelona 1992.
29. The measure of recruitment of their own electoral base (relation between the number of members of socialist parties and that of socialist voters), which we have developed elsewhere (*Le Social-démocratie de 1945 à nos jours*, Table 1), better accounts for the electoral status of a party than the measure constructed on the basis of the *total* electorate (used by Voerman in 'Le paradis perdu'). The latter underestimates the organizational density of parties with an average or weak electoral influence (case of the PSI or the PvdA). Thus, according to the measure of recruitment of their *own* electoral base (classically employed by Maurice Duverger), the rate of adhesion for the SPD was 6.6 per cent in 1989 (against 9.1 in 1949); for the PvdA 3.4 in 1989 (against 9.5 in 1948); and for the PSI 11.4 in 1987 (against 13.0 in 1973). These figures indicate that the SPD is closer, as regards its organizational penetration, to the most classically social-democratic group of parties as well as the PSI, whose membership rate differs profoundly from that found in the other countries of southern Europe. By contrast, the PvdA is markedly closer to parties like the French PS (3.0 in 1993),

PSOE (3.1 in 1986), and PASOK (3.7 in 1994). Thus, if one establishes an organizational dichotomy between northern/central European socialism and southern European socialism, the two truly 'abnormal' cases would be the PSI and PvdA (see *La Social-démocratie de 1945 à nos jours*, pp. 32–5).

30. For a more global approach to the sociology of the social-democratic organizations, see Part II below.

31. Emmanuel Leroy-Ladurie, quoted in Nonna Mayer and Pascal Perrnieau, *Les Comportements politiques*, Armand Colin, Paris 1992, p. 45.

32. Otto Kirchheimer, 'The Transformation of the Western European Party System', in Joseph La Palombara and Myron Weiner, eds, *Political Parties and Political Development*, Princeton University Press, Princeton, NJ 1966, p. 184.

3

Social Democracy in the Electorate

'Any sociological study of voting behaviour', Matei Dogan has written,

> is inevitably caught in a vicious circle. A thorough analysis should not be limited to such gross categories as the working class and middle class. . . . Nevertheless, the more one takes into account the actual social diversity, the more one is limited to rough guesses and surmises. . . . Thus, paradoxically, the more one looks for precision in the social infrastructure, the more one risks being imprecise in analysing the social bases of each party.[1]

The inherent limitations of the present study oblige us to proceed by 'gross categories', and the numerical data for different countries must not be taken to the decimal point because of the different criteria employed. Analysis will nevertheless make it possible to identify the main trends, especially given that some similarities or contrasts are too marked not to be significant.

Working-Class Support and the Majority Vocation

One of the postulates of the 'catch-all' thesis, which highlights the *mutation in partisanship* in developed societies, is that during the 1960s parties of social integration gradually abandoned any ambition to mould populations intellectually and morally, and simply sought to expand and diversify their electoral base. In the event, the tendency to form *voter, 'catch-all' parties*, largely confirmed in terms of the actors' programmes and strategic objectives, is only *very partially* confirmed at the level of the socio-electoral support for European social-democratic parties.

Whether we are talking about the Scandinavian countries, Austria, Great Britain, or even the FRG or Belgium, the sociological content of social democracy's electoral make-up is unambiguous. In the 1960s, parties of the social-democratic type remained parties of the working class on two counts. First, the largest part of their mass electoral base derived from the working class (Table 3.1). Second – and above all – *the majority of this class*, and sometimes a *very large majority*, supported the parties in question (Table 3.2). Despite a tendency to become increasingly interclassist in their physiognomy, parties of the social-democratic type were constructed during the period under examination as specific coalitions whose main ingredient and central bloc remained the working class.

Table 3.1 Social composition of the social-democratic electorate

	SAP 1968	SD 1966	DNA 1969	SPD 1972	Labour 1966	SPÖ 1955
Workers	67	72	65	50	81	61
White-collar workers/managers	29	23	26	35	–	25
Self-employed	4	5	9	8	19	14

Sources: For the Scandinavian social democracies, see Gøsta Esping-Andersen, *Politics against Markets: The Social Democratic Road to Power*, Princeton University Press, Princeton, NJ 1985, pp. 128–9. For the SPD, Gerard Braunthal, *The West German Social Democrats, 1969–1982*, Westview Press, Boulder, CO 1983, p. 165. For the British Labour Party, Bo Salvik and Ivor Crewe, *Decade of Dealignment*, Cambridge University Press, Cambridge 1983, p. 89. For the SPÖ, Wolfgang Muller and Peter Ulram, 'The Social and Demographic Structure of Austrian Parties, 1945–93', *Party Politics*, vol. 1, no. 1, 1995, p. 148 (for the SPÖ, the category of 'self-employed' contains self-employed, professionals and farmers. The percentages have been established by us after excluding housewives, pensioners and the unemployed.)[2]

I think the essential point to emphasize is that the most successful social-democratic parties electorally are precisely those that are most distinctively working class. The long social-democratic ascendancy in Scandinavia was inextricably bound up with the decisive influence of the socioeconomic cleavage and, as a consequence, the development and persistence of class voting. 'One of the paradoxes of Scandinavian political development', Francis Castles has written, 'is ... that the reformist Social-Democratic parties of Scandinavia offer the only empirical confirmation of Marx's view that the politics of social class leads to the inevitable political victory of the working class.'[3] The majority status of these parties was often linked less to their capacity to attract the middle classes than to their impressive entrenchment among the working class. The case of Swedish social democracy is exemplary here.

Table 3.2 Working-class electoral penetration of five social-democratic parties (1960s)

Country	Date	Party	Working-class vote %
Sweden	1968	Social democrats	77
Denmark	1968	Social democrats	65
Norway	1965	Labour	69
Great Britain	1964	Labour	64
FRG	1969	Social democrats	58

Sources: See Table 3.1.

The Swedish Case

The hegemonic role – in the Gramscian sense – of the SAP, established before the Second World War, was based, among other things, on the 'unique advantage' (in Eric Hobsbawm's phrase) of the party's entrenchment in the working class. Despite its quasi-hegemonic influence, its spirit of openness, its remarkable trade-union implantation among white-collar workers, and despite the fact that the SAP 'has never been a socially isolated labor party' – despite all that, and contrary to conventional opinion, the SAP's electoral influence remained comparatively limited outside the working class.[4] Fundamentally, the enduring political hegemony of the SAP – possibly the most powerful party western Europe has ever known – had as its spinal column the stability, at a very high level, of social-democratic influence among the working class.

Table 3.3 Social-democratic penetration among manual and non-manual workers in Sweden (1956–76)

Date	SAP share of the manual vote	SAP share of the non-manual vote
1956	74	22
1968	74	32
1976	62	28

Source: Christine Buci-Glucksmann and Göran Therborn, *Le Défi social-démocrate*, François Maspero, Paris 1981, p. 281.

Throughout the 1960s, the relative progression of the SAP among non-manual strata – significant in itself, given their growing numerical importance – accompanied and supported the extraordinary stability of social-democratic penetration of the working-class milieu (Table 3.3).

The 1976 elections, and the bourgeois parties' accession to power after forty-four years of social-democratic governments, marked the end of – or possibly an interlude in? – the SAP's impressive domination of Swedish political life. As Table 3.3 demonstrates, the SAP's electoral crisis was essentially due to the defection of a *significant number of workers*, and hence to losses deriving from the party's 'natural' social base. This electoral erosion, which crystallized very clearly during the difficult years of the economic crisis, reflected the erosion of social-democratic hegemony in Swedish society.

The British Case

From the viewpoint that interests us here, the case of the British Labour Party is even more interesting.

In the 1960s, Labour's arrival in power after three consecutive defeats depended on two things. The first was the stronger propensity of manual workers to vote Labour – a propensity that approached the symbolic 70 per cent mark at the 1966 election. The second was Labour's increased penetration among the new salaried strata. But just as the 1964 and 1966 victories were primarily the indisputable result of the party's advance among the manual workers, so the defeat of 1970 derived from extensive disaffection among working-class voters, Labour's share of the non-manual vote having scarcely changed relative to 1966, and having increased compared with 1964.

Table 3.4 The British Labour Party's penetration among manual and non-manual workers (1959–70)

Date	Labour share of manual vote	Labour share of non-manual vote
1959	62	22
1964	64	22
1966	69	26
1970	58	25

Source: Bo Salvik and Ivor Crewe, *Decade of Dealignment*, Cambridge University Press, Cambridge 1983, p. 87; my adaptation.

If, on the basis of the data in Table 3.4, we establish the average Labour share for the 1960s according to elections won/lost and the categories manual/non-manual, we can better illustrate the relationship between the manual vote and the Labour Party's majority status. Table 3.5 clearly indicates that there is a close connection between the level of the working-class vote and the majority status of the party. The picture that emerges from these data allows for little interpretative hesitation: Labour's victories were strongly correlated with increased working-class support, and its defeats with a reduction in this support.

Table 3.5 Elections won and lost by Labour and the manual/non-manual vote (1960s)

1960s	Share of manual vote (average)	Share of non-manual vote (average)
Won: 1964/1966	66.5	24
Lost: 1959/1970	60	23

Source: See Table 3.4; my calculation.

The German Case

In the social-democratic universe, the SPD constitutes a paradigm of its own. Despite their great working-class tradition, German social democrats suffered the repercussions of the religious divide and the division of the country, and were restricted to a level of penetration of the working-class population markedly inferior to that of their Swedish, or even British, counterparts. While it had a majority within the working class, the SPD stood below the 60 per cent threshold of the working-class vote.

The SPD's progress to power was a long process, marked by a gradual and almost continuous improvement in its influence among all segments of the population, and in the first instance the salaried middle classes.

The German social democrats achieved a competitive status that allowed them to rule the country[5] in two phases. In 1969, an initial quantitative and qualitative leap forward derived from a *differential* advance, whose main distinguishing feature was the SPD's spectacular breakthrough among salaried middle strata. In 1972, by contrast, professional categories shifted in their entirety towards social democracy, demonstrating that the party of Willy Brandt had enhanced its powers of attraction in an extremely diversified electoral field (Table 3.6).

Table 3.6 Electoral penetration of the SPD (1953–72)

	1953	1961	1965	1969	1972
Workers	48	56	54	58	66
Employees/civil servants	27	30	34	46	50
Self-employed	11	14	18	17	23
Farmers	4	8	–	16	10

Source: Ilias Katsoulis, in Helga Grebing, *L'histoire du mouvement ouvrier allemand*, Papazissi, Athens 1982, p. 413.

Overall, we could say that the SPD – which, since the Second World War, had been of a less distinctively working-class character than the most important social-democratic parties – owed both its strong electoral growth after 1969, and its constitution as a 'natural' party of government, largely to the new salaried strata.

Hence this party appears to be *very sensitive to fluctuations in the vote of the middle strata*, and this was to be the source of many anxieties in the future. But it continued to be a political formation whose electoral and social base remained, in its majority, the working class.

Social Democracy and the Middle Classes

Referring by definition to a scalar – and ternary – structure of social stratification, the term 'middle class' derives its force from an intuitive perception of the reality of social classes which is very widespread and long-standing. From the standpoint of electoral sociology, however, it conceals extraordinary disparities of behaviour and ideology. In accordance with the variety and fragmentation of the social groups composing them, it is preferable to speak of the middle classes in the plural – something I shall do throughout the present work.

The Uncertain and Uneven Adhesion of the Salaried Middle Strata

The first question we should address concerns the evolution in the postwar period of the propensity to vote social democrat among the middle classes, provisionally construed as an internally undifferentiated statistical unit. Now, the social-democratic or labour constituency grew significantly with time, the arithmetical progression of these classes in the population being accompanied by an increase in social-democratic influence among them (Table 3.7).[6]

Table 3.7   The middle-class vote in Norway, Denmark and Sweden

	Farmers	Small businessmen	Senior managers	White-collar/ Middle managers	Total electorate
Denmark 1971					
Radical Left	0	2	12	18	10
Social Democrats	2	19	9	31	34
Centre Parties	79	27	43	21	35
Conservatives	19	52	36	31	20
TOTAL	100	100	100	101	99
Norway 1969					
Radical Left	1	0	9	5	6
Labour	9	42	21	40	44
Centre Parties	84	27	28	31	31
Conservatives	6	31	42	25	19
TOTAL	100	100	100	101	100
Sweden 1970					
Radical Left	2	5	1	2	3
Social Democrats	9	18	24	47	47
Centre Parties	85	57	53	40	40
Conservatives	5	21	22	10	10
TOTAL	101	101	100	99	99

Source: See Francis Castles, *The Social Democratic Image of Society*, Routledge & Kegan Paul, London and Boston, MA 1978, p. 109.

However, the electoral fate of parties of a social-democratic type, at least in Scandinavia, was very different depending on whether the relevant subset was the 'self-employed' or salaried strata (Table 3.7). In their great majority, the 'self-employed', whether farmers, small businessmen, or members of the liberal professions, cast their votes for the parties of the centre and the right; the same applies to senior managers.[7] In contrast, the electoral behaviour of the salaried middle strata, especially the lower fraction, was more nuanced: a significant proportion of them – something in the region of 40 per cent – turned to social democracy. Thus, in their electoral behaviour the salaried middle strata presented themselves as the *principal partner* – albeit an uncertain and hesitant one – of the working class within the social-democratic coalition. It should, however, be stressed that the propensity to vote social democratic among the salaried middle strata was almost identical to the national average in the three countries concerned (Table 3.7). This demonstrates the ambiguous and, in a sense, 'undecided' character of their electoral behaviour.

This general impression is largely confirmed in West Germany, where, as we have indicated, the SPD, a less working-class and more interclassist party than its cousins in other countries, comfortably passed the 40 per cent threshold in the category employees/middle management from 1969 onwards (1969: 46 per cent; 1972: 50 per cent).

During the 1960s and up until recently (with the exception of the elections of 1997 and 2001), Labour followed a rather different pattern of electoral development, making Great Britain a partially 'atypical', borderline case. Compared with other countries, British society is characterized by a more assertive and rigid differentiation between workers and the middle classes as regards lifestyles and, more generally, what are called 'life chances'. This means that there has traditionally been a very strong middle-class vote for the Conservative Party. 'In largely rallying to the Conservative banner,' Monica Charlot has written, 'the middle classes defend a *status* and a lifestyle that they consider to be under threat from a majority working class.'[8]

Thus, Labour's marked inferiority among not only the upper middle classes and self-employed but also among salaried middle strata, which contrasts with the politico-electoral 'uncertainty' of the latter in other countries with a strong social democracy, makes Britain a rather special case. Yet in Great Britain, too, a more subtle analysis, based on socioprofessional categories other than the conventional distinction between manual and non-manual workers, yields a picture with greater contrast. In the 1964–70 period, Labour's penetration in the category of employees (which, in its majority, forms part of the popular classes) is situated at a level very nearly equivalent to that of the social-democratic-type formations examined in this work (31 per cent in 1964, 42 per cent in 1970).[9]

Analysis based on examination of 'gross categories' indicates that from the perspective of electoral sociology, the space occupied by the middle classes, rather than being a zone of convergence and absorption of 'extremist' attitudes in some kind of intermediate electoral behaviour, is traversed by pronounced disparities and oppositions. The middle classes are politically *extremely* divided – something that is underestimated by approaches that employ a 'scalar' schema of social stratification. These approaches attribute a resolutely intermediary role to the middle classes, which are regarded as forces of moderation and consensus – a kind of *third party* challenging a supposedly bipolar social antagonism. Now, this schema does not correspond to the complexity of societies in advanced capitalism. From the viewpoint of electoral sociology, the image of an 'intermediate' middle class, privileged depository of social peace, is a myth. It is a myth based on – and, in turn, justifying – the notion of solidarity between medium-sized and small capitalists on the one hand, and the lower 'middle' classes on the other – a 'solidarity' that does not withstand the test of actual political behaviour. In addition, Nicos Poulantzas's hypothesis of a 'quasi-class' – the petty bourgeoisie – with two fractions, the *traditional* petty bourgeoisie and the *new* petty bourgeoisie, is justified by their common polarization *vis-à-vis* the bourgeoisie and the working class. However, Poulantzas's approach underestimates the incontrovertible empirical fact that these two components of the petty bourgeoisie are *highly polarized*, electorally and culturally, among themselves, before being polarized *vis-à-vis* the proletariat and the classical bourgeoisie.[10] In this respect, the key distinction seems to us to be that between those who *own* their means of labour (medium and small businessmen, shopkeepers, artisans, liberal professions, etc.), as well as senior managers, and the middle and lower bands of the *salaried* middle strata (junior and middle managers, civil servants, employees, salaried intellectual professions). Thus, the urban middle classes are *politically* structured around two major poles: on one side, the traditional middle and petty bourgeoisie, which is a pole of *minimal* support for social democracy and the left in general; on the other, the salaried middle strata (broadly, the famous 'new petty bourgeoisie'), which act as an intermediate pole of support for social democrats, and as the second major pillar, alongside workers, of their electoral strength. Within the category of salaried middle strata, which is an internally fragmented group, two components – or, better, *two types of voters* – seem to constitute the epicentre of social-democratic influence.

The first is essentially found among *employees*, all those who do not occupy a position in the social division of labour which confers on them a certain status and authority. The orientation of this category to the left is 'instrumental', and reflects its relative 'marginality' within the middle classes – a 'marginality' that brings it closer to the working class. The firm entrenchment of the social-democratic parties among employees and minor public officials underlines the *popular* character of the social-democratic enterprise.[11]

The second type of voter comes from the intermediate or higher scales of the salaried middle strata. This type is characterized by the practice of a professional skill, often involving duties of supervision and authority, and is principally – but not exclusively – located in the public and para-public sector. It broadly corresponds to what sociologists call 'new middle strata'. This group comprises the professions of teaching, social work, health, and public officials, as well as artistic professions. Its value-orientation, regarded by Frank Parkin as 'altruistic',[12] is often associated with a highly structured left-wing ideology. A 'radical-altruistic' electorate, it corresponds in part to what the 'post-materialism' school, following the pioneering work of Ronald Inglehart, was subsequently to characterize as an electorate with *post-materialist* values.[13] The most distinctive characteristic of this well-educated group (which refers not to a unified social category, but to a socially disparate jumble) is its 'cultural liberalism', according to 1980s French electoral sociology, or 'radical liberalism', according to David Jary.[14] This liberalism or radicalism is linked to a relatively well-articulated left-wing political ideology. In fact, during the 1960s this group became the privileged vector of the two ideological dominants that would seem to be specific to the left-wing electorate: 'traditional left-wing values' and 'cultural liberalism'. Both are strongly correlated with voting for the left – the former more so than the latter, obviously.

The shortage and heterogeneity of available data certainly complicate any attempt to establish the characteristics and real arithmetical weight of this group in the social-democratic electorate with any rigour. It nevertheless seems to be established that the most consistent share of support for social democracy from the higher and middle ranks of the middle classes derived from the new middle strata. This support was an expression – and, at the same time, a demonstration – of the ability of social-democratic parties in the postwar period to expand *well beyond the poor and poorly educated strata of the population*. Social democrats' tendency to pose as a vehicle of 'cultural modernization' in the European societies of the 1960s encouraged – and was encouraged by – the left-wing leanings of this group. It was also furthered by a certain cultural 'archaism' on the part of the centre-right parties (particularly Christian Democrats and conservatives). Hence the support in question was used by the social-democratic elites as the marker of a certain identity, as an *index of modernity*. In this instance, where 'modernity' was the value connoted, the support of new middle strata became a source of strength – a source that was a good deal more important than their electoral weight in the population (ultimately limited) betrays. In the 1950s, and especially in the 1960s, social democracy – mature social democracy – truly and fully acquired its specificity solely through this 'modernizing' aspect. In the 1960s, social democracy established itself, and blossomed, as a force for social *equality* and *redistribution*, but also as a '*modern*' and *culturally liberal* force – more modern and liberal, at any rate, than its conservative opponents. Thus, the firm entrenchment of parties of a social-democratic type among minor employees and new salaried strata, particularly their most educated fraction, highlights and confirms the simultaneously *popular* and *culturally modernizing* character of the social-democratic approach in the initial postwar period. The social democrats' ability to ally egalitarian demands with liberal demands for cultural modernization underlay their strength and consolidation as parties of government.[15]

We cannot offer a sharper image of social-democratic penetration of the salaried middle strata here. The rapid analysis above does not, therefore, enable us to avoid 'contemplation of an ocean of uncertainties', as the French political scientist Philippe Braud might say. Even so, everything indicates that two types of non-manual voter, socially and culturally distinct, gave their support to social-democratic parties. Everything also indicates that this advance among the middle classes allowed social-democratic and labourist formations to constitute themselves as *natural governmental forces*, and to play an important, or even central, role in the political system. However, they did not establish themselves as dominant forces among these classes, not even within the segment most inclined towards them, the salaried middle strata (treated here as a statistical whole without internal differentiation). In their electoral behaviour, these strata were intermediate between a working class strongly inclined to the left, and 'self-employed' and upper middle classes strongly inclined to the right.

Thus, even during the 1960s the adhesion of the middle classes remained a minority and uncertain affair. The structure of the social-democratic electorate confirms the *uncontested predominance of the working class*.

Electoral Social Democracy: Working-Class or Interclassist?

Class Parties and Parties *of the Class*

Given the arithmetically minority status of the working class *stricto sensu*,[16] working-class parties in the 1920s and 1930s were soon faced with a crucial, ideologically formidable electoral dilemma: either to remain class parties and run the risk of being doomed to permanent minority status; or to transform themselves into interclassist parties and claim a majority position in the political system. Condemned to ambiguity, to be strategically Janus-faced, the social-democratic parties 'cannot remain a party of workers alone and yet they can never cease to be a workers' party'.[17] What ensued, particularly after the Second World War, was the gradual dissolution of their class appeal and their constitution in accordance with a format that tended towards the interclassist. Social-democratic parties are *coalition* parties, but not all 'coalitions' are identical.

What constituted the *specificity* of each coalition was the fascinating and peculiar interaction of the combinations that were constructed, the particular mix in the components of a partisan electorate. Otherwise, the electorates of left-wing parties in the countries of advanced capitalism – constituted, as a general rule, by the crucial contribution of two social groups, workers and salaried middle strata – would all have to be treated as equivalent.

The social character of a party is largely conditioned, first, by its social penetration (the percentage of the class or social category that supports the party in question); second by the 'concentration' or 'social cohesion' of its electoral base (the percentage of its electorate that belongs to a single social class); and – even more, perhaps, since what is at stake is then the party's development – by the evolution of these over time.

The great majority of parties of the social-democratic type are, in Richard

Rose and Derek Urwin's classification (developed using the criterion of cohesion or concentration, not penetration), either homogeneous class parties, or parties with 'mutually reinforcing loyalties', constructed around a working-class and a secular component.[18] This criterion, however, does not make it possible to account for the fundamental difference – very rich in its implications – between *class parties* and *parties of the class*. This distinction is highly significant for understanding the representative capacity of social-democratic political forces, and the place they occupy within the party system. A *class* party is one whose electoral base is *socially homogeneous* (in the sense, following the criterion of *cohesion*, that the great majority of its voters belong to a single social class). But a class party is not necessarily a *party of the class* (because it may be the case, following the criterion of penetration, that only a small minority of the relevant social class supports this party). Consequently, a left-wing party can be constituted as a *working class* party without thereby being the party *of the working class*. It can also be a party of the working class without thereby being a working-class party.

The criterion of social penetration, prioritized here, enables us to measure and grasp the entrenchment – the real influence – of the social democrats in society and, in so doing, their role in the political system.

Social Democracy as an *Enlarged* Coalition of the Working Class

If we follow the indications given throughout this chapter, a number of conclusions follow.

1. In all the cases examined, the *central electoral bloc* in the social-democratic electorate is focused on the working class, social-democratic penetration of which is very deep. Alongside the central bloc, a *second bloc* is formed by the salaried middle strata, which, in terms of electoral support, represent an intermediate pole. Thus, the electoral strength of social-democratic-style parties during the 1950s and 1960s was articulated around a central working-class pillar and a secondary pillar, based on the most 'popular' and 'radical-liberal' segment of the middle classes.

2. Given that a *clear majority* – and in some cases an *imposing* majority – of the working class supported social-democratic parties, with the assistance of a substantial minority of the middle classes, we shall call these political formations *enlarged coalitions of the working class* from the standpoint of electoral sociology. We shall distinguish two categories:

    (a) The first (Sweden, Norway) is characterized by a social-democratic penetration that approximates or exceeds *two-thirds* of the working-class vote. These are the parties of *maximum working-class penetration*, and their prototype is obviously the SAP.

    (b) The second is characterized by a penetration situated around the *three-fifths* mark (Great Britain, Denmark) or, in the borderline case of the FRG, clearly exceeding the threshold of 50 per cent of the working-class vote. These are parties with *high working-class penetration*,[19] and it is possible to identify two variants: *strong working-class concentration* – not penetration – whose most characteristic example is the British Labour Party; and a *more interclassist format*, of which the SPD is the most developed specimen.[20]

3. Parties of a social-democratic type are clearly distinguished in the 1950s and 1960s from working-class parties which are *class parties*, but not *parties of the class* (e.g. the PCF and other communist parties). They are also distinguished from parties which, though they belong to the great European social-democratic/socialist family, are neither class parties nor parties of the class, but *interclassist formations* (e.g. the SFIO, the French PS, the PSI, PASOK in the 1970s, the Portuguese PS).

4. The social fabric of electoral behaviour, which we have explained very briefly, demonstrates that social-democratic-type parties did *not* conform to the model of the catch-all party in their electoral sociology.[21] In the initial postwar period, these parties certainly strove to present themselves as great 'popular' formations, as 'coalition forces', in electoral competition. But if the programmatic profile, the social-democratic *scaenae frons*, evolved firmly in a catch-all direction, the hard core – the sociological pillar – was based on the working-class matrix. During the 1960s, the massive sociological reality of social democracy remained essentially centred on the working class.

5. Unquestionably, the so-called 'catch-all' policies of the social-democratic parties proved effective not 'although', but precisely 'because', they were interclassist. But at the same time, these interclassist policies proved effective not although, but *because*, they were centred on the working class. The sub-standard performance in the 1950s and 1960s of parties without deep working-class roots, like the SFIO and PSI, constitutes *a contrario* evidence for this claim. In reality, what a number of political scientists – including myself, for the sake of terminological convenience – have referred to as the social-democratic 'catch-all' strategy of the 1950s and 1960s was not a catch-all strategy, or a working-class strategy, or a 'dual' strategy (which, by definition, is impossible). It was a 'semi-working-class' and 'semi-catch-all' strategy: a strategy of 'sociological broadening'.[22]

In short, the gradual crystallization of a significant audience among some segments of the middle classes (employees, new salaried strata), and the preservation of the working-class mould, form the two sides of social-democratic vitality, of the politically stable and electorally triumphant social democracy of the 1950s and 1960s. Compared with the beginning of the twentieth century and the interwar years, social democracy changed substantially in this period. But the architecture of its electoral space retained the structure – and depth – of yesteryear. The change was gradual and partial; the mutation was not a metamorphosis: it represented an evolution, not a revolution.

From this perspective, the very significant contribution of the salaried middle strata to the social-democratic electoral coalition was that of a pivotal social force. Without it, social democracy would never have had a majority. But without the working class, the very idea of social democracy would have been inconceivable. Its electoral core consisted in the working class, the primary and primordial source of power and effectiveness for a social democracy that was increasingly interclassist.[23]

Notes

1. Matei Dogan, 'Political Cleavages and Social Stratification in France and Italy', in Seymour Martin Lipset and Stein Rokkan, eds, *Party Systems and Voter Alignments: Cross-National Perspectives*, Free Press, New York and Collier-Macmillan, London 1967, p. 129.
2. The exclusion of housewives, pensioners and the unemployed leads to a certain underestimation of blue-collar workers in the social structure of the SPÖ. According to the data cited by Muller and Ulram, 75% of SPÖ voters in 1961 and 68% in 1969 came from a blue-collar occupational milieu (occupational milieu is the occupation of the 'head of the household') (Wolfgang Muller and Peter Ulram, 'The Social and Demographic Structure of Austrian Parties, 1945–93', *Party Politics*, vol. 1, no. 1, 1995, p. 148).
3. Francis G. Castles, *The Social Democratic Image of Society*, Routledge and Kegan Paul, London and Boston, MA 1978, p. 118.
4. Göran Therborn, 'A Unique Chapter in the History of Democracy: The Social Democrats in Sweden', in Klaus Misgeld *et al.*, *Creating Social Democracy: A Century of the Social Democratic Labor Party in Sweden*, Pennsylvania University Press, Pittsburgh 1992, p. 11.
5. In reality, the SPD has been supported by even a relative majority of the electorate only once – in 1972, when it secured 45.8% of the vote against 44.9% for the CDU–CSU. Even during its best period (1969–80), the SPD always came second and its electoral averages range from 43.3% in federal elections to 40.8% in European elections (as against 46% and 49.2%, respectively, for the CDU–CSU). See Henri Menudier, *Les Élections allemandes, 1969–1982*, Centre d'Information et de Recherche sur l'Allemagne Contemporaine, Paris 1982, pp. 37, 81.
6. See also Gerassimos Moschonas, *La gauche française (1972–1988) à la lumière du paradigme social-démocrate. Partis de coalition et coalitions des partis dans la compétition électorale*, doctoral thesis, University of Paris II, 1990, p. 61.
7. In Norway we observe a stronger propensity, by European standards, for the old middle classes to vote for the left. Given, as in most European countries, the weak arithmetical weight of these classes (11% of the population in 1957; 8% in 1989), Norway may be regarded as a particular case, without thereby being distinguished from the general trend. Italy and Greece may also be regarded as separate instances. A feature of Italian and Greek society is the high proportion of self-employed work. The influence of the left (PCI and PDS in Italy, PASOK and KKE in Greece) among the old middle classes is far from negligible.
8. Monica Charlot, ed., *Élections de crise en Grande-Bretagne*, Presses de la Fondation Nationale des Sciences Politiques, Paris 1978, p. 19.
9. Anthony Heath, Roger Jowell and John Curtice, *How Britain Votes*, Pergamon Press, London 1985, pp. 32–3.

10. For a deeper, more detailed analysis of the electoral bond between the left and the middle classes, see Moschonas, *La gauche française*, pp. 59–70, 249–82, 300–12.

11. Working with a very large sample of *non-manual* Labour voters, Colin Rallings demonstrated that 70.7% of its non-manual electorate belonged to the category of 'employees' and 56.3% regarded themselves as part of the working class. He also showed that the more a middle-class voter resembled a working-class voter in sociological terms, the more likely she or he was to vote Labour ('Two Types of Middle Class Labour Voter', *British Journal of Political Science*, vol. 5, 1975, pp. 108–9). Butler and Stokes, for their part, reported that in 1963 68% of those in the category of 'lower non-manuals' regarded themselves as belonging to the working class (*Political Change in Britain*, Macmillan, London 1970, p. 70). The ideal-typical model of this type of non-manual Labour voter, a modified and expanded version of Richard Rose's model, comprises the following five characteristics: (1) possession of a minimal level of education; (2) non-performance of supervisory tasks; (3) membership of a trade union; (4) council house tenancy; (5) working-class origin in respect of intergenerational mobility (Colin Rallings, 'Political Behaviour and Attitudes among the Contemporary Lower Middle Class', in J. Garrard *et al.*, eds, *The Middle Class in Politics*, Saxon House, London 1978, p. 205; Richard Rose, *Class and Party Divisions: Britain as a Test Case*, University of Strathclyde, Glasgow 1969).

12. Frank Parkin, *Middle Class Radicalism*, Manchester University Press, Manchester 1968.

13. Ronald Inglehart, *The Silent Revolution*, Princeton University Press, Princeton, NJ 1977.

14. David Jary, 'A New Significance for the Middle Class Left? Some Hypotheses and an Appraisal of the Evidence of Electoral Sociology', in J. Garrard *et al.*, eds, *The Middle Classes in Politics*, Saxon House, London 1978, p. 140.

15. Alain Bergounioux and Marc Lazar, *La Social-démocratie dans l'Union européenne*, debate in Les Notes de la Fondation Jean Jaurès, no. 6, Paris 1997, pp. 10–11.

16. Adam Przeworski and John Sprague, *Paper Stones: A History of Electoral Socialism*, University of Chicago Press, Chicago 1986, p. 35.

17. Adam Przeworski, 'Social Democracy as a Historical Phenomenon', *New Left Review*, no. 122, 1980, p. 44.

18. Richard Rose and Derek Urwin, 'Social Cohesion, Political Parties and Strains in Regimes', in Dogan and Rose, *European Politics*, Macmillan, London 1971, p. 221. The authors regard the Swedish and Danish social democrats, and the British and Norwegian Labour parties, among others, as homogeneous class parties; and formations like the SPD, SPÖ, PCI and PCF as possessing mutually reinforcing loyalties.

19. It might be argued that the distinction between social-democratic-type parties with *maximum working-class penetration* and those with *high penetration* corresponds, in large part, to the distinction between *successful* and *less successful* parties of the working class.

20. Regarding these two variants, constituted by the criterion of *social cohesion*, my distinction coincides in the main with the conclusions of Rose and Urwin in *European Politics*, pp. 221–5.

21. My analysis broadly coincides with the conclusions of Bartolini: 'if a "golden age" of class alignment and of social homogeneity in socialist support ever existed, this was certainly not the early phase, but rather the intermediate period of the 1930s–1950s' (*Electoral, Partisan and Corporate Socialism. Organisa-*

tonal Consolidation and Membership Mobilisation in Early Socialist Movements, Estudio/Working Paper 83, Juan March Institute, Madrid 1996, p. 44).

22. See Moschonas, *La gauche française*, pp. 493–4. Kirchheimer does not identify the catch-all party with the interclassist structure of its electorate (see Otto Kirchheimer, 'The Transformation of Western European Party Systems', in Joseph La Palombara and Myron Weiner, eds, *Political Parties and Political Development*, Princeton University Press, Princeton, NJ 1966, p. 185). For a presentation and critique of the thesis of the catch-all party in Kirchheimer, see Steven B. Wolinetz, 'The Transformation of Western European Party Systems Revisited', *West European Politics*, vol. 2, no. 1, 1979, pp. 4–28. See also Karl Dittrich, 'Testing the Catch-all Thesis: Some Difficulties and Possibilities', in Hans Daalder and Peter Mair, *Western European Party Systems*, Sage, London 1985, pp. 257–66, especially pp. 258–9; also Daniel-Louis Seiler, *De la comparaison des partis politiques*, Economica, Paris 1986, especially pp. 94–9.

23. The precondition for the realization by social democrats of their 'dual' function as *parties of the working class* and *national parties of integration* (Leo Panitch, 'Profits and Politics: Labour and the Crisis of British Capitalism', *Politics and Society*, vol. 7, no. 4, 1977, p. 478), resides in their working-class entrenchment. It is thus not surprising if the most spectacular successes or the most crushing defeats of social-democratic parties have often been associated with fluctuations in the vote of 'low-paid social groups'. For – to invoke Geoffrey Hodgson – I shall say that this is 'surely the lesson' of the 1960s: 'Those who must live by the labour movement can also die by that movement' (*Labour at the Crossroads*, Martin Robertson, Oxford 1981, p. 122). *Some decades later, this was perhaps no longer true.*

4

Social Democracy in Competition

Uses of the term 'social democrat', from the strictest to the loosest, implicitly or explicitly refer to political behaviour of a 'right-wing' sort, characteristic of certain working-class/popular parties in northern and central Europe.

Adoption of a 'moderate' ideological and programmatic profile, and implementation of interclassist strategies, are its two most important expressions. The distinctively social-democratic traits that facilitate – and follow from – this behaviour (which is not always 'right-wing'), and constitute the specificity of social democracy as an *electoral operator*, are the focus of this chapter.

Legitimate Parties

If parties of a social-democratic type are to be able to develop their full dynamic in competition, they must not only be masters of the left of the political scene – something we shall see later – and have a privileged link, both electoral and organizational, with the working class; they must also be accepted as *legitimate contenders for government*. This is all the more important in that historically socialist or communist parties have been *outsiders*, 'ideological' parties positioned outside the dominant pragmatism and the terms of what is ideologically admissible.

If governmental legitimacy is – currently – a constitutive element in the identity of social democracy, in the first phase of social democracy's career it was neither given, even in the case of electorally powerful parties, nor produced in quasi-mechanical fashion by the 'natural' operation of competitive democracy. It was the result of a full-scale confrontation over conflicting images of what is legitimate, it was a product of ideological and political struggle. Parties of a social-democratic type became wholly 'competitive' only gradually, by adopting a political profile that was intrinsically close to the *status quo*.

From the beginning of the twentieth century, while the centre of political life in western countries overall moved to the left (in the sense that certain left-wing ideas became the 'fund of ideology' common to the whole of society), left-wing parties, and especially the social-democratic parties, shifted to the right. This shift had as a corollary the *de-radicalization* of the social-democratic parties, a reduction in the distance between the political changes desired and advocated by them and what the British call '*status quo* policies'. John Clayton Thomas has shown that in the period 1911–62, this shift 'to the right', common to all left-wing forces, was most pronounced in countries with a classical social democracy, like Sweden, Austria and Germany.[1] Indeed, the ideological and political trajectory followed by the Marxist social democrats of the beginning of the century was marked by more ruptures and renunciations than that of the labour parties of the Commonwealth, which were more moderate from the outset; or of the communists, whose anti-capitalism was more consistent and enduring.

Once acquired, this legitimacy separated social democracy from other 'reformist' political forces and equipped it, at the level of competition, to present itself as:

(a) the natural force of alternation;
(b) the force capable of neutralizing a possible 'regime vote'.

The Natural Force of Alternation

Presenting itself as the natural force of governmental alternation allowed social democracy, *inter alia*, to attract the protest vote against the incumbent government when it found itself in opposition – almost mechanically so in two-party systems. Traditionally non-socialist social categories and political tendencies broadened the electoral bases of the social-democratic parties, associating themselves willy-nilly with the social-democratic electoral coalition by virtue of the latter's competitive position. This vote – cast for social democracy not only because of its ideological principles or its concrete programme, but also as a function of the 'pivotal position' it occupied in the disposition of opposition forces – was directed less to social democracy as such than to 'the opposition'.

The ability to 'identify itself' (to use this term) with 'the opposition' was characteristic of every social democracy in the 1960s, but not of every opposition party. 'Anti-systemic' parties (Georges Lavau) – or those perceived as such, we should add – devote themselves totally and continuously to the critique of the system, its values and norms, its authorities.[2] But as for fitness to 'take over' from these authorities, they find themselves in a difficult situation. The cases of 'reformist' communist parties like the PCF or the PCI are good examples of oppositions that were incapable, for different reasons, of identifying themselves with 'the opposition'. The case of the SPD – a party that was not anti-systemic – in the initial postwar period is another instance. Suffering the damaging consequences of the division of Germany, and pursuing the model of 'oppositional' socialism after 1949, the SPD soon found itself accused of not looking after the nation's interests. The remarkable accumulation of successive electoral defeats (1949, 1953, 1957, 1961, 1965), despite its regular electoral progress (from 1953 onwards), furnished proof of the SPD's inability to establish itself as a 'natural' – because legitimate – force of alternation. The symbolic 'brutality' of the turn at Bad Godesberg (1959), like the policy of the Grand Coalition (1966–69), made the SPD one of the most 'right-wing' social-democratic parties in the European socialist family of the era. The implementation and dramatization of this radically moderate strategy had as its main objective dispelling the hesitations and fears of the electorate, and reassuring the various 'centres of power and authority'. The SPD undertook, with great success, to 'divest itself of all the repulsive attributes of the identity it had constructed',[3] in order to establish itself as a legitimate claimant to power. In effect, these attributes prevented it being identified with the German opposition (in the sense defined above), despite the fact that it represented the main opposition in the German party system. Hence the SPD's excessive moderation directly corresponded – and responded – to the excessive domination of its opponent's ideas, to the fact that this opponent, and it alone, represented governmental legitimacy.

If, in the FRG, it was necessary to pass via Bad Godesberg, and then the Grand Coalition, for 'sole possible alternative' and 'natural alternation' to coincide, in Italy the Historic Compromise and, considerably later, the PCI's transformation into the PDS were required. In France – where the SFIO was unable to identify itself with the opposition not because it was not moderate, but because it was too moderate – it was necessary to operate via the Union of the Left (1972–81) and especially, thanks to the Union, a whole process of marginalization of the PCF, historically the most important left-wing party in France. In other words, in France radicalization of the left (through the Common Programme), and then its *de-radicalization*, as indicated by the marked displacement of the balance of forces in favour of the PS, was the condition for the 1981 victory.

In this perspective, the term 'natural alternation' designates a *political aptitude*, not a particular and specific way of structuring the space of opposition (where the only organized opposition is the left). For to be the sole – or principal – recipient of the protest vote against the incumbent government, and to attract that vote effectively, are not the same thing. Being the sole possible alternative, and constituting oneself as the 'natural' alternative, are not the same thing.[4] Now, it is clear that the 'typical' social democracy of the 1960s – 'mature' social democracy – proved capable of constructing itself as a political force that was in a position to compound the effects of the left dynamic and the opposition dynamic. It thus imposed itself as a force capable of *establishing its majority/governmental vocation*.

The social-democratic parties were moderate forces of a specific type and structure. Precisely because they occupied virtually the whole of the left part of the political scene, and precisely because they enjoyed massive support from the world of labour, they were simultaneously in a position, through a strategy of moderation, to attract 'centrist' and 'barely politicized' bands of the electorate effectively. For not every strategy of moderation is effective, or effective in an identical manner and to the same degree, simply by virtue of being moderate. The cases of the SFIO, the PSI or, much later, the Portuguese PS – parties that did not control the left part of the political scene to the same extent as the parties of a social-democratic type, or enjoy the unequivocal support of the world of labour – demonstrate that moderation does not necessarily betoken electoral effectiveness. There are different ways of being 'moderate', just as there are different ways of being 'revisionist', 'reformist', or merely 'modernizing'.

The Force Capable of Neutralizing a Possible 'Regime Vote'

By 'regime vote'[5] I mean that share of the vote cast for the 'conservative' party[6] best placed to confront the left-wing adversary, when the latter – as a result of its electoral strength and radical policy – seems capable of challenging the equilibrium of the whole sociopolitical system. This type of vote is not an act of loyalty towards the chosen 'conservative' party, but *a gesture of support for the system*, the beneficiary being merely the appropriate vehicle, the most effective political instrument, to respond to the competitive challenge from the left.

A system really or allegedly at the crossroads between capitalism and socialism is the basic causal factor underlying the emergence of a 'regime vote'. Its preconditions are the presence of a left-wing party which is, first, an irreconcilable enemy – real or supposed – of the existing system; and, second, sufficiently strong to accede to government. The existence of this type of vote prevents the left-wing party (socialist or other) fully benefiting from the exhaustion of the incumbent government, and thus constituting itself as a rallying point, and hence as a pole of government. The 'regime vote' rests on the quasi-opposition – or what is experienced as such – between the left-wing party and the social system. Now, the exhaustion of social democracy's anti-capitalist spirit, and its renunciation of its anti-systemic objectives, were precisely what contributed to surmounting definitively the obstacle represented by this type of vote. Stripped of its anti-capitalist temptations, social democracy discovered a new competitive vitality – in the 1930s in some instances (Scandinavia), in the 1940s for a majority of parties, and the 1960s for others (FRG). As soon as the barrier of the 'regime vote' was breached, it could thus amass the lion's share of the protest vote against the government, presenting and constructing itself as a majority/governmental force.

The attainment of legitimacy, opening the way to government, was mainly the product of – and, in a way, compensation for – ideological de-radicalization. Whether the compensation was commensurate with the ideological 'sacrifice' demanded is a question that does not lend itself to an unequivocal response.

Parties Largely Dominant on the Left

In the countries that are most advanced on the social-democratic path (Scandinavia, Austria, the FRG and, in variant forms, Great Britain and the Benelux countries), the most striking thing about the structuration of the left in the period 1945 to 1973 was the domination of *virtually the whole* of the left of the politico-ideological continuum by the social-democratic-type party. The absence of a significant left competitor is not only a constant of the successful social-democratic experiences, but seems to condition the success itself. For the competitive status and role of the party in the party and political system are heavily subject to the presence or absence of a competitor of some arithmetical significance, whether communist or other. This is so for four reasons. (1) With no significant rival on its left, the party of a social-democratic type can, *at no great risk*, initiate a political strategy *orientated towards the centre* with a view to attracting more moderate segments of the population. (2) This positioning more to 'the centre', and the moderation that accompanies it, lead (as we shall see) to the success of the tripartite 'social pact', one of whose essential bases is precisely a culture based on conciliation and pragmatism. (3) Having consolidated its electoral entrenchment in the working class, the social-democratic party can, in the absence of a significant left wing competitor, pursue a strategy of attracting the middle classes, without courting the danger of being destabilized. (4) With no electorally influential opponent on the left, the social-democratic-type party can legitimately take advantage of its representativeness, sociological and political, to establish itself as a natural party of government.

It is certainly no accident if the social-democratic parties with the most pronounced governmental character were those that were both *most working-class* in the social composition of their electorate, and *faced with no important rival on the left*. Measuring the 'governmental power' of the socialist/social-democratic parties for the period 1945 to 1979, Anton Pelinka has ranked the parties of the following countries in the top five: (1) Sweden, (2) Norway, (3) Denmark, (4) Austria, and (5) United Kingdom.[7] It should be noted that the five parties concerned are socially the most working-class, and have no important competitor on the left – with the exception of the Danish social democrats since 1960 (SF: 6.1 per cent) and especially 1966 (SF: 10.9 per cent). It is perhaps not irrelevant to signal that in the same study Pelinka ranks lowest the socialist parties of France (SFIO, PS) and Italy (PSDI and PSI), which are highly interclassist and flanked on their left by powerful communist formations.

Thus, if the social-democratic parties proved able to solicit the centrist vote successfully, it is because they were able to consolidate their traditional electorate, the electorate situated most to the left on the left–right continuum. Anchorage and domination on the left were invariably the *first step* in an ambitious centripetal strategy. In fact, largely dominating the left of the political scene represented a condition of any successful strategy

orientated towards the centre. Parties of a social-democratic type established themselves as central parties in European political systems only
because they were able to penetrate the centre effectively; and *they were able
to penetrate the centre effectively only because they were not centrist.* In a seeming
paradox, a quasi-monopoly on the left was the *precondition* of moderation.
But this quasi-monopoly made the social-democratic parties, for all their
moderation, popular *left-wing* parties, not intermediate political formations
equidistant from the extremes.

The existence or emergence of an important competitor on the left is a
factor of *structural destablilization,* for the competitor tends to test the way in
which the whole social-democratic political edifice is constructed, and
operates. In effect, the 'opening' to the middle classes, or the pursuit of a
politics inflected to the centre, truly succeeded only once social democracy
had established its unequivocal preponderance over the whole of the left.
The presence, alongside the socialist or social-democratic party, of a strong
communist party represented either a major obstacle to such 'sociological
openness', or the central factor in the failure of such initiatives. The
examples of the SPD before 1933, or the SFIO after the war, are evidence
enough.[8]

The consolidation and blossoming of such left-wing rivals, and the
constant pressure exerted by them on social democracy, weaken it sociologically, politically and ideologically, rendering it incapable of fulfilling its
'role' in the party and political system. Implicitly at stake in the existence
of significant left-wing competitors is the destabilization – or frustration –
of the dominant socialist party's strategy.

The 'mechanical', but often effective, response to this left-wing challenge
is the *displacement of the social-democratic party's ideological centre of gravity to the
left.* It is well known in the political literature that the existence of
comparatively strong communist parties has often led the social-demo-
cratic/socialist parties to adopt a more radical profile. More recently, the
appearance of the Greens in the FRG and the strong rise of the popular
socialists in Denmark have prompted the social-democratic parties in those
countries to position themselves markedly more to the left than before.
The more radical profile of PASOK in Greece, and of PSOE (during the
immediate post-Franco era) in Spain, attest equally, in their fashion, to
the impact of an electorally and politically significant left-wing pole on the
mechanism of competition.

Thus, the number – and especially the level of influence – of parties to
the left of social democracy had a far from negligible impact on its
ideological and political evolution, and on its capacity to implement the
tripartite 'social pact'. This was not without its consequences for the future.

Degree of Domination on the Left, Structuration of the Trade-Union Movement and the Effectiveness of Interclassist Strategies

The strategy of opening up to the middle classes, a constant of social-democratic politics after 1945, was furthered and refined in line with the increasing arithmetical weight and internal differentiation of this highly heterogeneous social group.

This strategy brought with it, however, the risk of disharmony between the party's natural base and the middle classes, since greater influence among the latter had the potential to weaken working-class support. Were that to have transpired, it would have been as if the social-democratic parties, ensnared by their own strategy, had sacrificed any possibility of a majoritarian politics, since any policy of 'openness' risked becoming very costly, and hence intolerable.

Przeworski and Sprague have shown that a 'trade-off' between votes of working-class origin and votes of 'middle-class' provenance did exist, and that in at least some instances it weighed heavily in the frustration of interclassist politics.

In countries with an influential communist party, a fragmented trade-unionism, and/or a significant religious divide, an interclassist strategy risked proving very costly.[9] The reason was that in political systems with a *divided* left, workers had the alternative, *as workers*, of shifting to the communist parties, which naturally pursued a specifically working-class counter-strategy.

By contrast, in countries without a significant religious divide, with a weak communist party, and a dense, unified and relatively centralized trade-unionism, *the costs of the interclassist strategy were significantly reduced.* There, it proved effective in winning votes from the middle classes. The contrast between these two scenarios enables us to appreciate the practical importance of the social-democratic actor occupying virtually the whole of the left part of the left–right continuum. The identity of social democracy (ideological, programmatic, sociological) was profoundly marked by the presence or absence of this competitive attribute.

To some extent, the adoption of an interclassist appeal indicates abandonment by the social-democratic party of its role as explicit *political organizer* of the working class. The absence in the second group of countries of an influential left-wing party, able to substitute itself for social democracy and address the working class *as a class*, allows social democracy to remain, *faute de mieux*, the representative of the working class without undue cost. Moreover, very strong unions operate as 'the effective mechanism of class organization', establishing the salience of class in political conflict and public debate through their activity and power. We might even say that if this salience is called into question by interclassist electoral strategies, it is continually re-established – albeit only in part – by trade-union action and, even more, by the existence of the system of corporatist representation (see below). Thus, given the absence of *politically* competing class interpellation and the role of class organizer assumed by 'friendly' unions, the weakening of working-class politics at the level of electoral strategies in countries with a strong social democracy does not lead to the creation of a wide gulf between the social-democratic elites and working-class strata. Were that to change, everything might change.

Notes

1. John Clayton Thomas, *The Decline of Ideology in Western Political Parties: A Study of Changing Policy Orientations*, Sage, London 1975, pp. 21–2, 41–3.
2. Georges Lavau, 'Partis et systèmes: interactions et fonctions', *Canadian Journal of Political Science*, II, vol. 1, March 1969, p. 40.
3. Georges Lavau's words, referring to the PCF, in *À quoi sert le Parti communiste français?*, Fayard, Paris 1981, p. 423.
4. An interesting illustration is the British Labour Party in the 1980s.
5. See Marcello Fedele, *Classi e partiti negli anni 70*, Editori Riuniti, Rome 1979, p. 120 for 'voto di régime'.
6. It need not be a conservative party in the traditional sense of the term, but simply the party that is best placed, regardless of its ideological profile, to guarantee continuity, to *preserve* the system. The vote for the DC in Italy in 1976 and the PS in Portugal in April 1975 (in both instances to thwart the 'communist threat') are good examples of a 'regime vote'.
7. Anton Pelinka, *Social Democratic Parties in Europe*, Praeger, New York 1983, p. 80.
8. See Adam Przeworski and John Sprague, *Paper Stones: A History of Electoral Socialism*, University of Chicago Press, Chicago 1986, pp. 71–2. Studying the electoral results of the left in fifteen countries (1917–43, 1944–78), Stefano Bartolini has shown that there was a correlation between the communist vote and the socialist vote, an increase in the one very often entailing a decline in the other. In countries with a strong communist party (Italy, France, Finland, Iceland), a rise in the communist vote was accompanied in 58.3% of cases (in 1944–78) by a decline in the socialist vote, whereas the converse (increase in the socialist vote, decline in the communist vote) was true in only 37.5% of cases. It is important to signal that in the group of 'other countries' the corresponding statistics were 57.5% and 62.2% ('The European Left since the Second World War: Size, Composition and Patterns of Electoral Development', in Hans Daalder and Peter Mair, eds, *Western European Party Systems*, Sage, London 1985, p. 154, Table 6.4).
9. Indeed, Przeworski and Sprague have found that the SPD (before 1933), the SFIO (before 1968), and the Finnish party (before 1972) paid very dearly for their interclassist strategies. For each voter from the middle classes, the SPD lost on average – for the whole period examined – 16.7 workers, the French socialists 9.3, and the Finnish 1.41. The respective figures for Sweden are 0.77, for Norway 0.02, and for Denmark 0.13. See *Paper Stones*, p. 70, Table 3.3.

5

The Social-Democratic Compromise

The Social-Democratic/Keynesian Symbiosis and Neo-Corporatism

With the Cold War, we suggested, the anti-capitalist vocation of social democracy was blurred completely, and it henceforth became synonymous with 'reformism'. The blossoming of mature social democracy was deeply bound up with the expansion of the role of the state and Keynesianism. The discrediting of *laissez-faire* capitalism following the interwar depression, the highly active role of the state during the war, and the enormous tasks of reconstruction thereafter created an economic and intellectual framework which was conducive to the legitimation of state intervention. In addition, Keynesian policy imparted a 'rational' economic foundation to the postwar egalitarian surge: *the smooth operation of the economy henceforth depended on strengthening domestic consumption through a more equitable distribution of income and wealth, in the framework of an economically and socially active state.*[1] More particularly, through the public financing of investment and the maintenance of demand by means of budgetary policy, the state could satisfy simultaneously the imperative of economic growth and the aspiration to social justice. Here various ideas dear to left-wing parties (active state, wealth redistribution, prioritization of consumption, protection of the weakest) found an ideal ground – and the appropriate economic techniques social democracy had lacked in the interwar years – for their implementation.[2] In circumstances of rapid growth and a significant increase in living standards, the social democrats' main objectives were full employment, increases in the real income of wage-earners, development of a social security system, equal participation in all the benefits of the education and health system, and improvement in public infrastructure.[3]

These objectives found support in a whole institutional apparatus – of varying complexity and efficiency, depending on the country – of consultation, negotiation and decision-making between the social partners (employers, unions), under the auspices of the state (*social corporatism* or *neo-corporatism*). The mainspring of this institutional apparatus, as well as of the symbiosis between social democracy and Keynesianism, was the social-democratic *compromise*, involving the institutionalization of a mode of regulation of social conflict based on the multiplication of bi- or trilateral arrangements between unions, employers and state.

As a general rule, the bi- or trilateral system, often dubbed neo-corporatist, had the following characteristics, as described by Ferdinand Karlhofer:

- small number of labour and employer organizations (monopoly or oligopoly);
- high degree of concentration and organizational centralization;
- a certain degree of autonomy of the elites from the rank and file (upward delegation, downward control);
- existence of inter-organizational networks of interest representation ensuring stable and calculable political exchange;
- co-ordination and synchronization of sectoral collective bargaining by the national peak associations;
- collaboration of worker and employer organizations with the government in macro-economic steering (in particular concerning income policy).[4]

The neo-corporatist apparatus is a system of 'regulated exchange'.[5] Wage moderation, industrial peace, profit rates sufficiently high to maintain and strengthen the competitiveness of firms – more generally, the acceptance by the organized working class of the capitalist logic of profit and the market – these constituted the *first plank* in this 'system of exchange'. Solidaristic wage-bargaining, the establishment of an ambitious social state, an expansionary budgetary policy, the strengthening of 'workers' collectives' in the firm, and often an active labour-market policy – these constituted the *second plank* of the exchange, the plank of compensation.[6] In effect, the system of bi- or tripartite negotiation, whether centralized or semi-centralized, aimed at more than the mere regulation of industrial conflict. Combined with an economically active state, it formed part of a more general economic and social order, the 'Co-ordinated Market-Economies' or, in a different terminology, the 'Organized Market Economies'.[7] Their distinguishing characteristics were a capitalist economy with high wages, relative egalitarianism, a well-designed social state, a high level of competitiveness, and an absence of major industrial conflicts. On these grounds they differ from the 'Liberal Market Economies' of the Anglo-Saxon variety, which are less egalitarian, possess a less active state, and have fragmented systems of negotiation.

Thus defined, the institutional set of 'social partnership' was not really established outside central and northern Europe. Strictly applied, this definition covers Sweden, Austria, Norway and, in a less structured version, Denmark. In the Netherlands and Belgium, too, the *consociational* process of decision-making approximated to neo-corporatism. Germany shared some of these characteristics, notably during the period of 'concerted action' (1967–76). The superficial unity of British trade-unionism and its extremely decentralized (or, better, minimally articulated) structure, as well as the matching inability of the British employers' associations 'to enforce collective agreements on employers',[8] largely account for the less developed and very unstable character of 'corporatist' arrangements in the United Kingdom.

In Finland, Italy, and France (after the left's arrival in power in 1981), in Spain and, to a lesser extent Portugal and later Greece (the 1990s), steps were taken towards the adoption of a more neo-corporatist format.[9] But while the results were not always disappointing (the Finnish experience being the most advanced), they fell short of the objectives.

From the perspective of day-to-day co-operation – but also from a strictly institutional and juridical viewpoint – there were very considerable differences between the various national types of institutionalized collective bargaining. From the more decentralized model of German 'co-determination' to the more egalitarian, solidaristic and 'inclusive' Scandinavian system, via the less egalitarian and more consensual Austrian Chambers system, the scenarios of national and sectoral macro-negotiation were many, varied, and original.[10] However, the pact between capital and labour found its consummate expression in Sweden, a country whose social system was profoundly marked by this grand 'coalition for growth'.

This compromise, whose first significant appearance dates back to Sweden and Norway in the 1930s, reached a peak in the period 1960 to 1973.[11] Thus, approximately fifty years after the first revisionist crisis, in its practice and ideology social democracy implemented a dual compromise between capital and labour on the one hand, the state and the market on the other.[12] The social-democratic synthesis was of great significance in the formation of a *fundamental consensus* after the Second World War. It established the social-democratic model of problem-solving, the social-democratic paradigm, as the central reference point for a whole period. This was the era of the social-democratic 'consensus' or, as some had it, 'civilization'. For indeed, as Alan Wolfe has emphasized: 'What is surprising about social democracy is not that it exists in a capitalist world system, but that in some ways *it actually organizes that system and defines its priorities.*'[13]

The Social-Democratic Compromise: Capitalist Regulation or Expression of the Strength of Labour?

The social-democratic model of social compromise becomes possible only when the social partners accept the capitalist order and contribute to its macro-economic management. In other words, the horizon of social-democratic reformist action, and of neo-corporatist regulation, is determined by an *impassable boundary*, though the latter varies depending on the particular period and society: protection, in the macro-economic sense, of capitalist accumulation, and hence profit. This border puts property in a position of strength *vis-à-vis* the unions. The privileged position of capital consists in the fact that investment decisions – a necessary condition for the production of wealth – are a private prerogative, attaching to property, and have as their purpose profit. 'Society's structural dependence *vis-à-vis* capital' is the origin of the deterrent – and persuasive – power of employers. 'Businessmen do nothing more than persuade,' Charles Lindblom has written.[14] Thus the satisfaction of working-class interests, like those of every social group, depends largely on their compatibility with the private profits of the owners of capital. When such compatibility does not exist (e.g. the

Swedish trade-union left's option for 'wage-earner funds', which was perceived as hostile to employers' interests), capital gets out.

An invariably unstable *balance between unequal forces* constitutes the prior given framework, 'past, present and to come', of the social-democratic compromise. The flourishing of this 'tripartite' policy was undoubtedly linked in part to the intellectually and economically propitious postwar context. For the social democrats it supplied an electorally effective and economically coherent response to the major difficulty – and basic contradiction – of the social-democratic project: 'constraining business while relying on it to maintain high investment'.[15]

For all that, was the social-democratic compromise, as well as the whole neo-corporatist consensus bound up with its most advanced forms, a mere shadow theatre bereft of utility for the working class?

The most advanced forms of 'policy-making' of a neo-corporatist type unquestionably seem to be linked to national situations characterized by a powerful working-class movement. According to Walter Korpi's calculations, the group of countries where the working class was strongest in 1946–76 – strength being calculated according to three quantitative indicators (rate of unionization, electoral support for left-wing parties, length of time in government) – comprised Sweden, Austria and Norway, countries with a long social-democratic tradition. These same countries were, however, also 'highly corporatist'. The 'power resources' of the working class, its union and political strength, exerted significant influence on the establishment and development of the neo-corporatist apparatus: growth in this power seems to act positively, and its decline negatively, on the stability and productivity of the apparatus. In this sense, the neo-corporatist participatory process is not simply a 'means of control and integration' of the working class. No doubt it is that too. But at the same time, it *translates and validates the political and trade-union strength of wage-labour at an institutional level.*[16]

Moreover, it exercised significant influence over public policies, which were more 'sensitive' to the interests of wage-labour (active employment policies, wage solidarity, a more developed social state than elsewhere, protection and enhancement of trade-union rights). Thus, particularly in *social-democratic regimes*,[17] the neo-corporatist apparatus – supported by, and in turn supporting, the Keynesian social state – 'partially decommodified labour insofar as it reduced workers' dependence on the market for economic security'.[18] Paul Boreham and Richard Hall's data point in this direction:

> Both macroeconomic and microeconomic advantages appear to flow to labour *where a sustained strategy of political unionism is pursued.* By contrast, where union strategy remains locked into the level of the enterprise only, whether through strategic choice, the influence of policy conditions or institutional design, significant gains for labour at both levels remain elusive.[19]

Thus everything suggests that a weak degree of contractual regulation of class confrontation and, consequently, a high level of industrial conflict are often – but not always – a *sign of weakness*, rather than an expression of the strength of the working-class movement. Moreover, one reason for the ongoing destabilization of corporatist structures today is the weakening of the political and, above all, trade-union left.

The Decisive Role of the Party/Union Pair

The participation of labour unions in the 'generalized exchange' represented by the neo-corporatist process is shaped, *inter alia*, by two conditions. The first consists in the unions' capacity to control a potential crisis of representation within the organized working class. For compromise to be possible, union organizations must be representative and 'centralized'; or the relationship between the base and the leadership must at least be '*well-articulated*' in the sense that 'any activism of the rank and file is contained within forms and goals consistent with and interdependent with the strategy of the national leadership'.[20] Such unions are in a position to have the commitments they make in their name respected by their base and the mass of workers.

The second condition – which we shall discuss at greater length – relates to the existence of a powerful, favourably disposed – that is to say, socialist or social-democratic – government. Such a government not only represents the guarantor of the results anticipated from the exchange: like every government, it puts pressure on the two social partners to reach agreement. This pressure is exerted in the name of the general interest, and particularly of 'third parties', who are usually the 'innocent victims' of labour disputes and bipolar confrontation.[21] Such a government also – and above all – acts on the formation of coalitions within the triangle and, as a result, on the *outcome* of the tripartite negotiation. Working-class and trade-union interests are given more weight when left-wing parties 'occupy the seat of power'. According to Francis Castles, class co-operation 'can only be advantageous to the working class when the dominant political force in society is either an agency of working-class interests as such or is, at least, quite explicitly not a creature of the political Right'.[22] It is equally clear that the presence of a *powerful* social-democratic party in government – and, consequently, the *perspective of an extended period of social-democratic government*, is an *effective motive* for trade-union participation in neo-corporatist arrangements. The 'contractual' process of regulating class confrontation is nearly always, implicitly and explicitly, a *three-sided game*. The political 'complexion' of the third party – that is, the state – largely determines the strategic calculation of the working-class partner. Basically, despite a widespread thesis to the contrary, the requirement of mutual reciprocity – the principle of 'I give so that you will give' (*Do ut des*) – governs the logic of centralized or semi-centralized collective bargaining *only partially*. This exchange 'involves "univocal reciprocity" where A may give to B but receive from a third party, and B may receive from A but give to another party, rather than "mutual reciprocity" where A and B both give and receive'.[23]

In this sense, if neo-corporatism contributes to short-circuiting the power of the state; if private associations (unions and employers) find themselves accorded 'an authority in place of the state in whole sectors of public life',[24] the role of the state remains directly or indirectly central.

Thus, the likelihood of a union adopting a 'confrontational' strategy would appear less if union density is high, the union is unified and centralized, its relations with the socialist or social-democratic party are close, and the 'governmental fitness' of this party is high. The quasi-exception to this tendency is British trade unions, which are among the most 'conflict-oriented' despite their close links with Labour, a party with a high governmental quotient until the late 1970s. The main explanation for this is the superficial unity of British trade-unionism, and its decentralized structure. The French case, an instance of 'concertation without labor', affords *a contrario* proof of the tendency. The problem of 'class struggle' trade-unionism in France lies not in some option for 'class struggle', but in its representative weakness. Marked by the vicious circle of its contradictions (division, politicization, weakness), and confronted (in George Ross's excellent expression) with the 'dilemma' of being 'hostage to a friendly opposition',[25] French trade-unionism before 1981 directed its mobilizing powers not towards the institutionalization of social conflict but towards open conflict, in the perspective of the left's accession to power. After 1981, the absence of a social-democratic-type structure, the socialists' difficulty in managing a fratricidal trade-union pluralism, and adverse economic circumstances objectively encouraged – as in Spain, Portugal and Greece – a policy of seeking to outbid rivals and reversion to the logic of governmental regulation. The weakness and fragmented texture of French trade-unionism, combined with the representative weakness of the employers' organizations, were among the factors that led to weak institutionalization of social conflict.[26]

Class Compromise and the
Social-Democratic Configuration

By making the welfare state and growth their aim, and Keynesianism and tripartite decision-making the appropriate instruments, social-democratic parties could finally reconcile the imperative of efficiency and the aspiration to equality in pragmatic fashion. They could thus perform the dual function – which was electorally very rewarding – of being simultaneously *working-class* parties and parties of *all the people*, presenting and often establishing themselves with voters as guarantors of working-class interests and the general interest alike.

Thus, the social-democratic experience of the 1950s and 1960s represented a particular way of managing the social question. And the 'social-democratic regime'[27] was not – to adopt an Aristotelian term while altering its sense – that of the 'median', but of the 'mixed' polity. A widespread view to the contrary notwithstanding, it was not a project for the promotion of a 'third social force', that is, the middle classes (*to meson auxein* – 'to increase the middle class' – as Aristotle put it), but a *modern* version of the classical bipolarity between the propertied and the unpropertied. The logic of the social compromise thus rested firmly on the institutionalization – and hence the *enhancement* – of organized capital, organized labour, and the conflict between them. Social-democratic logic did not challenge class antagonism; it presupposed partners with specific identities and interests, not amenable to some Rousseau-style 'general will'.

In its neo-corporatist form, the social-democratic compromise was not, therefore, an antidote to the class mentality. Obviously, this experience was not the only possible version of modern class struggle, and perhaps it is only a borderline case. But in its fashion, it clarifies an important dimension of modern class struggle. Within this mode of managing things, class struggle became a central institutional element of the *'normal' daily operation* of the economic and social system. The class system in each society is, by definition, unique, and precludes any 'block' reflection and interpretation. But at least in Scandinavia – to varying extents, depending on the country – the visibility and transparency of class structuration was strong, and was further strengthened – even if this might initially seem paradoxical – by 'triangular', and often peaceful, regulation of the social question. Ironically, with neo-corporatism class fronts were strengthened, but head-on class confrontation abated.

If the institutionalization of social conflict enhanced its visibility, it simultaneously rendered the emergence of a 'revolutionary consciousness', involving perception of the capitalist order as fundamentally illegitimate, more difficult. Institutionalized collective bargaining strengthened the *ideology of moderation* (taking account of the interests and logic of the opponent/partner), and the *ideology of the national interest*, within trade-union federations, thus considerably strengthening their bureaucratic character and organizational conservatism. In this system the working class was regarded as a tranquil force, rather than as the dangerous class. In this sense, the social-democratic experience represents the example of a class struggle *without revolutionary potential*, without a 'universal class', without red banners, without 'everything or nothing', and without a 'final' break.

Even so it was a class struggle. It was a class struggle that did not challenge the capitalist mode of production, and did not only *not* seek to eliminate the old 'machinery of oppression' constituted by the state, according to Marx, but attempted to utilize it. In the social-democratic experience, however, the working class was neither an 'atomized' class, nor a class with a 'trade-unionist' culture whose horizon was limited exclusively to the economic struggle. *It was more than a 'class in itself':* it was a class constituted as a class, as an autonomous force, and proud of so being. It did not simply intervene on the political front, but tended to influence and shape the whole political system, intervening in its macroeconomic options. It was thus entitled to speak in the name of the general interest. Trade-unionism became a *popular-national institution* with the right – and the duty – jointly to administer the public interest. And in the countries of 'labour dominated corporatism' (Sweden, Austria, Norway, Denmark), it established itself as an important pillar of the political system.[28]

So the social-democratic compromise emerges as a *class* enterprise closely bound up with the distinctive characteristics of social democracy:

(a) it was a *class* compromise, since it instituted a 'pact' between the two central poles of the classic economic and social cleavage, capital and labour;

(b) it presupposed, as a condition of its success, social-democratic entrenchment in the world of labour, and hence the constitution of the social-democratic party as a working-class/popular party;

(c) its foundation consisted in the conjunction and synergy of party and union, the veritable *dual centre* of the social-democratic 'constellation';

(d) its precondition was a culture of moderation and pragmatism. Now, this pragmatism, a distinguishing characteristic of social-democratic culture, reflected the strong domination exercised by the party of a social-democratic type over the 'left' part of the electoral and political spectrum. It was this domination, and the persistent absence of a significant left-wing competitor, which widely encouraged the adoption of moderate positions, and hence negotiation and compromise.

Thus, the distinctive features of social democracy (party/union link, anchorage in the popular electorate, control of the left of the political scene, pragmatic and consensual culture) lay, to a considerable extent, at the foundation of the neo-corporatist edifice. The logic of this centralized co-operation was in part linked to the 'identity specificity' of the social-democratic parties. Their more or less enduring character traits, and their macro-policies – of which tripartite systems of negotiation were an expression and a supporting structure – were 'dynamically consistent'. These institutional-political characteristics imparted coherence to public policies that varied significantly, and were implemented in highly diverse economic and political circumstances. From this perspective, social democracy is a particular species, and therefore *rare*, and trying to find it amid the immense variety of existing political forms would inevitably lead to the dilution of the concept, stripping it of any distinctive power. Social democracy is identifiable with neither moderation nor 'reformism', even if social democrats are profoundly moderate and reformist. Before being a doctrine, ideology, mentality, or mode, social democracy is a *specific and original mode of structuring the left*. The social-democratic compromise was in large part simply a particular product – the 'output' – of this structuration.

Notes

1. Stephen Padgett and William Paterson, *A History of Social Democracy in Post-War Europe*, Longman, London and New York 1991, p. 12.
2. Alain Bergounioux and Bernard Manin, *Le Régime social-démocrate*, Presses Universitaires de France, Paris 1989, pp. 65–6.

3. See Fritz W. Scharpf, *Crisis and Choice in European Social Democracy*, trans. Ruth Crowley and Fred Thompson, Cornell University Press, Ithaca, NY and London 1991.

4. Ferdinand Karlhofer, 'The Present and Future State of Social Partnership', in Günter Bischof and Anton Pelinka, eds, *Austro-Corporatism, Contemporary Austrian Studies*, vol. 4, 1996, p. 120.

5. Thomas Janoski, *Citizenship and Civil Society*, Cambridge University Press, Cambridge 1998, p. 118.

6. It is superfluous to point out that the content of the exchange, the terms of the *quid pro quo* as described here, is only indicative. National traditions, the balance of forces, the conjuncture, and institutional forms mean that centralized or semi-centralized systems of negotiation produce different results. For example, policies of solidaristic wage-bargaining were of great importance in Scandinavia, whereas the objective of wage solidarity was never central in Austria, a country with very considerable wage diversity.

7. See Torben Iversen, 'Wage Bargaining, Hard Money and Economic Performance: Theory and Evidence for Organized Market Economies', *British Journal of Political Science*, no. 28, 1998, p. 34.

8. Bruce Western, *Between Class and Market: Postwar Unionization in the Capitalist Democracies*, Princeton University Press, Princeton, NJ 1997, p. 47.

9. Colin Crouch, 'The Fate of Articulated Industrial Relations Systems: A Stock-Taking after the "Neo-Liberal" Decade', in Marino Regini, ed., *The Future of Labour Movements*, Sage, London 1992.

10. For a more detailed analysis, see below, Chapter 10.

11. The first major experiment in the postwar period was undertaken in Britain in the years 1945 to 1950. Through the adoption of Keynesian methods and the establishment of a mixed economy, the Labour Party was able to pave the way for the welfare state, the centrepiece of which was the National Health Service. A number of industries and utilities were nationalized, and full employment was provisionally achieved with a significant improvement in working-class living standards.

12. Bergounioux and Manin, *Le Régime social-démocrate*, p. 69.

13. Alan Wolfe, 'Has Social Democracy a Future?', *Comparative Politics*, October 1978, p. 103; emphasis added.

14. Charles Lindblom, *Politics and Markets*, Basic Books, New York 1977, p. 185.

15. Andrew Glyn, 'The Assessment: Economic Policy and Social Democracy', *Oxford Review of Economic Policy*, vol. 14, no. 1, 1998, p. 16.

16. Walter Korpi, *The Democratic Class Struggle*, Routledge & Kegan Paul, London 1983, pp. 40, 181.

17. Gøsta Esping-Andersen, *The Three Worlds of Welfare Capitalism*, Polity Press, Cambridge 1990.

18. Philip O'Connell, 'National Variation in the Fortunes of Labor: A Pooled and Cross-Sectional Analysis of the Impact of Economic Crisis in the Advanced Capitalist Nations', in Thomas Janoski and Alexander Hicks, eds, *The Comparative Political Economy of the Welfare State*, Cambridge University Press, Cambridge 1994, p. 220.

19. Paul Boreham and Richard Hall, 'Trade Union Strategy in Contemporary Capitalism: The Microeconomic and Macroeconomic Implications of Political Unionism', *Economic and Industrial Democracy*, vol. 15, Sage, London 1994, p. 342; emphasis added.

20. Crouch, 'The Fate of Articulated Industrial Relations Systems', p. 170.

21. Mario Telo, 'Les représentations de l'adversaire et compromis social dans la politique de la social-démocratie allemande', AFSP, Fourth Congress, Paris, September, 1992.
22. Francis G. Castles, *The Social Democratic Image of Society*, Routledge & Kegan Paul, London and Boston, MA 1978, p. 125.
23. Peter Ekeh, quoted in Janoski, *Citizenship and Civil Society*, p. 77.
24. Dominique Pélassy, *Sans foi ni loi? Essai sur le bouleversement des valeurs*, Fayard, Paris 1995, p. 277.
25. George Ross, 'The Perils of Politics: French Unions and the Crisis of the 1970s', in Peter Lange *et al.*, eds, *Unions, Change and Crisis: French and Italian Union Strategy and the Political Economy, 1945–1980*, George Allen & Unwin, London 1982, p. 73.
26. Ross has described the 'cycle of contradictions' in the French trade-union experience as follows: division – weakness – unity-in-action – growing power – politicization – division – weakness (*ibid.*, p. 16).
27. See Bergounioux and Manin, *Le Régime social-démocrate*.
28. Basically, the social-democratic experience offers a dual challenge to the Marxist equation trade-union = reformism, party = revolution (an equation which, moreover, does not derive from Marx, as Étienne Balibar has rightly stressed). It obliges us to reflect on a very controversial aspect of class theory: the different 'levels' of class consciousness. In fact, the social-democratic experience illuminates the elliptical and reductive character of the distinction between 'class in itself' and 'class for itself' – a distinction which, at least in some of its applications, raises more questions than it answers.

Part II

Contemporary Social Democracy

6

Electoral Weakening:
'Magical Return' of the Big Loser?

In the eye of the storm from the mid 1970s onwards, and victim of the great changes shaking modern societies, social democracy currently seems to be in the ascendant again, and is the principal governmental force in the EU countries today. A social democracy that was in crisis – and, according to some, in decline, decay, or a kind of coma – has been transformed, as if by a modern Circe, into a triumphant force at the beginning of the new century. Does this betoken what René Cuperus and Johannes Kandel have called the 'magical return'[1] of a political current which, only a little while ago, seemed to be in the grip of a 'historical decline'? Or is it an ultimately insignificant conjunctural oscillation in a cycle of electoral decline or stagnation?

Table 6.1 measures the electoral strength and governmental 'capacity' – what Wolfgang Merkel calls the power 'quotient' – of the main socialist/social-democratic parties, grouped in three categories, over various periods. The first, 1960–73, corresponds to the phase of social democracy's blossoming; the others – 1974–89, 1980–90, 1990–99 – to phases of uncertainty and retreat, but also of the new social democracy's accession to power (in particular, 1990–99).

The parties in the first group possess more of the distinctive characteristics of the social-democratic model than the others; despite striking national specificities, they more or less represent the historically most accomplished and (in the sense defined in this study) 'modelled' form of social democracy. Formations with a very high competitive status, fluctuating within an electoral zone of influence usually exceeding 35 per cent of the electorate, these parties represent *governmental social democracy par excellence*.

The second group contains social-democratic parties which, while not very distant from the first in their identity traits, are distinguished by their *intermediate* competitive status.

Finally, the third group, commonly referred to by the dubious term 'southern European socialism', comprises parties presumed to be different from typical social democracy on account of their overall constitution and history.

Several conclusions emerge from these data.

Table 6.1   Electoral performance (legislative elections) and governmental quotient of socialist parties in western Europe (average)

	1960–73		1974–89		1980–90		1990–99	
	EP	GQ	EP	GQ	EP	GQ	EP	GQ
Austria	46.3	2.3	48.1	3.94	44.6	2.5	37.3	2.0
Denmark	38.7	3.0	32.7	1.94	32.2	1.0	36.0	2.1
Norway	42.9	1.8	38.6	2.75	37.4	1.8	36.0	2.8
Sweden	46.8	4.1	43.3	2.5	44.5	3.0	39.8	2.8
Germany	41.0	1.3	40.2	1.69	37.9	0.7	36.9	0.3
Great Britain	45.1	2.0	33.6	1.88	29.2	0.0	38.8	1.5
Averages	43.5	2.4	39.5	2.45	37.6	1.5	37.5	1.91

	1960–73		1974–89		1980–90		1990–99	
	EP	GQ	EP	GQ	EP	GQ	EP	GQ
Belgium	30.0	1.2	27.2	0.75	28.2	0.7	23.2	2.0
Netherlands	25.9	0.3	31.5	0.88	31.0	0.3	26.5	2.5
Finland	24.0	1.1	24.9	2.0	25.4	2.7	24.4	1.2
Averages	26.6	0.9	27.86	1.21	28.2	1.23	24.7	1.9

	1960–73		1974–89		1980–90		1990–99	
	EP	GQ	EP	GQ	EP	GQ	EP	GQ
Spain	–	–	39.3	2.69	44.0	3.6	38.0	2.4
France	16.8	0	32.1	1.69	34.7	2.7	20.7	2.1
Greece	–	–	34.4	2.88	42.2	3.5	42.3	3.0
Portugal	–	–	28.9	1.38	27.2	0.7	39.1	1.6
Averages	–	–	33.67	2.16	37.0	2.6	35.02	2.27

Sources: 1960–73, 1980–90: Wolfgang Merkel, 'After the Golden Age: Is Social Democracy Doomed to Decline?', in José Maravall *et al.*, *Socialist Parties in Europe*, ICPS, Barcelona 1991, pp. 215–18. Averages per party (with the exception of the SPD) established by Merkel; 1974–89, 1990–99: Wolfgang Merkel, 'The Third Ways of Social Democracy', in René Cuperus, Karl Duffek and Johannes Kandal, *Multiple Third Ways*, Friedrich-Ebert-Stiftung, Amsterdam, 2001, pp. 34–5. Group classification of parties and averages for each group calculated by the author.

Note: The governmental quotient is calculated as follows:
5 points: socialist governments with a parliamentary majority
4 points: socialist governments without a parliamentary majority (minority government)
3 points: socialists as dominant partner in a coalition government
2 points: socialists as equal partner in a grand coalition
1 point: socialists as junior partner in a government coalition
0 point: socialists in opposition

1. Straightforward observation of the electoral performance and governmental quotient of the three groups offers a timely reminder of the
reductive character of the diagnosis of a general electoral regression in
the 1980s – or a general advance in the 1990s – by the socialist and
social-democratic left. The data in Table 6.1 display the *diversity of
national situations*, and the interpretative difficulties generated by the
electoral pattern. The period 1974–89 emerges overall as a phase of
significant electoral weakening for the group of great social-democratic
parties, culminating in the 1980s. At the same time, as indicated by the
negative evolution of their governmental quotient, their transition to
opposition (or shared governmental power) becomes more frequent,
more protracted, and – not surprisingly – makes itself felt more in the
same period. By contrast, the 'southern European socialism' group plays
its hand well, and experiences an unprecedented electoral upturn.
Situated between these two groups with contrasting electoral records, we
have the social-democratic parties of intermediate competitive status.
The Belgian PS is in clear retreat, whereas the PvdA marks an appreciable advance in its level of electoral influence (only to lose ground again
in the 1990s), and the Finnish SDP progresses weakly.
2. This first impression (which takes no account of post-1990 developments) is partially modified, without being fundamentally altered, in the
period 1990–99. The first group of parties sees its losses confirmed and,
in general, proves incapable of recovering the electoral ground lost in
the 1980s. Obviously, this impression of overall electoral stability conceals highly distinct – even opposed – trends at the national level. For
the three traditionally most powerful parties within this group – the
SAP, DNA and SPÖ – the trend is a marked increase in their regression,
particularly in the case of the Austrian social democrats, for whom all
signals are at danger. By contrast, a long dose of opposition in the case
of the Danish social democrats, and British Labour translates into a
sharp recovery of influence and reversion to a more customary balance
of forces in the relevant countries. In sum, the period 1990–99 witnesses
a very interesting *contraction effect*, with the gap between the strongest
and weakest parties in the group closing significantly. This contraction
against a background of overall electoral stability (but with strong
fluctuations from country to country) is in marked contrast to the
impression of disorderly upheaval for the period 1974–90. On the other
hand, it is remarkably close to that of the years 1960–73. It is as if, from
1990 to 1999, social democrats – who were initially surprised, hesitant,
lacking in inspiration and, in some cases (Denmark or Great Britain),
enormously 'affected' by changes in economic rhetoric or the advent of
'new politics' (or 'semi-new politics') – are in the process of *absorbing the
shock*, and getting a better grip on the new political and ideological
order. At the same time, the 'social-democratic image of society' having
ceased to be dominant, the great robustness of the Swedish and Austrian
social democrats and, to a lesser degree, Norwegian Labour, is impaired.
Henceforth, 'banalization' of their electoral performances, formerly exceptional, is

the rule. The example of the SAP is striking in this context. Having been in government since 1982, and won three consecutive elections, in 1991 the Swedish social democrats achieve their lowest electoral score since 1928 (39.5 per cent), picking up again in 1994 (46.1 per cent), only to plummet in 1998 (36.4 per cent). In its electoral performances, 'the west's most successful electoral party of any political stripe'[2] has become a 'commonplace' party: henceforth it is a party 'like the others'.

3. The parties of southern Europe, classed among the great victors of the 1980s, consolidate their strong electoral positions in the 1990s, despite an *appreciable but ultimately limited retreat.* Once their electoral 'maturation' is complete, around the mid-1980s, we observe a type of electoral pattern that tends to be analogous to that of the most classically social-democratic parties. Analysis by country reveals the very great instability – and fragility – of the French PS, traditionally capable of the best and the worst, as well as the resurgence of the Portuguese PS. In contrast, PASOK appears relatively robust – like the PSOE, which, although noticeably weakened, remains powerful despite its long period in government and the electoral setback of 1996.

4. The group of parties of intermediate electoral status, having enjoyed increased support in the period 1980–90, registers some important losses in the 1990s, especially in the case of the Belgian socialists and the PvdA. Here, too, a *narrowing* is visible, the margin of the average influence of the three parties concerned tending strongly to converge.

5. In sum, the parties of the first group, with a disappointing electoral 'harvest' in the period 1980–90, stabilize at the same level in the 1990s overall. But compared with the 1980s, they strengthen their governmental presence. The parties of the intermediate group fall back appreciably relative to the 1980s, but they, too, improve – and strongly – their governmental quotient! Only the southern parties, following their extraordinary electoral performances in the 1980s, regress at both electoral and governmental levels, albeit slightly. If one compares the average performance by decade of the thirteen parties represented in Table 6.1, nine register electoral losses compared with the 1980s, and only four (the Danish SD, the British Labour Party, PASOK, the Portuguese PS) progress. Obviously, the unit of comparison employed here – the electoral *average* by decade – does not measure short-term fluctuations (from one election to the next), which alone determine a party's transition to opposition or its accession to government. Nevertheless, taken overall, as a political family, *socialist parties recede electorally (albeit moderately) not only compared with some distant electoral 'golden age', but also relative to their worst electoral decade: the 1980s.* Significantly however, the great majority of them find themselves in power. Socialism dominates governments in Europe, even if the electoral base of this domination, compared with that of the period 1960–73, is less broad and less solid.

6. Let us try to refine the analysis above. Comparing the electoral results of socialist parties in three parliamentary elections before June 1999,

Table 6.2 Election results of socialist parties in the three most recent legislative elections (as of June 1999), according to whether or not in government

	Ante-penultimate elections	Elections before last	Last elections	General evolution
In government throughout				
Austria	42.8	34.9	38.1	−4.7
Belgium	25.5	24.5	19.7	−5.8
Denmark	37.4	34.6	36	−1.4
Spain	39.6	38.8	37.5	−2.1
Norway (except 89–90)	34.3	36.9	35	+0.7
Netherlands	31.9	24	29	−2.9
In opposition and then government since the elections before last				
Greece	38.6	46.9	41.5	+2.9
Sweden	37.7	45.2	36.6	−1.1
In government and then opposition since the elections before last				
France	37.5	19.2	23.5	−14
Finland	24.1	22.1	28.3	+4.2
In opposition throughout				
Germany	33.5	36.4	40.9	+7.4
United Kingdom	30.8	34.9	43.2	+12.4
Ireland	9.5	19.3	10.4	+0.9
Italy (PDS)	16.1	20.4	21.1	+5
Portugal	22.3	29.3	43.8	+21.5

Source: Stavros Skrinis, 'Electoral Performance and Governmental Power of the European Socialist Parties (1990–1999)', in Skrinis et al., *Elections in the European Union 1977–1998*, Pantheion University, Athens, 1999 (in Greek).

Table 6.2 demonstrates that the fact of being in government or opposition in the parliament preceding the election is a 'key' to explaining socialist electoral performance.[3] *Participation in government constitutes an important factor in electoral weakening; opposition a factor in electoral strengthening.* This broadly explains the variations and contrasts by country. Without making such participation the exclusive foundation of the differential competitive trend of the socialist and social-democratic parties, the data in Table 6.2 tally in indicating its importance. Obviously, this phenomenon – the corrosive effect of office – is standard in the political history of democratic societies, and nothing new. It forms part of the basic democratic game and conventional wisdom. But it currently seems to involve *a high electoral price – in all probability, higher than in the past*. Like their non-socialist opponents, socialists in government are dependent on the very difficult general conjuncture, which is inauspicious for parties in power. They are thus subject to the hazards and reversals typical of electoral cycles.[4]

7. Yet the corrosive effect of being in power, linked to the specific logic – and exacting character – of the act of governing, operates more as symptom than cause: it makes it possible to take stock of the shortcomings and inadequacies of the social-democratic political project. Accordingly, while there is no point in ignoring its particular contribution to increased socialist weakness, it would be unwise to overestimate its significance. In reality, participation in government generated, triggered or accelerated a weakening which, in 'creeping' or 'blatant' fashion, began to rack the social-democratic parties successively, to different degrees and at different rhythms and moments, from the beginning of the 1970s. From this point of view, it is indicative that the parties closest to the classical social-democratic model, which historically represented governmental social democracy *par excellence* (the first group in Table 6.1), started to waver. They were suffering. Over the last twenty-five years they have, on average, lost 14 per cent of their electoral strength. Electoral performance is always 'a feeling thermometer evaluation of political parties'.[5] In this sense, statistics are not simply statistics: they are the tangible sign and echo of the political weakening of social-democratic-type parties. They disclose, confirm and reflect their political 'destabilization'.

On the basis of these findings, the analysis above might be summarized as follows:

(a) The mixed and contrasting character of the socialist electoral record does not support the hypothesis of a general decline in the period 1974–90 (compared with 1960–73); still less does it corroborate the thesis of the 'historical decline' of social democracy.[6] The hypothesis of an overall electoral advance for the 1990s, compared with the already very testing 1980s, is not verified either. 'The report of my death was an exaggeration,' said Mark Twain. But recent reports of a social-democratic resurrection are equally exaggerated.

(b) Over the long term, if we compare 1974–99 with 1960–73, the socialist parties are less strong electorally, without this preventing them from exercising power, particularly during the second half of the 1990s.

(c) Given their losses, a destabilization and weakening peculiar to *the most classically social-democratic parties*, or those close to them, appears to influence their electoral performance and governmental power significantly.

(d) The weakening of these parties seems bound up as much with a crisis of social-democratic political logic as with a crisis of *governability* of European political systems, the one compounding the other.

(e) The most recent electoral results (post-1990) do not allow us to
establish a dichotomy between electoral destinies according to the
north/south divide, or according to a division between socialist parties
of a social-democratic type and non-social-democratic socialist parties.
The impression conveyed by the 1980s (an electorally prosperous
south, a mediocre or disappointing 'harvest' in the north) was the
effect more of a *two-speed* electoral development than of the greater
'strategic flexibility' of the southern parties.[7] In this sense, the
'southern socialists' and 'northern social democrats' resemble one
another electorally more than ever – not only because they structure
political systems in analogous fashion, as key forces with a governmental vocation in their respective countries;[8] but also because their
electoral dynamics, the sequence of highs and lows, seem to conform to the same political logic, and would not appear to differ
significantly.

Placed in historical perspective, the electoral weakening and rapid exhaustion of left-wing governments reveal a profounder malaise affecting socialist
forces: they manifestly lack robustness, and their intervention is faltering.
Can we, therefore, talk about an electoral crisis of European socialism? If
the present is judged in the light of past performance, indeed we can. But
if the present is judged relative to itself, certainly not. For from the
viewpoint of the electoral balance of forces – let me stress: the electoral
balance of forces, *not* electoral history – a party's strength is a direct
function of its opponents' strength, and its stability is a function of their
stability. All political actors fashion their identity (of which electoral
influence is a constitutive element) *in and through the adversaries facing them.*
It is in confronting them that a party becomes itself. And faced with their
strength, its strength assumes political significance. From this angle – the
position of *relative* strength – the weakening and reduced stability of socialist
parties, while they are significant in themselves, do not betoken an electoral
crisis, in so far – and only in so far – as their conservative opponents are,
today, even weaker and more unstable than they are. This explains why, in
a political landscape that is more fragmented than previously, socialists
could simultaneously lose votes and increase their governmental quotient
in the 1990s.[9] Today's socialists are not as powerful as they were in the
1960s; overall, they are even less powerful than they were in the 1980s.
Nevertheless, everything suggests that they are less weak than their
opponents. As a result, in relative terms, socialists are strong – strong, but
weakened!

Notes

1. René Cuperus and Johannes Kandel, 'The Magical Return of Social Democracy',
   in Cuperus and Kandel, eds, *European Social Democracy: Transformation in Progress,*
   Friedrich Ebert Stiftung, Amsterdam 1998, p. 11.

2. Winton Higgins, 'Social Democracy and the Labour Movement', *South African Labour Bulletin*, vol. 17, no. 6, 1993, p. 74.
3. The construction of Table 6.2 by Stavros Skrinis is inspired by the work of Alain Bergounioux and Gérard Grunberg, and in fact updates their data (*L'utopie à l'épreuve. Le socialisme européen au XXe siècle*, Éditions de Fallois, Paris 1996, pp. 271, 277).
4. Some notable exceptions require us to restrict the scope, and stress the limits, of this assertion. Having held power alone for eleven years, despite its weakening the PSOE succeeded in securing a fourth consecutive electoral victory in 1993, only to be removed from power in 1996 after obtaining a very respectable electoral score (37.4%). Again, the Finnish SDP, a governmental party *par excellence*, was able to improve its electoral performance while being in government virtually without interruption in the 1970s and 1980s, despite an important falling-off (22.1%) in the March 1991 elections, which brought a 'bourgeois' coalition to power. Profiting from the economic crisis, attributed by the social democrats to the bourgeois coalition, the SDP received 28.3% of the vote in the 1995 legislative elections, thus attaining a peak it had exceeded only in 1939. By contrast, in 1992 the British Labour Party confirmed – for the fourth consecutive time, and despite a considerable electoral advance – its status as a party of opposition (before returning to power in 1997). In the same way the SPD, out of power since 1982, became a party of government again only in 1998. At all events, on this very fluid terrain, where a whole host of parameters is in play, and where the share of hypothesis and deduction is large, prudence is required.
5. John Coleman, 'Party Organizational Strength and Public Support for Parties', *American Journal of Political Science*, vol. 40, no. 3, 1996, p. 811.
6. According to Bergounioux and Grunberg's calculations, comparing the averages of electoral percentages for all the socialist parties (excluding Spain, Portugal and Greece) for the years 1945–74 and 1975–95, it seems that the decline is slight: 31.7% in the former period as against 30.4% in the latter, or a difference of 1.3%. If we add the three parties of southern Europe, the drop is no more than 0.7% (*L'utopie à l'épreuve*, p. 271). Wolfgang Merkel reached about the same conclusions; see his 'The Third Way of Social Democracy', pp. 34–35.
7. See Herbert Kitschelt, *The Transformation of European Social Democracy*, Cambridge University Press, Cambridge 1994, pp. 324–6.
8. With the notable exception of the French PS, characterized by a congenital fragility and an extraordinary capacity for bouncing back.
9. For a fuller analysis of the socialists' return to power, see Chapter 9.

7

The Transformation of
Social Democracy's Electoral Base

There can be no question of offering a detailed electoral sociology of the social-democratic parties here. My aim is more modest and precise: to present some basic sociological data identifying the main features of social-democratic electoral development; and to furnish, as and where necessary, what I regard as essential elements for an initial explanation of the loosening of the link between the working-class and social-democratic parties, which was complex and ambivalent, but politically vital. To this end, I have chosen to study principally – but not exclusively – six national cases: the British Labour Party, the Danish SD, the Norwegian DNA, the German SPD, the Austrian SPÖ, and the Swedish SAP. The analysis will be rounded off by a study of the French left, which is assumed to be 'atypical' given the absence of a 'classical' social-democratic party.

None of these scenarios by itself represents the 'truth' of the social-electoral mutation of the left in Europe, but each, in its fashion, illuminates an important dimension of that mutation. These cases are, as it were, privileged observation points from which we can 'catch in full flight' the characteristics of the relationship between the working class and voting for the left. In Great Britain and Denmark, where the examples are (or are considered) extreme, the upheaval initially assumed the dimensions of a sociological earthquake. In Norway the decline in the working-class vote was gradual, smooth and silent, like a sociological mechanism that starts up gently and produces its effects imperceptibly but inexorably. In Sweden and Austria, two models of working-class social democracy, the social-democratic vote among workers also declined, but the contrasts between these two countries underline the impact of political factors on the evolution of class voting. In Germany the trend was rather towards stability, despite slight disturbances, thus contributing to the 'steady crisis' of the SPD. In France, fluctuation in the working-class vote was at the centre of political upheavals, making this country a model case where, more conspicuously than elsewhere, the fluctuation in class voting is conditioned by changes and variations in the interplay of partisan competition.

Social Democracy and the Working-Class Electorate: The Weakening of a Vital Link

Great Britain

(i) *The Trends*

Analysis of Labour's penetration of manual strata makes it possible to identify an evolution in four phases: an expansive phase, a downturn in two successive stages, and renewed expansion.

(a) During the first period, 1959–70, the level of Labour's penetration of manual strata reaches a peak (62 per cent in 1959, 64 per cent in 1964, 69 per cent in 1966).
(b) Retrospectively, in spite of Labour's two electoral victories in 1974, the period 1970–79 may be considered as *the first stage of a major uncoupling.* In the context of a general electoral low-water mark, Labour's penetration of manual workers falls back below the 60 per cent threshold and settles at a level markedly inferior to that of the previous decade (58 per cent in 1970, 57 per cent in 1974, 50 per cent in 1979). Compared with 1959, the party's constituency among non-manual workers remains fairly stable (22 per cent in 1959, 22 per cent in 1964, 25 per cent in 1970, 23 per cent in 1979). Relative to the 1960s, only Labour's penetration of manual strata undergoes marked decline, its support among non-manual workers remaining virtually intact (Table 7.1).
(c) In the third phase (the 1980s) the party crosses a new quantitative threshold in its downturn, despite a slight recovery in 1987. Now *all social groups turn away from Labour,* and manual workers rather more than the others (index of evolution of Labour's penetration: 65.41 per cent among manual workers; 77.08 per cent among non-manual strata).
(d) At the 1992 election, after three consecutive defeats, the Labour Party

Table 7.1   British Labour Party penetration according to the manual/non-manual cleavage (1964–97)

	M	NM		M	NM
1964	64	22	1979	50	23
1966	69	26	1983	42	17
1970	58	25	1987	45	20
1974 (Feb.)	57	22	1992	51	24
1974 (Oct.)	57	25	1997	58	40

Source: See David Sanders, 'Voting and the Electorate', in Patrick Dunleavy *et al.*, *Developments in British Politics 5*, Macmillan, London 1997, pp. 55–7.

lost once again. Its electoral recovery was insufficient to repair the electoral damage caused by its last period in government (1974–79) and its political options in the 1980s. It did, however, improve its influence appreciably among both non-manual and manual strata (Table 7.1). But despite this improvement, working-class and popular support for British Labourism (measured by its penetration of manual workers) was markedly inferior to its influence in the 1960s, and even the first half of the 1970s (index of evolution 1992/1960s: 76.69 per cent). By contrast, Labour's influence among non-manual workers, despite the preceding fluctuations, was at exactly the same level in 1992 as the average for the 1960s.

The 1997 election was a veritable landslide for 'New Labour'. The party of Tony Blair advanced on all fronts and terrains, regardless of region, type of constituency, or social class. But it made its most spectacular break-through in the C1 category (skilled non-manual workers), where it obtained 47 per cent of the vote (+19 points compared with 1992). This result disrupted the 'classical norms' of British electoral behaviour inasmuch as traditional Conservative supremacy within this category made Britain a partially 'atypical' case among European countries. Similarly, Labour once again became the unquestionable leader (54 per cent) within the C2 category (especially among skilled manual workers, according to the statistical categories used by opinion pollsters) – a category that had swung, according to the dominant approach among British psephologists, in favour of the Conservatives during the previous twenty years (Labour's advance relative to 1992: +15 points).[1] In consolidating and reinforcing its traditional pre-eminence among semi-skilled and unskilled manual workers (61 per cent, or +9 compared with 1992), Labour re-established itself as the unchallenged party of the working class following the painful wilderness years of the 1980s. We should nevertheless emphasize that Labour's penetration of manual workers remained *below* the level achieved in the 1960s, despite Blair's exceptional electoral performance in 1997. Compared with the general election of 1964 (an election precisely comparable to that of 1997 in terms of the national vote obtained by Labour: 44.1 per cent in

Table 7.2   Index of evolution of the Labour vote according to the manual/non-manual cleavage (1964–97)

	(averages by decade; base 100 for the 1960s average)	
	Manual	Non-manual
1970s/1960s	83.45	98.95
1980s/1960s	65.41	77.08
1990s/1960s	81.95	133.33

Sources: See Table 7.1; my calculation.

Table 7.3 Labour's electoral penetration according to social class (1964–92)

	Salariat	Routine non-manual	Petty bourgeoisie	Foremen/ technicians	Working class
1964	19	26	14	46	68
1966	25	41	19	61	71
1970	29	41	19	56	61
1974 (Feb.)	22	29	19	40	60
1974 (Oct.)	23	32	13	52	64
1979	22	32	13	43	55
1983	13	20	12	28	49
1987	15	26	16	36	48
1992	20	30	17	45	56

Sources: 1964–87: Anthony Heath *et al.*, *Understanding Political Change*, Pergamon Press, London 1991, pp. 68–9; 1992: David Denver, *Elections and Voting Behaviour in Britain*, Harvester Wheatsheaf, London and New York 1994, p. 73.

1964 as against 43.3 per cent in 1997), Blair's party obtained 58 per cent of the manual vote (against 64 per cent in 1964) and 40 per cent of the non-manual vote (against 22 per cent in 1964)! So, if the gap in Labour voting between manual and non-manual categories was reduced from 42 per cent in 1964 to the still significant figure of 27 per cent in 1992, it was only 18 per cent in 1997.

(ii) *Discussion*

According to the dominant approach in British electoral sociology, changes in electoral behaviour in Great Britain since the 1970s have made it one of the best examples of class dealignment. The authors of *How Britain Votes*,[2] however, have challenged this interpretation. Undertaking a redefinition of the schedule of socio-professional categories, which is doubtless closer to the real world of social classes, they have argued that *relative* class voting is not in decline. What is involved is not a decline in class voting, but 'trendless fluctuations', with circumstances and electoral appeal mainly explaining working-class behaviour. Given the importance of the issue, and the fact that it has a direct bearing on the nature of the argument advanced throughout this chapter, we shall take up certain aspects of the history – this *other* history – of class voting in Great Britain.

Two different but complementary impressions emerge from scrutiny of Table 7.3. The impression for the period 1970–79 – and hence prior to the political trauma of 1983 – is too clear to be open to ambiguity: Labour fell back among workers and foremen/technicians, considered by Heath *et al.* to be close to the working class, and *solely* among them. It was precisely in the social zone traditionally identified with Labour that the great electoral

Table 7.4   Social classes and index of evolution of the Labour vote
(1964–92)

	(averages by decade, base 100: average for the 1960s)				
	Salariat	Routine non-manual	Petty bourgeoisie	Foremen/ technicians	Working class
1970s/1960s	109.09	100	96.96	89.25	86.33
1980s/1960s	63.63	68.65	84.84	59.81	69.78
1992/1960s	90.90	89.55	103.03	84.11	80.57

Sources: See Table 7.3. Indices of evolution calculated by the author.

migration commenced. By contrast, Labour held its position or advanced, albeit marginally, among all other classes or social groups (see the indices of evolution in Table 7.4).

In contrast to this first impression, the 1980s reveal a Labour Party suffering general electoral discredit. In the context of an unprecedented drop, Labour lost part of its electorate among all groups in the population. The losses among foremen/technicians – 'a kind of blue-collar elite', according to Heath *et al.*[3] – were the most important on average, but did not reach levels unknown among other social groups (see Table 7.4).

Basically, the Labour coalition in its 1960s form was 'shattered' – initially by the considerable erosion in working-class support (the main moments of decline being 1970 and, in part, 1979, which 'capped' undistinguished governmental records); and then by a generalized decline of British Labourism in nearly all sectors of society. In addition, the 1992 result indicates that, compared with the 1960s, Labour's working-class influence was fixed at a level proportionately below its influence in other social groups, when likewise compared with that of the 1960s. This difference in workers' behaviour, however, is not as important as conventional approaches have maintained (indices of evolution of Labour's penetration 1992/1960s: working class: 80.57 per cent, foremen/technicians: 84.11, routine non-manual: 89.55, salariat: 90.90, petty bourgeoisie: 103.03 – see Table 7.4). The contrast becomes sharper, however, if we compare the election of 1992 with that of 1964: Labour strengthened its penetration of all non-manual groups as well as the petty bourgeoisie; it remained stable among foremen/technicians; it fell back only among the working class.

Various conclusions follow from this analysis:

(a) Since the beginning of the 1970s, a significant section of the broad category of manual workers – or a less extensive but far from negligible part of the working class in the strict sense – has deserted the Labour Party. It is common sense to observe that as regards the electoral behaviour of workers, what is involved is class dealignment, at least 'in the absolute, as opposed to the relative, sense'.[4] Regardless of all other considerations, this decline in *absolute* class voting among workers is in itself significant: it affects Labour's class basis; it weakens its positions and place among its 'natural' electorate. With its influence in the working class reduced by at least 20 per cent compared with the 1960s, Labour in the 1980s is not the Labour of the 1960s, even if we accept that its *relative* class anchorage changed only marginally. *An 'unsuccessful class party'* (Heath *et al.*) *is different from a successful class party, precisely in terms of its class anchorage and class identity.*

(b) The general and non-class-specific regression of Labour in 1983, partly confirmed in 1987, was added to an already deteriorating situation whose principal and primordial element – as well as its common denominator – was *working-class disaffection.* This disaffection is not – and cannot be considered – a merely 'static' statistical datum that could just as simply be compensated or cancelled by other, subsequent statistical data. It is not, as Patrick Dunleavy would say, 'context-free'.[5] The dynamic process that the class dealignment of the 1970s generated, or in which it was involved, partially prepared the ground for the subsequent general decline of British Labour among all social groups. In fact, the initial erosion of the links between Labour and manual strata in the 1970s, which contributed to calling the party's governmental vocation into question, subsequently (in the 1980s) favoured the defection of marginal non-manual voters from Labour, as well as the electoral breakthrough of the Liberal/SDP Alliance, creating 'an across-the-board reduction in support'.[6] A sociological and electoral dynamic was set in train by the phenomenon of the class dealignment of the 1970s, whose effects, although difficult to measure, should not, on that account, be ignored.

(c) Nevertheless, when all is said and done, it remains the case that throughout the period 1964–97 – and even during the 1980s, the dark years of British Labourism – Labour's overrepresentation within the working class, as defined in the *narrow* sense of Heath *et al.*, was a constant that was never seriously challenged. Compared with its penetration among the whole electorate, Labour's penetration of the working class – what we might call Labour's *relative* working-class penetration – underwent fluctuations, but was not – over the long term – in decline (Table 7.5). This overrepresentation constitutes a weighty argument for defenders of the thesis of 'trendless fluctuations'.

(d) New Labour, such as it emerged from the 1997 election, is a party close to the catch-all model, having proved capable of enhancing its influence in novel social territory, while re-establishing itself – and this time in incontestable fashion – as the 'natural' party of the working class. *Class dealignment through Labour's advance among non-manual strata, particularly evident from 1959 to 1974 and arrested thereafter, becomes spectacular in 1997* (especially among skilled non-manual voters). This influx of non-manual voters into Labour's electoral ranks is explained by the corrosive effect of government on the Conservatives and, obviously, by Blair's modernization strategy. Basically, Blair was able to

Table 7.5 Specificity of Labour's working-class vote relative to the Labour vote of the total electorate (1964–92)

Year	1964	1966	1970	1974(F)	1974(O)	1979	1983	1987	1992
Index of specificity	154	148	142	161	163	149	178	152	163

Source: Labour's electoral results in Yves Meny, *Politique comparée*, Montchrestien, Paris 1988, p. 207. For Labour's working-class vote, see Table 7.3. Indices of originality calculated by the author.

create a 'new interpretive order' concerning not only the identity of Labour (and the perception of it by the public and 'centres of authority'), but also the whole electoral game in the United Kingdom. Here, the strategy of 'natural party of government' – to borrow a term from Ivor Crewe[7] – largely explains the interclassist character of the new Labourist coalition of 1997. And – should such a thing be necessary – it demonstrates the role of *political factors* in the establishment of new class alignments or the consolidation of 'old' ones.

(e) In Great Britain, the classical class divide has lost some of its former strength, as is clearly indicated by the increase in cross-class voting, the reinforcement of centrist formations, and greater fluctuation in voting behaviour. However, the factor of 'social class' has not lost its pre-eminence in the British political system. More specifically, in terms of the Labour Party's ability to represent the working class electorally, analysis of the trends has demonstrated on the one hand that it varies considerably according to political conjunctures, and on the other that it has partially but significantly diminished (something that is indicated by the marked decline in *absolute* class voting among workers). Labour's overrepresentation among the working class, as well as the 'ecological paradox' of class voting in Great Britain (the so-called 'area class effect'), unquestionably mean that even during the 1980s, Labour remained the 'natural' representative of the working class. In truth, Labour found itself in a paradoxical position. It was a 'natural' party of the working class that had in part lost – at least conjuncturally and temporarily (in the 1980s) – the principal attribute attaching to its nature: the capacity to represent the *great majority* of this class electorally.

To summarize, observation of the whole period 1964–1997, which is not homogeneous, reveals that Labour's positions within the working class have been weakened. The party became considerably more vulnerable within its 'natural' electorate than previously, while ultimately proving victorious (as 1997 clearly demonstrated) among the most peripheral sections of the 'natural' electorate of its Conservative opponent (particularly the lowest group of non-manual workers, those designated C1).[8] Are we dealing with 'class dealignment' or 'trendless fluctuations'? The question is complex, and in some respects too technical to be dealt with here.[9] Even so, it is hard to deny that since the beginning of the 1970s the working class, sociologically and organizationally the most structured – and structuring – element in Labour's electorate, has proved to be *politically more fragmented, ideologically more undecided, and electorally more unstable than in the past.*

Denmark

Working-class disaffection with the Danish social democrats occurred in two distinct phases.

At the beginning of the 1960s, a section of manual workers turned in fairly enduring fashion to parties to the left of the SD, and in the main to the newly formed Socialist People's Party (the social democrats' working-class penetration registered an appreciable reduction, falling from 64 per cent in 1964 to 54 per cent in 1971).

At the beginning of the 1970s, and particularly after the electoral 'disaster' of 1973 (37.3 per cent of votes cast in 1971, 25.6 per cent in 1973), another fraction moved to the 'bourgeois' parties – in particular, the Progress Party (right-wing populist in allegiance) in 1973 and 1975, and the conservative party in 1984 (social-democratic working-class penetration fell from 54 per cent in 1971 to 41 per cent in 1987). Although it can be regarded as a continuation of the sequence that began in the 1960s, this second phase exhibited a new qualitative threshold on the path of decline, inasmuch as it expressed a certain class *dealignment.* (In 1984, the influence of the bourgeois parties among manual workers was 36 per cent, as opposed to 22 per cent in 1964; the index of evolution for 1964–84 [1964 base = 100] was 164!).

Certainly, in the 1990s the social democrats, profiting from a long spell in opposition (from 1982 to 1993 the SD experienced a continuous period in opposition for the first time since 1929), recovered some of their working-class losses (56 per cent in 1990, 45 per cent in 1994). But this recovery, which was very relative, was not of such a nature as to challenge

Table 7.6 Electoral penetration of the Danish social democrats according to social class (1964–94)

Year	64	66	68	71	73	75	77	79	81	84	87	88	90	94
Blue-collar	64	59	53	54	41	46	52	52	46	47	41	41	56	45
White-collar	33	30	25	25	18	24	34	36	27	24	23	26	33	30
Self-employed	13	9	6	7	5	6	9	13	7	6	8	11	8	7

Source: See Lars Bille, 'The Danish Social-Democratic Party', in Robert Ladrech and Philippe Marlière, eds, *Social-Democratic Parties in the European Union*, Macmillan, London 1999, p. 49.

Table 7.7   Social classes and index of evolution of the social-democratic vote in Denmark (1964–94)

	(Averages by decade, base 100: average for the 1960s)		
	Blue-collar	White-collar	Self-employed
1970s/1960s	83.53	93.41	85.74
1980s/1960s	74.58	85.23	85.74
1990s/1960s	86.08	107.39	80.38

Sources: See Table 7.6. Indices of evolution calculated by the author.

the fundamental fact of the 1970s and 1980s: the *weakening* of their popular entrenchment. For the whole period 1964–94, one of general electoral downturn for the social democrats, losses within the different socio-demographic categories were not evenly distributed. Analysed by decade, the erosion of the SD's electoral penetration compared with the 1960s is systematically more pronounced among manual than among white-collar workers (Table 7.7). In the 1990s the SD even improved its influence, albeit marginally, among these workers (indices of evolution 1990s/1960s: 86.08 per cent for blue-collar workers, 107.39 for white-collar workers). Thus the differential of the blue-collar vote for the SD, compared with the white-collar vote, went from +31 points in 1964 to +15 points in 1994. In addition, the socialist bloc as a whole (SD + SFP) appears very well entrenched among non-manual salaried strata, essentially because of the attraction exercised over this category by the SFP.[10] Thus, if the socialist bloc is much more resilient among non-manual wage-earners than among workers, this serves to confirm the picture of a class dealignment in the Danish political system.

The central position of the SD since 1924, making it the focal point of the Danish party system, was due largely to the unfailing *loyalty* of the working-class electorate. This is certainly no longer the case today. The slight improvement in the working-class penetration of Danish social democracy during the 1990s, which accompanied the strengthening of its overall electoral influence, remains markedly inferior to the level of the 1950s, and even the 1960s.

Norway

For a long time, and well before many European countries, Norwegian society was politically structured by the class cleavage. For several decades after the Second World War, the political domination of the Norwegian Labour Party (DNA) was based largely on the stable support of the great majority of the working class, which approached or surpassed two-thirds of the working-class vote. Indeed, during the *trente glorieuses* the penetration

Table 7.8 Electoral penetration of the 'socialist bloc' in Norway according to social class (1965–89)

Year	1965	1969	1973	1977	1981	1985	1989
Workers	75	74	70	68	61	63	58
New middle class	40	40	42	38	35	38	44
Old middle class	29	33	28	24	24	18	30

Source: Olga Listhaug, 'The Decline of Class Voting', in Kaare Strom and Lars Svasand, eds, *Challenges to Political Parties*, University of Michigan Press, Michigan 1997, p. 81.

of 'bourgeois' political forces among the working-class segment of the population remained consistently below the 30 per cent level. By contrast, until the end of the 1960s the vote of workers for the 'socialist bloc' (DNA + left-wing socialists) was invariably massive: 77 per cent in 1957, 75 per cent in 1965, 74 per cent in 1969. From the beginning of the 1970s, however, the working-class vote for the left fell off, the trend being characterized by a gradual and almost continuous decline (70 per cent in 1973, 68 per cent in 1977, 61 per cent in 1981, 63 per cent in 1985, 58 per cent in 1989). For the whole period 1957 to 1989, the 'socialist bloc' lost 19 points among the working class,[11] whereas it dropped only 7.3 points among the electorate as a whole (going from 51.7 per cent to 44.4 per cent). Symmetrically, working-class penetration of the 'bourgeois bloc' improved appreciably, going from 23 per cent in 1957 to 42 per cent in 1989[12] in a tangible sign of class political dealignment, at least as far as the electoral behaviour of the working class is concerned.

This picture is confirmed by the data in Table 7.9. First of all, taking the average for the 1965 and 1969 elections as a base, we should note that the Norwegian left, traditionally stronger among the old middle class than the left in other countries, declined sharply among this segment of the population. Next, we note that the influence of left-wing forces in Norway declined markedly – in stages – among the working class, while it remained fairly stable among the new middle strata. Thus, the differential between the socialist vote of workers and the socialist vote of the new middle strata

Table 7.9 Social classes and index of evolution of the socialist vote in Norway (1965–89)

	(Averages by decade, base 100: average for the 1960s)		
	Workers	New middle class	Old middle class
1970s/1960s	92.61	100	83.87
1980s/1960s	81.43	97.5	77.41

Sources: See Table 7.8. Indices of evolution calculated by the author.

went from +35 points in 1965 to only +14 points in 1989, a development that can be explained more by working-class disaffection than by the rallying of the new middle strata. This fraying of the bond between the working class and left-wing parties – occurring, as it did, in a slow, uninterrupted fashion – differs from the model of strong fluctuations in the working-class vote observed in countries like Denmark, Great Britain or, in another context, France.

Germany

Finally – and somewhat against the trend of what occurred in the great majority of countries with a powerful social democracy – the SPD was able to maintain its overall position within the working class, despite a minor tendential decline. In the late 1960s, German social democrats were certainly distinguished within the universe of European social democracy by the *weakness of their working-class penetration* (a weakness bound up in part with the importance of the religious divide and in part with the division of the country), and their relatively important influence among salaried middle strata. It is above all to the latter that the SPD owes its strong electoral growth and its constitution as a 'natural' party of government, particularly since 1969.

Roughly speaking, in the period 1969 to 1987 the German social democrats proved able to preserve their traditional electoral base (working-class penetration of the SPD: 58 per cent in 1969, 60 per cent in 1976, 62 per cent in 1980, 55 per cent in 1983, 59 per cent in 1987). In the 1990 election, the first to be held after reunification, in the context of a general decline in social-democratic influence (33.5 per cent, or the SPD's worst electoral result since 1957), we observe a very important contraction in the SPD's working-class penetration.[13] In fact, the reduction of its influence among the working class (45.8 per cent in the western half of the country, as against 59 per cent in 1987) was *considerably greater* than among the electorate as whole (the SPD's electoral decline in the territory of the former Federal Republic was only 1.1 per cent). It was linked to the inability of the SPD, and its leader Oskar Lafontaine, to live up to the exceptional historical moment of reunification, which was controlled with a firm hand by Chancellor Kohl. Indeed, this poor election result is principally explained by the centrality of 'national' issues and the relegation of socioeconomic questions to the background. In the 1994 election, however, the SPD made its biggest breakthrough in the traditional industrial constituencies of the western part of the country.[14] It thus proved capable of re-establishing its working-class influence in the main (the social democrats obtained 55.9 per cent of the working-class vote – a good performance given that a new left-wing party from the east, the PDS, obtained 2.2 per cent of the working-class vote in western Germany).

By contrast, it is among the new middle classes – a rather volatile social sector in Germany – as well as the young that the SPD has lost most ground

Table 7.10   Electoral penetration of the SPD according to social class (1961–94)

Year	1961	1965	1969	1972	1976	1980	1983	1987	1990*	1994*
Workers	56	54	58	66	60	62	55	59	45.8	55.9
Salaried Employees	30	34	46	50	43	50	43	37	33.1	39.4

* Western Germany

Sources: 1961–72: see Ilias Katsoulis, 'La nouvelle vision "de classe" de la social-démocratie', in Helga Grebing, *L'histoire du mouvement ouvrier allemand*, Papazissi, Athens 1982, p. 413; 1976–87: see Ursula Feist and Hubert Kriegel, 'Alte und neue Scheidelinien des politisches Verhaltens', *Aus Politik und Zeitgeschichte*, B12/87, 21 March 1987, p. 38; 1990: see Russel Dalton and Wilhelm Bürklin, 'The German Party System and the Future' in Russell Dalton, ed., *The New Germany Votes*, Berg, Providence and Oxford 1993, p. 244; 1994: see Russell Dalton and Wilhelm Bürklin, 'The Two German Electorates', in Russel Dalton, ed., *Germans Divided*, Berg, Oxford 1996, p. 187.

since 1983. The appearance of a new challenger – the Greens – in the 1980s, positioning themselves on the left of the political spectrum, is not irrelevant in the disaffection of a segment of the new middle strata and the younger generations with the SPD (Table 7.10). The threat presented by this – albeit peripheral – political actor destabilized German social democracy. Indeed, in its specificity the German case underscores the formidable challenge to parties of a social-democratic variety represented by the strong emergence of the materialism/post-materialism cleavage.

Nevertheless, despite the relative preservation of the SPD's working-class bases and its stagnation (since 1983) among the new salaried strata, the dynamic governing the behaviour of the two main components of the SPD electorate in the long term does not differ fundamentally from that in other European countries. The SPD is more resilient among the new salaried strata than among the working class (Table 7.11). In the 1998 election, when it returned to power, the SPD only slightly improved its vote among workers (between 1 and 4 per cent *for the whole of Germany*, according

Table 7.11   Social classes and indices of evolution of the social-democratic vote in Germany (1961–94)

	(Averages by decade, base 100: average for the 1960s)	
	Workers	Salaried Employees
1970s/1960s	112.5	126.84
1980s/1960s	104.7	118.20
1990s/1960s	90.80	98.88

Sources: See Table 7.10. Indices of evolution calculated by the author.

Table 7.12 Working-class penetration of the SAP (1956–94)

Year	1956	1960	1964	1968	1970	1973	1976	1979	1985	1994
Blue-collar	74	77	75	77	70	69	68	66	64	63

Sources: 1956–79: see Gøsta Esping-Andersen, *Politics against Markets*, Princeton, University Press, Princeton, NJ 1985, p. 126; 1985–94: in Christoph Kunkel and Jonas Pontusson, 'Corporatism versus Social Democracy', *West European Politics*, vol. 21, no. 2, 1998, p. 17; 1991.

to the different polling organizations), and among the unemployed (44 per cent against 42 per cent in 1994), despite the spectacular losses suffered by the CDU among the working class in the east (leading to the end of the 'inverted social profile' of class voting there). The SPD advanced more noticeably among the middle classes (particularly public servants, or *Beamten*) and the self-employed, groups traditionally close to the CDU, where it secured 4 per cent more than in 1994 (respectively 37 per cent and 22 per cent, according to *Der Spiegel*'s statistics). In addition, it achieved a rather disappointing vote among farmers; at 15 per cent, it progressed only marginally by comparison with 1994.[15]

Sweden and Austria

If the 'spell' between workers and Swedish social democrats has been broken, the drop in their working-class penetration remains fairly modest. The proportion of workers voting SAP fell from 74 per cent in 1956 to 66 per cent in 1976 and 63 per cent in 1994 (Table 7.12). The consequent weakening of the Swedish social-democrat party – party of the working class *par excellence* – is considerably less marked than elsewhere, but no less real for all that – and all the more so since the SAP has serious difficulties attracting new generations, a trend that is observable in all Scandinavian countries.[16] It is important to stress that contrary to the Austrian pattern, most voters who abandon the SAP switch to the Left Party, restricting the sociological groundswell of class dealignment in Sweden, at least as far as the working-class vote is concerned. Great fluctuation in the electoral performance of the SAP – which is likewise struck by the 'electoral instability syndrome'[17] – is certainly accompanied by increased volatility in working-class electoral behaviour (as indicated by the SAP's working-class vote in 1991, when an important percentage of workers went for non-socialist parties).[18] More specifically, in the period 1979 to 1994 the SAP's decline among workers – particularly private-sector workers – is clearly visible. In the same period, however, it gained ground strongly among white-collar workers, especially in the public sector (Table 7.13).

Working-class support for the SPÖ (which habitually secured something over two-thirds of the working-class vote) registered a considerable drop,

Table 7.13 Electoral penetration of the SAP and SPÖ according to social class (1979–95)

Year	SAP				SPÖ		
	1979	1985	1994	Change	1986	1995	Change
Total vote	43	45	45	+2	43	38	−5
Blue-collar	66	64	63	−3	57	41	−16
White-collar*	33	35	41	+8	40/49	32/48	−8/−1
Self-employed	13	14	17	+4	14	18	+4
Private sector	46	43	43	−3	51	36	−15
Public sector	43	43	51	+8	51	44	−7

* For Austria, the first figure refers to *Angestellte*, the second to *Beamte*.

Source: Kunkel and Pontusson, 'Corporatism versus Social Democracy', p. 17.

falling from 64 per cent (average for 1971–75) to 57 per cent in 1983 and 41 per cent in 1995 (Table 7.13). Part of the working-class and popular electorate currently supports the FPÖ, a national-populist party which has established itself in the Austrian system as a right-wing party with strong popular ties and a socio-demographic profile close to that of the SPÖ.[19] Thus, this migration to the right of a significant band of Austrian workers, particularly those employed in the private sector, expresses a considerable class dealignment. At the same time – and contrary to the Swedish pattern – from 1986 to 1995 the SPÖ recorded sizeable losses among white-collar workers, with the notable exception of civil servants. These, however, were considerably more modest than the drop in the working-class vote *stricto sensu* (−8 as against −16).

Historically, the SAP and the SPÖ are characterized by their working-class/popular ties and the institutional role allotted to trade unions as a force representing the interests of wage-earners. The electoral shifts indicated above clearly tend in the direction of a marked weakening in the popular entrenchment of these parties. The fall in the working-class vote in Sweden is all the more significant in that the last three decades have witnessed increased unionization. The considerably more pronounced decline in the working-class vote in Austria, where trade-unionism has been weakened in the same years, demonstrates that while high union density cannot reverse the trend to working-class disaffection, it remains a positive factor in influencing workers to vote for the left.[20]

France

In France, fluctuations in the working-class vote were central to the political and social upheaval that accompanied the transition from the Fourth to the Fifth Republic. The two great breaches in the continuity of working-

Table 7.14 Electoral penetration of the French left according to socio-professional group (1956–97)

	Workers	Middle managers/ white-collar employees		Workers	Middle managers/ white-collar employees
1956	66	–	1981Pb	72	62
1958	55	–	1981	69	63
1965Pb	55	45	1986	61	52
1967	54	44	1988Pb	68	61
1968	57	43	1988	60	55
1969Pa	50	36	1993	46	46/43d
1973	68	44	1995Pb	52	44/42d
1974Pb	73	53	1997	52	51/54d
1978	70	54c			

a: first round; P: presidential election; b: second round; c: salaried non-workers; d: intermediate professions/white-collar

Sources: 1956–73: Gerassimos Moschonas, *La Gauche française (1972–1988)*, doctoral thesis, University of Paris II, 1990, pp. 233, 255; 1978 and 1995: Daniel Boy and Nonna Mayer, eds, *L'électeur a ses raisons*, Presses de Sciences Politiques, Paris 1997, p. 109; 1974, 1981 and 1986: Gérard Le Gall, 'Mars 1986: des élections de transition?', *Revue Politique et Parlementaire*, no. 922, 1986, p. 11; 1988: SOFRES, *L'état de l'opinion*, Seuil, Paris 1989; 1993 and 1997: Fondation Saint-Simon (collective), *Pour une nouvelle république Sociale*, Callmann-Lévy, Paris 1997, p. 154.

class electoral behaviour can be clearly located in 1956 and 1973, which constitute the point of departure for two contrasting developments. The year 1958 marked the beginning of a period of class dealignment, whereas 1973 initiated a phase of new and strong class polarization (Table 7.14). By contrast, the 1990s saw a new decline in class voting among workers, comparable to – but rather more pronounced than – the Gaullist period of the 1960s (Table 7.15).

The specificity of Gaullism – or, at least, the presidential Gaullism of de Gaulle – derived from its ability to attract an electorate from diverse ideological and social horizons, from the centre-left to the 'extreme left' (as it was then called). The high level of Gaullist influence among the working class, the attachment of a number of voters of communist origin to the 'enlarged' or 'maximal' electorate of Gaullism, the use of referenda as an instrument of partisan dealignment – these are so many indices of the socially and politically 'disruptive' role of de Gaulle's approach. Gaullism was unquestionably the great unifier of the conservative firmament in France. But it was a singular, almost atypical conservatism. Its strong representation among workers, and relative weakness among higher executives, the liberal professions and, at the outset, the rural heartland, are

Table 7.15   Socio-professional groups and indices of evolution of the left-wing vote in France (1956–97) (averages by decade)

	Workers (base 100: 1956)		Workers (base 100: average for 1965–69)	Middle managers/ white-collar employees (base 100: average for 1965–69)
1960s/1956	81.81			
1970s/1956	106.56	1970s/1960s	130.24	119.84
1980s/1956	98.73a	1980s/1960s	120.67a	136.90a
1990s/1956	75.75	1990s/1960s	92.59	111.90/110.31

a: The two elections in 1981 have been taken together, as have those in 1988. To calculate the index of evolution for the 1980s, I have used the average for each of the pairs of elections in question.
Source: See Table 7.14.

among the factors that emphasize the *original* character of electoral Gaullism.[21]

If the Gaullist adventure appears unintelligible without reference to the working-class penetration of Gaullism, the Union of the Left is no less so without reference to its ability to attract an overwhelming majority of the working-class electorate from the time of its formation in 1972. It was precisely by reconquering its 'natural' social territory that the French left, in the shape of the Union, broke the vicious circle in which it had been trapped during the initial period of the Fifth Republic. In fact, different social groups rallied to the Union in *two phases*: the first was marked by an adhesion of working-class strata which was so rapid and massive as to be disconcerting; the second by the gradual adhesion of salaried middle strata (Table 7.14). Thus, at the heart of the left coalition's expansion, chronologically and qualitatively, was the working-class strata's turn to the left. Everything cohered around this: the Union's achievement of competitive status allowed it to present itself as a natural force of political alternation; this triggered a process of adhesion by the salaried middle classes to a pole that was credible and possessed of a governmental vocation.

Thus, strengthened class voting in France during the 1970s was matched only by weakened class voting – or *absolute* class voting, at any rate – in countries like Great Britain or Denmark in the same years.

In the 1980s and 1990s, in the context of a general decline of the French left, a dual dynamic ensued: on one hand, considerable working-class disaffection in 1986, which was very 'discreet' in *relative* terms (the left actually fell back among all social classes), but very visible in *absolute* terms, and became massive – not to say spectacular – in 1993; on the other, much *greater resilience* on the part of the left among intermediate professions and middle management. This trend is accentuated if we take into account the electoral behaviour of higher executives and intellectual professions, where we observe a greater tendency to vote for the left in 1995 and 1997 (43 per cent and 49 per cent, respectively, as opposed to 31 per cent in 1978), despite the worse overall performance of the left in those years.[22] In sum, the differential in the left vote between blue-collar and white-collar workers diminishes appreciably, falling from 24 points in 1973 to 10 points in 1995, to approach zero in 1997! Accordingly, if swings of the electoral pendulum describe the electoral behaviour of the working class accurately enough over a long period (1956–97), the traditional opposition between waged workers and non-workers gradually loses its salience because of salaried middle strata's greater attachment to the left. By contrast, the opposition in terms of electoral behaviour between the self-employed and wage-earners (workers and non-workers) persists, because in their clear majority the self-employed (shopkeepers, artisans, farmers) remain attached to the right.[23] What must be stressed is the fact that the most significant reductions in the left's working-class influence – important losses in 1986, violent contraction in 1993 – follow their inglorious governmental experiences. In addition, there is evidence of a veritable realignment of workers towards the National Front, which obtained 13 per cent of the vote in 1988 (11 per cent of the whole electorate), 18 per cent in 1995 (13 per cent overall), and 24 per cent in 1997 (15 per cent overall). This realignment is all the more significant in that it is the workers most integrated into the working-class universe (that is to say, children and spouses of workers) who support the extreme-right party most strongly. Likewise, Chirac's strong showing among the French working class in the 1995 presidential election was manifestly linked to the candidate's decision to conduct a campaign against *la pensée unique*, and put himself forward as champion of the struggle against social inequalities. Thus – more visibly, perhaps, than elsewhere – class voting by workers is punctuated in France by the political appeal of the opposing parties and the bad governmental record of the left. *Politics counts; it even counts a lot – that is the great lesson of the history of the last forty years of class voting in France.*

Class Voting and the Impact of Political Action

The Major Trends

An overview of the pattern of class voting clearly indicates that a process of class dealignment has occurred in the great majority of cases considered. More specifically, we can identify in this process two dynamics, which are simultaneously complementary and distinct.

(i) *Class political dealignment by social democracy's downturn among manual strata*

The first major trend to be registered is the erosion in working-class penetration by social-democratic parties (with the small but ambiguous

exception of the SPD). As a general rule, this erosion benefits the traditional 'bourgeois' parties or new right-wing 'populist' parties, and in
some cases – but only partially – formations to the left of the social
democrats (to some extent this is the case in Sweden, Denmark and
Norway). The nature, extent and rhythm of working-class defection vary
according to country and political-electoral circumstances. But the basic
bond of mutual trust between these parties and the working class – what
Hobsbawm called a 'unique advantage' – risks disintegration.

The second major trend to register is an *increased instability* in the electoral
behaviour of workers. Overall, their support for the left is more fragile, more
subject to conjunctural factors and the interplay of competition.

Nevertheless, measured over an extended period (1990s/1960s or by
decade), and thus setting aside short-term fluctuations, the social-democratic downturn among the working class is *fairly moderate.* All in all, the
picture that emerges is of social democracy in the 1980s and 1990s
establishing itself at a level appreciably below that of the 1960s, with its
working-class influence fluctuating around 80 per cent of the total for the
1960s. Relative stabilization at this level confirms the impression of a *non-
conjunctural class dealignment.* However, this decline is neither imposing nor
spectacular. Moreover, nothing points to a growing deterioration in the
links between socialists and the working class in recent years; nothing
indicates a more or less brutal aggravation of the trend. On occasion,
working-class disaffection has certainly assumed extraordinary proportions
(Denmark in 1973; Great Britain in 1983) – and will probably do so again
in the future. This has often created the impression of a cataclysmic
change, the definitive 'end' of class voting. But such a picture sins by
exaggeration. It is unquestionably true that working-class attachment to the
left no longer possesses the vigour, power, durability and political substance
of yesteryear. But it exists. Social-democratic parties remain the 'natural'
parties of the working class. Yet their capacity to represent it electorally has
definitely diminished significantly.

(ii) *Class dealignment by the advance – or greater resilience – of social
      democrats among the salaried middle strata*

Over the last thirty years, increased penetration (in relative terms, but often
also in absolute terms) of social democracy among these categories is
clearly apparent. The social democracies are increasingly sustained by votes
from the salaried middle classes, allowing them to limit the damage done
by working-class disaffection and the fall in working-class numbers in the
population. This influence is essentially concentrated among the 'new'
middle classes or the 'salaried middle strata' (office workers, intermediate
executives and professions, technicians and engineers, teachers, health and
social service workers, etc.) – categories that are undergoing strong arithmetical expansion. More particularly, the most cultured band of the new
middle classes – the intellectual professions (academics, teachers, and the
information, arts and entertainment professions) – are categories that

display an increased tendency to vote for the left (social democrats, left socialists, ex-communists, or ecologists). *There is nothing to suggest that this is a conjunctural shift.* The *cultural liberalism* of these highly cultured categories ('moral' permissiveness, anti-authoritarian/participatory political values, universalist/anti-ethnocentric attitudes) makes them suspicious of the cultural conservatism of much of the traditional right, and unsusceptible to the authoritarian and anti-universalist discourse of the extreme right.[24]

Thus, the structure of social democracy's electoral development in the period 1960 to 1997 seems clear enough: in phases of electoral breakthrough it gains rather more ground among the salaried middle strata than among workers; and in phases of downturn it is more resilient among the former than the latter. We should also note that in a majority of the countries considered here, the level of social-democratic influence among the salaried middle strata in the 1990s is either higher than or equal to that of the 1960s, even though the electoral performance of socialist/social-democratic parties is often inferior.

The progress of socialist/social-democratic parties among the salaried middle strata is partially challenged, however, in countries where formations of a 'new politics' (or semi-new politics) type emerge strongly. Such formations tend to root themselves primarily in these strata, restricting social-democratic influence there (examples are Germany, Norway, Denmark and Sweden).

We should also underline a marked tendency towards a *relative* strengthening of social-democratic penetration of *public-sector strata*, regardless of their manual or non-manual character and hierarchical status. The salaried strata of the public sector – and, more especially, those who work in nationalized enterprises, education, health, research, communications, social services in general (the 'state service sector', as Wright and Cho term it)[25] – are becoming the *new epicentre* – alongside the working class – *of the left's electoral strength.* The 'state service middle class' is characterized by a pronounced attachment to left-wing values, and is significantly further to the left than the middle classes in the private sector. The influence of the sectoral divide on the left-wing vote is strong in the majority of the cases studied in this chapter. It is particularly strong in the Scandinavian countries (notably Denmark, but also – and in descending order – Norway and Sweden), France and Greece. It is visible in Austria and Great Britain. Public-sector salaried employees in part represent the new conquered land of the social democrats, and could prove even more of an acquisition in the future, if social democracy succeeds in neutralizing the influence of parties representing varieties of 'new politics'.

(iii) *The social democrats are the object of a persistent rejection by the traditional middle and petty bourgeoisie, as well as – in a majority of cases – small farmers*

Relative decline in traditional commerce and craft industry is accompanied by an expansion in new commercial and artisanal categories of a higher social and cultural level. The relative embourgeoisement of the traditional 'new' petty bourgeoisie, as well as the increased salience of the tax issue, explain its rejection of the left and electoral support for the right.[26] The small and medium bourgeoisie, attached to the culture of the firm, remain the solid, central electoral bloc of the right – in some cases more so than in the past, in others a little less. With the exception of a very limited number of countries (notably Norway, Italy and Greece), the world of small and medium-sized enterprise acts as a stable bloc with extraordinary political cohesion. Thus, if we take as our point of departure and reference the classical Marxist division between bourgeoisie (petty, medium and large) and working class, which is still valid, we observe that class dealignment is restricted to the political behaviour of the working class. We are dealing with a *unilateral class dealignment*.[27]

The Working-Class Electorate and the Importance of Politics

The 'class' factor has partially lost its former pre-eminence in European political systems. According to a comparative analysis by Paul Nieuwbeerta, who has studied the relationship between social class and electoral behaviour in several countries (measuring absolute as well as relative class voting), 'a fairly monotonic decline in the countries' levels of class voting has occurred, but around this trend fluctuations are visible'.[28] This is broadly in keeping with the findings of the preceding analysis. The 'social psychology' of class voting has changed,[29] although there is nothing to suggest the end of the electoral class struggle.

How, then, are we to interpret the 'lost' loyalty of part of the working class, and the variations in its political options?

Clearly, the transformation of the societies of advanced capitalism does not favour 'old-style' class political polarization. Some basic sociological factors (arithmetical decline of the working class *stricto sensu*, increased professional fragmentation, unemployment, ethnic diversification of the most marginal sections of popular strata, considerable growth in the number of people with an 'uncertain status', the development of 'flexible' forms of employment), as well as some specifically political factors (the adoption of a catch-all profile by left-wing parties), lead to a further attenuation of the link between the working class and voting for the left. However, while the Keynesian equation proved effective, neither social changes – which have been going on for a long time – nor catch-all strategies – which date back to the 1950s – resulted in working-class disaffection, except marginally or in circumstantial fashion. 'Structural' explanations, the '"bottom-up" approaches to the structuring of political divisions' dominant in political sociology, often ignore the fact that the effects of social change on voting are very uncertain. In addition, they underestimate – just as they always did – the *impact of political action*, and political actors' capacity to adapt. 'The most interesting characteristic of Norway's party system', Kaare Strom and Lars Svasand have written, 'lies in the magnitude of the drama we shall observe: the scale and rapidity of social change and the vigour of the organizational response.'[30] Are workers' political choices independent of the action of political organizations – of the 'organizational response'? Are they reducible to the *social change* experienced by the countries of advanced capitalism? Are they principally to be explained by 'subterranean' developments in social structure? On this vast subject, which is scarcely new, I shall restrict myself to some past and present examples, in order to bring out the importance of political action in the establishment – and testing – of class political alignments.

The theme of the 'embourgeoisement' of the working class found its most fervent adepts in the late 1950s and early 1960s. Following three consecutive defeats for Labour, the 'affluent worker thesis' was particularly in vogue in Britain. In France, René Mouriaux took it as an established fact in 1970 that 'workers increasingly vote for the candidates of the right. This is a transnational phenomenon that has assumed greater magnitude in France than elsewhere and a particular complexion with the presidency of General de Gaulle.'[31] Likewise, André Philip asserted: 'we are currently witnessing the decline of working-class parties to a certain extent everywhere. I am not referring to the crisis of the SFIO in France ... I am thinking mainly of Germany and Great Britain. . . . Labour has lost three times, the SPD has lost three times.'[32] In the event, I am obliged to observe that after the great debate on the 'historic decline' of Labour, it recovered and succeeded in exercising power for eleven out of the next fifteen years, before being plunged into a very serious crisis after the electoral defeat of 1979. Similarly, the SPD was able to establish itself as the main party of government in the FRG throughout the 1970s. Moreover, in 1966 and 1972 respectively, the parties in question achieved one of their *best* electoral performances among the working class.

As for France, the thesis that the decline in working-class 'leftism' from 1959 to 1969, and more generally the rise of Gaullism, was caused by social change and an 'embourgeoisement' of the working class (established according to the classical equation between economic prosperity and lower class consciousness), was contradicted by the facts. For the great shift to the left among workers occurred in 1973 – still a time of exceptional prosperity. In reality, it was factors of a *political* nature that made possible the detachment of a significant – though not central – part of the working class from the left. Gaullism's ability to make non-economic issues (decolonization, institutional modernization, European integration, the Atlantic Alliance) salient questions in French political life, plus the General's exceptional charisma, explain the trend in question. Thereafter, it was modification of the 'electoral alternatives', conditioned by the events of May 1968, the retirement of the man of 18 June, and especially the *formation of the left alliance*, which led to the strong *resurgence* of the 'class' factor on the French political scene. Thus, in a period of 'post-industrial change' and 'class dealignment', the left found itself on the verge of power in 1974, thanks in large part to *strengthened class voting*. This represented the veritable 'revenge' of the electoral class struggle which, after a fifteen-year delay, got the better of the interclassist political groupings that had dominated the initial stages of the Fifth Republic – even if this revenge proved (for good reasons) short-lived.

In fact, it would appear that in France, as in Great Britain and elsewhere, whether in the 1960s or today, basic sociological factors ultimately play only a background role. They can certainly help to account for the 'intensive' or 'diffuse' type of support given to political parties by workers, or for the emergence of new electoral issues and political divisions; but *on their own* they cannot explain the major or minor shifts among working-class electorates that have occurred, or are occurring, in European countries. Let us take an example. Sociologically, the united left in France was structured in a similar fashion to 'classical' social democracy, at a time (the 1970s) when the latter was commencing its own dynamic of 'de-structuration'. If the Union of the Left fundamentally changed the realities of electoral competition in 1970s France, and contributed to strengthened class voting, the failure of governmental socialism in terms of social policy encouraged a sharp decline in the left-wing orientation of workers – a decline that was very evident in the 1993 election. Working-class defection followed an administration marked by deflation and austerity. We can see the same decline in class voting in Great Britain at the end of the 1960s and 1970s, when the unpopularity of outgoing Labour governments became obvious, and there was ruthless head-on confrontation with trade-unionism. The hypothesis formulated by Bruno Cautrès and Anthony Heath in their study of the decline of class voting in Great Britain and France would seem to be of *more general relevance*: 'class voting ... loses its intensity at moments marked by the striking unpopularity of outgoing left-wing governments ... the support of working-class voters for left-wing governments unquestionably [being] more pragmatic than ideological, unlike the middle strata'.[33]

Indeed, the available statistics seem to indicate that disaffection with socialist/social-democratic parties on the part of a far from negligible proportion of the world of labour and disadvantaged sections of the population tends to accelerate after a governmental failure by the left, especially in social policy. Thus, in some countries the downward trend in left-wing voting by workers was marked by brutal 'ruptures', and often by reverse – but not commensurate – subsequent swings of the pendulum (Great Britain, Denmark, France in part). In other countries, working-class defection was more linear, although not necessarily less pronounced (Norway), and not without 'minor' ruptures (Austria; Sweden to some extent).

The slower, more gradual character of the loosening of the link between the working class and socialist voting in Norway might seem – in this instance, at least – to lend more weight to a sociological than a political explanation – all the more so given that Norway experienced stronger economic growth than other countries during the 1970s and 1980s, largely linked to exploitation of the 'black gold'. Since the 1980s, Norway has been among world leaders in terms of indicators of prosperity (gross domestic product per capita, wage levels, life expectancy, medical cover).[34] When the development of Norwegian political life is examined more closely, however, we see that the political situation and the issues at stake in it – economic circumstances become a dimension of the political conjuncture once they are perceived as a matter for political action[35] – did not favour the Norwegian Labour Party. Thus, the slowdown in growth and the considerable deterioration in the trade balance coincided with the DNA's presence in government (1977–81). The Labour government found itself obliged to pursue a policy restricting total demand and freezing prices and wages (September 1978). Between 1978 and 1981, workers' real wages fell, and Labour, converted to austerity, was driven from office. The DNA's return to power in 1986, in the teeth of economic crisis, was again accompanied by a dose of austerity as well as rising unemployment, particularly following the major recession of 1988. As a consequence, *the electoral cycle weighed heavily on the fate of the DNA*, unable to benefit from the economic boom of 1983–86 because it was confined to opposition.[36] In fact, even in the case of Norway the weakening left-wing inclinations of the working-class electorate appear to be largely bound up with the political conjuncture and the performance, particularly in social policy, of Labour governments. Here, too, an explanation in political, and not purely sociological, terms seems more pertinent. Moreover, the marked acceleration in working-class defection during this precise period appears to favour this line of explanation.

The case of the Greek PASOK confirms this analysis *a contrario*. Its first stint in power (1981–85) – rather than weakening the party's popular bases, as happened in countries with a socialist government during the recession – strengthened its popular anchorage. This novel development was bound up with the fact that the first genuine attempt to construct a welfare state in Greece coincided with PASOK's arrival in government. Enshrined in PASOK's *populist* logic, the satisfaction of narrow sectional demands, accompanied by the establishment of a clientelistic socialist state, certainly led to the state getting deeply into debt in an adverse economic situation, destabilizing and partially delegitimizing the whole enterprise. But even if it was a 'bad manager', and politically cynical, the *image of a socially 'generous'* PASOK allowed the Greek socialists to put up better resistance among working-class and popular strata in their electoral defeats of 1989 and 1990. On the other hand, having adopted a managerial profile, and enjoying an incontestable advantage over its conservative opponent on the terrain of 'European pragmatism', PASOK alienated important sections of the socially and culturally disadvantaged in 1996, notwithstanding its electoral victory and breakthrough among well-off sections of the population.[37] This alienation was generally confirmed and magnified in the 1999 European elections, and in one sense in the legislative elections of April 2000. Returned to power, PASOK, despite a certain recovery of influence among popular strata, increasingly presents itself as the party of 'the contented'.[38] This is a remarkable development for a party often regarded in the not too distant past as 'populist'.

Lost Comrades: The Working-Class Vote and the Extreme Right

The breakthrough by the populist extreme right among the working class seems to confirm the thesis of the salience of political factors. Indeed, in some countries the extreme right increasingly begins to appear to a significant percentage of the popular electorate as a 'natural' political alternative. Today, it is unquestionably true that the formations of the populist right are (in Dominique Pélassy's words) 'expanding by popularizing themselves'.[39] In Europe, part of the 'plebeian public sphere' increasingly speaks the language of the extreme right, which is establishing itself as an 'exit option' for workers and culturally disadvantaged strata.

The class profile of parties of the new populist right (e.g. the FPÖ in Austria, the FN in France, the Progress Parties of Denmark and Norway) exhibits 'an increasing deviation from conventional bourgeois parties'.[40] As late as the 1980s, the FPÖ's electorate comprised more executives, self-employed, members of the liberal professions and graduates than the average for the population. However, Jörg Haider's accession to the party leadership (1986) drastically altered the structure of its support: a remarkable increase in its influence among workers (in its social make-up the FPÖ is as 'popular' today as the SPÖ); an improvement in its penetration among employees; and a drop among educated sections of the population.[41]

In France, the 'popularization' of the FN is more pronounced still, and an analogous pattern has occurred in Denmark and Norway. The three parties in question are overrepresented among the working class and the traditional petty bourgeoisie (though the latter's participation in the electorate of the Norwegian Progress Party is similar to its weight in the total population), and significantly underrepresented among the new middle classes. In addition, we should note that the electorate of the populist right is not ideologically extremist on all issues and in every respect. In France, Le Pen's electorate in 1995 was *further to the left* in its economic ideology than the electorate of the moderate right. Ideologically, it is genuinely 'in-between' the electorates of the left and the traditional right.[42] According to Gérard Grunberg and Étienne Schweisguth, the ideological complexion of the French extreme right 'can in no way be described as simply being more right-wing than the moderate right . . . but . . . owes its characterization as extreme right to its extreme rejection of universalist values'.[43] The electorate of the Danish Progress Party is also less hostile towards the welfare state than that of the other non-socialist parties.

Typical 'anti-tax', anti-bureaucratic and anti-establishment formations, which initially defended the freedom of the private sector, the Danish and Norwegian parties (particularly the former) have gradually become more moderate on all these points. During the 1980s the Danish Progress Party adopted a noticeably more social profile (supporting increases in pensions and health expenditure) and, at the same time, a more 'anti-immigrant' stance.[44] More faithful to its customary campaign themes, the Norwegian Party is evolving in the same direction, as was evident in the parliamentary elections of 1997. In Denmark and Norway 'it is probably more correct to speak of "welfare state chauvinism" than of anti-welfare attitudes: the welfare services should be restricted to "our own" '.[45] In France, too, an originally very neoliberal discourse has gradually given way to a socio-economic platform mixing neoliberalism, state interventionism and socializing measures.[46] Furthermore, the FPÖ, after the weakening of its liberal wing following a split in 1993 (and the creation of an authentically liberal party, the Liberal Forum), while advocating a reduced economic role for the state, has put more emphasis on the populist and protest aspects of its policies (violent rejection of the European Union and its domination by multinational companies and 'unrestricted neoliberalism'; reform of the Austrian political system).

Despite their originally neoliberal profile and strangely archaic conception of the role of public power (fewer economic and social functions, more police), the parties of the extreme right are today typically in the process of adopting – albeit slowly, and in a highly equivocal fashion – a more composite ideological-programmatic profile, less marked by neoliberal pro-capitalism.

There can obviously be no question here of analysing the distinctive features of a very heterogeneous political family. But given our aim, one observation is necessary: the parties of the new extreme right, whose doctrine is inegalitarian and anti-universalist, at a less conspicuous but increasingly explicit level produce an egalitarian 'ambiance', which is not (or not yet) an articulated discourse. In attacking the 'powerful', the 'establishment' and the 'coalition of elites' in the name of ordinary people and the 'small man', in timorously adopting a more 'social' discourse, they are becoming the perverted expression of a certain anti-egalitarian egalitarianism.[47] They are becoming the political instruments of a *populist 'egalitarianism'* – selective, diffuse and badly articulated – which coexists with a *liberal-capitalist anti-egalitarianism* (in marked retreat) and an aggressive, domineering *ethnocentric anti-egalitarianism*, the strongest and most distinctive element in the ideological/programmatic profile of the new extreme right.

In fact, in every instance the extreme right's strongest niche is the issue of immigration and ethnocentrism. The parties of the populist extreme right are unquestionably protest formations that garner the protest vote against the traditional parties. But above all, they are organizations that 'capitalize on the neglected issue'.[48] This applies even to the parties in Scandinavia, where immigration became a salient issue 'only after the Progress Parties were established'.[49] It is on immigration, 'law and order' and, more generally, attitudes towards universalist values that these parties find the most fertile ground for establishing and consolidating themselves, before finally blurring the division between left and right. Within a system comprising 'authoritarianism, ethnic particularism and market liberalism',[50] immigration and ethnocentrism ('anti-universalism' according to Grunberg and Schweisguth) play a major role in differentiating the extreme right from left and moderate right alike.

But why does a far from insignificant percentage of the working-class and popular strata turn to the new extreme right? Can this shift be explained by the notorious 'cultural traditionalism' of workers, or the historically greater diffusion of 'anti-universalist' values among them? Is it a product of 'working-class fascism'?

Historically, social democracy, and the left in general, established itself as a central, strategic pole within the popular milieu – as an 'attractor' (to borrow a term from Luc Boltanski). It was an 'attractor' that was certainly political, but also *cultural*, contributing to the formation of the collective identity of the subaltern classes. Historically, the left was not simply a force for the representation of socioeconomic interests but also a force for *civilization*, bearer of an 'ethical' project and universalist, egalitarian values. Thus, if in the past there was a certain discrepancy between left-wing values and 'spontaneous working-class consciousness' (the famous – very controversial – 'working-class authoritarianism'), the effectiveness of 'economic leftism', as well as the ideological efforts of left-wing organizations, played a decisive role in the attraction, unification and attachment of the working class to left-wing parties that 'aimed at broader and anti-authoritarian goals'.[51] Class interests took precedence over value orientations – or better: left-wing parties (and trade unions), possessing a remarkable capacity for the ideological and cultural orientation of *their* class, were in a good position to influence – almost to fashion – value orientations in popular milieux. Today, by contrast, the economic and social policy of the social-democratic left no longer polarizes social groups sufficiently, because it is no longer perceived as *sufficiently distinct from its neoliberal opponents*. The left 'no longer succeeds as readily in inflecting demands of an economic kind to the left ideologically'.[52] Because of its 'failure' in social policy, it does not succeed in carrying workers in its ideological/cultural wake either. With the ideological, cultural and organizational decline of the political and trade-union left, and its traditional networks of influence, a political and cultural space has opened up. A new polarization has been created, which is most conspicuous in France: the ideological centre of gravity of popular strata (even those who do not vote FN) has partially shifted towards the values of the right and extreme right (xenophobia, ethnocentrism, anti-universalism), while the cultivated upper classes maintain universalist positions that verge on a certain left-wing humanism.[53]

Basically, the absence of a clearly perceptible left-wing *differentia specifica* in economic and social policy distances a section of workers not only from the left, but also from the 'universalist' values it represents. Moreover, the increased weight in the social-democratic parties of the new 'cultural class' – liberal, often neoliberal, in its value orientation – shatters the solidarity between the 'people' and social-democratic elites, between apex and base of the social-democratic pyramid. Now, in the absence of a strong and strongly shared left-wing ideological framework today, this gulf between social democratic 'elites' and 'masses', between those 'above' and those 'below', is a supplementary factor in the defection of the workers. Basically, a vicious circle is initiated, the cultural effects of political options being compounded by the political effects of cultural 'predispositions'. When the impact of the traditional socioeconomic divide on voting decreases, the *libertarian versus authoritarian political dimension* assumes greater salience and importance. The result of socioeconomic disappointment among workers is thus added on to the result of *popular authoritarianism*, and it is not always easy to disentangle the two.

Voting for the populist extreme right by popular strata is largely the *indirect* result of what is today perceived as an 'illusory choice': it springs from great disillusionment among a section of the popular classes.[54] Thus, at the geometrical centre of several reasons for the consolidation of the popular bases of the new extreme right, at the core of its dynamic, is the major failure of its principal opponent: the egalitarian project of the left. In this respect there is no better gauge of the social defeat of the left in government than the extreme right's breakthrough in working-class milieux.[55]

The Breakdown of the Keynesian Equation and Working-Class Defection

We cannot understand the electoral link between social democracy and the working class, its nature and political significance, without considering a large number of parameters from which this link derived. Consequently, the hypothesis foregrounding political factors requires much more corroboration. Nevertheless, it seems clear that it was with the *'breakdown' of the Keynesian equation* that social democracy's position was significantly weakened in the world of labour. For the period that runs from the beginning of the 1970s to the present, considered from a macroscopic angle, the trend is pronounced and unambiguous. Basically, the decreasing propensity of workers and disadvantaged strata to vote for the left exposed the social-democratic parties' inability to manage the 'social question' effectively. Dependent on the very difficult general conjuncture, which was unfavourable to parties in power, socialists in government paid a high price. The corrosive effect of being in power was nothing new. What was new was that it appeared to exact a *higher social cost than in the past* (see Chapter 6). In this respect, the minor and partial German exception is not really such an exception. Out of power from 1982, the SPD was largely able to maintain its positions within the world of labour. This will not necessarily be the case in the future.

In reality, if workers are less susceptible than before to the social-democratic political appeal, it is partly because this political appeal is less sensitive to working-class demands.[56] Depending on social circumstances, the success or failure of a governmental experience, the structure and dynamic of the conservative 'opponent' and 'opposition bloc' – in short, the conjuncture of electoral competition – the working-class influence of social-democratic parties can decline or recover. But in every instance, today as in the 1950s and 1960s, the political appeal and governmental performance of left-wing parties appears to play a very important role.

So, at a time when working-class attachment to the left is proving less strong and stable, less total and intense, more episodic and conditional – in short, 'instrumental' – largely owing to the social and cultural recomposition analysed by supporters of the 'structural' thesis, the 'political strategy', 'electoral appeal', and especially 'governmental performance' of the left become central factors in accounting for the electoral behaviour of workers and subaltern classes.

It is absurd to oppose a 'vote on the issues' whereby an individualist worker, free of all social/cultural constraints, makes his or her choice according to the questions of the hour and the programme on offer, and a 'sociological' vote to which each elector is compelled in so far as she or he is constrained by the weight of class, religion and family tradition.[57] The 'sociological' vote does indeed exist; without it, the structure of party systems in Europe would be utterly unintelligible. Accordingly, foregrounding the political and conjunctural factors that determine working-class voting does not entail that we can thereby clearly demarcate 'conjunctural' from 'structural' determinants. A specific political conjuncture does not constitute 'a short-term political force' with only temporary effects.[58] When it comes to partisan identification, the 'conjunctural' is often the vector of the 'structural'; it can result in stable electoral behaviour, especially if a 'conjuncture' lasts a long time, as was the case after 1973. Moreover, political factors are all the more important when they affect a social class's 'potential for mobilization'. Political action and the effects of political action are decisive in the construction of class identities. In this sense, the attenuation of class voting by workers as a result of political factors is primarily a political phenomenon with social consequences. But it can become a social phenomenon with political consequences.[59]

Class politics is in retreat. It is in retreat because of the transformation (not the decline) of classes, but also because of the politics of the left. The analysis above does not prove that the electoral class struggle is at an end. Instead, it shows that the mediating role of political factors – and actors – between class structure and the act of voting is very important – in all likelihood, more important than it was in the past.[60]

The Social-Democratic Electorate: The Internal Sociological Dialectic

The Social Profile of the Social-Democratic Electorate

The social profile or social specificity of an electorate describes its class *cohesion*. It thus represents a useful indicator for identifying the social character and, indirectly, the cultural character of a party, as well as its ability to adopt a coherent class politics without clashing with whole sections of its own social base.

Moreover, focusing not on the electoral behaviour of classes, but on the *class composition* of electorates, not on the political specificity of social classes but on the class specificity of electorates, makes it possible to understand the internal sociological dialectic of the social-democratic coalition, by identifying the social groups within it which are in the ascendant or in decline.

If we look at the data in Table 7.16, we see that the *class cohesion* of electoral social democracy has been strongly affected since the 1960s, confirming the hypothesis of a significant recomposition of the social-democratic electorate.

A sizeable displacement in the sociological centre of gravity of this electorate towards the salaried middle strata has occurred, such that *two social poles of almost equal importance* now seem to coexist within the social-democratic space. This being so, the arithmetically massive and dominant presence of workers, which was *constitutive of social democracy*, faces significant challenge. As a consequence, the class character and *social cohesion* of this political force are considerably diluted.

This development seems to be in line with the gradual modification in the class equilibrium of modern societies over the last thirty years, and the strategic issue it raises: establishing an 'alliance' between workers and the expanding new middle strata, which, in the long run, would mean the sociological conversion of social democracy from a working-class/popular party into a party of salaried strata relatively close to the catch-all model.

The increased interclassism of contemporary social democracy is unquestionably a phenomenon of *adaptation*, but it also results from workers' reduced propensity to vote social-democratic, and the electoral weakening that ensues. Considered from this viewpoint, it is – albeit in the second instance – a *retreat*. But at the same time, in that it signals social democracy's implantation on new social terrain, it is primarily – in a paradox that is merely apparent – an interclassism of conquest, of *expansion*. This new, profoundly interclassist profile is the infallible sign of a mutation in social democracy's electoral space. The composition of this space, its mould, has changed considerably.

Conclusion: The New Diversity of Electoral Social Democracy

Following the data we have just presented, some reflections on the 'new' face of social-democracy-in-the-electorate suggest themselves:

1. As in the past, social democracy is essentially constituted socially around two pillars: the working class and the salaried middle strata. But the architectonic and balance of the edifice have been modified.
   (a) The relative weight of the traditionally central bloc of the social-democratic electorate, constituted by the working class, has dimin-

112   CONTEMPORARY SOCIAL DEMOCRACY

Table 7.16   Social composition of the social-democratic electorate

	Denmark		Austria*		Germany	
	1966	1987	1969	1995	1967	1994**
Workers	72	50	68	39	61	43
Salaried middle strata	23	46	25	50	32	46
Self-employed	5	4	7	4	8	5
	Norway		Sweden		Great Britain***	
	1965	1989	1960	1994	1966	1992
Workers	64	48	76	52	81	63
Salaried middle strata	22	37	18	43	19	37
Self-employed	14	15	4	4		

* In reaching these figures, we have excluded housewives and retired people from our calculations.
** West Germany.
*** The class composition of the Labour Party is established according to the manual/non-manual distinction.

Sources: For the Danish Social Democrats, see Gøsta Esping-Andersen, *Politics against Markets*, Princeton University Press, Princeton, NJ 1985, p. 128 for 1966, and Jorgen Goul Andersen, 'Denmark: Environmental Conflict and the "Greening" of the Labour Movement', *Scandinavian Political Studies*, vol. 13, no. 2, 1990, for 1987. For the SPD, see Anton Pelinka, *Social Democratic Parties in Europe*, Praeger, New York 1983, p. 46 for 1967, and Russell Dalton and Wilhelm Bürklin, 'The Two German Electorates' in Russell Dalton, ed., *Germans Divided*, Berg, Oxford 1996, p. 199 for 1994. For the SPÖ, see Anton Pelinka and Fritz Plasser, *The Austrian Party System*, Westview Press, Boulder, CO 1989, p. 75 for 1967, and Kurt Richard Luther, 'The Social-Democratic Party of Austria', in Robert Ladrech and Philippe Marlière, *Social-Democratic Parties in the European Union*, Macmillan, London 1999, p. 25. For the Norwegian Labour Party, see Jorgen Goul Andersen and Tom Bjorklund, 'Structural Changes and New Cleavages', *Acta Sociologica*, vol. 33, no. 3, 1990, pp. 208–9. For the SAP, see Nicholas Aylott, 'The Swedish Social-Democratic Party', in Ladrech and Marlière, eds, *Social-Democratic Parties in the European Union*, p. 196. For the British Labour Party, see Bo Salvik and Ivor Crewe, *Decade of Dealignment*, Cambridge University Press, Cambridge 1983, p. 89 for 1966, and David Denver, *Elections and Voting Behaviour in Britain*, Harvester Wheatsheaf, London and New York 1994, p. 11 for 1992.

ished markedly. This is due to two factors: (i) an important reduction, both absolute and relative, in the number of workers in the population; (ii) the proportionately greater dissatisfaction of workers with parties of a social-democratic type. Given that working-class defection is fairly moderate, the first is more important.[61]

(b) A second grouping – the salaried middle strata – has gradually asserted itself alongside the working class, which remains an important pole of support, but whose centrality has diminished significantly. Social-democratic influence within this large and very heterogeneous category is concentrated mainly among two subsets: the first comprises salaried employees in the public and para-public sector; the second, only partially coinciding with the first, comprises the intellectual professions that increasingly occupy a privileged position in the social base of the left, on account of their cultural weight.[62]

2. The logic of this evolution tends to attach the salaried middle strata to the *centre* of the social-democratic coalition, although the great diversity of national situations dictates prudence on this score. The lines of force of the new social penetration by socialists confirm the coexistence within the same coalition of voters from two major social groups, which are internally heterogeneous. Because the value priorities of these two central components of the social-democratic coalition differ sharply (the well-educated middle strata evince a strong adhesion to post-materialist values and cultural liberalism, workers a rather weak adhesion, if not a certain cultural conservatism), an evident dissymmetry opens up at the heart of the social-democratic electorate. Potential tension between these two universes, which are culturally distinct and electorally 'allied', is an important *source of weakness* for parties of a social-democratic type.

3. The emergence and consolidation of the divide between materialism and post-materialism, or (according to Walter Korpi) 'ecology' and 'technology', contributes to reducing the salaried middle strata's propensity to vote social-democratic. The influence of the 'green' parties or certain left-wing socialist parties (Denmark, Norway) tends to check social-democratic penetration among these categories. Everything indicates that this new line of division did split the social-democratic coalition of the 1950s and 1960s, making it possible to detach from it a politically significant proportion of educated sections of the population and youth. As a result of this divide, social democracy does not always fully benefit from the culturally post-materialist segment of the electorate, whose epicentre is often located in the public sector, a segment essentially composed of youth and white-collar employees.

4. Meanwhile, notwithstanding marked national disparities, a number of indicators reveal that social democracy tends to become, *par excellence*, the representative of social forces most attached to the state, and especially the welfare state, despite differences of emphasis and interest. These forces are obviously workers, who remain orientated towards the state and its redistributive functions, and salaried public-sector employees, whose interests are inextricably bound up with the fate of the state. Accordingly, socialists find themselves confronting a paradoxical and quasi-schizophrenic situation: at a time when they are adopting policies of neoliberal inspiration for reducing the role of the state, they simultaneously present themselves as the political actor representing the

social forces connected with the state or demanding its intervention. This relation and contradiction – a source of both socialist strength and weakness – renders adoption of a 'pure' neoliberal strategy too costly in electoral terms.

5. The working class is no longer the privileged sociological marker of social-democratic electorates. Their internal socio-demographic balance has shifted in the direction of a *relative equalization* of the working-class and 'salaried-middle-strata' components. As a result, the class specificity of these electorates, which historically confirmed the predominance of the working class, is being dissolved in a socially heterogeneous body. This drastically diminishes the social democrats' ability to adopt coherent class policies, since it inevitably increases the potential electoral cost of such policies. It also enables us to appreciate how much more difficult dealing with political options becomes with such diverse clienteles.

6. Compared with their own past, contemporary social-democratic parties are constructed on the basis of a profoundly interclassist format, by far the most interclassist in the whole history of social democracy. Their 'natural' sociological inclination is their *definitive* mutation into 'leftist catch-all parties'. At the present time, this is confirmed in terms both of the social composition of their electoral base and of their ideological/ programmatic orientation. Moreover, such a pattern partially invalidates Przeworski and Sprague's hypothesis according to which social-democratic parties tend to abandon interclassist strategies when they lose votes among the working class.[63] To be sure, 'perfect' catch-all parties, large formations that are able to attract 'everything' in the strict sense of the term, are virtually unknown in Europe. The sociology of the great left-wing parties remains 'a preferential sociology'.[64] The social-democratic parties cover a broad social spectrum, but none of them 'catches all' the positions in this space in some undifferentiated, homogeneous fashion. None has been able to penetrate in depth the central core of the opposing electorate (large bourgeoisie, traditional petty bourgeoisie, liberal professions, in part the rural world), just as no conservative party has been able profoundly and enduringly to penetrate the central kernel of the left-wing electorate. In this sense, contemporary social-democratic interclassism is incomplete and, most probably, incapable of being completed. During the initial postwar period, however, social-democratic interclassism was considerably more limited, and to a certain extent was even a 'projected', rather than an 'accomplished', interclassism (see Chapter 3). The discrepancy between the 'programmatic' and the 'sociological' is significantly less marked today. In a dual, complementary dynamic, the decline in class voting among workers and the increasingly left-wing orientation of salaried non-workers lead to this result.

7. The relative disaffection of workers and popular strata with social democracy is directly linked to its inability to 'pilot' the socioeconomic system and implement its commitment to the principle of 'rectifying' inequalities. Social-democratic formations unquestionably remain popular electoral forces, but their capacity to represent the working-class and

deprived sections of the population has diminished significantly. As a result, the first group of social-democratic-type parties identified in this study (see Chapter 3) – those with maximum working-class penetration (systematically approaching or surpassing two-thirds of the working-class vote) – is in the process of disappearing from the electoral map. The SAP, party of the working class *par excellence*, certainly remains very strong among manual workers, despite some falling off. Yet its constituency has manifestly been weakened, losing the stability and imposing density of the past. Today, the majority of social-democratic formations belong to an intermediate group whose main feature is the fluctuation of their working-class influence around the symbolic threshold of 50 per cent of the working-class vote (between 40 per cent and 60 per cent). The SPÖ, the SPD, the DNA, and the British Labour Party now belong to this category. The Danish SD, formerly very strong, appears to be doomed to languish below the 50 per cent bar. From the perspective of electoral sociology, it is no longer a valid generalization to say that social-democratic parties are parties of the working class.

8. The major phenomenon of the last thirty years is the advance – or greater resilience – of the left among non-manual salaried employees. 'Pools of attraction' have been constituted around the great socialist/social-democratic parties containing social categories that are less and less the 'natural' social categories of the left. The advance is considerable enough to compensate for the retreat of the left among workers, as well as the electoral effects of the reduction of the working-class group in the population. The scale of the consequences of this historically unprecedented development could be fully appreciated only towards the end of the 1990s when – despite the decline of the traditional working class – socialist parties dominated the European political scene.

9. 'Labour is nowadays the "natural" party of the minority social class in Britain,' Anthony Heath *et al.* have written, 'but that was the cross the Conservatives bore until well into the 1960s and it never stopped them from regularly winning elections.'[65] This is true not only of the British Labour Party, but of all the parties in the European socialist/social-democratic family. It is true on one condition: that we avoid the error of imagining that the 'nature' of a political formation can be constituted independently of the social bases that give it electoral 'materiality', dynamism and health. If the *overall economy* of the social bases of social-democratic parties is in the process of changing, then – even had social-democratic working-class penetration remained unaltered (which is not the case) – the 'nature' of these parties, regarded as the 'natural' parties of the working class, cannot fail to be affected. Even during the 1990s, parties of a social-democratic type were able to preserve their privileged relationship with the working class (as is indicated by their consistent overrepresentation within this category). But the lines of force of their overall social penetration have been significantly – one could say structurally – disrupted. Neither *class parties* nor, at times, parties *of the class*, social-democratic formations have changed. From

enlarged coalitions of the working class they have been transformed into *interclassist coalitions with a strong working-class influence*. And the difference is not insignificant.

Compared with the beginning of the twentieth century and the interwar period, social democracy in the 1950s and 1960s changed considerably in adopting a catch-all ideological and programmatic profile. But despite increased penetration among the middle classes, the sociological architectonic of its electoral space still remained massively structured by the working class. Significant as it was, the social-democratic mutation of the 1950s and 1960s was not a metamorphosis. Today, this architectonic finds itself altered and, with it, the very mould of social-democracy-in-the-electorate. Whether 'left-' or 'right-wing', the new social democracy is resolutely different from 'old-style' social democracy in terms of electoral sociology.

Notes

1. Colin Rallings and Michael Thrasher, 'Old election certainties buried in the avalanche', *The Sunday Times*, 4 May 1997.
2. Anthony Heath, Roger Jowell and John Curtice, *How Britain Votes*, Pergamon Press, London 1985.
3. Ibid., pp. 15–16.
4. Anthony Heath, Roger Jowell and John Curtice, 'Trendless Fluctuation: A Reply to Crewe', *Political Studies*, vol. XXXV, no. 2, 1987, p. 257.
5. Patrick Dunleavy, 'Class Dealignment in Britain Revisited', *West European Politics*, vol. 10, no. 3, 1987, p. 415.
6. See ibid., pp. 415–17.
7. Ivor Crewe, 'On the Death and Resurrection of Class Voting: Some Comments on *How Britain Votes*', *Political Studies*, vol. XXXIV, no. 4, 1986, p. 637.
8. Perhaps here we should examine the pertinence of the notion, firmly established among specialist political scientists and sociologists, that junior white-collar workers form part of the 'natural' electorate of conservatism. While this group is very clearly distinguished from the working class in the strict sense, it is yet more distinct from the world of senior management and the traditional large, medium and petty bourgeoisie. Thus, to consider the political orientation of a rather 'undecided' group, over which left and right fight in a majority of countries, as 'naturally' conservative, is to remain 'ensnared' in an Anglocentric vision of class alignment. (In Great Britain, the lower ranks of non-manuals have traditionally remained on the side of the Conservatives.) It is also to remain 'ensnared' in an outmoded conception of class voting that is at odds with reality, judging the present on the basis of criteria fashioned in and for the past.
9. Obviously, in this work I have tackled only one aspect of the approach of Heath and his colleagues, neglecting other, highly innovative aspects of their work. As a general rule, academic discussion of class voting is focused on overall levels of class voting, and the electoral behaviour of each class (class-specific trends) is often not studied separately. This results in a number of misunderstandings.
10. Gerassimos Moschonas, *La Gauche française (1972–1988) à la lumière du paradigme*

social-démocrate. Partis de coalition et coalitions de partis dans la compétition électorale, doctoral thesis, University of Paris II, 1990, pp. 162–4.
11. Ola Listhaug, 'The Decline of Class Voting', in Kaare Strom and Lars Svasand, eds, *Challenges to Political Parties: The Case of Norway*, University of Michigan Press, Michigan 1997, p. 81.
12. Ibid.
13. Russell Dalton and Wilhelm Bürklin, 'The German Party System and the Future', in Dalton, ed., *The New Germany Votes*, Berg, Oxford and Providence, RI 1993, p. 244.
14. Russell Dalton and Wilhelm Bürklin, 'The Two German Electorates', in Dalton and Bürklin, eds, *Germans Divided*, Berg, Oxford 1996, pp. 186–7.
15. These estimates concern the whole of Germany (east and west). See *Der Spiegel*, October 1998, p. 34; *Die Zeit*, 1 October 1998, no. 41.
16. Marit Hoel and Oddbjorn Knutsen, 'Social Class, Gender, and Sector Employment as Political Cleavages in Scandinavia', *Acta Sociologica*, vol. 32, no. 2, 1989.
17. David Arter, 'Sweden: A Mild Case of "Electoral Instability Syndrome"?', in David Broughton and Mark Donovan, eds, *Changing Party Systems in Western Europe*, Pinter, London and New York 1999, p. 143.
18. See ibid., p. 153.
19. Richard Kurt Luther, 'Austria: From Moderate to Polarized Pluralism?', in Broughton and Donovan, eds, *Changing Party Systems in Western Europe*, p. 133.
20. Christoph Kunkel and Jonas Pontusson, 'Corporatism versus Social Democracy: Divergent Fortunes of the Austrian and Swedish Labour Movements', *West European Politics*, vol. 21, no. 2, 1998, pp. 20–28.
21. Moschonas, *La Gauche française . . .* , pp. 215–18.
22. Daniel Boy and Nonna Mayer, 'Que reste-t-il des variables lourdes?', in Boy and Mayer, eds, *L'électeur a ses raisons*, Presses de Sciences Politiques, Paris 1997, p. 113.
23. Ibid., p. 114.
24. See Gérard Grunberg and Étienne Schweisguth, 'Recompositions idéologiques' and 'Vers une tripartition de l'espace politique', both in Boy and Mayer, eds, *L'électeur a ses raisons*.
25. Erik Olin Wright and Donmoon Cho, 'State Employment, Class Location and Ideological Orientation: A Comparative Analysis of the United States and Sweden', *Politics and Society*, vol. 20, no. 2, 1992.
26. Daniel Boy and Nonna Mayer, 'Secteur public contre secteur privé: un nouveau conflit de classe?', in Mayer, ed., *Les Modèles explicatifs du vote*, L'Harmattan, Paris 1997, p. 117.
27. Like all my other conclusions, this derives from calculation of the electoral statistics. However, the accumulation of corroborating indices reveals that a percentage of the upper middle classes and large capital is drawing ever closer to contemporary social democracy. There is no reason to suppose that these indices are insignificant, but they cannot be dealt with here.
28. Paul Nieuwbeerta, 'The Democratic Class Struggle in Postwar Societies: Class Voting in Twenty Countries, 1945–1990', *Acta Sociologica*, vol. 39, no. 4, 1996, p. 368.
29. David Sanders, 'Voting and the Electorate', in Patrick Dunleavy *et al.*, eds, *Developments in British Politics 5*, Macmillan, London 1997, p. 56.
30. Kaare Strom and Lars Svasand, 'Political Parties in Norway: Facing the Challenges of a New Society', in Strom and Svasand, eds, *Challenges to Political Parties*, p. 23.

118   CONTEMPORARY SOCIAL DEMOCRACY

31. Quoted in Robert Ponceyri, *Gaullisme électoral et Vᵉ République*, Doctorat d'État, IEP, Paris 1984, p. 539.
32. André Philip, 'La pensée politique des partis ouvriers', in Léo Hamon, ed., *Les nouveaux comportements politiques de la classe ouvrière*, Presses Universitaires de France, Paris 1959, pp. 205–6.
33. Bruno Cautrès and Anthony Heath, 'Déclin du "vote de classe"? Une analyse comparative en France et en Grande-Bretagne', *Revue Internationale de Politique Comparée*, vol. 3, no. 3, 1996, pp. 566–8.
34. Strom and Svasand, 'Political Parties in Norway', p. 24.
35. Alain Garrigou, 'Conjoncture politique et vote', in Daniel Gaxie, ed., *Explication du vote*, Presses de la Fondation Nationale des Sciences Politiques, Paris 1989, p. 359.
36. Lars Mjoset *et al.*, 'Norway: Changing the Model', in Perry Anderson and Patrick Camiller, eds, *Mapping the West European Left*, Verso, London and New York 1994, pp. 62–70.
37. Gerassimos Moschonas, 'The Panhellenic Socialist Movement', in Robert Ladrech and Philippe Marlière, eds, *Social-Democratic Parties in the European Union*, Macmillan, London 1999.
38. Gerassimos Moschonas, 'PASOK: From the "Non-Privileged" to the "Contentment Society"', *Epochi*, 21 May 2000 (in Greek).
39. Dominique Pélassy, *Sans foi ni loi? Essai sur le bouleversement des valeurs*, Fayard, Paris 1995, p. 218.
40. Jorgen Goul Andersen and Tom Bjorklund, 'Structural Changes and New Cleavages: The Progress Parties in Denmark and Norway', *Acta Sociologica*, vol. 33, no. 3, 1990, p. 213.
41. Daniel-Louis Seiler and Romain Meltz, 'Autriche', in Guy Hermet *et al.*, eds, *Les Partis politiques en Europe de l'Ouest*, Economica, Paris 1998, p. 65.
42. Pascal Perrineau, *Le Symptôme Le Pen*, Fayard, Paris 1997, p. 115.
43. Grunberg and Schweisguth, 'Vers une tripartition de l'espace politique', p. 187.
44. Lars Bille, 'Danemark', in Hermet *et al.*, eds, *Les Partis politiques en Europe de l'Ouest*, p. 124.
45. Andersen and Bjorklund, 'Structural Changes and New Cleavages', pp. 214, 212.
46. Perrineau, *Le Symptôme Le Pen*, p. 225.
47. Emmanuel Todd, *L'illusion économique. Essai sur la stagnation des sociétés développées*, Gallimard, Paris 1998, pp. 283–5.
48. Rudy Andeweg, 'Elite–Mass Linkages in Europe: Legitimacy Crisis or Party Crisis?', in Jack Hayward, ed., *Elitism, Populism and European Politics*, Clarendon Press, Oxford 1996, p. 152.
49. Christopher Anderson, 'Economics, Politics and Foreigners: Populist Party Support in Denmark and Norway', *Electoral Studies*, vol. 15, no. 4, 1996, p. 501.
50. Herbert Kitschelt, *The Radical Right in Western Europe*, University of Michigan Press, Ann Arbor 1995, p. 277.
51. Andersen and Bjorklund, 'Structural Changes and New Cleavages', p. 214.
52. Grunberg and Schweisguth, 'Recompositions idéologiques', p. 148.
53. Ibid., p. 177. In France, the lack of a degree explains anti-universalism better than it explains voting for Le Pen (people with a low level of education are characterized by their anti-universalist values, even if they do not vote FN). On the other hand, unemployment explains voting for Le Pen better than it explains anti-universalism (Grunberg and Schweisguth, 'Vers une tripartition de l'espace politique', p. 205).
54. The split in the Front National in France in 1999 will doubtless test Jean-Marie

Le Pen's implantation in the working-class electorate. The Front National now risks appearing to voters as a party 'like the others', which will reduce its ability to attract the protest vote as well as the impact of its networks of cultural influence. A directly *political* factor, the split is of a sort to sign away the working-class future – perhaps the future *tout court* – of the French extreme right.

55. In France, as indicated above, the frequency of the working-class vote for the extreme right increases with the number of working-class attributes. Workers who vote most for Le Pen are better inserted into the working-class milieu and, as a result, have the *same social profile as those who formerly voted for the PCF* (Boy and Mayer, 'Que reste-t-il des variables lourdes?', p. 112). This being so, can the Le Pen vote of what is certainly a minority of workers be regarded as an expression of the decline in class voting? Or, perhaps, as a *new* – and surprising – form of class voting: as (in a sense) an *inverted class vote*? If a working-class right-wing vote has always existed, the 'intense' (as opposed to 'diffuse') support currently given by workers to the extreme right is probably the portent of a rare phenomenon in electoral history: a *working-class right-wing vote* that is not 'deviant', but a *perverted class vote*, a class vote that does not conceive itself as such.

56. Moschonas, '*Quo vadis* social-démocratie?', in Michel Vakaloulis and Jean-Marie Vincent, eds, *Marx après les marxismes II: Marx au futur*, L'Harmattan, Paris 1997, p. 310.

57. Ronald Cayrol, 'L'électeur face aux enjeux économiques, sociaux et européens', in Pascal Perrineau and Ysmal Colette, eds, *Le Vote surprise: les élections législatives des 25 mai et 1er juin 1997*, Presses de Sciences Politiques, Paris 1998, p. 97.

58. Garrigou, 'Conjoncture politique et vote', p. 358.

59. See also Crewe, 'On the Death and Resurrection of Class Voting', p. 622.

60. See also Kitschelt, *The Radical Right in Western Europe*, p. 279.

61. Wolfgang Merkel, 'Between Class and Catch-all: Is There an Electoral Dilemma for Social Democratic Parties in Western Europe?', in Merkel *et al.*, *Socialist Parties in Europe II: Class, Popular, Catch-all?*, ICPS, Barcelona 1992, p. 25.

62. Some examples can illustrate the political heterogeneity of the salaried middle strata. Professions located in the 'repressive' apparatus of the state (army, police) typically vote for the right, despite belonging to the public sector. The category of 'welfare and creative professionals' inclines markedly to the left, despite the fact that a proportion of this category belongs to the private sector. In addition, teachers and lecturers are, in their large majority, completely behind the left in France, whereas teachers in Great Britain vote Conservative and higher education lecturers vote Labour in greater numbers (Boy and Mayer, 'Secteur public contre secteur privé'; Anthony Heath and Mike Savage, 'Middle-class Politics', in Roger Jowell *et al.*, eds, *British Social Attitudes: The Eleventh Report*, Dartmouth, Aldershot 1994).

63. Merkel, 'Between Class and Catch-all', p. 26.

64. Alain Bergounioux, in Bergounioux and Marc Lazar, *La Social-démocratie dans l'Union européenne*, debate in Les Notes de la Fondation Jean-Jaurès, no. 6, Paris 1997, p. 10.

65. Anthony Heath, Roger Jowell and John Curtice, 'Can Labour Win?', in Heath *et al.*, eds, *Labour's Last Chance*, Dartmouth, Aldershot 1994, p. 284.

8

Inside Social Democracy:
Organization in Mutation

The New Sociology of the Organization

The Ascendancy of the Salaried Middle Classes

The trend towards social diversification is more sharply pronounced among social-democratic members and activists than among voters. Sociological change seems to deliver a hard blow to the party's internal social and cultural cohesion and, more specifically, to its 'working-class mainspring'. The 'de-proletarianization' of the social-democratic membership base is spectacular (but not surprising), while the weight of the new salaried strata, especially their higher echelons, becomes very important, even central.

Indeed, in a majority of countries the social structure of social-democratic membership conveys an impression clearly marked by the dominant presence of non-manual salaried strata. Their imprint on the membership *far exceeds* their salience in the social-democratic electorate (where working-class/popular representation remains strong), affecting the social and cultural identity, and fundamental structure, of socialist organizations. The cases of the SPD, the SPÖ and the Danish SD offer an exemplary illustration of this general trend. In 1952, 56 per cent of SPD members were workers and 23 per cent were employees and executives. By 1966 the proportion of workers had fallen to 49 per cent, by 1977 to 37 per cent, and by 1991 and 1996 to 34 per cent and 35 per cent respectively; whereas the participation of white-collar strata increased from 23 per cent (1952) to 42 per cent in 1966, to 45 per cent in 1977, reaching 49 per cent in 1991 and approaching 60 per cent in 1996 (salaried employees and civil servants). The analogous sociological trajectory of Austrian social democracy makes it possible to measure the irresistible rise of the salaried middle classes in social-democratic organizations. Whereas workers constituted the great majority of the SPÖ in the 1950s and 1960s, relaying the party's working-class/popular entrenchment, the salaried middle classes have since invaded the socialist organization *en masse*, progressively establishing their domination. A strong swing towards them has occurred, deepening from one decade to the next (31 per cent in 1955, 38 per cent in 1970, 44 per cent in 1978, 54 per cent in 1990), and gradually assuming the character of a veritable mutation in inner-party power relations (in the same period, the proportion of workers declined appreciably: 59 per cent in 1955, 54 per cent in 1970, 42 per cent in 1978, 42 per cent in 1990).[1] In a clear majority in the Danish SD in 1971 (76 per cent), workers had dropped to 34 per cent by 1990, while the salaried middle strata spectacularly increased their representation, which rose from 22 per cent in 1971 to 58 per cent in 1990.[2]

The same picture emerges in Great Britain, where a sharp contrast in social profile was established between Labour's electorate and its membership. Whereas in 1987, 64 per cent of Labour's electorate belonged to the working class in the broad sense (workers, foremen, technicians), and only 14 per cent to the category of senior managers, teachers and liberal professions, *the relationship within Labour's organization was reversed.* The arithmetical weight of privileged and educated strata becomes imposing (49 per cent), while working class representation falls to 31 per cent (of which 26 per cent belong to the working-class in the strict sense and 5 per cent to the category of foremen and technicians). At the same time, we should emphasize the impact of the *sectoral factor* on the social composition of Labour's organization, which was far from negligible: out of the entire party membership, two-thirds work, directly or indirectly, in the public sector of the economy – central and local government, public services and industries.[3] The trend is not very different in Sweden. There, too, while the weight of workers within the membership body remains significant, it also decreases significantly: 80 per cent in 1960, 79 per cent in 1970, 65 per cent in 1985, and only 49 per cent in 1994. And the weight of the salaried middle strata progresses steadily: from 15 per cent in 1960 to 21 per cent in 1970, 30 per cent in 1985, and 44 per cent in 1994.[4]

The picture that emerges from these data is of an organization progressively gravitating into the orbit of the salaried middle classes. Yet given the *cultural ascendancy* of these strata, usually recruited from public service and the 'educated bourgeoisie', as well as their considerable individual and collective *mobilizing potential,* we are witnessing a *much greater decline in the influence of working-class culture* than the strictly arithmetical relations of force disclose.

The extent of this cultural ascendancy reinforces the position of those associated with it and, consequently, the *'aristocratic' character* of social-democratic organization. A *cultural quota* is operative within it[5] – as in society – which weakens the political engagement and role of workers and the most disadvantaged strata.

The Declining Influence of Working-Class Culture

The effects of the rise of salaried middle strata, and especially their most educated fraction, are felt in most aspects of organizational life with the production of new codes, new signs, new *habitus.* Once carried out primarily by workers turned 'full-timers', leadership tasks are increasingly taken over by these new categories, privileged possessors of the 'power of speech'.

Thus, a new cultural and sociological framework has gradually and imperceptibly been established, whose main consequence is a reduction in the role and power of the working-class component of the party. The significance of this infiltration of the social-democratic organization and apparatus by the new middle classes should not be underestimated: the party's identity is affected, and its overall balance is disturbed. It leads to a redefinition of the 'nature' of the social-democratic membership body and a challenge to the party's role as a structure 'intermediate', and 'mediating', between the state and the working class.

As the figures demonstrate, the working-class presence is obviously not residual; it is not – as Aragon put it – a 'scrap of tarnished metal' in an organizational edifice constructed by others, dominated by others, and serving others. But this presence – and influence – becomes increasingly *indirect*; it is down to the trade unions (and trade-union activists in the social-democratic organization), and hence to institutions that are, after all, 'external' to the political organization (and themselves weakened). Socialist organization is no longer – or is not sufficiently so any more – a site of *social integration and sociability*; neither is it a site for the attainment of *individual material and symbolic recompense* (elected posts, responsibilities, prestige) *by workers and ordinary people*.

Basically, it as if this loss of influence, and relegation to a secondary status, prompt an acceleration of the working-class 'exodus' through a mechanism of cumulative defection. Indeed, it would appear that a 'trade-off' has operated within social-democratic organizations between working-class recruitment and participation and the recruitment and participation of the 'middle classes'; and this has weighed heavily on the social character of social-democratic organization. By the terms of this trade-off, increased participation by the salaried middle strata seems to accentuate working-class defection, which in turn reinforces middle-class predominance. All the available statistics indicate that the reduction in the density of social-democratic membership derives from reduced participation by workers (as well as the young). The demographic weakening of the working class, as well as the mutation in its culture and way of life, underlie this phenomenon. But the desertion is also explained by social democracy's adoption of liberal economic ideas and methods in government, which is often experienced as traumatic. The entry of well-educated strata – teachers, technicians, administrators – into the party in force seems to lead, via a kind of 'spiral of silence', to the passivity of working-class members, even to their exit, and sometimes – as in the case of the PvdA – to their marginalization pure and simple.[6]

'Silence without departure'[7] on the part of workers is often followed by their departure in silence, confirming inner-party relations of domination that are disadvantageous to its popular element. If this is correct, we can anticipate that the working class, which today is letting go of the reins, will in future increasingly desert social-democratic organizations.

The Redistribution of Power in Social-Democratic Organization

Leaders, Members, Bureaucrats and Experts

Since the second half of the 1960s, observers of 'modern' electoral competition, particularly the election campaigns of the *great* political parties, have
highlighted three novel phenomena characterizing the means and methods
employed: (a) the central role of television, 'the most universal campaigning method'; (b) the quasi-systematic use of communications professionals
and 'experts' of every sort; and (c) the use of scientific methods of opinion
polling.

These changes could not leave the socialist and social-democratic parties
adopting them untouched. With the renewal of their 'communication' and
working methods, the endo-organizational distribution of power, the political rhetoric, even the traditional mode of existence of these parties has
been affected.

Four changes, presented here in 'ideal-typical' fashion, assume a particular importance.

The first relates to the *elevation of the party leader*. As the political
importance of television increases, the leader's role in the election campaign and party operation is enhanced. Leaders find themselves projected
to the centre of the public stage and the party stage, while intermediate
structures, like the membership body, fade.[8] Much more so than in the
past, today the leader is both a *team leader* and an important *issue* in
the election.

What ensues is a centralization of the main decisions, with decision-
making becoming the privilege of a small group revolving around the party
leader. Within this group, the role of *specialists* and *professionals* with
multiple qualifications expands, the 'modern' kind of centralization differing in that respect from 'old-style' centralization. Moreover, particularly
during election campaigns, this modern group of *custodes novellarum*
('guardians of information') often appeals to independent advertising
agency advisers, sometimes even involving them in its work by more formal
links. In the 'latent conflict' between 'organizers' and 'experts', which takes
place in every political party, it is the latter who emerge strengthened.
Whether it takes an institutionalized and publicly recognized form or an
unofficial form (belonging to the leader's entourage, making decisions in
'kitchen cabinets'), this influence is limited to certain questions, invariably
exercised on an occasional basis, and always under the supervision of the
party leadership or leader in person. This does not make a real power *the*
real power. But whether institutionalized or not, enduring or precarious,
the enlistment of experts into – or alongside – the party's decision-making
bodies is liable to reduce the influence of members and the traditional
bureaucracy over management of the party's ideological and programmatic
identity.

The third change consists in the significance accorded to opinion research, which plays a role of paramount importance in the party's strategic and tactical positioning. In the same way as (and sometimes more than) members, the body of qualitative and quantitative research produced seems to play a key role in the formulation and reformulation of the political/programmatic options of the great political parties, both right- and left-wing.[9] It creates a 'surrogate electorate' alongside the real elector- ate, one whose expectations are given maximum priority in socialist headquarters.[10]

From this set of changes, especially the preponderance of television, a fourth results: a *new inner-party culture*. The logic of 'televisual appeal', emphasizing leadership and debate between elites rather than the 'abstract mediocrity' (Max Weber) of programmes and ideologies, contributes to the emergence of a new intra-partisan spirit. This is more focused on personalities and their rivalries, more 'fragmented' and less 'collective'. The underlying cohesion – and fundamental divergences – entailed by intensive programmatic/ideological work lose their former value. The modern social-democratic spirit, the soul of the organization – *to tès psuchès èthos*, as the Ancient Greeks put it – is no longer based on an ethic of *strong integrating bonds* of programme, ideology or class.

These developments tend progressively to short-circuit the traditional sites of social-democratic endo-organizational power. The systematic util- ization of television strengthens the role of the leadership at the expense of the organization and its 'internal' leaders. The systematic employment of opinion research is carried on regardless not only of the organization, but also – a dimension largely underestimated by analysts – of the *media* as a relay of opinion to party elites.[11] The upshot is a reduction in the importance of the membership. It is *doubly weakened*, as a structure serving to transmit the party's policy to voters and voters' expectations and reac- tions to the party, to the advantage of 'direct', unmediated contact – direct but 'from afar' – between the leader and the electorate. The role of mass socialist organizations as institutions buttressed by trade-union power and a strong associational presence – associations constructed specifically to produce, and benefit from, the *effect of proximity* (by their strong presence and work on the social ground) – is significantly reduced.

Conceived as a hierarchical network that was extended, dense and active, classical social-democratic organization is giving way; and, with it, the traditional bureaucracy that represented the pillar on which party cohesion, mobilization and solidity were built. The increase in the number of 'full- time' personnel surrounding the party leadership[12] is merely a symptom of the gradual – and partial – *displacement of the organizational centre of gravity* towards the leadership circle. What follows, especially at election time, is a diminution in the operational autonomy of intermediate and local bodies, which find themselves more subordinate to the 'centre' than they were in the past. A characteristic of the 'postmodern' electoral campaign is pre- cisely the fact that even 'decentralized' actions are frequently 'nationally co-ordinated'.[13]

But it is not only new technologies and new methods of electoral campaigning and doing politics that underlie and sustain reinforcement of the leadership's status. Other powerful factors, possibly more concealed, tend in the same direction.

In current circumstances, a deep uncertainty about *identity* on the one hand, and doubts about *electability* and increased electoral instability on the other, enhance the importance of leaders as essential and sometimes irreplaceable links between the organization and the electorate. A leader with celebrity status and greater freedom of manoeuvre presents himself as a palliative for the *identity deficit*, but also the *competitive deficit*, of the contemporary social-democratic parties.[14] The ongoing slackening of the ties between socialist parties and trade unions tends in the same direction. As soon as the union stops 'identifying' with the party and the party with the union, once the link is loosened without being broken, the margin of freedom of the party – and of the leader who imposes himself in it – widens.[15]

Finally, a redistribution of power and roles has occurred within social-democratic organizations. It can be summarized as follows:

(a) strengthening of the role of the party leader *vis-à-vis* the rest of the organization, party elites included;
(b) strengthening of the role of the 'minority' (of elites), and especially the leadership group, *vis-à-vis* the mass membership;
(c) strengthening of 'experts' *vis-à-vis* the 'representative bureaucracy' of the party.

Are Members Insignificant?
The New Complexity of Social-Democratic Organizations

'What has a party to do with so many members?' The political scientist M.N. Pedersen's question is provocative. And his response is cut and dried: the epoch of the great mass parties, parties of *social integration*, is irrevocably over. Formerly the expression *par excellence* of modernity in political organization, these parties have no option, according to a widely held view, but to become 'media parties' led by a group of professionals resolutely and almost exclusively orientated towards the electoral market.

Pedersen poses the same basic question raised by Otto Kirchheimer (1966) and Angelo Panebianco (1988) in different terms: that of the transformation of mass bureaucratic parties into 'catch-all' parties (according to the former), or 'electoral-professional' parties (according to the latter). Now, a noteworthy aspect – at once condition and consequence – of this transformation is the diminished role of the mass membership within the party organization. The changes we have just inventoried certainly point in that direction.

But what is actually going on? Can we assign an unequivocal meaning to the reduction in the mass membership's influence in social-democratic organizations? Nothing is less certain. Everything points to believing that 'activists count'. First of all, they count because they continue to play a significant role in the process of deciding and formulating policies. Next, they count because they contribute to the smooth operation and effectiveness of the organization, as well as to divisions, splits and crises. They thus count as a source of *strength*, but also – and this is scarcely surprising – as a *nuisance* factor.

To illustrate this thesis, I shall restrict myself to a brief examination of three examples, which demonstrate the complexity and ambivalence of organizational change, obliging me to qualify the conclusions set out above.

1. The British Labour Party, a formation with an indirect structure, was never a genuinely mass party – without, for all that, being a cadre party. Initially developed almost exclusively through territorial diffusion, it has never known the robust and strongly hierarchized bureaucracy of continental parties – for example, the SPD or SPÖ. Moreover, it was characterized by a dual internal power structure. On one side was its apparatus, directed by the National Executive Committee (NEC) and dominated by non-parliamentary components (union leaderships, local constituencies), which defined the party's policy. On the other were the leader and the parliamentary group, which in reality possessed autonomous power and were disinclined to attach much importance to Conference resolutions and the NEC. This badly 'integrated' and scarcely coherent structure was the vector of an inherent fragility. Labour had a tendency to display its divisions in public at the slightest opportunity, and – much more seriously – to be destabilized every time it found itself in government (with the exception of the Attlee administration of 1945–51). In this complex, largely 'confederal' arrangement, the trade unions traditionally represented the crossing point and quasi-obligatory partner for any tendency or group aspiring to lead the party. At the same time, the institutionalized presence of the unions within the organization contributed indirectly to Labour's membership crisis, some trade unionists and working-class activists judging it unnecessary to join the party on an individual basis given their collective affiliation.

Thus, the success of the offensive launched by the Labour left against the moderate leadership of the party towards the end of the 1970s was conditional first, on supremacy within the local constituencies and second, on an alliance with the unions. Now, the traditional weakness in membership rendered the constituency parties more vulnerable to this offensive; and the failure of the 1974–79 Labour government, unable to create a minimum of co-ordination between the economic and financial policy of the state and the incomes policy of the unions – what Fritz Scharpf has called 'the drama of incomes policy' in Great Britain – encouraged the alliance between the unions, which had shifted to the left, and the radical wing of the party.

Once this supremacy and alliance were established, following a reinforcement of its positions throughout the 1970s and a battle of 'unprecedented ferocity',[16] the left won a great victory at the special Wembley Conference of January 1981. At the price of a split, it was thus able to 'resolve', in its own fashion, the bundle of contradictions in British Labourism, though this resolution proved temporary and largely illusory. The electoral disaster of 1983, and Neil Kinnock's arrival at the head of the party the same year, marked the beginning of a period of ideological and programmatic reorientation at the left's expense.[17] In the 1990s, on the initiative of the moderate leadership, an organizational reform of the party was undertaken. The increase in individual membership, as well as in the rights of individual members, sharply reduced the importance of 'activists' (in reality, the *active* membership), who tended to be on the left, and of affiliated unions, which (according to some) tended to adopt 'vote-losing policy commitments'. New Labour has thus become 'a mass party of largely inactive individual members having a plebiscitary, rather than any organic, relationship with a leadership cadre of professional politicians'.[18] Finally, under the auspices of 'democratization' and 'modernization', the role of the leadership circle, and the leader personally, was once again strongly enhanced.

2. While the major mobilization of 'new left' militants in the SPD in the 1970s did not allow them to capture the party's local constituencies – privileged site of confrontation between 'right' and 'left' – and, thereby, the whole of an extremely centralized organization, it did geatly destabilize the oldest socialist party in Europe. As some searched for a position that would be more in tune with the working class and the moderate segment of the electorate, and others for one that would be more in touch with the new middle classes and youth, the SPD almost lost its bearings. Claus Offe wrote of the German social democrats in 1981: 'For years now ... on all politically contentious issues (peace, building policies, environmental protection, nuclear energy, steel crisis, unemployment) there are social democrats on both sides of the frontlines, and in the long run not even the strongest organization can take this strain.'[19]

Of course, the left lost. But at the end of a battle in which the methods employed on both sides might have made Machiavelli blush, the party found itself destabilized. Its cohesion and traditional profile had been challenged. The invasion of the organization by the middle classes and the new left, and its gradual conversion to ecological themes – accelerated by the consolidation of the Green pole in the Germany party system – led to the 'Balkanization' of one of the historically most centralized and working-class parties in Europe.[20] Over recent years, the SPD has presented the image of a 'decentralized' party, its structure even being described – doubtless with some exaggeration – as 'loosely coupled anarchy'.[21] The 'new politics' culture is noticeably stronger within it, and leadership autonomy has been considerably reduced.[22] Under the influence of the Greens, a participatory *mechanism* has been initiated that favoured the installation of a more 'anti-authoritarian' model of internal democracy in German social democracy, as in other socialist parties.[23] However, the selection of Gerhard Schröder as social-democratic candidate for chancellor in 1998, which took a quasi-plebiscitary form, has once again enhanced the importance of the leadership. Moreover, his selection is indicative of the organizational ambivalence of the German social democrats, who proceeded to a subtle and perilous division of roles, as formerly between Helmut Schmidt and Willy Brandt. This sharing of roles between a candidate elected by plebiscite because he had a winning profile (and who subsequently became chancellor) and a leader of the organization (Oskar Lafontaine) closer to the party's actual ideology, proved short-lived. Lafontaine's resignation in 1999 and Schröder's accession to the post of party president will strengthen – at least temporarily – the SPD's unity, as well as the plebiscitary character of its leadership.

3. From the point of view that concerns us here, the case of the Dutch PvdA is typical. From the second half of the 1960s onwards, a group of young militants identifying with the 'new left' (*Nieuw Links*) challenged the traditional paternalism reigning in the party. The 'wave of democratization' that shook the PvdA (end of the 1960s, beginning of the 1970s) contributed significantly to the *decentralization* of the system of decision-making, as well as the radicalization of the party's programmatic choices. This decentralization – particularly on the crucial question of the selection of candidates for elected positions – which in the main was to prove enduring, despite some constitutional amendments in 1992, reduced the national leadership's freedom of action and decision-making.[24] Within an 'unstable equilibrium between different power centres', the intermediate elite played a crucial role in the decision-making process.[25] It should be added that the influence of the new left, bringing in its wake recruitment of members from the middle classes and the 'exodus' and marginalization of the working-class element, changed the party's internal culture. The PvdA lost its 'communitarian character'. Since 1966, suspicion and conflict have become the norm, signalling the emergence of an important deficit in internal cohesion.[26] Thus, in the 'new' organizational system, in which the internal game became more complex and subtle, the role of representatives of the militant base was once again enhanced, contrary to the expectations of Kirchheimer and Panebianco. Since 1992, however, the party executive has been substantially strengthened,[27] and the PvdA has become a more centralized party in which 'the political power of the regional bodies as well as the political influence of the local branches were restricted'.[28] This development is no cause for surprise.

These three examples indicate that the presence of the membership body, even as a disruptive factor, is too important to be reduced to a mere complement, without any real weight in the normal course of party life, or a by-product of an organizational apparatus of an electoral-professional variety.

The cases of Labour, the SPD and the PvdA clearly signal that the ideological and programmatic positioning of a party, as well as its political credibility, are not – or not always – a matter for 'professionals' and 'spin doctors'.

But if these examples demonstrate that members 'count', they also indicate that the gap between assertion of their power and submission to the leadership's power can turn out to be *very narrow*. Such is the meaning of developments in the relevant parties during the 1990s: ultimately, despite more democratic constitutional norms, the swing of the pendulum of power has not favoured the mass membership. Indeed, the influence of the latter within the 'elite-dominated associations' represented by the parties proved to be unstable, fluctuating, and unduly dependent on electoral and intra-organizational circumstances. This does not make it any the less real.

More specifically, in Labour and the SPD (and, albeit less spectacularly, the PvdA as well), the 1990s were marked by a '*turn to the leader*'. Following the tumult and fracas of protracted internal struggles, a general trend to reinforcement of the leadership – described above – prevailed.[29] Indeed, the influential membership base of these two historic parties, long confined to opposition and obsessed by the fear of failure, finally accepted a leader with virtually unlimited power (in the first case), and a chancellor largely solitary in the exercise of his duties (in the second). From this perspective, Tony Blair is a 'textbook case'. Having become the leader of a Labour Party traumatized by a long series of electoral defeats, he has disciplined the party, reduced the weight of the left and the unions, imposed 'tight political control over all policy pronouncements', and abandoned or modified political commitments without prior decision by the party's collective bodies.[30]

The cases of Blair and Schröder clearly indicate that political circumstances, and the 'personal equation' of the men and women who are leaders (notably their 'winning profile'), play a very important role in the distribution and redistribution of internal organizational power. Consequently, it is unwise to overestimate the importance of organizational and sociological factors. These two cases also show that, regardless of the constitutional arrangements, the frontier between weak and strong leadership – or between influential and marginal membership base – is extremely porous; and that the same organization can rapidly pass from a distribution of power that is unfavourable to the leader to one that is highly favourable. At root, this 'porous' frontier and these redistributions of power attest to the *antagonistic* tendencies traversing – and governing – the internal *modus operandi* of contemporary social-democratic organizations.

Here it is worth noting that bit by bit, a novel trend has recently emerged within all social-democratic organizations: the reassertion – or a certain reassertion, at least – of the value of mass membership, conceived as a source both of *political legitimation for the leadership* and of *electoral strength*. In Europe, classical models of political and electoral mobilization, largely based on the mobilizing capacity of the party's membership network, have persisted, even though they have been weakened. And nowhere has 'the centralized use of new communications technologies entirely extinguished the local component of national campaign strategies'.[31] Indeed, it is now firmly established that elections 'are not won or lost solely at the national level';[32] and that the membership – not only the active membership, but also the *passive* membership – is a source of electoral effectiveness. Moreover, several parties, facing competing political appeals at the local level, have been obliged to strengthen their implantation and presence on the ground.[33] In fact, confronted with the greater discredit of political parties, the appearance of new protest parties, and the participatory ambitions of members or potential members, leaders again tend to value the mass membership increasingly, and to encourage participation in the organization. Thus, in order to involve individual members in the party's work, they change the party rules to allow members to exercise 'direct influence in selecting candidates and determining party policies'.[34] A potential aspect of these new structures is 'the development of a new, plebiscitarian type of party in which vertical, internal communications ... replace horizontal communications within areas, regions and constituencies'.[35] More members, more participation in the decision-making process, more influence in the selection of candidates and the leader, more decentralizaton. And more power for the leader! Such is the content of organizational change in a great number of socialist and social-democratic parties today. These parties oscillate and hesitate between recourse to the leader and a more democratic, participatory internal regime. And they play on *both* registers at once!

The Middle Classes, 'New Politics' and Leadership

Change in inner-party power relations is equally linked to the new sociology of socialist and social-democratic organizations. Their new 'social structure' leads to the 'emergence' of a membership body that is culturally more 'autonomous' and less subject to the 'centre'.

The massive entry of educated strata creates a *new type of member*. More individualist, less docile, often 'polemical' in style, and 'cognitively mobilized', she or he demands respect for her or his opinions, and wants more influence on the party's 'public' affairs.[36] More so than in the past, the party's modern bureaucracy is the product of the middle classes. Full-timers issuing from this social group are characterized by a higher level of education and a 'network of relations', personal or familial, attributable to their social origin, which affords them greater autonomy and less conformism *vis-à-vis* the party leadership.[37] This sociological change affects the organization's identity and *modus operandi*. Cohesion becomes less strong, disobedience – even dissidence – more frequent, and internal conflict is perceived less negatively.

It turns out, moreover, that the salaried middle strata, especially their young and educated elements, are principally concerned with the 'change in value priorities' among the populations of Europe. Those in favour of the 'new politics' are orientated towards a normative conception of participation very different from the one described by Robert Michels, which traditionally obtains within great mass organizations. 'Cognitive mobilization' and 'post-materialism' significantly increase the *anti-authoritarian* and *anti-oligarchical* propensity, and strengthen tendencies conducive to the adoption of less centralized and more flexible organizational schemas, which take greater account of the aspirations of the membership base. Thus, 'emancipatory distance', or the possibility of speaking and contradicting,[38] is extended within socialist organizations. 'A high level of cognitive mobilization', Ronald Inglehart has written, 'virtually quadruples the propensity of an individual to want to direct the elites.'[39] Regardless of their organizational structure, socialist parties attract supporters of the new politics in far greater numbers than their conservative and liberal opponents, because of their 'egalitarian' political culture.[40] The consequences for the operation and constitution of the organization are important. The intermediate elites of socialist organizations affiliated to the 'new politics' – the majority hailing from the educated middle classes, and particularly the public sector – are more orientated to the 'base' and 'constituency' than the centre in cases of conflict; they are 'constituency oriented'. By contrast, supporters of the values of 'old politics' are more sensitive to the line laid down by the centre; they are 'leadership oriented'. According to Robert Rohrschneider's data, this general trend involves all the socialist formations – with the exception of the British Labour Party – and primarily the SPD, PvdA (see above), and PSOE.[41]

Hence a proportion of these intermediate elites operates, in a sense, as the *elite of the majority*, restricting the scope of the iron law of oligarchy. The partial turn of the intermediate strata of the socialist and social-democratic parties to the 'base' acts more as a counterweight to the new intra-organizational centralization than as a vehicle of a new balance that is disadvantageous to the leadership circle. Nevertheless, the distribution of power roles is affected, and the content of old hierarchies is blurred. The leadership is less self-assured. This is certainly not the 'soft' law of democracy, as Rohrschneider maintains, but it is not the classical type of iron law of oligarchy dear to Michels, either. The membership base, actual or potential, is no longer as he described it: incompetent, immature, malleable, and submissive. Today's social-democratic elites have to confront a different membership. This membership is, of course, less 'necessary' for the effective performance of the party machine, and probably less active and motivated. But it is increasingly educated, informed, mistrustful, and 'anti-authoritarian'. Accordingly, party elites sometimes have to retreat, sidestep issues, and compromise with it.

And the Unions?

The battle between 'left' and 'right' in the British Labour Party and German SPD during the 1970s and 1980s unquestionably highlighted the importance of the 'membership base' as a factor. It also highlighted the significance of the *structures* (indirect structure in Great Britain, centralized apparatus in the FRG) and *actors* (trade unions) forming part of the genetic code of socialist organizations. Indeed – to return to these two examples – the impossibility of the German new left allying with trade-unionists strongly conditioned its strategy, its political options and its defeat; whereas the establishment of this alliance was the prelude to the Labour left's victory.[42]

There is no doubt that a ubiquitous and progressive loosening of the links between socialist parties and trade unions is currently in progress. 'Disinvestment of the political field by the trade unions',[43] and relaxation of these ties, as well as the erosion of trade-union power, naturally reduce union influence within parties of the social-democratic type. However, *reduced influence does not mean absence of influence.*

This became evident in the second half of the 1980s and at the beginning of the 1990s, in the course of the debate on 'programmatic renewal' within European social democracy (see Chapter 9). The last refuge of a social-democratic ideology abandoned by social democracy itself, the unions have often been (in Padgett's words) 'the revisionists' major target, since they symbolised traditional party orthodoxy'.[44] In a sense – according to Andrew Taylor – 'what emerges so strongly from the politics of programmatic renewal is the unions' relative powerlessness and quiescence'.[45] The unions displayed pragmatism not only in the Scandinavian countries but also in countries like Germany, and even Great Britain. They neither wanted, nor were they able, to block the process of renewal; but they were unable to inflect it in accordance with their objectives and wishes either. This pragmatic attitude is explained by their weakened position and their 'electoralism': 'they had no political option other than social democracy'.[46]

Nevertheless, it should be added that the unions, despite being weakened, were capable of exerting a far from negligible political influence. The result of their participation in the debate was 'to tone down proposals and arguments generating disagreement within the labour movement'. While they appeared to be 'flexible' and 'open', union leaders were able to impose significant modifications on the SPD, DNA and SAP – parties in which union representation is important – and to attenuate the new neoliberal orientation of programmatic documents.[47] Moreover, it is no accident if British Labour and the German SPD required a long spell in opposition for the radical revisionism of Blair and Schröder, as well as the reduction of union weight in Labour, to take effect. In addition, the minor inflection to the left of Schröder's electoral strategy, in the last stage of his campaign in the 1998 German election, is a good example of union influence (and the influence of the party membership). Likewise, the reanchorage of the French PS on the left would have been inconceivable without the great union movement of December 1995.

More generally, the varied reception of neoliberalism and the values of the 'new politics' in different parties was linked, *inter alia*, to the unions' position in the party hierarchy. In southern European parties, characterized by a weak trade-union presence, a marginalized membership network, and a strong leadership (PSOE, PASOK, French PS, Portuguese PS), the turn towards 'moderation' and liberal economic management in the 1980s was more rapid and marked (PASOK being a *partial* exception here) than it was in most central and northern European parties. This 'accelerated' neoliberalization occurred despite ideological positions that were initially noticeably to the left.[48] In the 1980s and 1990s, when changes in economic rhetoric and the emergence of 'post-materialist' values prompted socialist leaders to redefine their objectives and sever connections with their parties' Keynesian past, the unions frequently assumed the function of an intra- or extra-organizational counter-power (in Kitschelt's term, they were a 'conservative force').[49] And in cases where the tradition of co-operation between party and unions was relatively strong, and inner-party union positions were relatively assured, the unions influenced the content and rhythm of the programmatic reforms adopted, without ultimately blocking the process of renewal.[50]

In sum, the unions have not proved capable of decisively fixing their stamp on the current political profile of parties of a social-democratic type. But – albeit markedly less so than in the past – they continue to influence the political and ideological equilibrium, and internal power struggles, of social-democratic organizations. Without any optical illusion, these are the two incontestable lessons that can be drawn from the process of programmatic renewal within social democracy in the 1980s and 1990s.

The brief analysis above indicates that the role of the leader and party elite is less central than is usually assumed. With the recomposition of communications and technology, the weakening of the unions, the new sociology of organizations, the diffusion of anti-authoritarian values – with all these, the modalities of the exercise of power by the few, as well as the modalities of participation, submission and 'rebellion' by the many, have certainly altered. Today's leaders are obliged to take account of the interests, aspirations, expectations or prejudices of members, the intermediate bodies of the party, and the unions linked to it. This amounts to saying that these 'actors' retain a *significant* proportion of their influence, even though it has diminished (sometimes severely). The social-democratic organization remains a *structure of co-operation and compromise*, a 'system of reciprocal expectations' between party elites, various centres of influence, and the membership base.

Obviously, the disparity in influence and strength between elites and 'base' is, as ever, great: like the one between David and Goliath. And 'History' teaches us that David won. Ordinary members and minorities in contemporary socialist organizations make their voices heard, perhaps a little more strongly and a little more frequently than they did in the past. 'David did overcome Goliath,' Ralph Miliband once wrote: 'But the point of the story is that David *was* smaller than Goliath and that the odds *were* heavily against him.'[51] In organizational terms, this means that today's leadership plays a central role, more central than previously, but that minorities occasionally prevail[52] – or, better: leadership centrality is currently reinforced, but minorities win less rarely than they did in the past.

This situation is unique, and no doubt it will please lovers of paradox. For in fact, today, the adhesion of the 'many' to hierarchical systems dominated by elites and leaders turns out to be *largely 'instrumental'*. It is *limited* in character and duration. Let us examine the data.

Socialist Leadership: 'Holding a wolf by the ears'

Weakening

Does the fact that the leader currently holds centre-stage – does this 'blaze of power' – create, or correspond to, a more durable and enduring authority? This is far from certain. Socialist leaders today both enjoy and suffer a *paradoxical* status. While they benefit from exhaustive media coverage, and while they increasingly go it alone (or seem to), they nevertheless find it more difficult than in the past to establish themselves in the long term. The data in Tables 8.1 and 8.2 are unambiguous: in the long run (1945–99), despite the new 'centrality' of the leader in the party apparatus and public debate, the position of the socialist leaders is being destabilized. Indeed, since the 1970s their term of office has been considerably shorter, and their power more *fleeting*, than in the initial postwar period. While this trend is not uniform, it is general (with the significant exceptions of the SAP and Danish SD), conveying the impression of a more fragile leadership.

Socialist leaders no longer break records of longevity at the head of their parties, as did Erlander in Sweden, Gerhardsen in Norway, Norton and Corish in Ireland, Mollet in France or, to a lesser extent, Wilson in Great Britain, Schärf in Austria, or Buset (1945–59) in Belgium.[53] The times are thus not so kind to the 'sovereigns' of contemporary socialism, testing their term of office. Socialist leaders are more vulnerable today than before. Staying put becomes hard.

Nevertheless, it is important to qualify the degree of vulnerability. The cases of Bruntland (DNA), Carlsson (SAP), Vranitsky (SPÖ), Jörgenson (Danish SD), Spring (Irish Labour Party), Spitaels (PSB), Papandreou (PASOK) and Gonzales (PSOE) – as well as the extraordinary terms of Bruno Kreisky and Olof Palme, the two great 'overlords' of European socialism in the 1970s and 1980s – demonstrate that an incontestable weakening relative to the initial postwar period does not amount to enfeeblement. The change is important, but it is a matter of degree rather than kind.

Weakening and the 'Organizational System'

The weakening of socialist leadership, which crystallized very clearly during the difficult years of the economic crisis, largely reflects the structural erosion of social-democratic hegemony within European societies. Let me nevertheless make it clear that it is not a uniform trend: Tables 8.1 and 8.2 display some significant differences depending on the party considered. The leadership of parties that are distinguished by the density of their organizational network (very great density in the cases of the SAP and SPÖ; average in the DNA, PSB, SD);[54] a high degree of bureaucratization (SAP, SPÖ, PSB); and high leadership autonomy (SAP, DNA, PSB), or comparatively high autonomy (SPÖ) – this leadership, while weakened, is more resilient. By contrast, weakened leadership is much more evident in the case of parties with an organizational network that is weak (British Labour Party, French PS), or rather weak (SPD); a meagre bureaucratic structure (British Labour Party, French PS, PSP) or one that has recently been weakened (SPD); and less leadership autonomy (British Labour Party before Blair, SPD in recent years,[55] French PS after Mitterrand).

Obviously, successive electoral reverses for the German social democrats and British Labour, as well as the French socialists after 1988, contributed significantly to the destabilization of their leaderships. But the period 1973 to 1999 was also a phase of significant electoral retreat and, in some cases, very severe defeats for most of the formations in the first group, without this entailing excessive destabilization of their leadership. The differentiated weakening of socialist leaders seems to be bound up as much with the differentiated electoral weakening of national parties as with variation in their organizational structures. And everything suggests that *the vulnerability of the leader's position is less pronounced in the case of parties that remain close to the traditional social-democratic organizational model than in those whose organizational pattern historically deviated from it, or has done so recently.* Nevertheless, notwithstanding these distinctions and nuances, the trend towards leadership weakening is the 'preponderant' tendency of the last three decades. This explains why leadership destabilization is not confined to a type of 'organizational system', even though it varies according to the type of 'system'.

If destabilization is not restricted to a type of 'organizational system', neither is stability. Formations with such distinct organizational structures as the SAP, SPÖ, PASOK or PSOE exhibit relatively stable (SPÖ) or very stable (PSOE, PASOK, SAP) leadership. This similarity against a background of contrasts is sufficiently curious to warrant further attention.

The parties in the socialist family with greatest leadership autonomy are those of southern Europe (PASOK, PSOE, French PS, PSI), where the role of leaders and (re)founding fathers was fundamental.[56] This autonomy, which has facilitated great tactical and strategic flexibility, was doubtless bound up, *inter alia*, with the 'primal scene' of these parties, the conjuncture of their formation or re-formation, when the leader's position was of the utmost importance.[57] The leaders of the parties in question established themselves as veritable autonomous power centres. Their status was that of '*primus solus*' rather than '*primus inter pares*'.[58]

The organization of the Greek socialists in the 1970s and early 1980s

Table 8.1 Socialist leaders (1945–99)

DNA		British Labour Party	
E. Gerhardsen	1945–1965	C. Attlee	1935–1955
T. Bratteli	1965–1975	H. Gaitskell	1955–1963
S. Reiulf	1975–1981	H. Wilson	1963–1976
G.H. Brundtland	1981–1992	J. Callaghan	1976–1980
T. Jagland	1992–	M. Foot	1980–1983
		N. Kinnock	1983–1992
		J. Smith	1992–1994
SPÖ		T. Blair	1994–
A. Schärf	1945–1957		
B. Pittermann	1957–1967	**SPD**	
B. Kreisky	1967–1983	K. Schumacher	1946–1952
F. Sinowatz	1983–1987	E. Ollenhauer	1952–1964
F. Vranitsky	1987–1997	W. Brandt	1964–1987
V. Klima	1997–	H.-J. Vogel	1987–1991
		B. Engholm	1991–1993
		R. Scharping	1993–1995
Danish SD		O. Lafontaine	1995–1999
H. Hedtoft	1939–1955	G. Schröder	1999–
H.C. Hansen	1955–1960		
V. Kampmann	1960–1962	**SFIO/PS**	
J.-O. Krag	1962–1972	G. Mollet	1946–1969
E. Dinesen	1972–1973	A. Savary	1969–1971
A. Jørgenson	1973–1987	F. Mitterrand	1971–1981
S. Auken	1987–1992	L. Jospin	1981–1988
P.N. Rasmussen	1992–	P. Mauroy	1988–1992
		L. Fabius	1992–1993
		M. Rocard	1993–1994
PSP		H. Emmanueli	1994–1995
M. Soares	1973–1986	L. Jospin	1995–1997
V. Constancio	1986–1989	F. Hollande	1997–
J. Sampaio	1989–1992		
A. Guterres	1992–	**PASOK**	
		A. Papandreou	1974–1996
SAP		K. Simitis	1996–
T. Erlander	1946–1969		
O. Palme	1969–1986	**PSOE**	
I. Carlsson	1986–1996	F. Gonzales	1974–1997
G. Persson	1996–	J. Almunia	1997–

Sources: For 1945–92, and the DNA, Labour Party, and SFIO/PS, see *European Journal of Political Research*, vol. 24, no. 3, 1993, pp. 324–5, 258, 296, and 279 respectively. For 1992–99, the sources are various; for the SAP, SPD, Danish SD, and PSP, the international sections of the parties concerned; for the SPÖ, Wolfgang Muller and D. Meth-Cohn, 'The Selection of Party Chairmen in Austria: A Study in Intra-Party Decision-Making', *EJPR*, vol. 20, no. 1, 1991, p. 45.

Table 8.2 Socialist parties and leaders (1945–99): average duration*

	Period	No. of years	No. of leaders	Average duration	
DNA	1945–1975	30	2	15	
	1975–1999	24	3	8.5	(2)
British Labour	1945–1976	31	3	10.3	
	1976–1999	23	5	4.5	(4)
SAP	1946–1986	40	2	20	
	1986–1999	13	2	10	(1)
SPÖ	1945–1983	38	3	12.7	
	1983–1999	16	3	7	(2)
SPD	1946–1987	41	3	13.7	
	1987–1999	12	5	3	(4)
SD	1946–1972	26	4	6.5	
	1972–1999	27	4	6.7	(3)
SFIO/PS	1946–1971	25	2	12.5	
	1971–1999	28	8	3.7	(7)
PSP	1974–1999	25	4	6	(3)
PASOK	1974–1999	25	2	22	(1)
PSOE	1974–1999	25	2	23	(1)

Sources: See Table 8.1; calculations by the author.
* To establish average duration, I have obviously not included the present incumbent (the figure in brackets indicates the number of leaders that forms the basis of my calculations). The complexity of the situations that give rise to the replacement of a leader (e.g. death or illness) means that *average duration* possesses a merely *indicative* value.

differed from formations of a social-democratic type in its interclassist character, its weak links with the trade-union world, its lack of a 'coherent' profile, its tendency to clientelism, its nationalist accents, and in the extraordinary personalized power of Andreas Papandreou (and weakness of the party apparatus). PASOK was unquestionably constituted as a party all on its own in the European socialist/social-democratic family.[59] However, by gradually reinforcing its social anchorage, it was able to create an original – and effective – organization composed of elements from two different 'logics' of party-building. First, it was a mass structure relatively well entrenched in popular and rural milieux, and – particularly since the end of the 1980s – in the trade-union environment as well. This structure supported (and in part still supports), and was sustained by (and in part still is), a vast clientelistic network. Second, it was a structure that was highly personalized and centralized, rendering institutional operation of the bureaucratic type obsolete, with all the 'democratic' and 'oligarchic' ambivalence that involves. The *clientelistic mass structure* was a stabilizing factor, permitting a better insertion of the party into the political and social field.

So was *personalized centralization*, for all that it might prove an important factor of potential weakness. The dynamic of its construction conferred on PASOK 'the character of a *charismatic-clientelistic mass party*'.[60]

PSOE was a party with a remarkable electoral performance, which for many years after 1982 defied 'the law of electoral gravity'.[61] After the neutralization of the influence of the membership base (late 1970s), PSOE was marked by the centrality of its charismatic leader. Indeed, rare are the political personalities in western Europe who have been able to dominate the political life of their country as comprehensively as Felipe Gonzales.[62] However, the internal structure of PSOE, which is the southern European party *least distant* from the social-democratic model, meant that unlike that of Andreas Papandreou, his exceptional reign was not an undivided one.[63]

A federal structure crowned by a strong central organization, PSOE (like PASOK) has considerably strengthened its organization since the second half of the 1980s by widely relying on clientelistic practices. Today, PSOE is a party well anchored in society. That said, great leadership stability in PSOE and PASOK is due not to the structure of the respective organizations but to the charismatic personalities around which they were built.

The converse of PASOK and PSOE are the SAP and SPÖ, vast, complex organizations with large memberships, possessing a remarkable capacity for mobilization and orientation of their social base. The development of a well-delineated and politically coherent bureaucracy – while doubtless raising the issue of 'oligarchic' domination by the leadership group – contributed significantly to the effectiveness and robustness of these parties. In addition, the internal politics of the SAP and SPÖ are characterized by a remarkable consensus, despite the self-assertion of a 'libertarian left' sector in the former, and a certain decentralization of power since Kreisky in the latter.[64] Their mass structure, as well as the important role of internal leaders and full-timers, does not expose these parties to 'entryism', in the noble and less noble senses of the term, by activists with an 'iconoclastic' ideology. This strongly differentiates them from formations like the British Labour Party, the PvdA, or the SPD in the 1970s, when a limited number of new members – a small 'stage army' as Robert McKenzie would say – could politically unbalance a large number of constituency or regional parties.[65] Moreover, better career prospects for the elites (in the organization or the state) weakened the potential for dissidence within these parties, complicating the formation of counter-elites capable of challenging the leadership.[66] All these factors contributed to leadership stability. This remarkable stability was thus bound up both with the good electoral performance of the Swedish and Austrian socialists and with strong organizational cohesion, while we should not underestimate the weight of such important personalities as Palme, Kreisky, or Franz Vranitzky. The example of the SAP in 1991 is revealing: the very severe – almost humiliating – defeat of the Swedish social democrats, who achieved their lowest electoral score since 1928, did not provoke a challenge to Ingvar Carlsson. *The 'organizational system' of these parties* – parties that could be characterized as the 'bedrock' within the European socialist family (given their strong internal cohesion, stability and resistance, at least until recently, to the dynamic of 'demassification' and fratricidal struggles) – *functions as a structure that stabilizes their leadership.*

The secret of the long terms of Gonzales and Papandreou – but also of François Mitterrand, Bettino Craxi and, to a lesser extent, Mario Soares – lies in their personal prestige and their ability, frequently demonstrated, to win elections. Unlike the SAP or SPÖ, it was not the structure of a mass organization, with strong cohesion and discipline, that determined their longevity at the head of their parties, but this longevity that brought with it cohesion and discipline. Yet when strong leadership stability is not based on the substratum of an organization that is stable, institutionalized and well anchored in society, it can turn into its opposite – very great instability. The weakening of the French PS's leadership, particularly after 1988, is a good indication of this.

The future of the PSOE after Gonzales and PASOK after Papandreou – parties that are, anyway, better inserted into their respective societies than their French or Portuguese counterparts – seems fairly well guaranteed today. However, the influence of these parties, which once prided them-selves on their power, is currently reduced and becoming 'commonplace'. But the Spanish and Greek socialists, certainly the latter, seem successfully to have passed the test of the 'routinization of charisma'.[67]

Compared with the SAP or SPÖ, the southern parties lack density and depth. They lack a tenaciously nurtured sense of destiny and the slow progress that goes with solidity. They lack the stabilizing principle rep-resented by deep organizational and social anchorage. Yet PSOE and PASOK are two separate cases in southern European socialism. In various respects, the leadership of Gonzales and Papandreou was cataclysmic – and double-edged. But both, in their way, were able to construct relatively strong organizations, which are well rooted in society. A strong, durable and effective organization becomes such through a successful intermixture of collective histories and individual destinies. The Spanish and Greek socialists must prove that the foundation of the stability of their leadership – if not their entire organization – is something more than the 'charisma' of a founding leader (in the case of PASOK), or a refounding leader (PSOE). They must prove that the 'substance of the foundation' is not weak.

Factors of Weakness: 'The earth moves about, I can have no confidence in it'[68]

(i) *Extra-organizational factors*

When the Emperor Tiberius, one of the strangest figures in the history of power, was asked how he bore the burden, he invariably replied that he had the impression of 'holding a wolf by the ears' [*lupum se auribus tenere*].[69] My analysis has shown that the 'sovereigns' of contemporary socialism frequently convey the same impression. Behind the scenes, some profound changes are weakening the role of leadership. And the question that directly comes to mind is simple: why?

The electoral deficit: The 'ideal' leadership is one that is able to combine the imperative of maximizing votes in the electoral arena with that of maximizing support, and hence cohesion, inside the party.[70] But this ideal combination proves difficult to achieve. At a time when party apparatuses are more discredited, the leader most suited to winning on the electoral level is not always the person most identified with the organization and its internal affairs. In cases of latent or overt conflict between imperatives that are both attributes of effective leadership, the criterion of electoral 'success' tends to become – but is not always – paramount.

Since the second half of the 1970s, the 'breakdown' of the Keynesian equation – and the fiscal, managerial and legitimation crisis of the welfare state, which was the jewel in the crown of a culturally strong and electorally victorious social democracy – have deprived socialists of an electorally effective economic and social strategy. Now, in parties where pursuit of electoral success predominates, leaders risk being strong in so far, and only in so far, as they are successful. Hence their current insecurity, which is inherent in the notion and function of competitive 'palliative' evoked above. In an 'electoralist' party, those elected in the name of effectiveness will be replaced in the name of effectiveness. Those who live by the sword die by the sword: such is the law of 'proof' by performance.

The power deficit: Today, the internationalization of markets and economic constraints calls into question both the role of the nation-state and the historic social gains of the working-class movement. Within the European Union more particularly, the national state, as both economic actor and law-maker, is growing weaker. A set of 'systemic constraints', both external and internal, deprives all political formations of some of their power and impact – especially social-democratic formations that have 'traditionally made national public power the principal lever of [their] political and economic action'.[71] National parties have not managed to make up for the ground lost at a national level by occupying the European arena (which does not – or not yet – constitute a suitable framework for the exercise of democracy and authority). The reduction in national space remains without real compensation – or at least, without equivalent compensation – at the supranational level. This only serves to underscore the power – and credibility – deficit of parties in general, and socialist parties in particular. Now, it is scarcely necessary to enumerate the repercussions of this power deficit (in the state and parties) on the power of leaders, for the core of their strength is affected or bypassed: the party-institution they lead and the instrument (the state) by means of which their power is translated into deeds.

The novelty – and seeming paradox – of the current status of socialist leaders consists in the following fact: their '*internal*' political capacity – or ability to operate effectively and influence intra-party decisions – increases, whereas their '*external*' political capacity (their ability to influence social developments and inflect them in line with their designs) decreases. *Leaders are strengthened within an institution that is itself weakened.* They extend – or seem to extend – their ascendancy over an organization that is losing some of its ascendancy over its environment. The personalization of power they submit to (which is not simply impressionistic, or a mere artefact) has the effect of masking the weakening of the structure of the party and the nation-state on which leaders depend, since they are expected to sustain their action and supply mechanisms for effective action.

Thus, the synergetic fusion of the power deficit – bound up with the crisis of the nation-state – and the electoral deficit weakens socialist leadership.

Those who flaunt themselves do not always hold power, and those who hold power are not always strong. In reality, the 'personalism' that is in vogue is all the stronger, more immoderate and more ironic in that it is accompanied – and complemented – by a growing lack of power. More visible and more exposed, stronger and more disarmed than the 'erstwhile leader', the current socialist leader is charged with a mission that is beyond his or her means.[72] Frequently possessing an 'enormous collective author-ity' that they are not in a position fully to accept, today's leaders therewith run the risk of becoming the *ideal scapegoat*. And as the figures indicate, they frequently do become just that.

(ii) *Intra-organizational factors: What is happening to the 'party soul'?*

The factors I have just cited do not provide an exhaustive explanation, although their impact is not negligible. If the 'earth' around the party 'moves', so does the 'earth' of the organization, the party *intra-muros*, contributing to the destabilization of socialist leaders. Socialist organiza-tions become structures that *destabilize* their own leadership.

If socialist organizations, like every organization, are constructed as a 'system of reciprocal expectations' between party elites and ordinary mem-bers, this system has changed profoundly today in comparison with its own past. The massive entry of the middle classes, the growing anti-authoritarian ambiance and, more generally, individualism, which naturally extends even to left-wing organizations, affect the core of these collective entities. The loosening of the common ideological and sociological 'cement', as well as the 'increasing autonomization of the private life from the militant life',[73] call into question the *identity function* – ideological and 'associational' – of the organization.

To encourage participation and strengthen active membership, the 'old-style' social-democratic organization combined two types of incentive. The first was what is conventionally called the 'realization of objectives' ('rec-ompense' for participation is bound up with attainment of the organiz-ation's goals, implementation of its ideological and programmatic objectives). The second was what Peter Lange calls 'incentives of identity', in which he distinguishes two components: an *ideological* component (iden-tification with the ideology and symbols of the party) and an *associative* component (identification with the group, creation of interpersonal bonds that derive from sociocultural affinities linked with membership of the organization/collectivity).[74] This involves ideological satisfaction and socio-affective gratification attaching to the privilege of identifying, and being identified, with an ideological system ('ideological' component) and a solidaristic group ('associative' component). In this respect, the mass socialist organization was a *community of solidarity*, an affective community that bound 'the member to party over and above politics': it provided members with the *self-assurance* of an identity (ideological, associative).

Now, parties as sites of integration through ideology and sites of integration in the basic sense of the term ('a will to break with solitude, to broaden too limited a network of individual relations') find themselves devalued today.[75]

The reduction – not complete disappearance – of such rewards, which has been evident since the 1950s and accelerated since the second half of the 1960s, influences the character of participation in mass organizations and, as a consequence, the way in which organizations become organizations. The new system of incentives offered by socialist and social-democratic parties to their adherents is principally focused on the 'attainment of objectives' and 'material' stimuli (tangible rewards and benefits, including jobs and favours).[76] Pursuit of the party's programmatic aims, or of individual reward, now represents the essential motivating force of adhesion.[77]

In such parties, a *trade-off* prevails: trade-off in the noble sense, bound up with ideological and programmatic motives (achieving power in order to translate party policy into deeds); and trade-off in the less noble sense, linked with 'self-interested' motives (patronage, elective functions, etc.). Now, the alteration of expectations in a more *utilitarian* direction – is not an organization a system of reciprocal 'expectations'? – is not without its effects on the leadership's security. More so than in the past, its success and stability depend on a set of *exogenous* factors (economic constraints, possible alliances with other parties, circumstances of party competition, etc.), over which, by definition, control proves less easy. As a result, it is weakened, particularly in a period marked by the reduced effectiveness of the left's economic policies and the fiscal crisis of the state (and a consequent scarcity of posts and favours to distribute). At present, success, in its various dimensions and facets, is a more important criterion of leadership selection and evaluation than the fact of serving, defending and embodying a common 'cause'. But success is not always available. Basically, an *implicit pact of effectiveness* links the leader to the party-organization and the party-in-the-electorate. Ineffective leaders break this pact, and hence become weak. They mobilize the will of the party – which, in the interests of effectiveness, was initially with them – against them. In a sense, the party retrospectively 'recovers' the power – 'the enormous collective authority' – it had vouchsafed them to begin with.

As a result, contemporary parties and their leaders cannot respond as effectively as in the past either to the requirements of a utilitarian rationality (which encourages participation on the basis of realizing collective goals and distributing individual rewards) or to the requirements of an 'affective' rationality of human relations, of 'identity', which (itself 'utilitarian', according to some) likewise strengthens members' commitment.

In the past, a high level of participation on the basis of 'identity' or 'solidarity' facilitated greater leadership flexibility in the direction of the party's internal affairs. Members whose commitment revolved around 'identity' (particularly of an associative type) not only did not expect a 'trade-off' for their activity, but simultaneously – and above all – in some sense 'protected' the leadership from the demands of other members, whether politically interested or simply 'interested'.[78] *This protective screen has largely disintegrated today.* The arithmetical reduction and departure of members motivated by the incentives of solidarity (above all, workers), whose great loyalty was in large measure based on habit, leaves the leadership facing members mobilized by 'incentives of exchange'. We have thus passed from a system of delegation of power – resting on what Pierre Bourdieu, in connection with the PCF, has called a '*fides implicita*' – to a situation of permanent transaction.[79] Ulrich Beck expresses the same idea in a different idiom: 'Individualization destabilizes the system of mass parties from the inside, because it deprives party commitments of tradition, making them dependent on decision-making or, seen from the party perspective, dependent upon construction.'[80] Thus, once an organization's *esprit de corps* is weakened, the 'generous' (if not unlimited) confidence in the leadership diminishes, and internal tensions mount.[81] As a result, contemporary leaders are less capable of establishing their power, their status as leader, on an ethic of strong bonds of integration, on a spirit of discipline in a solidaristic and culturally and sociologically relatively homogeneous organization.[82] They are no longer the '*head*' *and representative of a fused community, or the living symbol of its values.* They are therefore more fragile.

With the decline of the party-community and the model of authority flowing from it, with the new sociology of the organization, with the diffusion of post-materialist and anti-authoritarian values, an important pillar of leadership stability disappears. By dint of becoming different, the organization creates a different (and, in part, indifferent) membership,[83] and a less solid leadership. The organization has, in a sense, become a structure that *destabilizes* its own leadership.

To conclude, we could say that the highly singular position of contemporary socialist leadership, composed jointly of strength and vulnerability, results from alterations affecting the means of communication, the effectiveness of the nation-state and economic policies, the organizational universe. Some aspects of the internal organizational modifications (weakening of the membership, reduced role of the bureaucracy, systematic recourse to experts) contribute to strengthening the status of the leader; others (end of the party-community, new sociology of membership, internal issues connected with the new politics) to weakening it. Once the complex of factors pointing in one direction or the other is partially clarified, an analogy comes to mind that will serve as a conclusion: in their relationship with their leadership, modern socialist and social-democratic organizations much resemble Herman Hesse's 'wolf-man', who 'was always recognizing and affirming with one half of himself . . . what with the other half he fought against and denied'.[84]

Concluding Remarks

1. Thanks to a network of collateral organizations, historical social democracy impinged on numerous spheres of social life. It offered its members the prospect of 'integration', particularly as regards education, political information, social security, and leisure. Today, the bases of this type of recruitment are profoundly – and possibly irremediably – eroded. Hence the reduction in membership density, and the marginal mobilization and habitual lethargy of current day-to-day organizational life. In the light of this new state of affairs, *to detect a 'crisis' in social-democratic organizational development is to judge the present on the basis of traditional criteria.* It is to ignore the new social, institutional and cultural influences that engender a novel reality and a novel organizational ethos. What appears to be a 'crisis' of activism and the activist life, a 'crisis' of the organization, is in reality simply a mutation. It is certainly seen and experienced as a 'crisis', and above all as a 'loss': a loss of reference points, effectiveness, ambiance and style, memory – in short, a loss of identity. However, like every mutation, it permits the emergence of a new organizational 'formula': new reference points, a new effectiveness (and ineffectiveness), another style, a different ambiance.

2. Indeed, the changes I have just inventoried (preponderance of new middle classes, weakening of working-class presence and culture, redistribution of internal power at the expense of the membership and traditional bureaucracy, a leadership at once both stronger and weaker, end of the party-community and strengthening of the culture of trade-offs, weakening of the 'identity incentives', reinforcement of anti-authoritarian tendencies and values, less dense membership fabric) – all these *tend in the direction of a profound change of identity*, rather than an internal reorganization of the social-democratic organizational mode of being.

3. An organizational structure is built through the combination of two complementary and inseparable 'logics': *local and sectoral implantation*, which produces segmented units; and *integration*, according to modalities of articulation specific to each organization, which confers on these units the unity that inserts them into a functional whole – which does not mean one devoid of contradictions. The peculiarity of the structure is precisely to envelop – and activate – in one and the same *modus operandi* different, even divergent, units. Today, the decisive weight, if not absolute predominance, within mass socialist organizations of integrative rationality (through a pyramidal armature,

bureaucracy, summary but strong and strongly shared ideology, the communitarian-associative spirit, central control of intermediate instances) is considerably reduced. These organizations become political structures in which conflict, disorder and instability are more pronounced and visible than in the past. They become a 'stage' for increased instability, or – worse – of stability through indifference, the diminution of their relevance as a stage.[85] The centre becomes stronger and the local, outside national election campaigns, more autonomous. Contact between the two becomes more direct and mediating structures are weakened.[86] The internal rules of the game are more democratic and decentralized, and the process of choosing leaders is more open and competitive.[87] Socialist and social-democratic organizations are less unified and compact, but also more democratic, 'open', supple and flexible.

4. The *unter uns gesagt* (between ourselves) mentality having long since been left behind, flexibility and 'openness' make these organizations capable of responding more rapidly to the stimuli of electoral competition. To take one example: the loosening of the link with the unions – as well as a certain weakening of the latter –weakens the social-democratic parties organizationally and electorally.[88] But in a society that is not classically bipolar, it simultaneously affords them greater freedom of action and greater openness to new sensibilities, which can be left-wing, right-wing, or 'neither left nor right' (e.g. feminist ideas, minority rights, ecology, neoliberal ideas). In addition, the increased autonomy of the leader facilitates a capacity for innovation 'from above' (whatever the political and programmatic content of this innovation) and, as a result, socialists' competitive capacity.[89]

5. This trend makes most of the contemporary social-democratic organizations *mixed* structures, halfway between the classical mass party model (described by Weber, Michels, Neumann and above all, Duverger), and the electoral-professional model (described by Panebianco).[90] Thus the thesis of the transformation of the mass social-democratic parties into electoral-professional parties is only partially confirmed. Moreover, in actual political life it is intermediate forms, not pure forms, that dominate. Socialist organizations bear marks inherited from the mass party model (reduced but still mass membership; persistence – albeit weakened – of the union link; associative network linked to the party; operational *habitus* belonging to the organization's genetic code) and marks pertaining to the electoral-professional party model (increased leadership power; enhanced role of experts/professionals; renunciation of any aspiration to 'intellectual and moral *encadrement* of the masses'; ever more interclassist internal format). The balance – and sometimes tension – between these organizational elements and orientations varies according to the internal relation of forces, conjunctures and national traditions. These two types of structure and practice are superimposed, intermingled, intertwined. And in complementing and

contradicting one another, they constitute the two faces of contemporary social democracy.

6. This development – which I have doubtless oversimplified somewhat here – is a conclusion whose premisses date from the beginning of the 1960s. If contemporary social-democratic organizations are developing as *mixed structures*, retaining certain aspects of the mass party while evolving towards the electoral-professional type of party, and thus as structures located in an organizational 'in-between', nothing suggests that we are dealing with *parties of integration*, whatever the meaning attributed to that concept. The 'comprehensive grassroots connections' of the past between these organizations and the 'public' have become '"functional connections" driven by immediate political needs'.[91] Today, parties of a social-democratic type are no longer in a position – and anyway, no longer have the ambition – to fulfil a function that was traditionally theirs: 'the creation and preservation of collective identities through ideology', in Panebianco's terms; or 'the intellectual and moral *encadrement* of the masses', according to Otto Kirchheimer. In this respect, the change is radical. Social democracy no longer assumes a central social function which forms part of its deepest political specificity.

7. This drastically diminishes its autonomy *vis-à-vis* its own environment and its ability to control it: social democracy is no longer constructed as a 'strong institution' capable of significantly influencing 'the value and attitudinal system' of contemporary societies, and has not been for a long time. 'Right-thinking' forces, social-democratic organizations, which today are weakened, 'are no longer able . . . to think beyond the next election'.[92] The archetype of 'rational' politics, based on the prioritization of the search for votes, which scarcely applied to the great membership organizations historically represented by the socialist parties, increasingly accounts for the current *modus operandi* of social democracy. As a result, these organizations are unable to leave deep traces in the collective imaginary. Their distinctive profile and values have been diluted.

8. In the aftermath of these changes, the social-democratic organization conceived as a 'community of solidarity' no longer exists, just as the political and especially social terrain that favoured its development no longer exists. Paradise is lost.[93] Today, only the shadow of the party-community, its outline, survives, despite the resistance and resurgence, here and there, of kernels 'with strong cohesion and great affective connotation' – of certain 'niches', as Jacques Ion would say.[94]

9. The sociology of social-democratic organization, which registers the hegemony of the middle classes today, differs profoundly from that of the working-class organizations of the prewar period, and even from the popular organizations (with strong working-class representation) of the 1950s. The change is sizeable. The 'contented majority' currently control social-democratic organizations, which distance themselves from the mass of the 'non-privileged' and still more from the growing

world of the excluded. The 'subaltern' classes are certainly still present in the organization, but they are reduced to a species of second estate and subsidiary force. In this sense, the famous *fracture sociale* also exists at the very heart of socialist and social-democratic organization. More precisely, those who are socially either on the 'periphery' or *extra muros* are organizationally *outside* the party. This development is historically novel. The organization's sociological continuity has, to a considerable extent, been shattered.

10. Social-democratic 'self-identity' is currently more political, and a good deal less ideological, sociological or cultural. Compared with the inter-war and immediate postwar periods, contemporary social democracy is in large measure a *different* social democracy – despite the incontestable fact that 'past organisational choices have enduring effects'. Even when they evolve substantially towards the model of 'catch-all entrepreneurial organizations', the strong structures that mass parties are by definition cannot be totally disowned. Once consolidated, a structure 'immobilizes time in its own way'. Thus, organizational change often takes the malleable forms bequeathed by the past, while on occasion taking quite new directions. However, the new organizational identity of social democracy, which is unquestionably composite and belongs to two distinct modes of party construction, is not – and will not be – a renewed identity, but a *novel* identity.

Notes

1. In reaching these percentages, I have excluded from my calculations retired people and housewives, and more generally the economically inactive population. This procedure, necessary in a comparative framework, affords an unduly simplified image of the occupational structure of the parties studied. In addition, it contributes to underestimating the weight of the working class, since a significant proportion of the categories 'housewives' or 'retired' derives, in all probability, from the working class. Sources: for the SPD (1952, 1966, 1977), in Anton Pelinka, *Social Democratic Parties in Europe*, Praeger, New York 1983, p. 48; for the SPÖ (1955, 1970, 1978), in William Paterson and Alastair Thomas, eds, *The Future of Social-Democracy*, Clarendon Press, Oxford 1986, p. 166; for the SPD (1991, east and west) and for the SPÖ (1990), in Wolfgang Merkel *et al.*, *Socialist Parties in Europe II: Class, Popular, Catch-all?*, ICPS, Barcelona 1992, pp. 138, 161; for the SPD (1996) in Johan Jeroen De Deken, 'The German Social-Democratic Party', in Robert Ladrech and Philippe Marlière, eds, *Social-Democratic Parties in the European Union*, Macmillan, London 1999, p. 86.
2. Lars Bille, 'The Danish Social-Democratic Party', in Ladrech and Marlière, eds, *Social-Democratic Parties in the European Union*, p. 48.
3. Patrick Seyd and Paul Whiteley, *Labour's Grass Roots: The Politics of Party Membership*, Clarendon Press, Oxford 1992, pp. 34, 39.
4. Nicholas Aylott, 'The Swedish Social-Democratic Party', in Ladrech and Marlière, eds, *Social-Democratic Parties in the European Union*, p. 195.
5. Pascal Perrineau, 'Introduction' in Perrineau, ed., *L'engagement politique, déclin ou mutation?*, Presses de la Fondation Nationale des Sciences Politiques, Paris 1994, p. 16.

6. Gerrit Voerman, 'De la confiance à la crise. La gauche aux Pays-Bas depuis les années soixante-dix', in Pascal Dewit and Jean-Michel De Waele, eds, *La Gauche face aux mutations en Europe*, Éditions de l'Université de Bruxelles, Brussels 1993, p. 80.

7. Michel Offerlé, *Les Partis politiques*, Presses Universitaires de France, Paris 1987, p. 80.

8. On changes in the activity of the leader in an electoral campaign, see, *inter alia*, the very important work by Peter Esaiasson, '120 Years of Swedish Election Campaigning', *Scandinavian Political Studies*, vol. 14, 1991, pp. 261–78.

9. Shaun Bowler and David Farrell, *Electoral Strategies and Political Marketing*, St Martin's Press, New York 1992, *passim*.

10. Danilo Zolo, *Democracy and Complexity*, Polity Press, Cambridge 1992, p. 163. The definition of a politics 'from afar', thanks to the body of research produced in the 'little world' of the specialists without always taking activists' experience in the field into consideration, creates as many problems as it is supposed to resolve. The inability of the socialist high command to anticipate the emergence and persistence of new social movements and political currents (e.g. the ecological movement, 'new politics' parties, new extreme right) is one expression of them. Moreover, the sublimation of the effects of new technologies has often led left-wing leaders to forget the importance of an active membership in *successfully resisting* a competing political appeal. Moreover, the latter becomes all the more hostile, and its effects more unpredictable, in that it manifests itself principally – what an irony! – on a local stage, *far from the television studios, and also far from the opinion pollsters*, prior to establishing itself on the national political scene (see Gerassimos Moschonas, 'L'éclat d'un pouvoir fragilisé. Force et faiblesse du leadership socialiste', in Marc Lazar, ed., *La Gauche en Europe depuis 1945*, Presses Universitaires de France, Paris 1996, p. 586).

11. Knut Heidar, 'The Norwegian Labour Party: "En Attendant l'Europe"', in Richard Gillespie and William Paterson, eds, *Rethinking Social Democracy in Western Europe*, Frank Cass, London 1993, p. 74.

12. On the expansion of this personnel, which is very sensitive to the ideas of the party leadership and assumes the function of technical support and active executant of its policy, see the case studies collected in Richard Katz and Peter Mair, eds, *How Parties Organize: Change and Adaptation in Party Organizations in Western Democracies*, Sage, London 1994.

13. Pippa Norris, 'Political Communications', in Patrick Dunleavy *et al.*, eds, *Developments in British Politics 5*, Macmillan, London 1997, p. 77.

14. Moschonas, 'L'éclat d'un pouvoir fragilisé', pp. 587–8.

15. Ibid., p. 589.

16. Eric Shaw, 'Conflict and Cohesion in the British Labour Party', in David Bell and Eric Shaw, eds, *Conflict and Cohesion in Western European Social Democratic Parties*, Pinter, London and New York 1994, p. 152.

17. Monica Charlot, *Le Parti travailliste*, Montchrestien, Paris 1992, pp. 125–48.

18. Colin Leys, 'The British Labour Party since 1989', in Donald Sassoon, ed., *Looking Left*, I.B. Tauris, London and New York 1997, p. 19.

19. Quoted in Thomas Koelble, *The Left Unraveled: Social Democracy and the New Left Challenge in Britain and West Germany*, Duke University Press, Durham, NC 1991, p. 5.

20. Stephen Padgett and William Paterson, 'Germany: Stagnation of the Left', in Perry Anderson and Patrick Camiller, eds, *Mapping the West European Left*, Verso, London and New York 1994, p. 124.

21. Quoted in Susan Scarrow, *Parties and their Members: Organizing for Victory in Britain and Germany*, Oxford University Press, Oxford 1996, p. 202.

22. Stephen Padgett, 'The German Social Democrats: A Redefinition of Social Democracy or Bad Godesberg Mark II?', in Gillespie and Paterson, eds, *Rethinking Social Democracy in Western Europe*, p. 36.

23. Thomas Poguntke, 'Parties in a Legalistic Culture: The Case of Germany', in Katz and Mair, eds, *How Parties Organize*, p. 211.

24. Ruud Koole, 'The Dutch Labour Party: Towards a Modern Cadre Party?', in Merkel *et al.*, *Socialist Parties in Europe II*, pp. 207–11.

25. Philip van Praag, 'Conflict and Cohesion in the Dutch Labour Party', in Bell and Shaw, eds, *Conflict and Cohesion in European Social Democratic Parties*, p. 137.

26. Ibid. See also Voerman, 'De la confiance à la crise', pp. 67–84.

27. Van Praag, 'Conflict and Cohesion in the Dutch Labour Party', p. 147.

28. Kees van Kerbergen, 'The Dutch Labour Party', in Ladrech and Marlière, eds, *Social-Democratic Parties in the European Union*, p. 158.

29. More particularly, in the Labour Party and SPD recourse to strong leadership with a 'winning profile' constitutes an exemplary instance of the leader's function as *palliative* for the deficits of identity and competitiveness.

30. Leys, 'The British Labour Party since 1989', pp. 20–22.

31. Scarrow, *Parties and their Members*, p. 110.

32. Charles Pattie, Paul Whiteley, Ron Johnston and Patrick Seyd, 'Measuring Local Campaign Effects: Labour Party Constituency Campaigning at the 1987 General Election', *Political Studies*, XLII, 1994, p. 479.

33. Susan Scarrow, 'The "Paradox of Enrolment": Assessing the Costs and Benefits of Party Memberships', *European Journal of Political Research*, no. 25, 1994, pp. 53–7.

34. Scarrow, *Parties and their Members*, p. 157.

35. Patrick Seyd, 'New Parties/New Politics? A Case Study of the British Labour Party', *Party Politics*, vol. 5, no. 3, 1999, p. 401.

36. The working-class sections of the SPÖ and SAP (in factories and popular suburbs) are more 'conformist' and more respectful of the traditional rituals of party life than sections in which the middle classes predominate (Herbert Kitschelt, 'Austrian and Swedish Social Democrats in Crisis: Party Strategy and Organization in Corporatist Regimes', *Comparative Political Studies*, vol. 27, no. 1, 1994, p. 19).

37. Angelo Pancbianco, *Political Parties, Organization and Power*, Cambridge University Press, Cambridge 1988, p. 228.

38. See Jürgen Habermas, *The Structural Transformation of the Public Sphere*, trans. Thomas Burger, Polity Press, Cambridge 1989.

39. Ronald Inglehart, *La Transition culturelle*, Economica, Paris 1993, p. 441.

40. Robert Rohrschneider, 'How Iron is the Iron Law of Oligarchy? Robert Michels and National Party Delegates in Eleven West European Democracies', *European Journal of Political Research*, no. 25, 1994, p. 212. 'In some ways,' Herbert Kitschelt has written, 'the libertarian assault on the European mass-membership party displays a political thrust similar to that of the "progressive" middle-class movements in the United States that attacked the urban party machines after the turn to the twentieth century' (Kitschelt, 'European Social Democracy between Political Economy and Electoral Competition', in Kitschelt *et al.*, eds, *Continuity and Change in Contemporary Capitalism*, Cambridge University Press, Cambridge 1999, p. 331).

41. Rohrschneider, 'How Iron is the Iron Law of Oligarchy?', *passim*. Let us reflect a little on the case of the British Labour Party. Since the 'treason' of Ramsay MacDonald, a certain mistrust of the leader has formed part of the genetic code and memory of British Labourism (Charlot, *Le Parti travailliste*, pp. 35–6). Moreover, the original structure of this party, which made the leader and parliamentary group autonomous, has contributed to the fact that the left wing historically identifies with the 'base'. The failure of moderate Labourism on the economic front, its persistent inability to keep its economic and social promises (1964–70 and 1974–79 governments), opened up a space for the 'old' left within the organization. Faced with this failure of the 'right', and in the absence of a 'new politics' pole in the British political field, the radical wing *ipso facto* represented the rival and challenger of the moderate party leadership. This explains the British exception, where, contrary to the pattern in continental parties, the intermediate elites orientated to 'old politics' are more focused on the constituency than the centre. The centrality of socioeconomic issues and themes, as well as the working-class and popular tradition of British Labourism, have determined the Labour left's political and ideological profile and its orientation to the 'base' and the constituency. This is a left which, from the heroic period of the Independent Labour Party up to the battle over Clause 4 and its victory at the 1981 Wembley Conference, has stirred itself strongly and 'sometimes . . . makes life difficult for the leaders' (Moisei Ostrogorski, *La Démocratie et les partis politiques*, Fayard, Paris 1993, p. 313).
42. Koelble, *The Left Unraveled*, p. 118.
43. Patrick Hassenteufel, 'Partis socialistes et syndicats: l'autonomisation réciproque', in Lazar, ed., *La Gauche en Europe depuis 1945*.
44. Padgett, 'The German Social Democrats', in Gillespie and Paterson, eds, *Rethinking Social Democracy in Western Europe*, p. 30.
45. Andrew Taylor, 'Trade Unions and the Politics of Social Democratic Renewal', in Gillespie and Paterson, eds, *Rethinking Social Democracy in Western Europe*, p. 150.
46. Ibid., pp. 149–50.
47. Gillespie and Paterson, eds, *Rethinking Social Democracy in Western Europe*, *passim*.
48. Gérard Grunberg, 'Existe-t-il un socialisme de l'Europe du Sud?', in Lazar, ed., *La Gauche en Europe depuis 1945*, p. 495.
49. Kitschelt, 'European Social Democracy between Political Economy and Electoral Competition', in Kitschelt *et al.*, eds, *Continuity and Change in Contemporary Capitalism*, p. 330.
50. Thomas Koelble, 'Recasting Social Democracy in Europe: A Nested Games Explanation of Strategic Adjustment in Political Parties', *Politics and Society*, vol. 20, no. 1; 'Intra-party Coalitions and Electoral Strategies: European Social Democracy in Search of Votes', *Southeastern Political Review*, vol. 23, no. 1.
51. Ralph Miliband, *The State in Capitalist Society*, Weidenfeld & Nicolson, London 1969, p. 165.
52. See Knut Heidar, 'The Polymorphic Nature of Party Membership', *European Journal of Political Research*, no. 25, 1994, Table 12, p. 80.
53. The same tendency towards weakening is visible since the beginning of the 1970s in the Belgian Socialist Party. However, the party's division in 1978 into Parti Socialiste (PS) and Socialistische Partij (SP), in accordance with the linguistic divide, does not allow a rigorous comparison with the initial postwar period. Prudence is therefore in order. On the tenure of socialist leaders in

Belgium, see Lieven de Winter, 'The Selection of Party Presidents in Belgium', *European Journal of Political Research*, vol. 24, no. 3, October 1993, p. 235.

54. On membership density, indicated by the degree of enrolment of the socialist electorate (rate of adhesion = relation between the number of socialist voters and of members), see Gerassimos Moschonas, *La Social-démocratie de 1945 à nos jours*, Montchrestien, Paris 1994, p. 33, Table 1. For a different but complementary approach, based on the relation between members and the total electorate, see Gerrit Voerman, 'Le Paradis perdu', in Lazar, ed., *La Gauche en Europe depuis 1945*.

55. According to Kitschelt, 'in the German social democrats, leadership autonomy has lagged': 'European Social Democracy between Political Economy and Electoral Competition', p. 333. See also Padgett and Paterson, 'Germany: Stagnation of the Left', p. 124. For a comparative treatment of the position of the Labour and Conservative leaders in Great Britain, see Giulia Caravale, 'Leader e sistema di partito in Gran Bretagna', *Politico*, vol. LVIII, no. 4, 1993, pp. 531–70.

56. See Herbert Kitschelt, *The Transformation of European Social Democracy*, Cambridge University Press, Cambridge 1994, p. 225.

57. See the excellent analysis by Grunberg, 'Existe-t-il un socialisme de l'Europe du Sud?'.

58. Costas Botopoulos, *Les Socialistes à l'épreuve du pouvoir*, Bruylant, Brussels 1993, p. 230.

59. See Moschonas, *La Social-démocratie de 1945 à nos jours*.

60. See Gerassimos Moschonas, 'The Panhellenic Socialist Movement', in Ladrech and Marlière, eds, *Social-Democratic Parties in the European Union*.

61. Patrick Camillier, 'Spain: The Survival of Socialism?', in Anderson and Camiller, eds, *Mapping the West European Left*, p. 259.

62. Ibid., p. 260.

63. During the 1980s, a certain 'dyarchy', with Gonzales representing the 'party-government' and Alfonso Guerra the 'party-organization', ensured a margin of internal party pluralism, albeit very limited. Moreover, the greater decentralization of the Spanish party system allowed some regional leaders (the so-called 'barons') to claim a power space of their own. The regional arena is an important site of conflict within the PSOE, at the expense of both the 'centre', which remains the critical instance for the exercise of power, and the 'local'. See Richard Gillespie, '"Programma 2000": The Appearance and Reality of Socialist Renewal in Spain', in Gillespie and Paterson, eds, *Rethinking Social Democracy in Western Europe*, pp. 80, 84; Gillespie, 'The Resurgence of Factionalism in the Spanish Socialist Workers' Party', in Bell and Shaw, eds, *Conflict and Cohesion in Western European Social Democratic Parties*, pp. 59–62.

64. Kitschelt, 'Austrian and Swedish Social Democrats in Crisis', pp. 13, 31–3. See also Jonas Pontusson, 'Sweden: After the Golden Age', in Anderson and Camiller, eds, *Mapping the West European Left*, p. 50.

65. Kitschelt, 'Austrian and Swedish Social Democrats in Crisis', pp. 18, 33–4.

66. Wolfgang Muller and D. Meth-Cohn, 'The Selection of Party Chairmen in Austria: A Study in Intra-Party Decision-Making', *European Journal of Political Research*, vol. 20, no. 1, 1991, p. 57.

67. Moschonas, 'The Panhellenic Socialist Movement', p. 116.

68. Quoted in Christopher Lasch, *The Culture of Narcissism*, Abacus, London 1980, p. 24.

69. See Pascal Quignard, *Le Sexe et l'effroi*, Gallimard, Paris 1994.

70. Muller and Meth-Cohn, 'The Selection of Party Chairmen in Austria', p. 59.
71. Mario Telo, 'La social-démocratie entre nation et Europe', in Telo, ed., *De la nation à l'Europe*, Bruyant, Brussels 1993, p. 48.
72. The case of François Mitterrand is exemplary in this respect. See Alistair Cole, 'Studying Leadership: The Case of François Mitterrand', *Political Studies*, XLII, 1994, pp. 453–68.
73. Jacques Ion, 'L'évolution des formes de l'engagement public', in Perrineau, ed., *L'engagement politique*, p. 33.
74. The distinction between incentives of finality and incentives of identity, which we are applying in the case of mass socialist parties, derives from Peter Lange, 'La théorie des stimulants et l'analyse des partis politiques', in J.-L. Seurin, ed., *La Démocratie pluraliste*, Economica, Paris 1981, especially pp. 253–8.
75. Henri Rey and Françoise Subileau, *Les Militants socialistes à l'épreuve du pouvoir*, Presses de la Fondation Nationale des Sciences Politiques, Paris 1991, p. 55. The expansion of political information through non-party channels (e.g. television), as well as the multiplication of non-party 'structures' of political participation, are additional factors in the weakening of political organizations. See Scarrow, 'The "Paradox of Enrolment"', pp. 50–51.
76. Lange, 'La théorie des stimulants et l'analyse des partis politiques', p. 249.
77. Rey and Subileau, *Les Militants socialistes à l'épreuve du pouvoir*, p. 27.
78. Alan Ware, 'Activist–Leader Relations and the Structure of Political Parties: "Exchange" Models and Vote-Seeking Behaviour in Parties', *British Journal of Political Science*, vol. 22, no. 1, 1992, p. 84. The abandonment by socialist and social-democratic parties of their traditional ideologies means that 'authoritarian' leadership of a party can no longer be justified by reference to ideology (see Jan Sundberg, 'Finland: Nationalized Parties, Professionalized Organizations', in Katz and Mair, eds, *How Parties Organize*, p. 170).
79. Lazar, in Bergounioux and Lazar, *La Social-démocratie dans l'Union européenne*, p. 12.
80. Ulrich Beck, *The Reinvention of Politics: Rethinking Modernity in the Global Social Order*, Polity Press, Cambridge 1997, p. 144.
81. Ware, 'Activist–Leader Relations and the Structure of Political Parties', pp. 89–92. The distinction between the different types of incentive is inevitably schematic, and only occasionally assumes an absolute sense. The motives behind partisan commitment are typically multiple and combined according to a 'chemistry' that is specific to each individual. But the fact that the distinction is not absolute does not reduce its *heuristic* value.
82. Nothing illustrates the end of the party-community better than the profound change in the 'nature' and functions of socialist and social-democratic local sections, which increasingly resemble the local sections of conservative and liberal parties. A very eloquent description of this change in the Scandinavian countries is provided by Jan Sundberg, 'Participation in Local Government: A Source of Social Democratic Deradicalization in Scandinavia?', in L. Karvonen and J. Sundberg, *Social Democracy in Transition, Northern, Southern and Eastern Europe*, Dartmouth, Aldershot 1991, pp. 135–8, Tables 10 and 11.
83. See Heidar, 'The Polymorphic Nature of Party Membership', pp. 61–86; Herbert Kitschelt, 'Austrian and Swedish Social Democrats in Crisis: Party Strategy and Organization in Corporatist Regimes', *Comparative Political Studies*, vol. 27, no. 1, 1994, p. 10.
84. In this respect our analysis differs from that of Richard Katz and Peter Mair, who maintain that contemporary parties, 'cartel parties', are characterized by a

model of internal authority of the 'top–down', rather than 'bottom–up', variety. We believe that while various influential factors considerably strengthen the 'top–down' dimension of intra-organizational authority, others tend to strengthen the 'bottom–up' dimension ('Changing Models of Party Organization and Party Democracy: The Emergence of the Cartel Party', *Party Politics*, no. 1, 1995 p. 20).

85. Knut Heidar, 'Towards Party Irrelevance? The Decline of Both Conflict and Cohesion in the Norwegian Labour Party', in Bell and Shaw, eds, *Conflict and Cohesion in Western European Social Democratic Parties*, pp. 96–112. See van Praag, 'Conflict and Cohesion in the Dutch Labour Party', in ibid., pp. 146–7.
86. Scarrow, *Parties and their Members*, pp. 202–4.
87. Two expressions of this 'openness' directly concern the leadership. First, leadership selection has become more 'competitive'. The 'poison of competition' is slowly making its appearance in socialist organizations – something that is not always status-enhancing for the image either of the party or of the leader. Second, the selection process has become more democratic. It is less than ever before a matter of a closed circle and an uninfluential, often restricted, selection body, where everything has been settled in advance in the closed universe of the 'few', i.e. the organization's most prestigious leaders. See *European Journal of Political Resarch*, 'Selecting Party Leaders', special issue, vol. 24, no. 3, October 1993; also Mair in Katz and Mair, *How Parties Organize*, pp. 5, 17.
88. See Christoph Kunkel and Jonas Pontusson, 'Corporatism versus Social Democracy: Divergent Fortunes of the Austrian and Swedish Labour Movements', *West European Politics*, vol. 21, no. 2, 1998.
89. For 'innovation from above', see Kitschelt, *The Transformation of European Social Democracy*, p. 213.
90. The conception of contemporary parties as 'groups of leaders', as 'partnerships of professionals' absorbed by the state, and no longer as 'associations of citizens' (the concept of the 'cartel party'), unilaterally – and exaggeratedly – accentuates certain features of the modern reality of parties, and takes only partial account of the composite reality of today's socialist and social-democratic parties. See Katz and Mair, 'Changing Models of Party Organization and Party Democracy', pp. 16, 21–2.
91. John Coleman, 'Party Organizational Strength and Public Support for Parties', *American Journal of Political Science*, vol. 40, no. 3, 1996, p. 807.
92. Donald Sassoon, *One Hundred Years of Socialism*, I.B. Tauris, London 1996, p. 690.
93. Voerman, 'Le Paradis perdu', p. 561.
94. Ion, 'L'évolution des formes de l'engagement publique', p. 31.

9

A Time of Competitive Insecurity:
'La modernité, c'est nous!'

Domination under Threat

I have said that the striking thing about the structuration of the left in the countries furthest advanced along the social-democratic path lies in the domination of most – often virtually all – of the left-wing political-ideological continuum by parties of a social-democratic type. Thus the strength of these parties in competition consists in: (a) their solid domination of the 'left' of the political scene, a natural consequence of the absence or neutralization of significant left-wing competitors; and (b) their capacity for 'openness' to the centre, the principal consequence of this domination.

Today, this domination is coming under challenge from the emergence of peripheral political poles representing a 'new politics'. Among these new actors, whose most well-known and widespread (but not exclusive) version is the 'green' parties, parties of a 'new left' variety predominate. In the origin of their memberships and voters, their programmatic and ideological options, their position on the left–right spectrum, these formations constitute a real challenge to the social-democratic parties, and to the forces of the established left in general. The appearance and relative consolidation of 'green' formations, and 'new politics' or 'semi-new politics' formations generally, as well as the importance of the themes they develop (environment, women's rights, minority rights of all sorts, peace, North–South relations, etc.), represent one of the most remarkable political developments of the last twenty years.

Without getting lost in statistical minutiae, we should note that the ecological/alternative parties occupy an important place in the European political landscape. They are strongly or moderately represented on various national political stages – in Germany (8.3 per cent in 1987, 4.9 per cent in 1990, 7.3 per cent in 1994, 6.7 per cent in 1998, and 6.4 per cent in the 1999 European elections); in Belgium (6.2 per cent [ECOLO + AGALEV] in 1985, 7.1 per cent [ECOLO + AGALEV] in 1987, 8.3 per cent [ECOLO + AGALEV] in 1991, 7.3 per cent [ECOLO + AGALEV] in 1995, 7.4 per cent [AGALEV] and 8.4 per cent [ECOLO] in 1999; in Austria (4.8 per cent in 1986, 4.8 per cent in 1990, 7.3 per cent in 1994, 4.8 per cent in 1995, but 9.2 per cent in the 1999 European elections); in Finland (4 per cent in 1987, 6.8 per cent in 1991, 6.5 per cent in 1995, and 13.4 per cent in the 1999 European elections); in Sweden (5.5 per cent in 1988, 3.4 per cent in 1991, 5.2 per cent in 1994, 4.5 per cent in 1998, but 17.2 per cent in the 1995 European elections and 9.4 per cent in the 1999 European elections); in the Netherlands (4.1 per cent in 1989, 3.5 per cent in 1994, 7.3 per cent in 1998, and 11.9 per cent in the 1999 European elections).

We might also note that in Denmark, a party of a semi-new left type (or, in Kitschelt's classification, 'left-libertarian'[1]) – the Socialist People's Party (SF) – has established itself as an important political actor since the 1960s, although its influence is waning (11.5 per cent in 1984, 14.6 per cent in 1987, 13 per cent in 1988, 8.3 per cent in 1990, 7.3 per cent in 1994, 7.5 per cent in 1998, and 7.1 per cent in the 1999 European elections). Similarly, in Norway, another Scandinavian country with a powerful social democracy, the left-wing socialists – politically close to their Danish counterparts, but with a very uncertain and unstable electoral record – have formed part of the Norwegian political landscape since the second half of the 1960s. (Under the title of the Popular Socialist Party [SF] they obtained 3.5 per cent in 1969 and 11.2 per cent in 1973; under that of the Socialist Left Party, 4.2 per cent in 1977, 4.9 per cent in 1981, 5.5 per cent in 1985, 10.1 per cent in 1989, 7.9 per cent in 1993, and 6 per cent in 1997).

Obviously, the electoral 'business' of these parties cannot be regarded as flourishing and expanding, and the increased volatility of their electorate in some instances translates into uneven results.

Meanwhile, in Sweden and Finland, the effect of their presence is reinforced by the existence of traditional left-wing (ex-communist) formations, which have been significantly renovated and converted to ecology and the themes of the new politics. (The Party of the Left [V] in Sweden scored 6.2 per cent in 1994, 12 per cent in 1998, and 15.8 per cent in the European elections of 1999. The Left Alliance [VAS] in Finland obtained 11.2 per cent in 1995 and 9.1 per cent in the 1999 European elections.)

In addition, in a southern Europe marked by a strong communist tradition, despite the general erosion in their influence, we observe a certain resilience of communist forces which to some extent is astonishing. In France, the PCF obtained 9.9 per cent in 1997 (but 6.8 per cent in the 1999 European elections as against 9.7 per cent for the Greens). In Spain, the United Left (IU) obtained 10.6 per cent in 1996 (and 5.8 per cent at the last European elections). In Italy, Rifondazione comunista obtained 8.6 per cent in 1996 (but only 4.3 per cent at the 1999 European elections). In Portugal, the communists and their allies secured 8.6 per cent in 1995 (and 10.3 per cent in the 1999 European elections). In Greece, the communist party (KKE) scored 5.6 per cent in 1996 (and 8.7 per cent in the 1999 European elections).[2] It is important to note that the left oppositions (communists, post-communists, left socialists, Greens) exceed 15 per cent of the votes cast in three EU countries, two of which (Sweden, Finland) are located in the northern part of the continent.[3] In the other three (Germany, Spain, France), the influence of the formations in question exceeded 10 per cent of the votes cast at the last legislative elections.

Of course, arithmetic must not take precedence over politics: these formations are part of a large, very heteroclite mass, lacking a common tradition and with a dispersed ideological framework. Their electoral support is unstable and their organizational structures are invariably weak. They possess neither the deep roots nor the stability of the old communist parties. The logic of the statistics, however, is illuminating: it indicates the reasonable electoral health of the left oppositions (new and old) and the 'neither left nor right' oppositions. They may not be flourishing electorally, but what is implicitly and explicitly at stake in the power of these poles (new and old) is the destabilization – even obstruction – of the strategy of the great social-democratic parties.

Indeed, the presence of such rivals on the left (or of the 'neither left nor right' variety), and the constant pressure that they exert on social-demo-cratic-type parties, weaken these parties politically, sociologically and ideo-logically. The 'left' segment of the political scene is no longer – as it so often was in the past – *a space with minimal political competition*, a terrain on which social democracy's writ essentially runs. It is now subject to the dialectic of confrontation, proper to every bi- or multipolar space. The *competitive security* of social democracy is affected. We have seen tangible signs of this in the recent past, and we also see them today, in Norway, Denmark, Germany, Sweden, Belgium, and, to a lesser degree, in Austria, Greece and elsewhere.

Doing Battle on Two – or Three? – Fronts

The emergence and consolidation of these challengers have prompted the social-democratic parties, often through the prior activation of fratricidal internal struggles, to make a *turn to the themes and options of the new politics*, a switch often perceived and accepted as a left turn. In particular, the Scandinavian, Dutch and German social-democratic parties – and, to a lesser extent, the Austrian – embarked during the 1980s, as did the Italian PDS during the 1990s, on a very important attempt at programmatic renewal, integrating the themes of the 'new politics' (especially ecological themes).[4] In Norway, for example, the emergence of social movements has made 'post-materialist' questions (particularly the environment and feminism) a central axis of Norwegian public debate.[5] Gro Harlem Brundtland, former leader of the Norwegian Labour Party, has even become 'the emblematic figure of a social democracy in the vanguard of ecological consciousness and the demands of a new feminist left'.[6] In Germany, where 'two SPDs' (one 'traditional', the other 'new politics') confront each other within the SPD, the 'ecological modernization of the economy' was a centrepiece of the party's programmatic renewal.[7] The SAP, traditionally distinguished by a long 'legacy of continuous reform and innovations', 'elevated a good environment to one of the four major goals for the decade' in its action programme for the 1990s.[8] The SPÖ's 'Social Democracy 2000' programme, adopted in 1989, contained a long chapter on 'ecological renewal in an industrialized society'.[9]

This conversion to the values and themes of the new politics (the 'greening of socialist parties') was in some instances a means of preventing the crystallization of an organizational schism between the 'traditional' left and the 'new' left. It was also a way of simultaneously neutralizing and conciliating the new parties and new social movements, precisely in order (in the words of German social-democratic leader Erhard Eppler) to render 'the Greens useless'. Thus, seeking to protect themselves from this novel threat and contest the 'new politics' parties on their own ground to prevent their consolidation, social democrats found themselves challenged and partially transformed.

In addition to the challenge represented by the rise of 'new political' values, socialists faced the *simultaneous* rise of neoliberal values in a context unconducive to social-democratic economic 'solutions'. Thus, contrary to the situation in the 1950s – when the pressure came above all from the right – and the 1960s and 1970s – when it came, rather, from the left – in the 1980s socialists had to respond to *unprecedented pressure*. In the face of the breakthrough and impact of neoliberal ideas, a 'neo-liberalization of the debate' occurred at the very heart of the social-democratic ideological universe in the course of the 1980s. The socialists' new rhetoric and practice (promotion of the market, competitive austerity policies, reform of the welfare state) have contributed significantly to the redefinition of social-democratic identity. In effect, confronted by the dual ideological competition of neoliberalism and the 'new politics', socialists and social democrats have doubly 'retreated': they have gradually become *simultaneously more 'neoliberal' and more 'new left'*. The defection of part of their traditional electorate, particularly the popular component, was the logical consequence of this *simultaneous dual turn*.

This turn has generated a deficit of self conception, a profound doubt about social-democratic identity. The key indicators that historically made up social democracy's *partisan imaginary* (e.g. its perception as a left-wing party confronting the right, as the party of labour and equality confronting the forces of capital and inequality, as the party of ideals confronting opponents bereft of an ideology, etc.) – these have been blurred. The result is a confusion about its identity. As Donald Sassoon has emphasized: 'it is not because of electoral losses or the collapse of the industrial working class that one can talk of a "crisis" of socialism. It is because the socialist movement was forced to renew itself *by going outside its own traditions and re-examining its own basic values*'.[10]

Accordingly – particularly in countries where 'new politics' formations have more or less consolidated their positions – social democrats have found themselves caught between *three* contrary pressures that are difficult to reconcile: one radical and post-materialist, deriving from the ecological/libertarian left; another moderate and pro-capitalist, deriving from the right; and a third hostile towards liberalism (and often mistrustful of

post-materialism), deriving from their 'privileged class' and their own
social-democratic tradition (now represented by the trade unions, the left
wing of the party and, in some countries, by communist and ex-communist
formations). In addition, we should note that the resonance of some 'old'
left themes (especially defence of the welfare state) has been amplified by
the fact that a large part of the 'post-materialist' and libertarian left
(whether Green or Red-Green in complexion), particularly influential in
the public sector, tended to adopt an ever more firmly social and anti-
neoliberal vocation. The new left, whose rhetoric has been largely 'pirated'
by the social democrats, has thus readjusted its position on the 'material-
ism/post-materialism' axis. It has progressively adopted a more composite
and rather more 'materialist' profile.

The Programmatic Response of the Socialists

If the socialists have retreated under the impact of the twin threat posed by
neoliberals and 'left-libertarians', they have done so in order to defuse the
dynamic of their competitors by appropriating some of their themes. They
have retreated, the better to counterattack. The fact that the great majority
of European countries were governed by socialists towards the end of the
1990s is eloquent testimony to the effectiveness of this counteroffensive.
But on the basis of what strategic formula?

With reference to the British Labour Party, Ivor Crewe has described the
new strategy of socialists and social democrats – the strategy of 'natural
party of government' – as follows:
  i. the abandonment of policies tailored to specific group interests and
      demands in favour of across-the-board appeals to the consensual
      values of the whole electorate
  ii. the substitution of electoral for ideological criteria in policy-making
  iii. the elevation of image management above policy detail as the
      centrepiece of the party's communication strategy ... with an
      emphasis on 'competence', 'responsibility' and 'respectability'.[11]
To these three characteristics of the 'natural party of government' strategy,
we might usefully add – or re-emphasize, at the expense of slight qualifications – the following features:
  iv. Occupation of the semantic field of 'modernity' and 'renewal'.
      Investment of the terms 'modernity' and 'modernization' by social-
      ists is not a new phenomenon. Did not the SPD win the legislative
      elections to the Bundestag in 1969 on a promise of 'creating a
      modern Germany'? Did not Harold Wilson's Labour Party, with its
      project of an alliance between science, technology and planning,
      and the ambition of modernizing the British economy, reproach the
      Tories with being 'reactionary' in 1964? Today, occupation of the

semantic field of 'modernity' – and the keywords associated with it ('new', 'renewal', 'competence', 'responsibility', 'efficiency', 'openness') – is the great socialist/social-democratic response to the 'modernity deficit', real or alleged, of 1980s and 1990s socialism. This deficit was due to changes in social stratification and contraction of the left's 'natural' social base, as well as the neoliberalization of debate within advanced capitalist societies. Hence the similarity of discourses on the 'modern' and 'modernization' throughout Europe. In reality, the themes of 'modernity', 'competence' and 'responsibility' possess the strategic advantage of attracting part of the conservative electorate, without alienating the hard core of the social-democratic electorate. This being the case, the historically highly polysemic terms 'modern' and 'modernity', which have a long and weighty political history on the left, are at present almost inevitably charged with markedly technocratic connotation and social-liberal overtones, in line with the spirit of the age.

v. The great value placed on the leader, whose 'personal' equation becomes the focal point of election campaigns, and whose autonomy is considerably enhanced. A famous leader with a 'modern' profile corresponding to the 'spirit of the age' becomes an irreplaceable political and electoral weapon.

vi. A political-programmatic formula developed around *three* themes: a more or less classically social-democratic thematic, directed towards growth (and the traditional values of the left: social equality, welfare state, employment); a 'post-materialist' and 'anti-authoritarian' thematic, sceptical of growth; and a third thematic of neoliberal inspiration (extolling market logic, monetary stability, obsession with austerity as well as a discourse of 'sacrifice'). This triple thematic, this series of options and priorities, yields an all-encompassing programmatic discourse of the catch-all variety, the product of several coexistent matrices that are distinct and ultimately contradictory. The upshot of this composite profile is often the sense of a symbolic and programmatic vacuum – or rather, since it always comes down to the same thing, an excess. In addition, in some cases (especially New Labour, the SPD under Schröder, and the PSB), a fourth thematic, focused on *moderate* exploitation of the traditional conservative theme of 'law and order' (notably anti-crime measures, tighter control of immigration), forms part of the programmatic apparatus of the 'natural party of government' strategy. Obviously, the balance between these three (or four) thematics varies appreciably from country to country, and changes according to the period and competitive stimuli, or whether the party concerned is in government or in opposition. Various combinations, decisions, priorities, symbolic routes are possible. But in all cases, social democrats/socialists are at present continuously zigzagging between these three (or four) thematics, which have become their main hobbyhorses.

vii. Within this diverse and complex programmatic apparatus, which does not convey the image of a coherent and stable synthesis, the neoliberal option (competitiveness, price stability, balanced budgets, reduction of social expenditure, privatization, deregulation and 'liberalization' of the economy, 'commercialization' of an increased range of activities, stabilization or reduction of the tax 'burden', greater labour flexibility, pragmatic management) *gradually but systematically* gains ground, establishing itself as a constitutive element in the distinctive new stamp of the contemporary social-democratic enterprise. *The neoliberal option ceases to be adopted as a 'constraint'*, as was the case during the 1980s. It stops being a barely welcome or badly tolerated alien intruder, disrupting the ideological/programmatic coherence of social democracy. Particularly in the second half of the 1990s, this intruder becomes a *natural* part of the universe of the new social democracy.

Nevertheless, notwithstanding some overhasty assertions, the 'social' (and associated keywords: solidarity, social cohesion, equality) remains at the heart of social-democratic programmatic options. Historically constituted as an emblem of the social-democratic parties, and serving as a rallying cry to their members and voters, the 'social' still remains the principal point of demarcation between right and left. The credit of these parties not only with their working-class electorate, but also with some of their middle-class voters, stems from their capacity to present themselves as a vehicle for rectifying inequalities. The work of ideological and theoretical innovation hitherto carried out by what is called the 'new' social democracy, however iconoclastic, does not really challenge the priority of the theme of solidarity. Thus – and this is more than symptomatic – *the 'social' was at the heart of the most recent election campaigns by socialist parties in Europe* (struggle against unemployment, preservation of an albeit reformed social security system, reduction in working hours in the case of some parties, measures to help the disadvantaged, etc.).[12] In the social-democratic rhetorical system, 'social cohesion', 'solidarity', 'social justice' are stipulated as prerequisites, at once moral and economic, of any well-governed society: 'neo-revisionism involves rejecting old policies, not old ethical principles, old ways of achieving desirable ends, not the ends', Donald Sassoon has written.[13] Yet this is only partially true. To take an example: the concept of equality has often become 'equality of opportunity' or 'equality of life chances' (particularly in Great Britain); and the 'right to work' has become 'employability'. In reality, the new social-democratic elites have only partly renounced the 'traditional' values and cultural codes of the postwar period. But seeking to reactivate the inherited partisan imaginary, without at the same time neutralizing it through all this labour of 'redefinition', 'reinterpretation' and 'enrichment', amounts to a Herculean task.

At root, the definition of the 'social' and of 'equality' by contemporary socialists/social democrats is largely conditioned by *acceptance of the neoliberal option*: their proposals in social policy like to think of themselves as 'realistic', and must submit to economic 'constraints' and the imperative of the national economy's 'competitiveness'. Thus, *neoliberal* and *anti-liberal* ingredients coexist, constituting a double-edged system of ideological/programmatic reference points. This system, within which different ideological/programmatic options are possible, produces stances adjusted to the circumstances of political competition and/or the interplay of inner-party power.

To summarize: ultimately, social democracy's move towards a moderate neoliberal discourse, embellished with a more traditionally social-democratic social discourse as well as a post-materialist sensibility,[14] creates a somewhat 'social-liberal' programmatic profile. With ever-increasing difficulty, neoliberal-inspired modernization is concealed beneath a rhetoric that merely condemns the 'excesses' of economic liberalism: 'unbridled liberalism' or 'ultra-liberalism'. And the struggle against poverty is increasingly reduced – even at a discursive level – to the struggle against 'social exclusion'.[15]

Of course, the semantics of discourse and those of action are not identical. This is an ordinary and routine law of political life. As for the 'semantics of actions', the neoliberal option ends up weighing heavily in socialists' governmental practice, despite a more composite discourse inflected to the 'social'. Moreover, implementation of the 'natural party of government' strategy occurs largely 'at the expense of the traditional blue-collar sector and especially workers in uncompetitive and declining industrial branches'.[16] Thus, moderate economic liberalism, which – particularly since the second half of the 1980s and still more in the 1990s – has infiltrated socialist programmes, sets its stamp very clearly on their actions in government (see Chapter 10). *At a governmental level, liberal economic logic is dominant*; neo-Keynesian and ecological compensations get the meanest share.[17]

viii. The objective of the 'natural party of government' strategy 'is to build an even broader social/electoral coalition than ... the social democratic "catchall" approach of the 1950s and 1960s because it appeals to groups outside the white-collar and blue-collar working classes ... by offering "something for everyone" to match the electoral appeal of conservative parties'.[18] In reality, this strategy, an updated and renovated formula of the semi-catch-all strategy of the 1950s and 1960s, constitutes the *historically most striking and emphatic social opening* to the middle classes and the world – and civilization – of enterprise. Simultaneously, at the level of rhetoric it represents the accentuation of an existing trend: socialist discourse addressing itself to either the whole electorate, or segments of the electorate, on the basis of a *less and less classist* semantics. Stress is clearly put on consensus, not class divergence. Hence the technocratic, 'responsible' and 'modernist' character of the current discourse. Hence also

the semantic shift, in the group orientation of the discourse, from
social classes and *quasi-classes* (high-, middle-, and low-wage earners,
employees and employers), to *individuals* (the citizen, the voter), to
non-classes (families with children, savers, women, youth, the elderly,
etc.), or to the entire '*nation*' (the people, the voters, etc.). Today,
socialist/social-democratic parties combine, and aim to combine, the
most advanced 'ideological de-polarization' with the most developed
interclassist sociological format in their history. But this does not
mean that they opt for 'pure' interclassist strategies.

Overall, then, and setting aside national specificities, these parties present themselves in ideological and electoral competition as – at one and
the same time – *moderately neoliberal, moderately close to 'old-style' social democracy, moderately attuned to the 'new politics', and – exceptionally – moderately 'law
and order'*. Simultaneously, they present themselves as resolutely 'modern',
'open', and 'competent' parties, parties 'of all the people'. 'Moderation'
and 'modernity', the distinctive and pervasive marks of the new strategy,
aim to produce a 'positive bandwagon' effect: reinforcement of socialist
influence among all social classes and categories, particularly blue- and
white-collar workers. Basically, the 'natural party of government' strategy
aims to make socialists the most 'modern' representatives of, and 'spokes-
men' for, the general interest. The socialist parties are *national parties of
government*, even when they are not in government.

The peculiarity of these strategies, which always bear the impress of
national history and the context of political rivalry, is that they are quite
often fleeting and uncertain about their boundaries, and fragment into an
extended series of particular cases. Today, however, unlike in the 1980s,
their centre of gravity is rather well-defined, as we have just described. In
fact, what the German social democrat Kurt Sontheimer wrote of the
imponderables in the SPD's programmatic debate in the 1980s more or
less applied to all the socialist formations of the period:

> The decision to embark on the programme review was taken in a situation in
> which it is extraordinarily difficult to arrive at a clear picture of developments
> in the world and in society. That is the dilemma in which the party finds
> itself. It knows that in these changing times, a reorientation appears necessary
> but change itself makes reorientation hard to accomplish.[19]

The 1980s were a decade of programmatic uncertainties, the absence of
any grand design, and pragmatic – and often opportunist – adaptation to
the constraints of governmental action ('governing as a learning experience'). The 1990s (particularly the second half) were years of *ideological
and programmatic clarification*. Today, although it is not definitive,
reorientation is sharper, more offensive than defensive, and tends to be
defined in more or less related terms across different countries.[20]

The Legitimacy and Variations of the 'Natural Party of Government' Strategy: The British, Italian and French Cases

New Labour and *Democratici di Sinistra*

In the second half of the 1990s, the social-democratic programmatic appeal was more clearly articulated, and its new contours became sharper. That is why I shall not attempt a systematic enumeration of the different national strategies, with a view to an exhaustive list: they will be defined comprehensively, not extensively.

Let me nevertheless make a small exception to examine three borderline cases more closely: the British Labour Party (and New Labour), the Italian Communist Party (and PDS), and the French Socialist Party. Absence of governmental legitimacy having been more pronounced here than elsewhere (for different, and often opposed, reasons), the strategic responses of these parties will make it possible – in and through their differences – to refine our analysis of the 'natural party of government' strategy.

During the 1980s, Labour's credibility gap assumed a cruel form for a party with a governmental vocation: a deficit in modernity and competence. Labour was seen as 'old-fashioned, incompetent and over-dependent on the trade unions'; as the party of 'a high-tax, inefficient and state-controlled economy'.[21]

In its strategy for government, the Blair group undertook a number of reforms. In the first place, it reformed the party organization (strengthening of party discipline, reduction in the influence of activists and trade-unionists, a politics of communication aimed at ensuring 'tight control over all policy pronouncements', a strong and quasi-plebiscitary leadership). Next, it redefined the ideological and programmatic positioning of Labour ('radical centre', abrogation of Clause 4, occupying the niche of 'renewal', 'change', 'realism' and the 'nation', major overture to the 'moderate middle-income majority' and the world of enterprise, an economic philosophy and programme strongly coloured by neoliberalism).[22] Through this profound (one might say 'unbridled') revisionism, Blair was able to create a clear and unambiguous contrast between 'old' and 'new'. The new options have been presented – and perceived – as a radical victory over the legacy of the past. Indeed, compared with the reorientation undertaken by the Kinnockites (Kinnock had likewise opted for the 'natural party of government' strategy), Blair's policy – following on from his predecessors, but dramatizing the design and complexion – sees itself, and is seen, as a project of transgression. Conferring high visibility on the revision in progress, Blair crossed a critical *psychological threshold*, and created a *symbolic rupture*: New Labour is a different Labour. The break is paraded, and infused with new references and ideas; on occasion it is even provocative. Thus, firmly brandishing its 'radicalism of the centre' and its politics of 'renewal', this great old party has ended up presenting itself as *the expression of moderation and modernity in the British party system,* as the *most modern* version of the public interest. New Labour, posing and imposing itself as a political force equipped to combine efficient technocratic management with political and institutional innovation, and these two objectives with the 'moral' exigency of greater social equity, has created a new 'interpretative order' in the British political system to its own advantage. And it matters little whether this fully pertains to the deregulatory paradigm imposed by Thatcher, with marginal modifications.

An identical project of transgression, in yet more radical form, was adopted during the transformation of the PCI into the PDS (1991). Electing to desacralize the past and its symbols, the Occheto leadership group clearly challenged Italian communists' 'sense of continuing identity'. The PCI, 'in transforming itself into a non-communist party of the left . . . removed the primary cause of a "blocked" party system'.[23] This was demonstrated by its accession to power in 1996, nearly fifty years after communist ministers were excluded from government by the Christian Democrat Alcide de Gasperi.[24] Certainly – at least since the spectacular strategy of the 'historic compromise' – the PCI was a party with a 'systemic' identity. Stamped with the seal of 'illegitimacy' on account of its communist character, with the historic compromise it had adopted a strategy of radical moderation, a strategy inconceivable for the overwhelming majority of European social democrats of the period, however resolutely moderate. Nevertheless, the *nome glorioso* remained a major obstacle on the PCI's path to legitimacy and power: the final obstacle for a party with a 'semi-social-democratic' ideology that dared not speak its name. The final obstacle – and the most important. For friends and foes alike, for the people and the elites, for every variety of power and counter-power, for communist militants themselves, the term 'communist' still designated a party that was different from the others, a party that could not be like the others. 'The name is our soul,' wrote a Greek poet. In effect, the abandonment of its name and symbols, symbols of identity, was a crucial victory on the score of legitimacy (and hence the 'natural party of government' strategy). As with the 'great revision' in the SPD symbolized by Bad Godesberg (1959) and the Grand Coalition (1966–69), in Italy the 'battle of the name' was above all a battle for the party's legitimation as a natural party of government.

The quest for governmental legitimacy, and the concrete content of this legitimacy, are always bound up with the national context, party-political and ideological, of competition. For the PCI, the important thing was its name: 'the importance of not being communist'.[25] For the Labour Party, the path to legitimacy goes through an affirmation – or rather, the emblematic exhibition – of its 'modernity' and 'competence': the importance of not being 'old-fashioned, incompetent and over-dependent on the trade unions'. For the SPD of the 1950s, legitimacy goes through its adaptation to the new national realities in a country traumatized by its division; it also, and simultaneously, went through exaltation of the party's 'modernity': the importance of not being 'red' and 'incompetent'. In all three instances, revision was *rectification* on the legitimacy front, an attempt to restore the electoral competitiveness of the parties in question.[26] Revision involved founding a strategy of large- or small-scale political conquests on a strategy of grand ideological renunciation. To revise is to turn 'handicaps' and 'defects' into positive weapons. It is to turn the 'pirated' rhetoric of competitors against them – even if that means largely adopting their way of seeing the world and society.

'The past is a scarce resource,' writes Arjun Appadurai.[27] But power is still more scarce.[28] The cases of Labour and the PCI (transformed into the PDS in 1991 and the *Democratici di Sinistra* in 1998) indicate that when the governmental illegitimacy – and electoral weakness – of a great left-wing party threatens to persist, the importance of the 'scarcity of power' tends to prevail over the 'scarcity of the past'. Hence a harsh settlement of accounts with the past. Hence the transgression of inherited party prohibitions and affinities. In both instances, the accusation of 'repudiating our past' has become the *cri de cœur* of the inner-party opposition – and justly so. The cases of New Labour and the PDS demonstrate what the 'natural party of government' strategy signified: 'we are moderation and modernity!'

La Gauche plurielle

In France, the persistent weakness of the left in the initial postwar period lay in its division, a direct result of the presence of a communist party that was powerful and sometimes hegemonic. This was the source of the socialists' inability to compete in enduring fashion in the centre, despite their 'right-wing' political profile. Thus, the SFIO was unable to establish itself as a credible force of government – not because it was not moderate, but because it was too moderate.[29] Now, the alliance between socialists and communists (sealed in 1972) turned out to be the appropriate political response to the congenital weakness of the French left, permitting it to establish itself as a natural force of government. Thus, the left's governmental vocation was established thanks to the revitalization of the left-wing discourse of the socialists, in and through a *left-wing* – not a right-wing – '*symbolic break*'. The governmental strategy of the Union of the Left in the 1970s (PS + PC + Left Radicals) was – by the standards both of France and of other European countries – a radical and somewhat centrifugal strategy. Obviously, the extraordinary skill of the socialist leadership of the time in managing the ambivalence, and in playing sometimes to the left and sometimes to the right, facilitated a rallying from both the 'left' and – above all – the 'centre' of the political scene: this was the 'centripetal paradox' of a centrifugal strategy.[30] It is therefore important to emphasize that the strategy of the Union operated only in part *conversely* to the other paradigms of the natural party of government strategy of the time (what Thomas Koelble called the 'socialdemocratic strategy').[31] Indeed, the strategy of the Union was 'paradoxical' and 'paradoxically' effective. It was paradoxical because it was simultaneously a strategy of 'oligopolistic competition', aimed at reducing the influence of the PCF, and one of 'vote maximization', aimed at making the left the majority in the country. It was paradoxically effective because, in making a strength of the contradiction, *it succeeded – almost simultaneously – on both counts.*[32]

Gérard Grunberg attributes the PS's return to power in 1997, following the dark years of the early 1990s, three factors:

(a) resolution of the central question of party leadership: only with the 1995 presidential election and Lionel Jospin's campaign did a genuine leadership impose itself at the head of French socialism, which until then had lacked an uncontested leader. Following his good showing in 1995, Jospin established himself as a leader who was competent, modern, popular, and – not least – largely uncompromised by the 'excessively liberal' economic policy of the preceding socialist governments (notably those of 1988–93);

(b) the policy of rallying the left (PS + PCF + small dissident formations), and its opening to the ecologists – something that had been stubbornly pursued by successive socialist leaders since the defeat of 1993;

(c) the reactivation of the left/right divide, particularly in the economic and social sphere, by advancing a political and programmatic platform inspired by a certain 'neo-Keynesianism'.[33]

Does 'French socialist voluntarism' – as Mario Telo called it[34] – represent a challenger to British 'new revisionism'? In certain respects, yes. For the French, the role of public power (national and, if possible, European) should not be restricted to protecting the market against its own excesses. Regulatory, redistributive and some entrepreneurial activity by the state is regarded as useful, even necessary.[35] Labour-market 'flexibility' is viewed with some mistrust. Commitment to a European power, economically active and in a position to guarantee the social state, is strong, and contrasts with the reserved attitude of British Labour, which conceives the EU as an economic zone largely unregulated by non-economic forces. Moreover, measures proposed before the elections (reduction of working time to 35 hours without loss of pay; creation of 700,000 jobs for the young, half of them in the public sector; a halt to privatizations, which in the event was not confirmed by governmental action; conditions on the franc's participation in the impending European single currency) conveyed the impression of a *moderate turn to the left.*

Thus, as in the 1970s, the French socialists' natural party of government strategy in the 1990s, combining an opening to the left with a 'rainbow coalition', is an original strategy by comparison with the majority of current strategic formulas for government. And it is no less effective electorally.

The success of the PS's governmental strategy can certainly be considered as a separate, isolated case, a sort of 'marginal' instance compared with the majority of 'normal' cases. Such an interpretation would reduce this strategy to the celebrated 'French exception'. However, this kind of explanation ignores the fact that the ideological course of the PS was not so 'exceptional', particularly after 1984. While it was in government (and particularly from 1984 to 1986 and 1988 to 1993), the PS contributed decisively to the legitimation of the neoliberal programme, and found itself in the vanguard of 'supply-side socialism'. It even found itself at the heart of European integration, and was among the promoters of the neoliberal-inspired Maastricht criteria. Moreover, this notorious 'exception' is only a semi-exception. Jospin's PS based its strategy for government on the same ingredients as socialists in other countries: an incontestable and popular leader; the register of 'modernity', 'responsibility' and 'competence'; 'across-the-board appeals to the whole electorate'; and a pragmatic, prudent and European approach to economic issues (which combined neoliberal logic with proposals derived from a 'soft neo-Keynesianism').

Nevertheless, it is still true to say that compared with what is proposed by New Labour or the majority of socialist and social-democratic parties, even compared with their previous record in government (1984–86 and 1988–93), the French socialists' programmatic and symbolic repertoire proclaims its left-wing credentials loud and clear, unquestionably containing dimensions that are scarcely neoliberal or non-neoliberal. As in other countries, the French PS's natural party of government strategy signified *la modernité, c'est nous!* However, this 'modernity' was not quite the same as that advanced by Tony Blair, Massimo D'Alema or Gerhard Schröder. The French case demonstrates that one 'modernity' is not necessarily much the same as another.

The 'Natural Party of Government' Strategy: The Factors Contributing to its Adoption

Thomas Koelble has pertinently demonstrated that the pace of adoption of the 'government party' strategy, and its concrete content (and the content matters!), depends on 'competing internal interests and the *intraparty games* played by politicians, activists and unionists'.[36] But this pace – and content – also depend upon international economic constraints, the swing of the ideological pendulum in a country, the intellectual climate, ideological struggle and, obviously, the 'articulation' of social interests. This remains true even where those interests do not participate in the 'intraparty game', because they find themselves virtually *outside* the socialist or social-democratic organization.

In this respect, the French and Greek cases are illuminating

'Today, there is room for a resolutely modern, authentically left-wing politics,' French Prime Minister Lionel Jospin asserted on 23 June 1998.[37] This space – whether rhetorical or real is largely beside the point – would have been inconceivable in France without the great strike movement of December 1995 and the 'social miracle' (Bourdieu) of the French unemployed movement. In effect, the impressive social mobilization of that December introduced other variables and considerations into the erudite discourse of the scientific-intellectual elite (particularly economists) and the strategies of political actors. This literally extraordinary demonstration proved a powerful advertisement against supporters of the neoliberal, modernizing and technocratic consensus, and served as a 'corrective' to it. As a result, the terms of a new rhetoric took shape on the French political scene and, more specifically, inside the PS – despite the fact that trade-union influence in the French PS is marginal, and consequently plays no more than an indirect role in the formulation of party policy. Thus, in a country where the neoliberal project seemed incapable of keeping its promises, and a society where the social movement was able to reactivate a whole 'egalitarian' cultural core, the formulation and deployment of a left-wing governmental strategy – or, to be more specific, more left-wing than the strategy of other socialist parties – was a perfectly 'rational' option. Basically, given the intellectual ambiance in the country, the presence of the PCF, the discredit of its own previous (neoliberal-inspired) adminis-tration, the PS could not have dreamt of presenting itself as the natural party of political alternation *without this left-wing option*.

Let us take another example. In the EU countries, the need to meet the convergence criteria stipulated by the Maastricht Treaty strongly encour-aged several left-wing parties in government to inflect their policy in a neoliberal direction during the second half of the 1990s. The risk of finding themselves excluded from participation in Economic and Monetary Union, which was often considered a major national political objective, made the 'race for the criteria' the vehicle of an important strategic repositioning (particularly in the three countries 'in danger': Italy, Belgium and Greece).

The case of PASOK is, in this respect, exemplary. Threatened with being held responsible for Greek estrangement from the EU, PASOK found itself 'compelled' to jettison its 'macroeconomic populism' of the 1980s, and work to enlarge the perimeter of the market (by privatizations) and reduce debt and the budget deficit.[38] Under considerable 'external' pressure (not missing the EMU train), particularly after 1996 PASOK conducted a major reorientation of its policy and ideological profile in a neoliberal direction.[39] PASOK, which has always been distinguished by its excessive 'tacticism' and frequent policy switches, definitively abandoned its initial strategy – the famous 'national-popular' strategy (with nationalist and populist overtones) – only in 1993 and, above all, from 1996 onwards. Basically, it has replaced the extraordinarily effective 'national-popular' strategy that established it as the 'natural party of government' with a different strategy conforming to the dominant model of the moment, and equally effective. Its very belated adoption was due less to the ultimately limited resistance of the trade unions and party organization (the great autonomy of its charismatic leader has allowed PASOK considerable tactical and strategic flexibility since its foundation in 1974) than to the extraordinary success of the previous strategy in electoral terms. This made a sizeable strategic turn far from rational, for in politics, as in sport, one does not change a winning team and strategy. However, the imperative of adaptation to the constraints of EMU, which rendered the 'populist' strategic posture of the 1980s utterly untenable, set up an irresistible dynamic without which PASOK's governmental credibility would have been irreparably jeopardized.

So, if it is clear that the adoption of a vote-maximizing approach 'is more difficult for parties with a strong organizational connection to blue-collar unions in declining industries',[40] it is equally clear that the content of this strategy and the timing of its adoption depend on various parameters (context of competition, ideological contest, 'external' constraints). Precisely in so far as it is a majority and governmental strategy, the 'natural party of government' strategy is linked in *constitutive* fashion to the representations and expectations of public opinion, as well as the ideological struggle within a society.[41] It is not a political/programmatic confection that emerges fully formed from the head of political decision-makers or intra-party games.

The 'Race to the Centre Ground' and Programmatic Convergence

The 'natural party of government' option has often been considered – not unreasonably – 'as the only choice social democratic parties have if they want to maximize votes'.[42] A rapid examination of the forms it has taken in the cases of Great Britain, Italy and France proves, however, that there is definitely 'a "leftist" and a "rightist" alternative within the government party strategy'.[43] This is confirmed by the Swedish social democrats' rapidly abandoned strategy of 'economic democracy' during the 1970s.

In the past, the distance between 'left-' and 'right-wing' alternatives was greater than it is today, and the contrasts were noticeably stronger (to take only three 'extreme' cases as examples: the SPD's Grand Coalition [1966–69] versus the French Union of the Left [1972–84], or the SAP's economic democracy strategy). At present, the distance between the different versions of the 'new' social democracy is considerably less. Ideological and programmatic convergence prevails over divergences. And even if he exaggerates somewhat, Laurent Bouvet is not very far from the truth when he claims that 'Blair often says out loud what numerous European social-democrat leaders think, or even do, on the quiet.'[44] To see in the divergences between 'Blairism' and 'Jospinism' an opposition between 'social-liberalism' and 'neo-Keynesianism' is thus to underestimate the many similarities between the French and British paths. The differences are certainly appreciable and significant at the level of discourse. Having rallied to the ideology of deregulation, and obsessed with embodying the 'centre ground', the British centre-left differs from the French socialists, who are closer to the 'people of the left' and a more interventionist logic.

But in terms of governmental practice, the two experiences do not diverge fundamentally (see Chapter 10). New Labour's strategy and the PS's 'plural left' strategy are different. But although they are distinct, they belong to a common genus, the same *eidos*. At present, a majority of socialist/social-democratic parties is situated between the French and British cases – two limit-cases – in a vast strategic and programmatic 'no-man's-land'.

Viewed from this angle, the French case, quite the reverse of blurring the distinctiveness of the governmental party strategy, only serves to bring out its content more precisely. As with the SAP's left turn in 1975 to an 'economic democracy' strategy – or, in another context, PASOK's 'national-popular' strategy in 1977–89, which made it a robust and quasi-dominant governmental force – the French experience proves that it would be erroneous to attribute a 'unique' content to the 'natural party of government' strategy. Hence, to identify it with different formulas for the 'race to the centre ground', as is generally done, is simply to perpetuate a misinterpretation. This misinterpretation certainly takes the facts into account, but takes account of only *some* of them. On the other hand, to regard the different socialist and social-democratic postures as irreducible to one another is to undervalue the *common* ideological, programmatic, cultural and sociological armature that unites socialism in Europe to an unprecedented degree.

The Magical Return of Social Democracy: From 'Ruse of Defence' to 'Ruse of Attack'

As I have shown, the electoral record of European socialism yields contradictory impressions and highlights the diversity of national situations. However, if we compare the period 1974–99 with 1960–73, socialist parties have experienced a noticeable erosion of their influence, without this preventing them from everywhere being in a position to exercise power, particularly in the second half of the 1990s (see Chapter 6). The majority of socialist and social-democratic parties are in, or have returned to, power. This is a 'magical return', in René Cuperus and Johannes Kandel's fine phrase.[45] Yet it does not constitute a miracle. This state of affairs permits some observations and justifies some hypotheses.

Considered over a long period, electoral socialism has unquestionably become more unstable and less robust. It has become weaker. But this does not necessarily betoken weakness. In systems of competitive democracy, strength or weakness is defined by a party's *competitive status*. This describes a *relative* position of strength whose true import depends on the electoral weight of the party, the electoral weight of its principal opponents, and the configuration of the 'opposing bloc', the rules of the game, the structuration of the party system. Now, even during the electorally very difficult

1980s, the socialist and social-democratic parties remained formations with a very strong competitive status. Their zone of electoral influence, which varied according to the party, was always *close to the governmental threshold*. This level of influence, however diminished in comparison with the past, allowed them either to be in power or legitimately to aspire to it in the comparatively short term, whether alone or as the dominant or equal partner in a coalition government. With the possible exception of the British Labour Party in the first half of the 1980s, social democrats were not a political force on the brink of catastrophe (notwithstanding approaches which exaggerate their 'decline'). To put it very simply: *they remained in the game of alternation*. Now, the first condition of success for major parties with a governmental vocation is precisely to be in the game of alternation. By continuing to present itself as the *natural* force of governmental alternation (for want of establishing itself as the left-wing alternative), social democracy was able to profit from the 'field of possibilities' – real and potential – peculiar to every electoral market.[46] If social democracy has not lost its role as the pole of alternation, it is largely because it did not lose its role as the dominant pole *within the left*.[47] This being so, social democrats have been well placed to attract the vote of those who become discontented with incumbent conservative governments – less as a function of their ideology or programme than because of their *central* (which does not mean *centrist*) strategic position in the disposition of party forces; and thus to renew their electoral vitality and governmental capacity.

If socialists and social democrats remained 'in the game', this was not solely down to them. It also depended on the opponent and the weaknesses of the 'opposing bloc'. The domination of neoliberal ideology has destabilized the whole of the left, but it has not installed a 'fundamental consensus' that enjoys the same legitimacy and stability as the postwar, social-democratic consensus. That consensus was based on an 'exchange', a veritable *quid pro quo* that allowed a conjuncture between three otherwise contradictory interests: the 'sectional' interests of the working class, the interest of capital in unfettered growth, and the interest of the national community in general well-being. By contrast, the conservative–liberal consensus was and is rather unilateral, divides society, and creates deep fractures. The base of consent has shrunk. Indeed, as Eustache Kouvélakis and Michel Vakaloulis have stressed, no new compromise seems set to take over from the defunct Fordism, because the 'capacity to define a common good that the "subaltern classes" would get something out of is in question'.[48] Thus, in so far as it exists, the new 'fundamental consensus' is passive and rather 'permissive'. Where it is active, it is solely at the level of the elites and those who find themselves 'on the "right" side of the social divide'. The neoliberal consensus among elites and strata which benefit from market liberalization has only partially found its logical continuation among the 'people'. In a sense, if the neoliberal wave has subsided fairly quickly, it is also because 'various sections of the middle classes did not identify with it'.[49] In other words, the nature of the conservative–liberal consensus was such that it precluded any transformation of the ideological and intellectual hegemony of the right into a durable political and electoral hegemony. The 'new right' has destabilized the traditional social zones of left-wing political-electoral influence, but it has not really been able to occupy them. The zones of 'social scorched earth' left behind by conservative/liberal administrations create, and re-create, *living* space for socialist forces. Peremptory diagnoses of the decline of social democracy have not taken stock of the reality – that is to say, the vitality – of this space.

Furthermore, the strong rise of the new populist extreme right in some countries certainly absorbs the left's natural social supporters, but it divides and hampers the classical right enormously. This facilitates the effectiveness of the socialists' natural party of government strategy. The 1997 victory of the 'plural left' in France would be inconceivable without the destabilization of the 'liberal-Gaullist' bloc by the rise of the Front National. Similarly, the electoral recovery of the Austrian social democrats in 1995 was greatly helped by the fear aroused by a possible post-electoral alliance between the ÖVP and the FPÖ.

In addition, the relative delegitimation of the communist and ex-communist parties, consequent upon the collapse of the 'planned economies', has lessened – at least temporarily – the possibility of formulating effective *class political appeals* to compete with social-democratic overtures – something that could have contributed to creating a wide and unbridgeable gulf between the social-democratic elites and working-class/popular strata.

All these reasons, however, would not be enough to explain the return in strength of the social-democratic parties without their labour of programmatic renewal. The new social democracy has won *not despite*, but *because* of, its novel programmatic profile.

'The game plan of the losing side', Norberto Bobbio has written, 'is to produce a synthesis of opposing positions with the intention in practice of saving whatever can be saved of one's own position by drawing in the opposing position and then neutralising it.'[50] Elsewhere (paraphrasing Machiavelli's language) I have dubbed the strategy described by Bobbio as *the objective 'ruse' of weakness*: the ideologically weaker party adheres to the stronger ideology of its opponent, 'copying' it *ideologically* the better to confront it *electorally*.[51] Thus, imitating the right, which partially adhered to its ideology in the initial postwar period, the moderate left has partially – that is, moderately – adhered to neoliberal ideology. In effect, confronted with the 'thematic victories' won by the supporters of neoliberalism and the 'new politics', social democrats have proceeded – as indicated above – to two major revisions: on the one hand, a neoliberal and 'modernist' *aggiornamento*, followed and complemented in some cases by a determination to occupy the 'centre'; on the other, an ecological and 'post-materialist' *aggiornamento*. In other words, they have 'copied' their opponents. But if this is the case, why have voters opted for the 'copy', not the 'original'? Why have they chosen social democrats who are in the throes of neoliberalization, not the neoliberals themselves?

Quite simply, because *social democracy is not – and cannot be – a copy*.

Take the example of neoliberalism. By virtue of its historical connection with the world of labour, its more popular profile and interventionist tradition, social democracy, even when it is 'neoliberalized', is *not neoliberal*. That is why, following an initial phase of profound ideological destabilization, it was able to establish itself as a force that is simultaneously both modern and equipped to *cushion the violence of neoliberal change*. Social democracy – neoliberalized social democracy – has precisely re-established its dominion in Europe *against* the neoliberals, amid the fears about inequality and insecurity provoked by the neoliberal project. The *fin-de-siècle* social-democratic victories were a reaction against the excesses of 'market fundamentalism'. To some extent, social democracy was able to integrate the neoliberal register, as well as the ecological/post-materialist register, into its own political rhetoric. This double 'grafting', ideologically questionable but electorally successful, indicates that contemporary social democracy is a political force with a great capacity for adaptation, not simply a short-sighted 'rustler' with narrow horizons. In all its versions (more or less liberal, more or less attuned to the 'new politics'), contemporary social democracy proves a formidable electoral operator. For it has been able to insert the 'pirated' rhetoric of its competitors, on both right and left, into its own programmatic-ideological rhetoric (orientated towards the social). It has thus turned the rhetoric of its opponents back against them. In other words – to persist with an idiom inspired by Machiavelli – it has shown itself brilliantly capable of *converting a 'defensive ruse' into an 'offensive ruse'*.[52]

Concluding Remarks

1. 'Typical' postwar social democracy, particularly the 'mature' social democracy of the 1960s, was able to construct and impose itself as a natural force of governmental alternation, as a political force with a majority vocation. In opposition, this allowed it, among other things, to attract the vote of those who were discontented with incumbent governments. It allowed it to 'identify itself with the opposition', even when it was not the only important organized opposition, and thus to attract the moderate and centrist vote. Now, this ability – which was neither given from the outset nor acquired permanently, and was not characteristic of every left-wing party – made parties of a social-democratic type 'competent' and 'moderate' *left-wing* forces (see Chapter 4). They were able – that is, legitimated – to exercise power.

2. However, in politics and ideology, nothing is ever definitively settled – particularly at a time when the adversary's ideas are dominant. The case of the British Labour Party in the 1980s or, in another register, the PCI (transformed into the PDS) – a semi-social-democratic party permanently in search of governmental legitimacy – has shown that the question of legitimacy remains (or can at any moment again become), at least for some parties, current. At present, the socialists/social

democrats, long identified with a political approach close to the *status quo*, do not have to prove, as they once did, that they have jettisoned their anti-capitalist credo. The radicalism of their project is no longer a genuine political issue. Instead, since the second half of the 1970s, the challenge – in some countries, at least – to their status as a natural governmental force has been due to the disillusionment caused by their inability to steer the capitalist socioeconomic system effectively. It is, above all, the shipwreck of 'economic leftism' that has dictated a labour of programmatic renewal, to effect a new conjuncture between the 'only possible alternative' and the 'natural alternative'.

3. Amid the growing penetration of neoliberalism, socialists had to prove their 'modernity' and 'credibility' if they were to be accepted (or once again accepted) as legitimate claimants to government by a large proportion of the electorate and the 'centres of power and authority'. Above all, amid conflicting pressures from left, right, or 'neither left nor right', they had to invent an electorally winning programmatic/ political formula, to (re-)establish their majority, governmental capacity. For that is the issue of issues for social democrats. It was the main engine *behind* the programmatic debate in the European socialist parties in the 1980s and 1990s. It was the great 'dark shadow' that hung over this debate.[53]

4. In adopting the 'natural party of government strategy' – better, in adapting it to new realities – socialists remained true to themselves. In largely abandoning their postwar programmatic options, they confirmed and perpetuated a constitutive element of their identity: their governmental vocation. Hence this paradox: ideological infidelity is not a sign of some break in continuity, but – and above all – a sign of *continuity*. Indeed, posing as the natural force of governmental alternation is an attribute that pertains to the deepest identity of the electoral operator called 'social democracy', such as we have known it during the postwar period. It is constitutive of the philosophy – and physiognomy – of social democracy, as of every political formation with a governmental vocation. Today, this vocation again imposes itself as a constituent that stems from the innermost being of social democracy. Socialists are attracted by the state, and 'strong attraction' has long formed part of their deepest being. Social democrats are like that. And in the final analysis, it would be 'non-social-democratic' for them to stop being like that.

5. Obviously, attaining natural party of government status, which opens the path to power, is not something that comes free of charge today, any more than it did in the past.[54] This access, as well as the ideological, programmatic and organizational costs it entails, moulds and remoulds socialist and social-democratic identity. Indeed, opting for the 'natural party of government' strategy appears to be the principal trigger or accelerator of the redefinition of programmatic choices and, often, of the reinterpretation of the values and symbols of great left-wing parties lacking governmental legitimacy or losing electoral momentum. It is at

the heart of projects of political innovation, whether these incline to the 'right' (most often), or the 'left' (less often). In a context of increased competitive pressure from left, right, or 'neither left nor right', and of social democrats' diminished ability to defend their identity and social and ideological territory, the programmatic and ideological 'response' has become more composite, more complex, full of internal tensions. The social democrats' position – and their degree of security – in the arena of party competition has changed. So has their response – and, with it, social democracy.

6. The new social-democratic 'appeal', product of a maturation that was gradual but, in the end, fairly rapid, makes the new social democracy a moderate force programmatically and ideologically: *moderately liberal, moderately anti-liberal, moderately ecological and 'post-materialist'*. The new social democracy contains a little bit of everything: some 'new politics', a little neoliberalism (no doubt a little too much!), a dose of social democracy. But it is radically 'modern'. In its programmatic identity, it is a '*trans-border*' force – capital and labour, liberalism and anti-liberalism, regulation and deregulation, materialism and post-materialism, 'security' themes and cultural liberalism, old politics and new politics. The new social-democratic discourse is, in the majority of cases, *minimalist*: profoundly catch-all, profoundly flexible, profoundly pragmatic, and profoundly middle-of-the-road (which does not mean centrist). To use Donald Sassoon's term, social democracy constructs itself as an ideologically 'modest' force. It is open to the ideas of competitors on the left, the right, and the 'neither left nor right'; open – and this is too often forgotten – to 'apolitical' ideas, and also open to 'things unsuspected and incongruous'.[55]

7. However, this social democracy with a 'trans-border' identity is not unaware of the danger of straying too far from its social and ideological roots. Hence its insistence (which is not merely rhetorical) on the social aspects of its political approach, and the frequent resort to traditional, and less traditional, left-wing themes (unemployment, the fight against social exclusion, social justice, equality, etc.). Even the most 'right-wing' social democrats do not really challenge the priority of the theme of equality (New Labour does so only in part). Even as redefined, equality is the theme – and site – where the left's identity is rooted, where its fidelity is rooted. Accordingly, insistence on it is not a subsidiary feature in social democracy's current programmatic identity. On the contrary, it is constitutive of that identity.

8. Nevertheless, the new programmatic 'solution' is not a mere pragmatic and moderate correction of the traditional social-democratic profile (which was already 'pragmatic' and 'moderate'). On the contrary, it is a *veritable redefinition* of it. For neoliberal-inspired modernization, as well as the implementation of policies of deregulation and competitive rigour by socialists in government, directly challenge the hard core of the postwar programmatic formula: the socially and economically active role of the state, and the interests of the most deprived sections of the

population. Thus, the latest phase of revision goes well beyond the political framework of postwar revisionism, even if its most conspicuous aspects come within its scope (see Chapter 17).

9. Having reacted to the dynamism of its competitors very effectively, and proved itself ready to envisage a real examination of its political and economic strategies, social democracy is clearly the victorious camp as we enter the twenty-first century. Unquestionably, this 'victory' is due in large measure to the weaknesses of the 'opposing bloc'. But it is also due to the extraordinary capacity for renewal of socialist formations. Everything suggests that this capacity for renewal – in the language of political punditry, 'strategic flexibility' – is today becoming an important feature of socialist and social-democratic parties (both 'left-wing' and 'right-wing'). It forms *part* of the new social-democratic identity. Possibly the most significant aspect of the new social-democratic programmatic profile is not the profile itself, but the very fact that it has been adopted.

10. The new social democracy has won because it has changed. It has not won despite its programme and 'new look' profile, but because of it. To deny this and expect social democracy, having won in this way, to behave as if it was not the '*new*' social democracy is to deny the profundity of its switch in identity. Without a doubt, it was an 'insipid' and extremely moderate socialism that won the elections in the second half of the 1990s, not an ideological, class socialism.[56] But it, and it alone, enjoys the legitimacy of the popular vote. And it is of little importance here if that legitimacy is fragile.

Notes

1. Herbert Kitschelt, 'Left-Libertarian Parties: Explaining Innovation in Competitive Party Systems', *World Politics*, vol. XL, no. 2, January 1988, p. 200.
2. The combined score of the left opposition in Greece (KKE + Left and Progressive Coalition + DIKKI) was 15.01% in the 1996 legislative elections, 20.7% in the 1999 European elections, and 11.41% in the 2000 legislative elections.
3. My calculations relate solely to legislative elections. On the map of communist influence after the 1999 European elections, see Marc Lazar, 'PCF: beaucoup de bruit pour rien . . .', *Le Monde*, 16 June 1999.
4. The British Labour Party, strongly marked by its working-class and popular tradition, and also by the role of socioeconomic issues in the structuration of its internal divisions, and highly 'protected' by the electoral system, has remained unreceptive to the emergence of post-materialist values and themes. This is also the case with the Belgian PS, which, before incorporating the ecological problematic into its programme (in the 1990s), 'resisted' the temptation of the 'new politics' more than other socialist parties. Confronted with the rise of qualitative demands, it invariably displayed 'the contempt of a hegemonic formation in the French-speaking part of Belgium and a traditional workerism due, in large part, to the pressure of the FGTB' (Pascal Delwit, 'Le Parti socialiste', in Delwit and Jean-Michel de Waele, eds, *Les Partis politiques en Belgique*, Éditions de l'Université de Bruxelles, Brussels 1996, p. 36).

5. Kaare Strom and Lars Svasand, 'Political Parties in Norway: Facing the Challenges of a New Society', in Strom and Svasand, eds, *Challenges to Political Parties: The Case of Norway*, University of Michigan Press, Ann Arbor 1997, p. 24.
6. Francine Simon-Ekovich, 'La gauche et l'écologie. Quelle adaptation possible?', in Marc Lazar, ed., *La Gauche en Europe depuis 1945*, Presses Universitaires de France, Paris 1996, p. 460. In Scandinavia, particularly Sweden, Norway and Finland, a 'green' centre constituted around an ex-agrarian centre has 'tapped' the ecological thematic, often trapping the social democrats, together with the 'new left' parties, in a vice (ibid., pp. 463–4).
7. Stephen Padgett, 'The German Social Democrats: A Redefinition of Social Democracy or Bad Godesberg Mark II?', in Richard Gillespie and William Paterson, eds, *Rethinking Social Democracy in Western Europe*, Frank Cass, London 1993, pp. 25, 33.
8. Diane Sainsbury, 'The Swedish Social Democrats and the Legacy of Continuous Reform: Asset or Dilemma?', in *Rethinking Social Democracy in Western Europe*, pp. 41, 52.
9. See Erich Fröschl and Karl Duffek, 'The Austrian Experience. Debates on the Austrian Social Democratic Platform', in René Cuperus and Johannes Kandel, eds, *European Social Democracy: Transformation in Progress*, Friedrich Ebert Stiftung, Amsterdam 1998, p. 184.
10. Donald Sassoon, *One Hundred Years of Socialism*, I.B. Tauris, London 1996, p. 679; emphasis added.
11. Ivor Crewe, 'Labor Force Changes, Working Class Decline and the Labour Vote: Social and Electoral Trends in Postwar Britain', in Frances Fox Piven, ed., *Labor Parties in Postindustrial Societies*, Oxford University Press, New York 1992, p. 42.
12. On the main campaign themes of the socialist parties in the most recent elections, see the excellent book by Guy Hermet, Julian Thomas Hottinger, Daniel-Louis Seiler, eds, *Les Partis politiques en Europe de l'Ouest*, Economica, Paris 1998. This book offers a practical guide to political parties in western Europe.
13. Sassoon, *One Hundred Years of Socialism*, p. 738.
14. The latter is more marked in Scandinavia, Germany, and the Netherlands, less so in Austria, and rather weak in Great Britain, Belgium or Greece.
15. Of course, in some cases the trend towards neoliberal themes is stronger (e.g. New Labour in Great Britain, PSOE, PASOK after 1996). In others, the tendency is less marked (e.g. SAP, DNA, Danish SD, Belgian PS, British Labour Party in the second half of the 1980s, SPD in the 1980s, French PS since 1995, PASOK up to 1989).
16. Thomas Koelble, 'Recasting Social Democracy in Europe: A Nested Games Explanation of Strategic Adjustment in Political Parties', *Politics and Society*, vol. 20, no. 1, 1992, pp. 65–6.
17. The domination of neoliberal logic in social-democratic governmental practice makes it necessary to qualify the assertion of Donald Sassoon, who writes that 'neo-revisionism cannot be viewed simply as a right-wing, social-democratic takeover of "genuine" socialist parties, as traditionalists have all too often lamented. Right-wing social-democrats were pragmatic, trade-union oriented, statist and gradualist socialists. They had little time for feminism or ecology, which they regarded as middle-class fads. In contrast, neo-revisionists often originated from the first "New Left", and had been deeply influenced by the new individualist politics of the 1960s and 1970s' (*One Hundred Years of Socialism*, p. 736).

18. Koelble, 'Recasting Social Democracy in Europe', p. 54.
19. Quoted in Padgett, 'The German Social Democrats', p. 35.
20. Socialist and social-democratic victories in Germany (1998), Great Britain (1997), Greece (1996 and 2000), in Italy with the PDS (1996), Portugal (1995), the Netherlands (1994), and in the Scandinavian countries, were secured along programmatic lines close to those described above.
21. Peter Kellner, 'Why the Tories were Trounced', Parliamentary Affairs, vol. 50, no. 4, 1997, p. 629.
22. See Dennis Kavanagh, 'The Labour Campaign', Parliamentary Affairs, vol. 50, no. 4, 1997, pp. 534–8; Colin Leys, 'The British Labour Party since 1989', in Donald Sasson, Looking Left, I.B. Tauris, London 1997, passim.
23. Martin Bull, 'The Great Failure? The Democratic Party of the Left in Italy's Transition', in Stefen Gundle and Simon Parker, eds, The New Italian Republic, Routledge, London and New York 1996, p. 159.
24. Ilvo Diamanti and Marc Lazar, eds, Politique à l'italienne, Presses Universitaires de France, Paris 1997, p. 100.
25. David Kertzer, Politics and Symbols: The Italian Communist Party and the Fall of Communism, Yale University Press, New Haven, CT 1996, p. 69.
26. The condition of respectability, allowing these parties to establish themselves (Italy) or re-establish themselves (Great Britain) as legitimate forces of government, involved outside forces: recognition by economic and intellectual elites, the media, and the moderate electorate of the identity change of the parties in question. In this respect, it says a lot that in Italy, in contrast to the favourable attitude of the electorate as a whole, a majority of communist sympathizers and voters was at the time (1989) opposed to the name-change proposed by the party's leadership (Jean-Yves Dormagen, I comunisti, dal PCI alla nascita di Rifondazione comunista, Editori Koinè, Rome 1996, pp. 74–6).
27. Quoted in Kertzer, Politics and Symbols, p. 158.
28. Party competition always takes place 'within a context of the structural "scarcity of power"' (Danilo Zolo, Democracy and Complexity, Polity Press, Cambridge 1992, p. 44).
29. If the difficult process of legitimating the left proceeded in Italy (and Germany) via a strategy of radical moderation, which was an 'extra-ordinary' strategy in the strict sense of the word – i.e. a strategy utterly inconceivable for the great majority of parties of a social-democratic type enjoying greater competitive security – in France it required the extraordinary reversal in the balance of forces between the PS and PCF.
30. Gerassimos Moschonas, La Gauche française (1972–1988) à la lumière du paradigme social-démocrate. Partis de coalition and coalitions de partis dans la compétition électorale, doctoral thesis, University of Paris II, 1990, p. 420. In the words of George Ross and Tony Daley, 'centrifugal centrism' ('The Wilting of the Rose: The French Socialist Experiment', Socialist Review, vol. 16, nos 87–8, 1986, p. 38).
31. A strategy that was 'the optimal vote-maximizing strategy in the postwar period until the end of the 1970s' (Thomas Koelble, 'Intra-party Coalitions and Electoral Strategies: European Social Democracy in Search of Votes', Southeastern Political Review, vol. 23, no. 1, 1995, p. 134).
32. From 1974 the PS established itself as the dynamic and dominant partner within the Union (to the detriment of the PCF). With Mitterrand's candidacy in the presidential election of that year, the Union turned in an exceptional electoral performance, only narrowly losing the election.
33. Gérard Grunberg, 'La victoire logique du Parti socialiste', in Pascal Perrineau

and Colette Ysmal, *Le Vote surprise. Les élections législatives des 25 mai and 1er juin 1997*, Presses de Sciences Politiques, Paris 1998, pp. 189–93.

34. Mario Telo, 'Europe et globalisation. Les nouvelles frontières de la social-démocratie européenne', *La Revue Socialiste*, no. 1, 1999, p. 138.

35. Henri Weber, 'Parti socialiste français et *New Labour* britannique: convergences et divergences', *La Revue Socialiste*, no. 1, 1999, p. 22.

36. Koelble, 'Recasting Social Democracy in Europe', p. 66. The SAP and PSOE have adopted this strategy since 1982, whereas the SPD and Labour Party adopted it only in 1988, after a long sequence of electoral defeats. More specifically, according to Koelble, 'the influence of trade union preferences are a crucial component of any understanding as to why some social democratic parties exhibit such difficulties in adjusting to new socio-economic and electoral conditions and why others do not' ('Intra-party Coalitions and Electoral Strategies', p. 145).

37. Quoted in *Le Figaro*, 24 June 1998.

38. Gerassimos Moschonas, 'The Panhellenic Socialist Movement', in Robert Ladrech and Philippe Marlière, eds, *Social-Democratic Parties in the European Union*, Macmillan, London 1999.

39. However, this was a reorientation that had already been conducted to a certain extent in the period 1985–87 and in more coherent fashion from 1993 onwards.

40. Koelble, 'Recasting Social Democracy in Europe', p. 52.

41. It suffices to observe the market in left-wing ideas in France and in Great Britain. On the 'London consensus', see the analysis by Philippe Marlière, 'Le "London consensus": à propos d'Anthony Giddens et de la "Troisième voie"', *Mouvements*, no. 3, 1998.

42. Koelble, 'Intra-party Coalitions and Electoral Strategies', p. 135; Crewe, 'Labor Force Changes, Working Class Decline and the Labour Vote', *passim*.

43. Koelble, 'Recasting Social Democracy in Europe', p. 54

44. Laurent Bouvet, 'Le blairisme est-il un socialisme?', *La Revue Socialiste*, no. 1, 1999, p. 62.

45. René Cuperus and Johannes Kandel, 'The Magical Return of Social Democracy', in *European Social Democracy*, p. 11.

46. It must be emphasized here that the representative democratic mechanism always tends to 'protect' parties that adopt a strategy of power: the key rule of the majority, and the *binary* (not *bipartisan*) logic of the competition that flows from it, favour great parties with a governmental vocation.

47. The recuperation by social democracy of the themes developed by 'new politics' formations contributed to its consolidation as the pole structuring the left, as the uncontested pivot-pole on the left.

48. Eustache Kouvélakis and Michel Vakaloulis, 'Le retour d'une affaire classée', *L'Homme et la Société*, nos 117–18, 1995, p. 27.

49. Arnaldo Bagnasco, *Le Monde*, 23 December 1997.

50. Norberto Bobbio, quoted in the *European*, 21–27 September 1998.

51. See Gerassimos Moschonas, 'tichii kai panourgia', journal TANEA, 28 November 1997 (in Greek).

52. These terms are borrowed from Pierre Manent, *Naissances de la politique moderne*, Payot, Paris 1977, p. 21.

53. 'A recurring theme in the presentation of the Freedom Debate was the necessity of making adjustments to "new circumstances" so that Labour would remain a "40 per cent party",' Knut Heidar has remarked of the programmatic debate in

the Norwegian Labour Party ('The Norwegian Labour Party: "En attendant l'Europe"', in Gillespie and Paterson, eds, *Rethinking Social Democracy in Western Europe*, p. 67). This sums up the frame of mind that characterized programmatic debates in several socialist parties during the 1980s.

54. The balance sheet of 'natural party of government' strategies is often uncertain. The success of such enterprises is not always – or not exactly – as anticipated, as the case of the PDS indicates. Certainly, in liberating themselves from their past and adopting a very moderate politics, the Italian ex-communists have been able to present themselves as the natural force of political alternation, and – finally – to assume the function of relief team in the Italian political system. But – was this the price to be paid? – they have opened up a large space on their left, into which the advocates of the 'old name', Rifondazione comunista, have swept. Despite the overly optimistic predictions of the PDS leadership, Rifondazione has constructed a left-wing space (ideological, organizational and electoral), which enjoys considerable influence and competes with the PDS (5.6% of the vote in 1992, 6% in 1994, 8.6% in 1996, and 5% in 2001). Challenging the capacity of the PDS (*Democratici di Sinistra*) to control the left segment of the political and ideological scene, this radical left-wing rival is of a kind to destabilize the PDS (Diamanti and Lazar, *Politique à l'italienne*, pp. 107, 110).

55. Beck, *The Reinvention of Politics*, p. 163.

56. Gérard Grunberg, *Vers un socialisme européen?*, Hachette, Paris 1997, p. 137.

10

In Search of New Prophets:
From Keynesianism to Liberalism

The Questioning of the Social-Democratic Compromise

The Keynesian Equation Jammed

In becoming the flagship of the socialist and social-democratic parties, Keynesian policies made possible what was, for them, the electorally ideal conjuncture of three otherwise contradictory interests: the sectional interests of the working class, the interest of capital in unfettered growth, and the interest of the 'national community' in general well-being.

With the slow-down in growth, however, the intellectual and technical framework of Keynesianism proved of limited effectiveness in the conduct of macroeconomic policy. Reflationary policies through strengthening internal demand or supporting investment – traditional Keynesian measures to sustain growth, and hence employment – were sooner or later punished, given external constraints, by capital flight and an inflation/devaluation spiral. The failure of the various attempts at reflation 'in one country', particularly in France (1981–82) and Greece (1981–84), are sufficient testimony. In the 1970s and 1980s, the great economic and social synthesis of the social democrats, thanks to which they had asserted themselves as a victorious and resolutely 'modern' political force, seemed to be exhausted. The 'parties of reform', previously hegemonic, found themselves without guidebook or compass. 'It is as if we were walking on quicksand,' observed Kent Carlsson, then leader of the Swedish Young Socialists: 'We did not know how to get out of it. We questioned what we had always defended and were not in a position to formulate new solutions.'[1]

With the explosion of the crisis, economic expansion seemed subject to the supply-side imperative of realizing high profits, and thus to a redistribution of wealth in favour of capital.[2] The social cost of the policies of *competitive deflation*, implemented by states under the constraint of international competition, was very high (unemployment, job insecurity, and deterioration of the welfare state and public services). The Keynesian equation appeared to be jammed. And as in the 1930s, social democrats found themselves boxed in by the economic 'crisis' engulfing the Western world.

The Tripartite Social Pact Fissured

In addition, a complex set of factors tested arrangements of the 'corporatist' variety.[3] A certain decentralization of bargaining institutions and, very often, an oscillation between centralization and decentralization, was a sign of the new situation in the majority of countries with a strong social democracy.

In Sweden, country of neo-corporatism *par excellence*, the system of national co-ordination became 'increasingly weak after 1983'.[4] The mistrust of an influential section of employers towards centralized wage bargaining, evident since the 1970s, finally prevailed, despite the resistance of the social-democratic government and some sectors of the trade unions and employers.[5] Moreover, the less compact structure of the trade-union movement favoured this development. 'Independent' unions (unconnected to the SAP) of white-collar workers in the public and private sectors had formed bargaining 'cartels' in the 1970s. Initially, 'these cartels rode on the coat-tails of the LO–SAF accords, but in the 1980s separate and distinctive agreements became more common'.[6] In the 1980s and 1990s, industrial conflicts, as well as conflicts between blue- and white-collar workers and private- and public-sector employees, became more frequent, as did government intervention to 'mediate'.[7] Here too, as in Denmark, a significant reduction in the cohesion of the trade-union movement, indicated by the decline in inter-confederal concentration (increase in the number of 'peak-level union confederations'), clearly worked in favour of a certain decentralization of the system.[8] In sum: 'despite considerable oscillation between centralized and decentralized forms of bargaining since 1983, the data support the view that 1980 marked a significant shift away from centralized bargaining'.[9] Considerably more so than in other countries, the Swedish class compromise developed in the 1930s was first and foremost a *great national accord*, progressively assuming the form of 'macro-bargaining' between social partners. It was precisely this accord and *quid pro quo* – not a system of industrial relations – which came under challenge from the 1980s onwards.

In Denmark, a system of 'centralized decentralization' was on the way to being established,[10] particularly from 1981, year of the 'first truly decentralized round since the early 1930s'.[11] Industrial conflicts became more frequent, and their resolution involved government intervention, notably by legislative means, whoever held the reins of power. These frequent interventions impaired the celebrated 'Danish model', which involved social partners resolving their own problems.[12] In the 1990s, according to Wallerstein *et al.*, Denmark was 'moving toward a new system in which the main actors are neither the national unions and industry-level employers' associations nor the peak associations, but five bargaining cartels – for industry, construction, transport and services, municipal employees, and state employees – and their counterparts on the employers' side'.[13] Establishment of these multi-industry or multi-professional cartels, covering the totality of blue-collar and a majority of white-collar workers, had two combined effects. On the one hand, it intensified the fragmentation of the system; on the other, it restricted the scope of the trend to decentralization. Henceforth a combination of moderate centralization and moderate fragmentation appeared to mark the Danish industrial relations system.[14]

Signs of decentralization were equally evident in the Netherlands. Here, the consociational process of decision-making was in some respects close to neo-corporatism. It was based on vertically organized, rigid confessional and sociopolitical subcultures (Calvinist, Catholic, socialist, liberal). With 'depillarization' there set in an erosion of the 'highly centralized incomes-policy-based system' – the great change taking place in 1968 – in favour of a more decentralized structure, marked by a preponderance of branch bargaining.[15] More recently, the so-called 'Dutch miracle' of the 1990s owes much to the co-operative attitude and wage moderation of the unions. For many observers, the 'Dutch model' has become the symbol of a third way between Anglo-American deregulation of labour markets and the more 'rigid' systems of countries like Sweden or France. This model, which has contributed to a spectacular fall in the rate of unemployment without an American-style aggravation of wage inequalities and poverty, allies fiscal conservatism, wage moderation, maintenance of universal social security but with reduced benefits, and an active labour-market policy favouring part-time employment.[16] One of the most perverse effects of this policy – one among others – was a marked deterioration in the Dutch welfare state, impaired by a long dose of austerity.[17]

Throughout this period, centralized tripartite bargaining has not ceased to play a co-ordinating role, 'but it does not have the same compulsory character as in the 1960s and the solidaristic profile of wage policies has weakened'.[18] In sum, while it remains active, the institutional form of bargaining has evolved in Holland. The balance 'has shifted from a tripartite pattern of centralized collective bargaining, towards bipartite organized decentralization under the shadow of (state) hierarchy'.[19]

Historically, British trade unions are among the most 'conflict-oriented', despite their close association with Labour, a party that was in government on a regular basis until the end of the 1970s. The superficial unity and decentralized structure of British trade-unionism, as well as the symmetrical inability of British employers' associations 'to enforce collective agreements on employers',[20] largely account for the historically undeveloped and very unstable character of 'corporatist' arrangements in the United Kingdom. The chronic ills of the British economy and the tendency of Labour governments, despite electoral promises, to adopt policies of deflation and monetary rigour, have undermined all attempts at lasting national co-operation with the unions. Doubly prey to the indiscipline of their base and the programmatic renunciations of the party, union leaderships have (e.g. in 1969 and 1978) abandoned midway their policy of 'voluntary wage restraint in return for social welfare and labor law reforms'.[21] Thus, Labour was the victim rather than the beneficiary of industrial mobilization, and 'has twice been ejected from office in the midst of strike waves (1970,

1979)'.[22] The great anti-union offensive launched by the Conservatives after their return to government in 1979 led to a profound political and institutional weakening of the union pole, without equivalent in Europe. The erosion of union power, as well as the new-found self-confidence of employers, have favoured the 'disorganized decentralization' of the industrial relations system. In truth, it is more accurate to speak of an 'institutional collapse' in the UK, 'as employers have simply chosen to opt out of branch-level arrangements'.[23]

In power once again since 1997, Labour seemed to follow in the footsteps of the Conservatives, despite a more skilful and amicable management of relations with the unions. Certainly, 'the style and appearance of governance is noticeably more consultative and consensual than previously', particularly over social security and welfare policies, and differs from the overtly hostile attitude of the Conservatives.[24] However, especially in the first phase of the Blair government, the unions were largely excluded from any significant political consultation on economic policy – something that strongly distinguished Blair from his continental socialist counterparts.[25] Today, the bellicose rhetoric current in the trade-union world during the Thatcher years is being transformed into a more constructive and open attitude towards employers. The era of systematic confrontation is possibly over. But given the structure of the TUC and CBI, given the unions' power deficit, and given a long tradition of failure and a traumatic 'institutional memory', the advent of a 'new industrial partnership', centralized and enduring, seems to be no easy matter in the UK.

In postwar Germany, the 'dual system' of industrial relations ('Works Councils in the factory and highly centralised and professionalised unions at the national and regional level') played a major role in the preservation of social peace. Bargaining at regional and sectoral levels, generally focused on wage issues, was complemented at the base by enterprise agreements, and thus by a sort of 'unofficial second round of negotiations' conducted by the works councils. Meanwhile, the leadership of IG Metall and the employers' federation provided an informal mechanism of national co-ordination. In effect, the German system gravitated around collective bargaining at the level of industrial sectors and co-decision at the level of enterprises.[26] In this respect, it was less centralized than the Scandinavian systems, and policies of wage solidarity were significantly less advanced than in Scandinavia. It was on the basis of this structure that a tripartism of 'concerted action' was developed in the period 1967 to 1976, a rather weak centralized form involving the peak associations at national level.

This system facilitated solutions that were more flexible and better adapted to the situation of the individual firm.[27] The flexible and more 'employer-driven' character of German neo-corporatist structures (better attuned than elsewhere to the needs of individual firms) was conducive to a *better adaptation* to the 1980s and 1990s. Certainly, greater decentralization marked the system of industrial relations from 1976 onwards. The diversification of interests, the rise of alternative social movements, and the flourishing of so-called 'qualitative' demands also led in this direction.

Decentralization was complemented by a strengthening of works councils, which assumed 'an increasing role in the implementation of industry-level agreements on wages and technological change'.[28] In the long term, this is a development that could encourage trends to greater deregulation, since the number of large firms (where unions are robust) is declining, and the number of small enterprises (which often have no works councils) is increasing markedly.[29] More generally, the importance of the central scale diminished with the end of 'concerted action', something that was further encouraged by German reunification. Thus, the system rediscovered its 'natural' structure: bargaining at branch level, although weakened, remains dominant.[30] But despite these developments, the system has displayed remarkable robustness overall. In addition, the Schröder government seems to be encouraging the social partners to conclude macro-level agreements (e.g. the Alliance for Jobs). The new economic environment, both national and international, and the unification of Germany have 'both challenged certain particulars and reaffirmed the basic strengths of the German model'.[31]

By contrast, neo-corporatist arrangements have more or less persisted in Norway and Austria. In the first half of the 1980s in Norway, we observe the same tendency towards decentralization, but marked by high and low points and considerable instability. In the second half of the 1980s, on the other hand, the system was recentralized in such a way that by the end of the decade, national collective negotiations were among the most centralized in Norwegian history. The persistence of centralized procedures seems to be connected with the rapid development of the oil industry and the need to restrict 'the country's high and increasing wage drift, which accounts for two-thirds of all wage increases'.[32] According to Torben Iversen's analysis, after 1986 'cost sensitive employers and workers in the exposed sectors allied themselves with an "activist" government to control the militancy of privileged "maverick" unions and restore the competitiveness to Norwegian industry'.[33] Thus, a coalition formed by a large proportion of employers and the LO union confederation, under the strong impetus of the Labour government, encouraged centralization of a system that nevertheless experienced strong pressure towards decentralized collective bargaining. In fact: 'bargaining returned to the sectoral level in the 1997 bargaining round for the first time in more than a decade'.[34]

As in Germany, the Austrian system of interest mediation is structured around a small number of very centralized organizations and works councils. The latter are, however, more integrated into the national union than the German works councils. In Austria, the process of wage-bargaining is traditionally conducted at industry level, despite the fact that the ÖGB, the trade-union confederation, is very centralized, its 'statutory authority' over its affiliated organizations being the strongest in Europe.[35] In this system of decentralized centralization, the 'centralized leadership acts more like a referee in a multilayer game than a player bargaining the outcome directly with employers'.[36] Thus, particularly in large competitive firms with powerful workers' collectives, the national agreement on wages is followed by wage-bargaining at factory level, which often challenges policies of wage solidarity and favours wage drift.[37] This system, which is certainly less conducive than the Swedish, Danish and Norwegian systems to reducing wage inequalities, has facilitated flexibility and adaptability in incomes policy. Thus, notwithstanding the corporatist structure, 'nominal and real wage flexibility in Austria is one of the highest among OECD countries'.[38] Austrian neo-corporatism combines national co-ordination (and the intro-duction of macroeconomic criteria into incomes policy), industry-wide bargaining, and greater variation in wages at the level of the firm. This flexibility has allowed it to absorb external pressures arising from inter-nationalization and technological change better, without generating global opposition to centralized collective bargaining, as in Sweden and Den-mark.[39] At the same time, the profoundly consensual culture of Austrian elites, product of the experience of devastating conflicts in the past, has favoured the maintenance of national structures of co-ordination. In addition, the persistence, as in Germany, of strong inter-confederal union concentration, and the increase in intra-confederal concentration,[40] tend in the same direction. Nevertheless, however, the vitality of the institutions of national co-ordination is in decline, 'while the power of individual bargaining units and of work councils rose'.[41]

The Trend towards Decentralization

Thus, everything indicates a descending curve of centralized bargaining. Systems of national collective bargaining, bi- or tripartite, experienced their moment of glory in the 1960s and endured, despite tensions, for the next decade. They have since fissured.[42]

The reasons, which differ with the circumstances from country to country, have been extensively studied. They include:

(a) The strong rise of 'white-collar' unions (particularly in the public sector), and the contraction and growing fragmentation of the tra-ditional working class, have led to a reduced role for trade-unionism as a national, cohesive and representative institution. The decline in inter-confederal concentration – very evident in the Nordic countries, but also in France and Italy[43] – has played an important role in the crisis of centralized bargaining in the Scandinavian countries, the classical instances of corporatism.

(b) Strengthening in the labour-market position of the highly skilled and educated segment of the labour force – the 'winners' from technologi-cal change – has favoured the development of phenomena of 'micro-corporatism' and the establishment of more flexible systems of remuneration.[44] This challenges *solidaristic wages* policies, which can only be managed centrally.

(c) The changed priorities of employers, who demand greater flexibility in the labour market (typically, wage cuts) in a context of intensified international competition, lead to a crisis of centralized tripartism. For some, employers are the major protagonist of the trend to decentralization.[45] The expansion in diversified quality production tends in the same direction. Micro-bargaining in the framework of the firm – a framework that is now generally (but not invariably) *advantageous to employers* – encourages 'differentiated, rather than uniform, responses'.[46] This change is an important factor – for some, even the crucial causal factor – in greater decentralization. To put it simply: 'many employers no longer view centralized bargaining as a good instrument for the control of wage costs'.[47]

(d) European integration diminishes the importance of 'national fora'. Various aspects of economic and social policy become subject to regulation within the Union and are largely directed by it.

(e) The state's increasing inability, during the crisis, to act as 'guarantor' of the benefits legitimately anticipated by the social partners in return for their conciliatory attitude constitutes an additional obstacle to corporatist integration.

(f) The end, in some countries, of prolonged social-democratic domination, and the advent of an era of frequent alternation (Scandinavia), or protracted confinement of socialists to opposition (Germany, United Kingdom), were not conducive to systems of centralized collective bargaining.

Thus, overall, everything points to the lesser stability and effectiveness of established corporatist systems, and a displacement of the centre of gravity of industrial relations systems to the sectoral level and the micro-level of firms.[48] But the trend towards greater decentralization is not uniform, and the thesis of an 'iron law' of decentralization is unsustainable. National situations are very diverse; toing-and-froing between different levels of bargaining is now more frequent, as is government intervention.

However, if, among the countries examined here, we identify those that have displayed the greatest centralization in the postwar period (Sweden, Denmark, Netherlands, Norway), only Norway partially retains a centralized structure of wage-bargaining, albeit in markedly more unstable form. The trend towards decentralization predominates, accompanied by greater instability. If we take as our comparative reference point the period of 'concerted action' (1967–77), from one angle Germany, a composite case with a considerably less centralized format, also figures among the countries *en route* to decentralization. On the other hand, in Austria, a classic case of corporatism, the somewhat less centralized system of wage-bargaining, which combines bargaining by industry with the participation of peak associations, still remains more or less operative.[49] Overall – to adopt Torben Iversen's terminology – the *new balance* of bargaining systems currently weighs more towards the German side ('monetarist semi-decentralization') than the Scandinavian ('Keynesian centralization').[50]

A Few Words in Conclusion

Neo-corporatist regulation is not enjoying its best years. The trend towards greater decentralization is incontestable. However, it is not general and, rather, takes the form of 'organized decentralization' (Great Britain being a case of 'disorganized decentralization').[51] We should nevertheless emphasize that crisis and instability do not issue in the triumph of 'pluralism', or a sort of chaos in industrial relations. After all, with the possible exception of Great Britain (and, in a quite different context, the United States), the weakening of union federations, one of the two poles in the capital–labour pact, does not appear to be either profound or irreversible.[52] Thus, the various forms of 'social partnership' have not disintegrated. The crisis or reduced stability of the central level leads predominantly to the assertion, activation and enhancement of 'varieties of meso-level corporatism'.[53] Collective bargaining systems thus become 'more sector-centered'.[54]

Moreover, in the 1990s signs emerged of a certain revitalization of social pacts, following the enormous difficulties of the 1980s. The agreements contained in this *new generation* of social pacts are representative of the unions' defensive attitude, since they often lead on to a kind of negotiated deregulation – what Negrelli termed 'deregulation by consent'.[55] At all events, compared with the 'Anglo-American' model or southern Europe, the countries traditionally considered exemplars of 'corporatist systems' (Sweden, Norway, Denmark, Austria, the Netherlands, Belgium, Germany) still retain wage-bargaining structures that are a good deal more centralized than elsewhere.[56] Their centralized and semi-centralized bargaining systems, which make them 'co-ordinated market economies', remain qualitatively different from the fragmented bargaining systems characteristic of the 'liberal market economies'.

Systems of consultation thus remain institutionally dominant, but the general tendency towards a more decentralized balance is certainly not 'distributively neutral'. Centralization tends to favour the weakest in the labour market, and wage solidarity is administered at the central level. In particular, the severe testing of Scandinavian centralism – 'Keynesian centralization', Iversen has written, 'became both a barrier to competitiveness (by inhibiting flexibility) and a vehicle for wage redistribution rather than wage restraint'[57] – is politically significant. Fundamentally, the relative destabilization and 'flexibilization' of corporatist arrangements challenges – at least in part – one of the boasts of postwar social democracy: an *alternative structure of regulation* which, while not revolutionary, or the most effective form of regulation in the world, could always serve as a corrective to market regulation.

What is to be Done? Social-Democratic Responses

Since Keynesianism allowed the social-democratic parties to reconcile the imperatives of greater equality and efficiency in a kind of *virtuous circle*, and thereby perform the dual function (very rewarding electorally) of being simultaneously working-class parties and parties of all the people, it was abandoned only some time after the onset of the crisis.

Attached to Keynesian regulation and protection of the gains of a whole political and economic career – and epoch – social democracy, a reformist force *par excellence*, began to convey the impression of a 'conservative' formation. Like those 'prophets of the past' who were unwilling to adapt to the evolution of circumstances and ideas, it emphasized the defensive aspects of its economic and social approach. Thus, initially (the 1970s), it more or less clung on to the Keynesian programme, trying to implement it even in adverse circumstances. And in a second phase (the 1980s), influenced by the restrictive international environment and the domination of neoliberal ideas, it was prompted to take measures of a neoliberal sort (prioritization of the fight against inflation, austerity policies, increase in the income of capital owners at the expense of workers' income, dismantlement of certain aspects of the social state in order to stabilize costs and lighten the tax burden on enterprise). But these measures were taken 'with a bad conscience and more under the cover of darkness than in the full daylight of ... programmatic debates'.[58] Renouncing a credo that was considered outmoded, social democrats found themselves bereft of an intellectual framework to underpin their new pragmatism.

Since the second half of the 1980s, the social-democratic/socialist parties have begun to explain – and take responsibility for – the key ideas underlying their new governmental practice. In this respect, the formula of the French Prime Minister, Lionel Jospin – 'yes to the market economy, no to the market society' – perfectly encapsulates the new orientation, and major contradiction, of the new social democracy. The urge to harmonize two seemingly contradictory registers – regulation *by* the market and regulation *of* the market – is now the most taut and fragile strand in the new social-democratic synthesis.

This does not prevent these distinctly different registers – and instincts? – going in tandem, in a state of overt or latent intellectual conflict, yielding new political syntheses that lack vigour and consistency. Now, obviously, in the absence of consistency, only governmental practice, which is the litmus test for any great party, can end up producing it. Moreover, this is the only consistency that counts. And it inclines markedly to neoliberalism.

Social Democracy on the Defensive:
The Sketch of an Initial Social-Democratic Response

My argument here pertains not to economics, but to political science. It is not my objective (and I am not competent) to analyse the economic effectiveness, and draw up a balance sheet, of the policies pursued by socialist governments in the 'new era'. Accordingly, there is no question of resuming in detail here analyses better formulated elsewhere – analyses, incidentally, whose conclusions remain uncertain and controversial. Even so, the interest of these policies is worth underlining. Their successes and failures are *politically* significant. I shall therefore briefly examine, on a purely illustrative basis, two pairs of governmental experiences. The first involves Sweden and Austria, two cases considered 'exemplary' for the 1980s by the great majority of specialists. The second consists of France and Great Britain, regarded as representative of contemporary socialism on account of their real or alleged rivalry.

(a) *The Swedish Case*

The 'third way' of the Swedish social democrats in the 1980s, which they presented as distinct both from the inflationary course of traditional Keynesianism – briefly pursued by the French and Greek socialists – and from the deflationary neoliberal route taken by the British Conservatives, initially proved effective.[59] According to Pontusson: 'from 1983 to 1988, the Swedish economy grew at an annual rate of 2.7 per cent, the balance-of-trade deficit turned into a substantial surplus, and the rate of unemployment fell from 3.5 per cent to less than 2 per cent'.[60] The Swedish recovery was based on a major devaluation of the currency (16 per cent in 1982) and the wage moderation of the unions, and it was helped in the second half of the 1980s by a more clement international conjuncture. In addition, an active labour-market policy and expansion of the public sector sustained employment.[61] Thus, confronted with the stagnation of private service-sector employment, expanding employment in the public sector – contrary to what occurred in Great Britain and the United States – was very important for the period 1970 to 1992.[62] All this appeared once again to confirm the extraordinary capacity of Swedish social democrats, as in the 1930s and throughout the postwar period, to create jobs. Historically, this capacity was an essential component in the long hegemony of the SAP. The Swedish model of the 1980s, wrote Mario Telo in 1992, 'demonstrated, at the height of the Thatcher decade, that modernization could be compatible with social policy and employment'.[63] The victory of the social democrats in 1988 was just reward for an economic success that seemed exceptional at the time.

However, the SAP's policy proved incapable of containing inflationary pressures, which were increased by the crisis of centralized bargaining and the extension of wage drift. In a more inauspicious international economic context, having deregulated financial markets in 1985–86, the social-democratic government of the early 1990s resorted – what a historical irony! – to the arsenal of governments without any trade-union base of support: price and wages freeze, anti-strike measures, reductions in social security expenditure.[64] It became increasingly difficult to distinguish the policy of the social democrats, converted to austerity, from that of the bourgeois parties. A historical model was in the process of being progressively diluted. The SAP's severe defeat in 1991 – after three consecutive electoral victories, it achieved its lowest electoral score since 1928 – dramatized the social democrats' difficulty in establishing a societal model that combined social solidarity and economic efficiency. Worse still, for the first time the Swedish social democrats' accession to power left the bitter taste of an 'ideological void'. An identical void was experienced in Great Britain towards the end of the 1970s, following the failure of the Labour government's 'social contract'; in Denmark at the beginning of the 1970s; or – in a quite different register – in Greece and France after the end of the socialist intendancy (in 1989 and 1993 respectively).

The SAP's return to government in 1994, amid grave economic difficulties (large budget deficit, weak currency, rising unemployment), led it to pursue a policy of severe austerity.[65] 'Market solutions' have become the central criterion of economic regulation in the SAP's new economic policy, implemented gradually and accentuated since 1994. Thereafter, 'Swedish macroeconomic policy [was] again mainstream'.[66] With the triumph of market logic, and a particularly strict budgetary and fiscal policy, the Keynesian inheritance has vanished. The anti-capitalist overtones inherent in the reformist offensive of the 'wage-earner investment funds' (1970s) now appear only too distant – as does 'the most pronounced keynesian experiment in any of the OECD countries during the 1970s'.[67]

Membership of the European Union has reinforced a restrictive budgetary policy (the deficit in the state budget fell from 12 per cent in 1994 to less than 2 per cent in 1997!); a strong currency policy (the krona was aligned with the ECU from May 1991); selective reduction in some social benefits; an increase in wage differentials; rising unemployment (the unemployment rate was 8.1 per cent in 1997 and 6.5 per cent in 1998, against less than 2 per cent in 1990). As for the indicator of social equality, the share of wages in GDP has declined appreciably since 1994.[68]

The neoliberal reorientation of the SAP's policy and the social deficit of its economic administration – one is inclined to say: the social-democratic deficit of its social-democratic administration – are not irrelevant to the electoral rout of the party in September 1998 (36.4 per cent of the vote against 45.2 per cent in 1994 and 37.7 per cent in 1991, the latter being regarded as the black year of social-democratic electoral history). The extraordinary electoral progress of the Left Party (12 per cent in 1998, against 6.2 per cent in 1994 and 4.5 per cent in 1991), which campaigned on a fairly social-democratic programme, only serves to underline the changed direction of social democracy and the relative disintegration of the Swedish model. Truly hegemonic until recently – 'a virtual state ideology', in Sassoon's words[69] – Swedish social democracy has lost its originality both as a force with a distinct social and economic project and as an electorally winning force.

(b) The Austrian Case

From 1973 to 1980, Austrian policies achieved some remarkable results, noticeably better than most Western countries when it came to unemployment, inflation and growth. Combining a 'hard currency' policy to control imported inflation (the schilling had been aligned with the mark since the 1969 devaluation), very moderate wage rises (thanks to bi- and tripartite bargaining), an expansionary budgetary policy (to sustain demand and maintain employment), a fiscal regime favourable to investment and public investment programmes, 'Austro-Keynesianism' was able to safeguard competitiveness and full employment.[70] In the more restrictive international environment of the 1980s and 1990s, however, the specificity of the model was gradually diluted. Since 1983, Austro-Keynesianism has been progressively abandoned.[71] Thus, 'while maintaining the stabilizing elements of the model, i.e. the hard currency and moderate incomes policies, deficit spending as a discretionary strategy has been given up'.[72] The priority was no longer employment, but reduction of the budget deficit. Active industrial policy (historically based on a very extensive nationalized sector, but facing painful problems of restructuration since the second half of the 1980s) was definitively replaced at the beginning of the 1990s by a policy of privatization. Adopted less out of conviction than under the constraint of the budgetary stabilizer, and pursued throughout the 1990s, this policy placed Austria in the first rank of European countries that have launched major privatization programmes. The macroeconomic performance of the Austrian economy remained rather good – at least as good as the average for the EU and OECD countries, and better than Sweden's. And unemployment, rising sharply since 1981, remains fairly low according to European methods of calculating it (9.1 per cent in 1998, 4.4 per cent according to the Eurostat calculation). But the distinctive features of the Austrian social-democratic road have lost their relief and visibility of yesteryear. The tenacious pursuit of a policy of gentle liberalization throughout the 1990s, and up to their passage into opposition (after the election of October 1999), allow us to assert that the economic 'miracle' of the Austrian socialists (renamed social democrats since 1991), as well as their specificity, must be reckoned to be at an end.

(c) The Failure of the Crisis Compromise

As the Swedish and Austrian experiences indicate, social democrats, faced with crisis, appeared – after a good deal of experimentation and hesitation, and despite great national differences – to be able to implement what amounted (compared with the performance of neo-conservatism) to a rather effective policy, particularly during the second half of the 1970s and first half of the 1980s. Wage moderation, a direct result of neo-corporatist systems of national bargaining, and a prudently (but not always) expansionary budgetary policy, were the two common elements in what has been called – doubtless with a trace of exaggeration – the 'social-democratic compromise of the crisis'.[73]

The effectiveness of these policies, which varied according to the country, was confirmed not only in Scandinavia and Austria, but also in Germany. The double German success against inflation and unemployment, following the first oil shock, stemmed from a combination of anti-inflationary monetary discipline (ensured by the Bundesbank), a budgetary policy of prudent support for demand, and the wage moderation of the unions.[74] The policy of the German social democrats, which proved effective up to 1979–80, did not survive the second oil shock, however, and was predictably abandoned (particularly its budgetary component) by the new CDU–FDP government in 1982.

What must be emphasized here is that these policies – in Scandinavia and Austria, at least – were in large part *linked to the distinctive features that make up the identity of the social-democratic parties.* They were consistent with social democracy's 'policy style' ('the standard operating procedures for handling issues which arrive on the political agenda').[75] Accordingly, although they were very prudent and moderate, they were policies of a social-democratic type. In fact, what lay at the base of the 'crisis compromise', as at the base of the social-democratic compromise of the 1950s and 1960s, was the *classical pair* of social democratic party/trade union on the one hand, and so-called neo-corporatist co-ordination on the other, privileged strategic instrument for the pursuit of a long-term incomes policy. This was the real foundation of the social-democratic response to the new economic situation, derived from the tradition of social-democratic policy-making.

Many specialist studies have sought to show that the problems of the welfare state and the economic crisis were *tackled better* after 1973, when powerful social-democratic parties and strong, centralized union organizations were in a position to co-ordinate their action.[76] This was a time when 'institutionalized' capitalisms, the 'organized market economies' – and not specifically social-democratic capitalisms – were hailed as possessing a competitive advantage over the Anglo-Saxon liberal model.[77] According to this approach, the best results in terms of unemployment and, to a lesser degree, inflation or growth were generally obtained in countries where there was neo-corporatist mediation under social-democratic auspices.[78] According to Colin Crouch, even for the period 1986 to 1990, 'both kinds of neo-corporatist economy – the employer-dominated and those with particularly strong labour – turn in the best performances' on unemployment and inflation combined. It is worth adding that countries with 'employer driven corporatism' (Germany, Belgium, the Netherlands) did better on inflation; whereas properly social-democratic countries – those with 'labour-dominated corporatism' (Sweden, Norway, but also Finland) – did better on unemployment (with the exception of Denmark). Austria, another country with 'labour-dominated corporatism', was highly successful on both inflation and unemployment fronts.[79]

So, according to a thesis widely held in the 1980s, the tripartite central-ized model, combined with a flexible economic policy of 'neo-Keynesian' inspiration (or, better, semi-Keynesian and semi-liberal), constituted a political-institutional alternative that was *economically superior* to typical neoliberal policies.[80] Now, in the light of developments in the first half of the 1990s, this first attempt at a specifically social-democratic solution to the crisis – the word 'model' would be too strong – could not endure. From the beginning of the 1990s, the economic viability of the Scan-dinavian, Austrian, or German models was called into doubt. Faced with the globalization and neoliberalization of economic priorities, the social-democratic 'solution' proved fragile and ephemeral.[81] And ironically, at the very moment when a body of academic work was highlighting the economic and social effectiveness of social-democratic institutions, 'social democracy was beginning to vanish'.[82]

Social Democracy on the Offensive?
Second Outline of a Social-Democratic Response

Drawing up an economic and social balance sheet of the ongoing social-democratic governmental experiences is difficult, since they have by no means yielded all their results. Right now, however, it is not a pointless exercise to try to evaluate the governmental practice of the 'new' social democrats. Two cases with different ideological and programmatic elab-orations – British New Labour and the French *gauche plurielle* – will make it possible, by way of illustration, to get a better sense of the progress of the new social democracy in power.

(a) *New Labour in Power*

Change in neoliberal continuity is the hallmark of the Blairites' governmental practice in economic affairs. In effect, the strategy implemented by the New Labour government hastened to respect the major lines of Conserva-tive policy (prioritization of the fight against inflation, independence for the Bank of England in fixing interest rates, adoption of the Conservative budgetary credo, selective withdrawal of the state from the economic and social domain,[83] the complete absence of any industrial policy,[84] the preservation of deregulation and labour-market flexibility).

This macroeconomic policy prioritizes economic stability, largely aban-dons anti-cyclical fiscal and monetary policies and restraints the redistribute use of the tax system while making considerable efforts to increase labour supply. Labour's macroeconomic management is *complemented* by a set of social measures of social-democratic inspiration intended to reduce feelings of insecurity, reactivate the traditional social dimension of Labourism, and maintain contact with the party's popular electorate. Among other things, we might cite the establishment of a legal minimum wage; a one-off tax on the 'windfall' profits of the privatized utilities to finance an unemployment programme; the 'welfare to work' programme, which includes several 'new deals', the main one directed at youth unemployment; measures to counter 'social exclusion'; increases in public expenditure on health and education; family tax credit; legal recognition of union organization in the workplace; a maximum 48-hour working week; and new laws on sickness, maternity leave and redundancy payments.[85]

Thus, neoliberal macroeconomic policy is combined with a number of 'left-wing' social reforms and measures which aim to 'limit the damage' of the Conservative legacy. Labour's option for addressing extreme poverty is to construct a highly targeted welfare state whose main role is to stimulate re-entry into the labour-market.[86] Yet the social planks of Blair's policy, part of an aggressive strategy that aims to liberate Labourism once and for all from the image of a 'tax and spend' party, are modest indeed – and often contradictory. In their prudence they contrast sharply both with the very assertive and robust neoliberalism of the macroeconomic management, and with Labour's constitutional reformism, which is simultaneously pragmatic and innovative.

More generally, traditional social-democratic economic policies, like the stimulation of demand and recourse to the state as *economic actor*, have been abandoned. Labour's administration thus confirms Eric Shaw's thesis, formulated in 1994, that 'post-revisionism regarded the central Croslandite proposition, that democratic government had the ability to prevail over the power of business, as false'.[87]

Even so, faced with the scourge of poverty, unemployment, social exclusion, and the deterioration of public services, any generalized withdrawal of the state is neither conceivable nor desirable, nor perhaps possible for the New Labourists. Such a withdrawal could, moreover, turn out to be electorally damaging. Hence a certain reaffirmation of the socially active role of the state – the state as promoter of *inclusion* and solidarity – in some sensitive areas (paralleling and complementing the policy of marketization). If Labour's social policy is constructed on the basis of reforms introduced by the Conservatives (and sometimes, as in education or aspects of the 'welfare to work' programme, reinforces their liberal dimension),[88] it simultaneously seeks – and in this it is innovative – the path of a politics that 'departs from the policies of Old Labour and New Tories', while here or there distilling elements of politics closer to the logic of 'Old Labour'.[89] Thus, Martin Hewitt's claim about social security seems to be of wider validity: 'in social security as elsewhere New Labour is seeking to tread a path marked by lines of continuity and discontinuity in a delicate balancing act. . . . It involves combining what under Old Labour and the New Right were seen as opposite attitudes and principles.'[90]

In reality, before and after attaining power, 'the trajectory of change for Labour has been overwhelmingly in one direction – that of convergence with the Conservatives on the basis of the dilution, weakening and selective abandonment of prior commitments'.[91] Arguments to the effect that the 'third way' is located 'beyond' neoliberalism and the 'old left' do not accurately describe the governmental practice of New Labour. Equidistance is not maintained, and the break with neoliberal agenda and 'old left' agendas is, rather, unilateral. What is rejected on one side is 'funda-mentalist' neoliberal rhetoric and the ultra-liberal practices induced by this rhetoric. But what is rejected on the other is the whole social-democratic tradition in economic policy,[92] as well as part of the social-democratic tradition as regards social security and social rights.[93] Likewise rejected is the whole tradition of social-democratic 'policy style', which gave trade unions a 'key position' in the decision-making process. This leads inevitably to the cancellation of the third way as a radically *different* course, a way that simultaneously transcends liberalism and the 'old' social democracy. Moreover, the 'timing' of the conversion of Labour-ism to liberalism (a moment marked by the balance of social forces established by radical and aggressive Conservative reformism) strongly determined the practical content of the British 'third way'. As Colin Hay and Mathew Watson have aptly emphasized: 'The timing of Labour's market conversion is in many ways as significant as that conversion itself. For to "accept the market" is not merely to accept a neutral mechanism of resource allocation. It is also to internalise and thereby normalise the form that the market took at the moment of that conversion.'[94]

In reality, the 'third way' represents an *enlightened and innovative adminis-tration* (not a mere updating) of *neoliberalism.* Blair has adopted the Conser-vatives' favourite themes, but combined them with reforms that go beyond Conservative logic.[95] The social measures set in train (often novel compared with the traditional social-democratic approach), like certain moves towards the requisite modernization of public services, are a constitutive element of this administration (and should not be underestimated). But this plan of action, apart from the fact that it is too modest when set against the explosion of economic and social insecurity, does not involve a rupture with, or resistance to, neoliberal logic.[96] The 'big picture' is *neoliberal.* The accompanying images are in large part *social-democratic,* even if they are not always social-democratic in the 'traditional' and habitual sense of the term.

(b) *La Gauche plurielle*

After a governmental experience too marked, especially in 1988–93, by liberal economic orthodoxy, the French left found itself in power once again in 1997. Victory was secured on a programme of moderate rupture with the economic and social orientation of preceding governments (right and left) and on a commitment to struggle against *la fracture sociale.*

If one of the first acts of the Blair government was to grant independence to the Bank of England, the calendar of the European Union meant that one of the first acts of the Jospin government was acceptance of the European stability pact, a less strict interpretation of which had been demanded by the left before the elections.[97] In accepting it without receiving anything real in return, France – and Europe – turned its back on the prospect of a Keynesian policy for stimulating economic activity. The subsequent resignation in March 1999 of Oskar Lafontaine, demonstrating the left's powerlessness to construct a social-democratic Europe, interred the neo-Keynesian project conclusively.

The French government's strategy has been based on a fourfold approach: a. budgetary consideration and price stability; b. actions to encourage stronger economic growth; c. targeting those unemployed who are the most alienated from the job market; d. multiplying the security-nets for those in extreme poverty. There are several signs of an economic policy that is more or less respectful of liberal orthodoxy:[98] respect for the letter – and no longer merely the 'tenor' – of the Maastricht Treaty; the adoption of budgetary orthodoxy; prioritization of the fight against inflation; the very slow progression, despite much more ambitious promises, in public expenditure (1 per cent over the years 2000–02, or 0.3 per cent per annum on average); a very moderate wages policy (though clearly more 'permissive' compared with previous austerity policies); multiple transfers of state interests in public enterprises.[99] Ultimately, the French left has not kept its engagement with a macroeconomic break. Despite some important 'corrections', the Jospin government *has not redeemed its promise to break with liberalism.*

Nevertheless, confronted with the 'collective fear' inspired by unemployment, poverty and social exclusion, a number of social measures have been taken 'to advance solidarity'. Let us briefly itemize some of them: establishment of 'universal sickness cover' (operative from 1 January 2000) – an important measure in the battle against exclusion, since it will ensure health cover for the six million French people who do not have basic and complementary sickness insurance schemes;[100] transfer of social contributions to the 'general social contribution'; increase in the guaranteed minimum wage of 4 per cent and in unemployment benefit of 2.2 per cent (1 July 1997); partial implementation of a youth employment project. Likewise to deal with social exclusion, the *Fonds d'urgence sociale* was set up during the winter of 1997–98 (close on the heels of the movement of the unemployed), followed – and, in practice, replaced – by the *Commissions de l'action sociale d'urgence*: structures that were more decentralized and better adapted to the enormous variety in the population affected by extreme poverty. Alongside these significant measures, other complementary steps have been taken, which are more limited in scope (if not symbolic, since their implementation falls well short of pre-election commitments): a slight increase in wealth tax; a tiny reduction in VAT to the benefit of the most modest households; light, temporary relief (two years) of taxation on businesses; moderately tightened taxation of savings.[101]

The launch of the 35-hour-week reform (an outline law was voted in June 1998, and a second law in January 2000), intended as the beacon of the new governmental team (if only for symbolic reasons), resulted in something rather different from what was promised before the elections. Thirty-five hours without loss of earnings, a promise that took its place in the framework of a moderately Keynesian policy (absorbing some unemployment without affecting internal demand), provoked the anger of employers, particularly at the outset. They characterized the reform as 'archaic', 'doctrinaire', and 'dirigiste', intent upon 'overburdening' enterprise – something that would be counterproductive, and have negative repercussions on employment. The enormous disparity of conditions (by enterprise and branch), the practical and legal problems encountered (annualization, overtime, work of executives, part-time jobs, etc.), government hesitation, the traditional weakness of French trade unions – these have progressively imparted a new content to the jigsaw puzzle of this reform, which was, in any event, very complicated to implement. Even so, its launch initiated major negotiations between social partners and the signing of thousands of enterprise accords. In reality, negotiations over the 35 hours affect all aspects of life in the firm and, regardless of the effects on employment, *illustrate an administration of the labour market wherein arbitration is not the exclusive prerogative of the laws of the market*, but also that of legislation and negotiation.

It is still not possible to sort out the positive and negative effects of the reduction in working hours, but there are already strong indications that employers have known how to turn certain aspects of the mechanism to their advantage, at least in part. At this stage it is not certain that it will trigger a powerful dynamic of job creation (hitherto, the repercussions on employment have been modest).[102] It nevertheless seems to be agreed that trends towards job flexibility are being reinforced (flexibility *endured* has become *negotiated* flexibility, which is something); that wage moderation will persist; and that a large number of heads of firms will have the luxury of hiring 'cheap' (thanks to public aid).[103] Among the effects of the reform we should emphasize the trend towards a gradual reduction in job insecurity (some enterprise accords anticipate the transformation of insecure jobs into contracts of unspecified duration); and the possibility offered to a large number of wage-earners – but not all – to enjoy more free time for life outside work.[104]

Thus, we observe that with the socialists, the state is continuing its partial withdrawal from the economic sphere, ceding an ever greater place to markets. However, the retreat from the 'social' sphere is a lot more difficult to effect and admit, especially in a country with a strong statist tradition and in a period of burgeoning social inequalities. The state thus appears to reassert, even *reinforce*, its presence in the 'social' sphere – its mechanisms of ultimate assistance – to counteract the effects of the explosion in poverty and job insecurity. Under a left-wing government, the state is simultaneously increasing the perimeter of the market and, faced with the emergency of social segregation, seeking to reinvest the 'social' in order to repair what can be repaired. It is therefore multiplying the 'ultimate safety-nets' of social security, which are directed not only at 'major exclusion' but at all those – in fact, the majority of beneficiaries – who are not in a position to secure decent living conditions for themselves.[105]

Profiting from a favourable international situation and the more accommodating monetary policy conducted by the European Central Bank, the 'plural left' can today pride itself on its comparative success on the unemployment, growth, and social deficit fronts.[106] Its policy, which aims to secure the support of the trade unions, differs in several respects from that of the French right. In its 'policy style' it is even fairly consistent with the social-democratic *modus operandi*. In terms of its content, however, it is closer to a soft neoliberalism than the prudent neo-Keynesianism pledged by the socialists before the election and bruited thereafter. In social policy the government has incontestably taken a number of measures to improve employment, social security safety-nets (especially to maintain the poorest of the poor), to increase the social minima, to extend the rights of the 'excluded'.[107] Moreover, it would be profoundly unjust to suggest that the two most important legislative initiatives – the youth employment programme (which has been a relative success),[108] and the reduction in working hours (distorted as it is compared with its original objectives) – are of neoliberal inspiration. They are fundamental reforms that directly affect daily life, and go *beyond market regulation*. If they achieve their objectives (which is far from guaranteed at the time of writing), their impact will transcend the borders of France. It is thus clear that the Jospin government is not submitting obediently and comprehensively to the general move towards liberalism. But it is also clear that it is not swimming against the current, that its policy does not represent a rupture with the neoliberal model of macroeconomic management. Accordingly, the French experience is marked by ambiguity. As usual, it is in France that the art of playing on two registers – deregulation and a certain re-regulation – is most flourishing today.

In adopting an 'orthodox' macroeconomic policy within the stabilizing framework of the European Union, the Jospin government has not really shown any inclination either to expand its budgetary room for manoeuvre, or to confront the power of the markets in order to sustain an economic and social policy more attuned to social-democratic aspirations. 'You in Greece', the French economist Jean-Paul Fitoussi said in an interview with the Greek journal *Avgi* – and you in England, we might add – 'see a great difference between Jospin's policy and Blair's policy. But in reality the differences are not important. Lionel Jospin has accepted the arrangements of the European stability pact, which present an obstacle to any active budgetary policy.'[109] If *change-in-neoliberal-continuity* seems to be the hallmark of the Blairites' governmental practice in economic affairs, change *in neoliberal continuity* also seems to mark the economic policy of the Jospin government. But when it comes to Jospin, there remains 'that margin of resistance that makes him appear – despite the renunciations – still anchored in the lineage of reform'.[110] Thus, the distancing from neoliberal logic (and the practice of previous left-wing governments in France) is more sharply and clearly asserted. And – as Henri Emmanuelli, former secretary of the PS, would say – 'objectively, if we observe what is going on in Europe, the French government appears the most left-wing'.[111]

The comparison with the Blairite *démarche* is illuminating here. On the level of discourse, the *gauche plurielle* is positioned distinctly and forcefully to the left of New Labour. On the level of governmental practice, it is equally to the left of Labour, but in much more discreet fashion. Thus, the more one passes from rhetoric to action, programme to performance, the more the distance narrows and convergences prevail. Accordingly, the import of this positioning to the 'left' should not be overestimated. But it should not be reckoned negligible either.[112] On both sides of the Channel, the new social democracy contains more neoliberalism than social democracy. Yet the proportions are not identical in Paris and London.[113] Nor is the policy style. And the style, as Jules Michelet would say, 'is simply the motion of the soul'.

(c)   *The Tradition Abandoned*

The social-democratic institutional configuration that sustained the Scandinavian (especially Swedish), German, or Austrian capitalist 'system' – to cite only countries with a strong social democracy – is more or less fissured today. Furthermore, at least since the second half of the 1980s, a steady *reorientation* of social-democratic economic priorities has occurred, largely regardless of the ideological make-up of the national parties, and of economic or political circumstances. This entitles me to assert that the characteristic specificity of left-wing public policies has been greatly diluted.

Initially, particularly in the first half of the 1980s, social democracy strove to preserve the specificity of its economic and social policies, at least partially, while gravitating towards neoliberalism. Subsequently, in the 1990s, it manifestly adopted the neoliberal agenda. Especially in the years 1995 to 1998, the convergence criteria fixed by the Maastricht Treaty further constrained the policies adopted, above all in their budgetary component. European growth has collectively suffered from the simultaneity of restrictive policies, the multiplier effect influencing economic policies decisively.[114]

As our brief examination of the French and British cases has shown, the social-democratic art of playing on both registers – deregulation and a certain re-regulation; the market and the state – is far from having been abandoned. And there are good economic and social reasons for that. In this sense, the new politics of the social democrats – left- and right-wing, south and north – could be summarized thus: *the 'economic' state withdraws in favour of the market and the 'philanthropic' state timidly re-emerges to reduce the social costs created by the market*. Obviously, arbitrations differ from country to country, and the dose varies. But the centre of gravity in this tricky – and quasi-schizophrenic – game of accommodating contrary logics and influences weighs clearly and heavily in favour of liberalism. From this angle, the latest period may legitimately be considered that of 'accommodation to the preferences of capital'.[115]

In the round, the adoption of orthodox policies and tendential decentralization of the structures of wage-bargaining have called into question *four central pillars* of the social-democratic approach: the policy of *wage solidarity*, which tended in the direction of the equality of wage-labour, and hence working-class unity;[116] the policy of *full employment*, which has been definitively jettisoned; the policy of *wealth redistribution* in favour of labour (though social democracy's impact on the distribution of income between wages and profits was traditionally modest); and the policy of *power redistribution* in favour of the wage-earning class and – above all – its trade-union representation (inside and outside the workplace).

I am therefore obliged to observe that the adoption by contemporary social democracy of policies of neoliberal inspiration, and the crisis of tripartite, centralized co-ordination – a *modus operandi* largely (but not exclusively) specific to social democracy – have *impaired the politico-economic originality of the social-democratic alternative*. It must equally be observed – drawing on Rand Smith's classification – that social democracy has passed from a 'market-modifying' type of strategy to a 'market-adapting' strategy. According to Smith:

> the market-modifying approach, like the market-adapting approach, accepts the basic capitalist framework, but seeks to modify that framework by enhancing organized labor's power within it ... The market-adapting approach accepts the market as the final arbiter ... allows more time for adjustment and is certainly more labor friendly than the *market-embracing* approach, because the goal is to restructure without causing widespread economic distress or community upheaval.[117]

Now, the adoption of a 'market-adapting' strategy (New Labour being located almost midway between 'market-adapting' and 'market-embracing' strategies) is an economic-social option that is largely *outside* the social-democratic tradition, and represents a *break* with it.

Obviously, the power of the working-class movement, both political and trade-union, remains an influential factor in economic solutions and distributive conflict. Particularly in the countries of 'labour-dominated corporatism', the bi- and tripartite compromises, and the co-ordination of wage policies – at least at sectoral level – still have a far from negligible role to play.[118] Even when it is fissured, this co-ordination remains an alternative structure of regulation that can always serve as a corrective to regulation by the market and unemployment.

But today's social democrats, their room for manoeuvre greatly limited by a liberal international economic system *and* their own liberal options of the last two decades, seem resigned to *choosing between different forms of inequality*. And in spite of their anti-unemployment discourse (and their support for the unemployed by more or less generous systems of compensation), they seem rather inclined to sacrifice employment with a view to limiting the damage at the level of wage differentials and inequality.[119] In this respect, Moene and Wallerstein's analysis seems highly relevant:

> There is probably no going back to the past, if the past is characterized as highly centralized wage setting that imposes a highly egalitarian wage distri-

bution. The unions have grown too heterogeneous and competitive with each other to agree to a common goal of increased wage equality. Employers have hardened in their insistence on the relaxation of constraints on the payment of wage differentials. To the extent that central wage setting continues, it will entail less wage equality and fewer constraints on wage increases at the plant level. Nevertheless, wage setting may remain sufficiently centralized to provide a floor that protects the income, but not the employment, of workers at the bottom of the labor market.[120]

The social and institutional achievements of societies with a powerful social democracy have not been erased from the map. Particularly in Scandinavia and Austria, across-the-board capitulation to neoliberal logic has been avoided.[121] The welfare state, which has not really been dismantled anywhere in Europe, has been even less so in countries with a social-democratic structure. The spread of extreme poverty has been avoided. Income inequality has certainly become greater, but 'the retreat from egalitarian outcomes has been fairly limited'.[122] And if unemployment is the enemy of the pay slip, the automatic mechanisms of the invisible hand remain – still – under political control.

But while the situation as regards extreme poverty and the divide between 'insiders' and 'outsiders' is better in Scandinavia, elsewhere the exposure to insecurity and risk is considerably greater. Social-democratic policies in Europe – particularly in France, Germany and Great Britain – do not seem to be equipped really to check deepening social inequalities and segregation. As Gøsta Esping-Andersen has written: 'if the opportunity structure for youth, women and the unskilled remains as blocked as it is today in much of Europe, we are more likely to see a rebirth of Disraeli's Two Nations than a pluralist haven'.[123]

Social Deficit and 'Identity' Deficit

Any economic option is assessed according to an economic calculus (effects on the dynamism of the economy), but also according to a calculation that is simultaneously political (electoral costs and benefits, costs and benefits in terms of ideological-political positioning) and social (whom does a policy benefit?, or costs and benefits according to social class). By the latter calculation, social democracy has not yet defined a new economic and social equation capable of producing *electoral and identity effects equivalent to those of the Keynesian equation.*

Unquestionably, there are no economic policies ready and just waiting for the left to adopt them. But for the first time since the Second World War social democrats do not possess a *politically plausible* social and economic strategy – that is, one both inspired by their own tradition and clearly distinct from that of their opponents. In this respect, regardless of its *raison d'être* and specifically economic value, the social-democratic economic response was not effective *politically*: it largely stopped being a *vector of left-wing identity* for the social-democratic parties and a *factor of political unification* for the subaltern classes, the natural social base of these parties. Socialist and social-democratic policies are no longer seen as making sense, particularly for popular strata. In this context the exercise of power has become a key factor in the destabilization and transformation of social-democratic identity.

In some sense there is a cause-and-effect relation between the diminished social effectiveness of social-democratic policies and their yield in terms of 'identity'. If a different political force was involved, this diminution would probably be less embarrassing. But it seems that the identification of social democracy with the welfare state and workers' interests holds great sway over European populations, disproportionate to the actual historical record (for it should not be forgotten that in several countries, conservative and Christian democratic parties contributed significantly to the advent of the welfare state). Now, once social democracy distances itself from Keynesianism and the welfare state, once it proves less capable of protecting the weakest – and hence its own social profile – it is because social democracy is no longer truly social democracy, or rather, is no longer held to be so. And this despite the fact that social-democratic neoliberalism is an inventive neoliberalism 'with a human face'; and the current enterprise of a certain re-regulation of the social domain offers a modest *corrective* to the laws of the market. But the overall impression does not change so long as restrictive budgetary policy remains dominant at the national and European levels; fiscal policy is scarcely used, or not used at all; and the instrument of national and European monetary policy is voluntarily downgraded in favour of an orthodoxy obsessed with inflationary fears.

A few words in conclusion. With the crisis and transformation of advanced capitalism, Keynesian regulation and neo-corporatist, tripartite consultation, two 'efficient causes' that helped to make social-democratic parties dominant political forces have been significantly challenged. However, social democracy has proved able to adapt to the new economic and social situation. Its specifically economic responses lack neither coherence nor technocratic effectiveness. But relative *to their own* social aspirations, they are extremely disappointing (particularly on employment and the reduction of inequalities). They are therefore *politically* inadequate. The dismantling of the model of economic and social policy bequeathed by social democrats from the first three decades of the postwar period means that the social-democratic social message is hopelessly indistinct. Social democracy has lost its influence as a force stemming from the working-class movement, and its attempts at a new synthesis create the impression that there is no new economico-social project to be substituted for the 'old' one. In the face of contemporary neoliberal reality, the 'loss' of the postwar project does not seem to be something that can be compensated for in the medium term. Combined with the social mutation of the new social democracy, and its opening to the middle classes and the world of big capital, this loss fuels its electoral instability and radically *challenges* the sociohistorical meaning of its project. The tragedy for social democrats, even for victorious social democrats at the dawn of this new century, even for those of them who do not experience it as a 'tragedy' – is that their urge (if only rhetorical) to act in accordance with a 'sense of justice' remains economically unarticulated. This renders their *identity* inarticulate. That is the great lesson of the last two decades.

Notes

1. *Le Monde*, 16/17 September 1990.
2. Fritz Scharpf, *Crisis and Choice in European Social Democracy*, trans. Ruth Crowley and Fred Thompson, Cornell University Press, Ithaca, NY and London 1991, p. 270.
3. Because of its protectionist and undemocratic connotations, the term 'corporatism' hardly accords with the spirit of the 'centralized bargaining system' characteristic of various countries with a powerful social democracy. See Karl Ove Moene and Michael Wallerstein, 'Social Democratic Labor Market Institutions: A Retrospective Analysis', in Herbert Kitschelt *et al.*, eds, *Continuity and Change in Contemporary Capitalism*, Cambridge University Press, Cambridge 1999, pp. 233–4.
4. Bruce Western, 'A Comparative Study of Working-Class Disorganization: Union Decline in Eighteen Advanced Capitalist Countries', *American Sociological Review*, no. 60, 1995, p. 184.
5. Jonas Pontusson, 'Le modèle suédois en mutation: vers le néoliberalisme ou le modèle allemand?', in Colin Crouch and Wolfgang Streeck, eds, *Les Capitalismes en Europe*, La Découverte, Paris 1996, p. 81.
6. Wallace Clement, 'Exploring the Limits of Social Democracy: Regime Change in Sweden', *Studies in Political Economy*, no. 44, 1994, p. 101.
7. Ibid.
8. See Miriam Golden, Michael Wallerstein and Peter Lange, 'Postwar Trade-Union Organization and Industrial Relations in Twelve Countries', in Herbert Kitschelt *et al.*, eds, *Continuity and Change in Contemporary Capitalism*, pp. 205–13.
9. Torben Iversen, 'Power, Flexibility and the Breakdown of Centralized Wage Bargaining', *Comparative Politics*, vol. 28, no. 4, 1996, p. 403.
10. Colin Crouch, 'Exit or Voice: Two Paradigms for European Industrial Relations after the Keynesian Welfare State', *European Journal of Industrial Relations*, vol. 1, no. 1, 1995, p. 73.
11. Torben Iversen, 'The Choices for Scandinavian Social Democracy in Comparative Perspective', *Oxford Review of Economic Policy*, vol. 14, no. 1, 1998, p. 66.
12. *Le Monde Diplomatique*, June 1998, p. 17.
13. Michael Wallerstein, Miriam Golden and Peter Lange, 'Unions, Employers' Associations and Wage-Setting Institutions in Northern and Central Europe, 1950–1992', *Industrial and Labor Relations Review*, vol. 50, no. 3, 1997, p. 395.
14. Crouch, 'Exit or Voice', pp. 73–4.
15. According to Wallerstein *et al.*, in practice 'the Dutch confederations have failed to conclude a frame agreement in most years since 1970'; and, following these failures, governmental regulation became more active, particularly towards the second half of the 1970s and at the beginning of the 1980s ('Unions, Employers' Associations and Wage-Setting Institutions', p. 394).

16. Anton Hemerijck and Jelle Visser, 'Quel "modèle hollandais"?', *La Revue Socialiste*, no. 1, 1999, *passim*; Torben Iversen, *Contested Economic Institutions: The Politics of Macroeconomics and Wage Bargaining in Advanced Democracies*, Cambridge University Press, Cambridge 1999. It should, however, be noted that the Dutch unions were opposed to the reduction of social benefits and very hesitant about part-time employment and flexibility. The reform of the social security system (particularly disability benefits), carried out against the unions' opposition, involved a confrontation between them and social democracy. It provoked a wave of mobilizations, the unions organizing (in The Hague) the largest demonstration since the Second World War in 1991 (Hemerijck and Visser, 'Quel "modèle hollandais"?', p. 74).

17. Christophe de Voogd, 'Pays-Bas: victoire et doutes de la coalition violette', in Alfred Grosser, ed., *Les Pays d'Europe occidentale*, Documentation Française, Paris 1999, p. 116.

18. Iversen, 'The Choices for Scandinavian Social Democracy', pp. 66, 70. See also Bruce Western, *Between Class and Market: Postwar Unionization in the Capitalist Democracies*, Princeton University Press, Princeton, NJ 1997, pp. 161–3.

19. See Frans Becker and René Cuperus, 'Dutch Social Democracy between Blair and Jospin', in Cuperus and Johannes Kandel, eds, *European Social Democracy: Transformation in Progress*, Friedrich Ebert Stiftung, Amsterdam 1998, p. 252.

20. Western, *Between Class and Market*, p. 47.

21. Ibid., p. 48.

22. John Kelly, *Trade Unions and Socialist Politics*, Verso, London and New York 1988, p. 101.

23. Colin Crouch, 'The Fate of Articulated Industrial Relations Systems: A Stock-Taking after the "Neo-liberal" Decade', in Marino Regini, ed., *The Future of Labour Movements*, Sage, London 1992, p. 181.

24. Martin Hewitt, 'New Labour and Social Security', in Martin Powell, ed., *New Labour, New Welfare State?*, The Policy Press, Bristol, 1999, p. 167.

25. Donald Sassoon, 'Le nouveau Labour, exemple ou contre-exemple?', *Esprit*, no. 251, 1999, p. 65; Peter Dorey, 'The Blairite Betrayal: New Labour and the Trade Unions', in Gerard Taylor, ed., *The Impact of New Labour*, Macmillan, London 1999, pp. 202–3. 'It is an open secret that the TUC leaders and the various heads of unions feel betrayed and outcast by Downing Street,' Lindsey German has written ('The Blair Project Cracks', *International Socialism*, no. 82, 1999, p. 29). The word 'betrayal' is certainly too strong, given that the promises were very modest. Moreover, the unions are not excluded from all consultation, although such consultation as has occurred involved subjects of little importance (Dorey, 'The Blairite Betrayal', pp. 202–3). It nevertheless remains the case that 'the fact that New Labour's pre-election pledges to the trade unions were so modest makes their subsequent downgrading and dilution even more offensive' (ibid., p. 207).

26. Pontusson, 'Le modèle suédois en mutation'.

27. Horst Kern and Charles Sabel, 'Trade Unions and Decentralized Production: A Sketch of Strategic Problems in the German Labour Movement', in Marino Regini, ed., *The Future of Labour Movements*, Sage, London 1992, p. 218.

28. Western, *Between Class and Market*, p. 159; also Crouch, 'The Fate of Articulated Industrial Relations Systems', p. 182.

29. Steve French, 'A "Third Way" through Social Pacts? Trade Union Weakness

and the Limits of German Corporatism', in Lothar Funk, ed., *The Economics and Politics of the Third Way*, LIT, Hamburg 1999, p. 114.

30. Western, *Between Class and Market*, p. 160.
31. See Richard Hyman, 'National Industrial Relations Systems and Transnational Challenges: An Essay in Review', *European Journal of Industrial Relations*, vol. 5, no. 1, 1999, p. 96.
32. Nils Elvander, quoted in Western, 'A Comparative Study of Working-Class Disorganization', p. 185.
33. Iversen, 'Power, Flexibility and the Breakdown of Centralized Wage Bargaining', p. 428.
34. Iversen, 'The Choices for Scandinavian Social Democracy', p. 71.
35. Wallerstein *et al.*, 'Unions, Employers' Associations and Wage-Setting Institutions', pp. 390–91.
36. Iversen, 'Power, Flexibility and the Breakdown of Centralized Wage Bargaining', p. 424.
37. Ferdinand Karlhofer, 'The Present and Future State of Social Partnership', in Gunter Bischof and Anton Pelinka, eds, *Austro-Corporatism, Contemporary Austrian Studies*, vol. 4, 1996, pp. 121–2.
38. Alois Guger, 'Economic Policy and Social Democracy: The Austrian Experience', *Oxford Review of Economic Policy*, vol. 14, no. 1, 1998, p. 53.
39. Iversen, 'Power, Flexibility and the Breakdown of Centralized Wage Bargaining', p. 426.
40. Golden *et al.*, 'Postwar Trade-Union Organization and Industrial Relations in Twelve Countries', pp. 208–9.
41. Guger, 'Economic Policy and Social Democracy', p. 55.
42. In countries without a neo-corporatist tradition (France, Greece, Spain), efforts in the direction of greater consultation were made by socialist governments – with very mixed and inconclusive results. The absence of a party structure of a social-democratic type, the socialists' difficulty in managing a fratricidal union pluralism, and an adverse economic situation objectively encouraged the politics of outbidding rivals and a return to governmental regulation.
43. Golden *et al.*, 'Postwar Trade-Union Organization and Industrial Relations'.
44. Iversen, 'The Choices for Scandinavian Social Democracy', p. 63.
45. Christer Thørnqvist, 'The Decentralization of Industrial Relations: The Swedish Case in Comparative Perspective', *European Journal of Industrial Relations*, vol. 5, no. 1, 1999, p. 83.
46. Marino Regini, 'Introduction: The Past and Future of Social Studies of Labour Movements', in Regini, ed., *The Future of Labour Movements*, p. 7.
47. Karl Ove Moene and Michael Wallerstein, 'How Social Democracy Worked: Labor-Market Institutions', *Politics and Society*, vol. 23, no. 2, p. 207.
48. Regini, 'Introduction', p. 7.
49. The tradition of relatively strong works councils (Austria, Germany), or the existence of an important privileged sector of 'cost-insensitive employers and militant "maverick" unions (the booming petrochemical sector in Norway)', seems to be a significant counter-incentive for employers – a sort of safety valve – inclining them against abandonment of central bargaining (Western, *Between Class and Market*, p. 160; Iversen, 'Power, Flexibility and the Breakdown of Centralized Wage Bargaining', p. 411).
50. Iversen, *Contested Economic Institutions*, pp. 163–5.
51. Thornqvist, 'The Decentralization of Industrial Relations', p. 72.
52. Golden *et al.*, 'Postwar Trade-Union Organization and Industrial Relations'.

The proportion of waged workers covered by collective agreements remains very high: more than 70% in the European countries, with the invariable exception of Great Britain. 'This is not to say that unions today bargain as effectively on behalf of their workers as they did earlier, but it does mean that their institutional role in the bargaining process remains largely intact and that they often continue to be able to take a large portion of wages out of competition' (ibid., p. 205).

53. Alan Cawson, quoted in Karlhofer, 'The Present and Future State of Social Partnership', pp. 119, 120.

54. Iversen, *Contested Economic Institutions*, p. 159.

55. Quoted in Hyman, 'National Industrial Relations Systems and Transnational Challenges', p. 95. The agreements concluded in Italy, Holland and Ireland represent examples of this trend (ibid., pp. 94–5). The agreement on a 35-hour week reached in France also tends in the direction of negotiated flexibility.

56. Wallerstein *et al.*, 'Unions, Employers' Associations and Wage-Setting Institutions', p. 392.

57. Iversen, *Contested Economic Institutions*, p. 164.

58. Scharpf, *Crisis and Choice in Social Democracy*, p. 323. See also p. 30

59. Pontusson, 'Sweden: After the Golden Age', in Perry Anderson and Patrick Camiller, eds, *Mapping the West European Left*, Verso, London and New York 1994, p. 34.

60. Ibid., p. 36.

61. In Sweden, active employment policy was traditionally exceptional in both its sophistication and its 'selective' and 'active' character. At the end of the 1980s, the 'proportion of labour market funds spent on *active measures*' to support employment was remarkably higher than the average for the OECD countries, making Sweden a truly 'deviant case' (Bo Rothstein, *The Social Democratic State: The Swedish Model and the Bureaucratic Problem of Social Reforms*, University of Pittsburgh Press, Pittsburgh, PA and London 1996, p. 60, Thomas Janoski, 'Direct State Intervention in the Labor Market: The Explanation of Active Labor Market Policy from 1950 to 1988 in Social Democratic, Conservative and Liberal Regimes', in Janoski and Alexander Hicks, eds, *The Comparative Political Economy of the Welfare State*, Cambridge University Press, Cambridge 1994, p. 55).

62. This was also true of the other Scandinavian countries.

63. Mario Telo, 'Les représentations de l'adversaire et compromis social dans la politique de la social-démocratie allemande', AFSP, Fourth Congress, Paris 1992.

64. Elie Cohen, 'La gauche et l'économie dans les expériences de pouvoir', in Marc Lazar, ed., *La Gauche en Europe depuis 1945*, Presses Universitaires de France, Paris 1996, pp. 645–6.

65. Juhana Vartiainen, 'Understanding Swedish Social Democracy: Victims of Success?', *Oxford Review of Economic Policy*, vol. 14, no. 1, 1998, p. 37.

66. Bernd-Joachim Schuller, 'The Swedish Third Way: Macroeconomic Policy and Performance', in Funk, ed., *The Economics and Politics of the Third Way*, p. 54.

67. Jonung, quoted in ibid., p. 41.

68. Ibid., pp. 46–8. In 2000, the Swedish economy was among the EU leaders in the fight against inflation, and seemed to have regained – if only partially – its position of 'low-unemployment country'.

69. Donald Sassoon, *One Hundred Years of Socialism*, I.B. Tauris, London 1996, p. 479.

70. Alain Bergounioux and Bernard Manin, *Le Régime social-démocrate*, Presses Universitaires de France, Paris 1989, pp. 157–9; Hans Seidel, 'Social Partnership and Austro-Keynesianism', in Bischof and Pelinka, eds, *Austro-Corporatism*, pp. 108–13.
71. Ibid., p. 114.
72. Guger, 'Economic Policy and Social Democracy', p. 56.
73. Bergounioux and Manin, *Le Régime social-démocrate*.
74. Ibid., p. 150.
75. Jeremy John Richardson, quoted in David Arter, 'Sweden: A Mild Case of "Electoral Instability Syndrome"?', in David Broughton and Mark Donovan, eds, *Changing Party Systems in Western Europe*, Pinter, London and New York 1999, p. 169.
76. In countries with a powerful trade-union movement (like Sweden, Austria, Germany), the development of real wages in the period 1960–90 matched the improvement in productivity, *even after 1975* (though to a lesser degree). In Italy, another country with a strong union movement, 'changes in inflation are most salient in predicting real wages' (Thomas Volgy, John Schwarz and Lawrence Imwalle, 'In Search of Economic Well-Being: Worker Power and the Effects of Productivity, Inflation, Unemployment and Global Trade on Wages in Ten Wealthy Countries', *American Journal of Political Science*, vol. 40, no. 4, 1996, p. 1245). By contrast, in countries with a moderately strong or moderately weak working-class movement (France, the Netherlands, Canada, Japan), it is unemployment that most influences the wage equation. The same is true of the United States, a country with a very weak union movement. More specifically, in the 1990s in the USA – recently bruited as a model of economic success – 'despite increased productivity, increased penetration of global markets, rising profits and low unemployment the real pay of the average production worker continued to decline' (ibid., p. 1248).
77. Colin Crouch and Wolfgang Streeck, 'L'avenir du capitalisme diversifié', in Crouch and Streeck, eds, *Les Capitalismes en Europe*, p. 13.
78. For purposes of information, the average unemployment rate for the period 1982–88 was 2.7% in Sweden, 2.7 in Norway, 3.5 in Austria, and 6.7 in Germany (3.5 in 1975–81 during the SPD–FDP government). In the same period the rate was 11% in the United Kingdom, 9.6 in France, 9.8 in Italy, and 10.4 for all the countries of the European Community (Moene and Wallerstein, 'How Social Democracy Worked').
79. Crouch, 'The Fate of Articulated Industrial Relations Systems', pp. 183–5.
80. According to Iversen, in the period 1973–93 two institutional configurations produced the best results as regards unemployment: 'a centralized mode of wage regulation where the government enjoys macro-economic flexibility and a decentralized (or semi-centralized) bargaining system in which the government is credibly committed to a non-accommodating monetary policy rule'. The first system (particularly the Scandinavian countries) is associated with a more egalitarian wages policy; the second (notably Germany, the Netherlands, Austria in part) is more inegalitarian ('Wage Bargaining, Hard Money and Economic Performance: Theory and Evidence for Organized Market Economies', *British Journal of Political Science*, no. 28, 1998). That said, the relative decentralization of bargaining systems and the adoption of orthodox monetary policies explain the recent intensification of wage inequalities in the Scandinavian countries.
81. The same picture is in part confirmed in the countries of southern Europe.

According to Andrew Glyn, socialist governments in France (1981–93), Spain (1981–95), and Greece (1981–89), 'all notoriously high-inflation countries, presided over noticeably larger increases in unemployment than the average for the OECD over the same period. Usually inflation was reduced by no more than the average fall, and this reflected the generally higher inflation to begin with: but the disinflation exacted a heavy toll in terms of lost jobs' ('The Assessment: Economic Policy and Social Democracy', *Oxford Review of Economic Policy*, vol. 14, no. 1, 1998, p. 12). Having undertaken policies of isolated reflation, which were abandoned in 1983 and 1984 respectively, and having proceeded to successive devaluations of their currencies, the socialist governments of France and Greece likewise finally opted for a strong currency strategy. However, in Spain and Greece, countries with a weak welfare state, a sharp improvement in social security and social rights was observed throughout the 1980s. From the second half of the 1980s the profits of capital, initially contested and then considered the principal condition for a recovery in investment, rose everywhere, and most especially in France (ibid., p. 13). The explosion of capitalist profits in Greece was considerably more tardy (second half of the 1990s), and occurred under a socialist government. It is indicative that PASOK, often accused of 'populism' and 'nationalism', was considered 'the party of the stock exchange' towards the end of the 1990s.

82. Karl Ove Moene and Michael Wallerstein, 'Social Democratic Labor Market Institutions: A Retrospective Analysis', in Kitschelt *et al.*, eds, *Continuity and Change in Contemporary Capitalism*, p. 232.

83. This takes the form less of traditional privatizations (e.g. the decision to privatize British air traffic control) than of the transfer of public-sector responsibilities to the private sector (public–private partnership in the domain of health and education, accelerated recourse to the private sector in the domain of pensions, encouragement to buy services previously supplied by the public sector). The progressive introduction of market criteria into the operation of the public sector is another aspect of the state's withdrawal.

84. The absence of an industrial policy is all the more significant in that British finance capital is 'risk averse, short term in its calculations and notorious for its unwillingness to support investment and innovation' (Colin Hay, *The Political Economy of New Labour: Labouring under False Pretences?*, Manchester University Press, Manchester 1999, p. 185).

85. Keith Dixon, *Un digne héritier: Blair et le thatchérisme*, Raisons d'Agir, Paris 2000, pp. 65–71; Jacques Leruez, 'Royaume-Uni: un "état de grâce" persistant', in Alfred Grosser, ed., *Les Pays d'Europe occidentale*, Documentation Française, Paris 1999; Sassoon, 'Le nouveau Labour'; *Le Monde*, 26 May 1999.

86. John Grahl, 'Le gouvernement Blair et le modèle social britannique', *L'économie politique*, no. 3, 1999; see also: Merkel, 'The Third Ways of Social Democracy', pp. 38–42; Andrew Glyn and Stewart Wood, 'New Labour's Economic Policy', in Andrew Glyn, *Social Democracy in Neoliberal Times*, Oxford University Press, Oxford and New York, 2001.

87. Quoted in Hay, *The Political Economy of New Labour*, p. 16.

88. 'Mr Blair represents his welfare reforms as a continuation of the spirit of Beveridge, but this is simply not the case', Stuart Hall has justifiably written ('The Great Moving Nowhere Show', *Marxism Today*, November/December 1998, p. 12). In several domains, like housing, New Labour has accepted part

of the philosophy and prescriptions of the Conservatives (Peter Kemp, 'Housing Policy under New Labour', in Powell, ed., *New Labour, New Welfare State?*, p. 146).

89. Powell, ed., *New Labour, New Welfare State?*, *passim.*
90. Hewitt, 'New Labour and Social Security', in Powell, ed., *New Labour, New Welfare State?*, pp. 150–51.
91. Hay, *The Political Economy of New Labour*, p. 140.
92. Dixon, *Un digne héritier*, p. 112.
93. 'To many commentators,' Eric Shaw has written, 'the modernization of Labour marks its long-delayed conversion to European-style social democracy. In fact the real ideological significance of "New Labour" is the abandonment of Keynesian social democracy in favour of pre-Keynesian orthodoxy' (*The Labour Party since 1945: Old Labour, New Labour*, Blackwell, Oxford 1996, p. 201).
94. Colin Hay and Mathew Watson, 'Neither Here Nor There?' p. 177.
95. John Crowley, 'Tony Blair: un modèle politique pour la gauche', *L'économie politique*, no. 3, 1999, p. 46.
96. See also Dixon, *Un digne héritier*, pp. 83–5.
97. Jospin opened his electoral campaign with a shock announcement: if the left came to power, there would be no new turn of the budgetary screw, even if meeting the convergence criteria imposed by entry into the euro required it. This position, coupled with other 'conditions' (among them we should mention the requirement of setting up an economic government to counterbalance the European Central Bank and a European pact for growth), allowed Jospin to position himself on the left, and reassert the 'French exception' in European affairs (*Libération*, 22 May 1997).
98. Gérard Desportes and Laurent Mauduit, *La Gauche imaginaire et le nouveau capitalisme*, Grasset, Paris 1999, *passim.*
99. According to the economist Elie Cohen, Jospin 'privatizes more than the previous right-wing governments', despite the pre-election rejection of any new privatization (Institut d'Études Politiques, Paris, oral communication, October 1999).
100. Desportes and Mauduit, *La Gauche imaginaire*, p. 82.
101. Ibid., *passim.*
102. Institutes of economic analysis (at least, the most optimistic of them) forecast the creation of 450,000 posts when all firms are applying the law. According to the government, in October 2000 more than 40,000 agreements had been signed since the first law in June 1998, with – at the end of it all – 232,000 promises of jobs created (88%) or preserved (12%). These figures, and a host of others, fuel the controversy, since it is very difficult to know the precise number of jobs created solely by virtue of the reduction in working hours.
103. Martine Bulard, *Le Monde diplomatique*, October 1999.
104. *Le Monde*, 21 May 1999.
105. *Le Monde*, 1 December 1998. A clear difference of philosophy distinguishes French socialists from British Labourists in their conception of social solidarity. Income support, proposed in December 1988 by the socialist government of Michel Rocard, is the social measure which, more than any other, attracted the attention of the major media. If from the outset the right wanted an 'activity in return' for the receipt of this benefit, so as not to trap the beneficiaries in welfare, the left conceived – and conceives – the *Revenu minimum d'insertion* as an *unconditional right* guaranteed by society and the state (*Le Monde*, 1 December 1998). By contrast, in the United Kingdom, New Labour's reduction of

single-parent benefits, and the reappearance via the 'welfare to work' programme of the classical conservative theme of the 'dependency culture' of the poor, are two examples of a social policy which is influenced by liberal philosophy.

106. Growth reached 2.7% in 1999 (but 3.6% in the last quarter of the year), after 3.4% in 1998 and 2% in 1997. Inflation reached 1.6% per annum in January 2000, placing France among the best performers of the European Union, but still behind Austria, the United Kingdom, Sweden, and the Netherlands. On the employment front, with a rate of unemployment standing at 10.5% at the beginning of 2000 – when the Netherlands posts 2.7% and the UK 4% – France comes twelfth out of fifteen in the EU (*Le Monde*, 17 March 2000). It remains the case that this rate is 2.1% less than the peak of summer 1997 (Françoise Milewski, 'La croissance', in OFCE, *L'économie française 2000*, La Découverte, Paris 2000, p. 51).

107. Desportes and Mauduit, *La Gauche imaginaire*, p. 191.

108. By the end of August 1999 208,550 posts had been provided and the rate of youth unemployment has fallen by 3% since 1997 (Oliver Brossard, 'L'emploi et le chômage', in OFCE, *L'économie française 2000*, La Découverte, Paris 2000, p. 60). By March 2000, according to the French government, more than 276,000 young people have been hired under the 'New Services – New Jobs' program.

109. *Avgi*, 21 March 1999.

110. Desportes and Mauduit, *La Gauche imaginaire*, p. 233.

111. *Le Monde*, 3 March 2000.

112. The conjunction of a number of specifically British factors has favoured the profoundly revisionist policy of the Blair team. Let us mention some of them once again: (a) Labour's deficit in managerial credibility and its long confinement to opposition ('the obsession with failure'); (b) the absence of an important competitor on Labour's left; (c) the historic defeat of the British trade unions, without parallel in continental Europe; (d) the traditional conservatism, considerably stronger than elsewhere, of the middle classes in Great Britain; (e) the great English liberal tradition that made the United Kingdom the weak link among the countries with a strong social-democratic presence. The *combination* of all these factors obtained only in Great Britain, making it ideal terrain for any radical 'revisionist' strategy.

113. By contrast, when it comes to 'cultural liberalism' the French left seems faithful to a long social-democratic tradition. The *Pacte civile de solidarité* (known as PACS), a measure that lifts the taboo on homosexuality and aims to strengthen the rights of couples, homosexual and heterosexual alike, who do not wish to, or cannot, marry, has created a clear divide between left and right. Similarly, legislation on the entry and stay of foreigners (1998) – legislation that was, however, criticized by some on the left – the law on parity of men and women (1999) and on nationality (1997), are indicative of a policy on societal questions that is a good deal more 'open' than the right's. In its tonality and content, this policy differs from the 'law-and-order and moralizing discourse' of New Labour (Dixon, *Un digne héritier*, p. 90). The latter has certainly introduced some liberal measures (e.g. relaxation of the draconian rules on the entry into the United Kingdom of the fiancés or spouses of foreign residents, or the abolition of the legal discrimination between heterosexual

and homosexual acts as regards the age of consent). But a 'law-and-order' approach marks its policy.

114. Milewski, 'La croissance', pp. 12–13.

115. Hay, *The Political Economy of New Labour*, p. 158.

116. According to Moene and Wallerstein: 'in the decade following the breakup of centralized bargaining in Sweden in 1983, wage inequality, as measured by the ratio of wages at the ninth and first decile of the wage distribution, increased by 9 per cent'. In these years the increase in wage differentials in Sweden was less strong than in Great Britain (14%) and the United States (23%), and markedly stronger than in Norway, Denmark, the Netherlands, Austria, and Germany, countries where social consultation did not break down ('Social Democratic Labor Market Institutions', p. 249).

117. Raud Smith, *The Left's Dirty Job*, Pittsburgh University Press, Pittsburgh 1998, pp. 11, 211–12.

118. Pontusson, 'Le modèle suédois en mutation'.

119. Iversen, 'The Choices for Scandinavian Social Democracy in Comparative Perspective', pp. 72–3. Some countries, like the Netherlands and Great Britain, have seen their unemployment rates fall spectacularly. These are countries that have undertaken profound reforms of their labour markets over the last ten years at least, either in a more or less negotiated fashion (the Netherlands) or violently, and while strongly exacerbating inequalities (Great Britain).

120. Moene and Wallerstein, 'How Social Democracy Worked', p. 207.

121. Glyn, 'The Assessment', pp. 16–17. See also Iversen, 'The Choices for Scandinavian Social Democracy'.

122. Glyn, 'The Assessment', p. 13.

123. Gøsta Esping-Andersen, 'Politics without Class: Postindustrial Cleavages in Europe and America', in Kitschelt *et al.*, eds, *Continuity and Change in Contemporary Capitalism*, p. 316.

Part III

The Logic of the
Social-Democratic Transformation
(A Synthesis)

Social democracy is a distinctive set of institutions and policies that fit together and worked relatively efficiently to reduce both the insecurity and the inequality of income without large sacrifices in terms of economic growth or macroeconomic instability.

(Karl Ove Moene and Michael Wallerstein)

11

The Postwar Social-Democratic Model
(1945–73)

Despite the comparative diversity that characterizes formations of a social-democratic type, between 1945 and 1973 they tended to share numerous traits in common. Let us recall some of them:

(a) a mass organization with great power in terms of activists and finances;
(b) a privileged link, whether institutionalized or not, with a working-class trade-unionism that was representative and often unified, well-articulated and centralized;
(c) a specific electoral make-up. Social-democratic parties were coalition parties, combining a very strong class base with a significant influence among sections of the middle classes. They were parties of the working class without thereby being working-class parties;
(d) these parties largely dominated the left of the political/ideological continuum;
(e) they were natural parties of government, capable of (i) identifying themselves with the opposition; and (ii) neutralizing – or not provoking – a 'regime vote';
(f) political liberalism, the welfare state, and the pursuit of social justice, as well as a culture of moderation, conferred on them an ideological *raison d'être* and a programmatic unity;
(g) the upshot of these characteristics of social-democratic identity was the social-democratic compromise, an important aspect of which was often – but not always – the establishment of a bi- or tripartite system of negotiation (neo-corporatist structures).

Thus defined, social democracy was not really established outside central and northern Europe. Strictly applied, this definition encompasses Sweden, Austria, Norway, Denmark, Germany, and, in a very 'atypical' – but well-modelled and distinct – version, Great Britain. The Belgian PS shared some of these characteristics, as did the Dutch PvdA in a less developed form.

The Party/Union Link and Social-Democratic Structuration

Social democracy in the first phase of the postwar period thus represented a particular model of constitution of the left, a specific and distinctive mode of existence.

At its heart, obviously, was the party/union link. This political/trade-union dual structure supported the whole edifice, and was partially responsible for its specificity. In the first place, the unions assumed the role of *partner* in the social-democratic political enterprise – something that allowed the party's leaders to pride themselves on a privileged position in party competition as the repository of 'social peace'. The implementation of bi- or tripartite negotiation under the auspices of social-democratic governments represented 'tangible' proof of this privileged, electorally beneficial position. Next, the unions took on the role of effective organizer of the working class, tending to re-establish – often in confrontation with the party – the importance of the class divide, fundamentally challenged by *interclassist* social-democratic strategies. Finally, they constituted a large 'reservoir' of voters and members for the party, since they facilitated social-democratic penetration of society. The party's electoral anchorage in the working class, its activist strength, and a significant proportion of its financial means – in other words, its sociological, organizational and, to a considerable extent, competitive status – were directly (though certainly not exclusively) attributable to the synergy of these two organizations. In the 1960s, the relation between the two basic historical component parts of the working-class movement was doubtless no longer that of 'one body, two wings'. In reality, each actor consolidated its power in the face of the other, in a subtle and sometimes conflictual game of mutual influence and permanent pressure – a game that often led where it did not wish to go. But as long as the link endured, this was something of an advantage. In a society that was not socially bipolar, it allowed the social-democratic party greater freedom of action and greater ambiguity as well.

Nevertheless, the reality of the social-democratic experience, now more than a century old, is not reducible to the party/union link. The thesis that correctly regards social democracy as a 'constellation' or 'configuration' often contains a significant drawback in practice. Social-democratic parties are not always considered in their electoral and strategic dimension; they are not always conceived in and for themselves, but essentially through their relationship with a more or less 'external' institution. Now, other parties – notably some of the major communist, Christian democratic, or 'non-social-democratic' socialist parties – have preserved, or still preserve, a link with large trade unions, which are often dominant, without thereby being (or becoming) social-democratic. Social-democratic reality unquestionably contains and 'condenses' in transposed form – that is to say, a properly *political* (electoral, ideological, organizational) form – the trade-union connection. The ideological or organizational reality of some major communist parties likewise – if not in identical fashion – involved this

connection. In fact, social democracy, with its own organizational, ideological and political tradition, its own social and cultural reference points, its
own memory and legacy – in short, its own identity – was constructed both
with this link and at the same time, to a considerable extent, *outside* it.
There exists a social-democratic type of *electoral constitution* and a social-
democratic type of *political operator* which, along with the party/union link,
are at the base of social democracy's specificity. For social democracy is
above all a *partisan form.*

Obviously, in suggesting here the importance of the social-democratic
type of electoral coalition and political entrepreneur, I have not discovered
America. In their general outlines these two dimensions are 'known' and
spontaneously or diffusely present in every representation of the social-
democratic phenomenon, whether intuitive or elaborated. They form part
of the 'obvious facts'.

But as with Cyrano's nose, there are numerous ways of referring to the
same obvious facts. What must be underlined is that if social democracy is
composed of the elements and structures I have just enumerated, these are
not reducible to the unity of some primary, preponderant element. Social democracy
is a whole. The singular 'links' composing it should not be considered
social-democratic as such but, rather, as *parts of a whole* which *alone,* in the
combination of its elements, is social-democratic. Thus, on bases that were
not wholly alien either to certain major communist parties or to some
Christian democratic parties, there progressively emerged an institutional-
political configuration whose components, unoriginal when taken separately, formed an original, unprecedented totality as a result of their
combination and precise weighting. And it is precisely this totality – and
not simply the party/union relationship – which is today in the process of
changing.

Social Democracy, Social Democracies

I do not intend to repeat the analyses above. However, let me give some
examples to illustrate the fact that what I have called social-democratic
attributes *are bound up with one another*, and account – or accounted – for
the cohesion and strength of social democracy.

(a) The link with the unions commands social-democratic domination of
    the world of labour, permits the implementation of the social-demo-
    cratic compromise, and partially facilitates social-democratic domina-
    tion of the left of the electoral and political spectrum.
(b) This domination, index of the absence of any important competitor
    on the left, facilitates social-democratic penetration of the working-
    class electorate and the trade-union world, and makes it possible to
    adopt a moderate ideological and political profile without excessive
    electoral cost.
(c) Moderation allows the social-democratic party to address the 'centrist'

segment of the electorate, to extend its audience well beyond the
working class, and to operate as a 'legitimate' political force with a
governmental vocation, in a position to identify itself as the opposition
and neutralize in advance the possibility of a 'regime vote'. It allows it
to conceive and implement 'natural party of government' strategies. In
addition, it favours the establishment of neo-corporatist structures, one
of whose essential foundations is precisely a culture of conciliation and
respect for the opponent-partner – in short, a culture based on
pragmatism.

(d) The institutionalization of social conflict through these structures
enhances and strengthens the role of unions. This, in return, allows
the latter to perform their role as 'mass relays' to the social-democratic
party more effectively, to exercise greater influence within the party
and thus, in these two ways, to strengthen the party's role as the
party of the class.

So, if we want to understand social democracy in the initial postwar period,
we must first of all ask what structure and coherence it rested on, rather
than how and to what end that structure was employed. It permitted various
ideological and political trajectories, depending on the national context
and the environment in which the social-democratic parties were operating.
Everything suggests that social democracy's continuity, its resilience over
time, was not exclusively (or even primarily) based on ideological *parti pris*.
Instead, it was founded on the continuity of a party, trade-union and
electoral structure. Social democracy was the product of a *mechanics of forces*
and a *set of structures*. Then, but only then, was it an *ideology*.[1] The pre-
eminence of this 'mechanics' reached a peak, and in part found its
embodiment, in the practice of the social-democratic compromise – particularly in its most complete version, the neo-corporatist system. This
system derived as much from a *mechanics* of structures, a logic of 'power
and counter-power', as from a culture of moderation – a 'psychology of
intentions', as Régis Debré would say. Postwar social democracy was postwar
social democracy only because it integrated all these particular dimensions
and planks, all these 'links' I have just mentioned, into a political totality
possessed of coherence – a coherence that was *practical*, not necessarily
logical.

Like any interpretation that refers to social democracy in the singular,
this one conceives it as an abstract and coherent political entity, and hence
somewhat unreal. The traits of this actor form a system – ideally, but not
always actually – and are all more or less present in the national social-
democratic parties, which are the only things with a 'real' historical
existence. Now, this 'more or less' is of the utmost importance: it determines the 'individuality' of each national party, as well as its effectiveness
(in politics, effectiveness is indirectly part of the identity of a political actor,
since it influences the roles a party does or does not assume). If these
elements are necessary for the *maximum effectiveness* of social democracy, it
does not follow that some intrinsic requirement preserves their links with

one another. Depending on the country, the socioeconomic context, the circumstances of competition, one or more of them comes under challenge. Thus, many are the parties that deviate, or have recently deviated, from this abstract description. To put it differently: the characteristic properties of social democracy thus defined are to be found in the national parties, but we cannot expect to find them all, in identical form, in every national party. Each 'individual' party draws on this collection of properties, which is not identical for any of them, yet not peculiar to each either. A party is a living part of its environment – a 'party-part'[2] whose specificity is largely related to this environment. In reality, there is no social democracy. Social democracy is a construction. There have been – there are – only social democracies.

Now, the presence of the maximum number of these distinctive features aids a better balance and greater effectiveness of the national social democracies on electoral and governmental levels, and in terms of legitimacy. Their absence leads to a destabilization of the social-democratic poles – and roles – in the political and party system.

Social-democratic parties must therefore do battle on several fronts to preserve their virtual monopoly on the left, their working-class influence, trade-union support; to remain a force with a governmental vocation; to implement the social-democratic tripartite compromise; to attract the middle classes. Like any self-respecting party, they must do battle to preserve or reinforce their political achievements, which are simply the result – the payout, as it were – of past battles. Now, the object and stake of this battle are not only political-electoral domination, but also the *identity* of social democracy. Like any partisan identity, social-democratic identity is in reality simply the product of battles won and battles lost. For, far from corresponding to a permanent state, it is changeable. Political identities are *events*, not 'essences'.

Notes

1. Michel Winock, *Le Socialisme en France et en Europe*, Seuil, Paris 1992, pp. 111–12.
2. Pierre Avril, *Essai sur les partis*, Payot, Paris 1990, p. 20.

12

Social Democracy in the
Process of Transformation

A Profound Transformation

As we have just indicated, in their 'mature', 1960s form, social-democratic configurations were shaped by the combination of a number of attributes and a practical ideology associated with them. In the crisis years, the social-democratic constellation was no longer the same.

At the obvious risk of repetition, let us retrace some aspects of the social-democratic mutation.

Changes within the organization (end of the party-community, preponderance of the new middle classes, reduced working-class presence and culture, weakening of 'identity' incentives at the expense of 'trade-off' incentives, strengthening of the participatory and anti-authoritarian culture, redistribution of internal power in favour of the leader and experts, a leadership at once stronger and weaker, a less dense membership fabric) – these prompted the emergence of a new social-democratic organizational identity. '*Integrative*' *rationality* (through the pyramidal armature, excessive bureaucracy, a summary but strong and strongly shared ideology, the communitarian-associative spirit, control by the centre over intermediate bodies) found itself considerably weakened. In addition, the increase in the leader's autonomy facilitated a capacity for innovation 'from above' (whatever its political and programmatic content) and, as a consequence, strategic flexibility. This set of developments made contemporary social-democratic organizations *composite structures*, halfway between the mass party model and the electoral-professional model. All this led to a profound change in social democracy's organizational mode of being.

The dominance of social-democratic parties on the left, which was often quasi-monopolistic, was challenged by the contraction of their electoral base and the emergence of peripheral, new political poles. Even in the second half of the 1990s, when Europe went pink once again, social-democratic electoral influence was inferior to what it was in the 1960s. More particularly, social democrats *stricto sensu* were stagnating electorally – not only relative to some distant electoral 'golden age', but also compared with their worst electoral decade, the 1980s. Taken as a bloc, socialist influence does not even match the level of the 1980s, a decade of mediocre electoral harvests. Socialism dominates the governments of Europe, but –

notwithstanding superficial analyses – the electoral base of this domination is becoming less solid. Moreover, new left-wing oppositions, or oppositions that are 'neither left nor right', are asserting themselves virtually throughout Europe, and threaten social-democratic predominance. The competitive security of social democracy, once the hegemonic operator on the left of the political scene, is partially – but not decisively – impaired.

The sociological characteristics of social democracy in the 1950s and 1960s account only in part for contemporary social-democratic identity. More specifically, three cumulative and convergent changes have resulted in a serious alteration in the sociological equilibrium of social democracy's political space.

(a) Within organized social democracy we observe a veritable inversion in arithmetical supremacy to the advantage of the salaried middle classes – urban, educated, and often from the public sector. Confirming the hegemony of the middle classes, the social structure of the organization differs profoundly from prewar working-class organizations, and even from the popular organizations of the 1950s. Still present in the organization, the 'subaltern' classes are reduced – particularly in their most plebeian fractions – to a species of second estate and subsidiary force.

(b) The tendency towards 'de-proletarianization' of the membership body is accompanied and complemented by a de-proletarianization – albeit less marked – of the social-democratic electorate. This contains two important aspects, among others:

(i) Social-democratic penetration among the working class has weakened significantly, though moderately. In addition, it has become less stable and less robust. The working class, sociologically the most structured and structuring component of the social-democratic electorate, proves politically more fragmented, ideologically more uncertain, and electorally more volatile than in the past.

Thus, the first category of social-democratic-type parties established in this study (see Chapter 3) – those with *maximum working-class penetration* (systematically approaching or exceeding two-thirds of the working-class vote: prototypes were the SAP and DNA) – is in the process of disappearing from the electoral map. Very strong among manual workers, the SAP is the last remaining representative – or survivor? – from this category. However, its audience has been appreciably weakened, and lacks the firmness, constancy and imposing solidity of the past. Today, a majority of social-democratic formations belong to an *intermediate* category whose principal characteristic is the fluctuation of its influence around the symbolic threshold of 50 per cent of the working-class vote (for the most part, between 40 per cent and 60 per cent). The DNA and SPÖ (parties with traditionally deep working-class penetration), like the SPD and the British Labour Party, now belong to this category. In addition, the Danish SD, once very strong, appears to be located systematically below the 50 per cent level. Certainly, social-democratic overrepresentation among the working class is a constant that has never been seriously challenged. But from the viewpoint of electoral sociology, the designation of social-democratic parties as parties of the working class no longer possesses *general* validity.

(ii) In addition, the *class cohesion* of electoral social democracy has been seriously eroded. Its internal socio-demographic equilibrium has altered in the direction of a *relative equalization* between the working-class and 'salaried middle strata' components. The reduction in the relative weight of the working-class group is attributable to two factors: an important, absolute and relative, decline in the number of workers in the population; and proportionately greater working-class disaffection with the social-democratic parties. Bearing in mind that working-class defection is not too serious, the first of these is more important.

In any event, the *class specificity* or *class cohesion* of these electorates, which historically registered the predominance of the working-class component, is being dissolved into a socially heteroclite mass. The current structure of the social-democratic voting coalition takes by far its most *interclassist* form in the entire history of social democracy. This drastically curtails social democrats' ability to adopt coherent class policies, since it inevitably increases the potential electoral cost of such policies.

All this confirms the hypothesis of a significant recomposition. Neither class parties nor – sometimes – parties of the class, social-democratic formations are changing. From expanded coalitions of the working class they are turning into *interclassist coalitions with a strong working-class influence*. And the difference is by no means negligible.

(c) The link between socialist party and working-class trade-unionism – which, more than a bond of kinship and blood, was one of self-interest, founded on calculation and trade-offs – is loosening. This affects both *organizational–institutional relations* (the link as a 'reciprocal penetration') and the *political trade-off* (the link as partnership, which finds its fullest expression in the neo-corporatist phenomenon). What is involved is certainly not some 'war of the roses' (David Arter), but the relationship between the two basic historic components of the working-class movement has altered substantially. Tending in the same direction, the decentralization and destabilization of tripartite systems of national negotiation in a sense *liberate the parties from the unions, and vice versa*. The trend to 'disinvestment of the political field by the unions' (Patrick Hassenteufel), and towards the disinvestment of the industrial terrain by the social-democratic parties, is the logical consequence of this development.

Similarly, in the majority of countries where it has been implemented, the social-democratic compromise, which is an inherent potentiality in every social democracy, finds itself destabilized and fissured. More specifically, today the system of consultation and bi- or tripartite decision-making is less functional, less effective and less legitimate.

At the heart of these developments lies the programmatic exhaustion of social democracy. Its values and economic competence are called into question by the discrediting of Keynesian solutions and the fiscal crisis of the welfare state. Social democracy is in the process of dismantling a historic capital, whose principal yield was the social and cultural well-being of disadvantaged strata and the institution of social capitalism.

With this set of changes, we observe a breach developing in the coherence that marked the social democracies of the 1950s and 1960s. Throughout this period, enduring institutional, political and sociological characteristics (electoral constitution as the party of the working class, party/union link, control of the left of the political scene, pragmatic and consensual culture) rendered the social-democratic parties, and their 'macro-policies', 'dynamically consistent'. These characteristics imparted coherence to significantly different public policies, which were implemented in highly diverse economic and political circumstances (e.g. Swedish or Austrian policy before and after 1973). They supplied a firm base and capacity for resisting the normal constraints of political life and economic administration without major ruptures and crises. But depending on the country concerned, they have progressively and variously been called into question. In the teeth of the macroeconomic crisis, this impressive construct withstood the new situation badly. In countries like Sweden or Austria, where social democracy was better equipped than elsewhere, the essentials were initially preserved (until the second half of the 1980s). But economic reality was stubborn. Locked in a stranglehold, and bereft of an adequate economic philosophy, social democracy exhibited strong signs of destabilization.

Obviously, as a specific institutional-political configuration, social democracy, although fissured, is still with us; it has not vanished into thin air. But its functioning and capacity for self-correction have been disrupted. Its economic *modus operandi* and its political-electoral *modus operandi*, largely interconnected, have been short-circuited. And in this sense, something important has been lost: the high degree of 'dynamic consistency-coherence'. Moreover, this loss is not attributable solely to the loosening of the party/union link, or to the deterioration in social democracy's electoral performance. The latter is simply the most visible aspect, and the most fraught with consequences, of the progressive but *quasi-generalized* mutation of the system of 'social democracy', which it simultaneously exposes and induces. In reality, the character traits of the social-democratic parties in their entirety are affected, as are their macro-policies, an example being tripartite bargaining systems that provided a structure of support for those policies. All the parameters that defined the social-democratic *partisan* space during the initial postwar period are more or less in the process of changing. This moulting process involves all levels of social-democratic life and reality. It simultaneously affects organizations, the union link, the composition of electorates, ideas – everything that goes to make up an identity.

Touched to the Quick: Social Democracy in a State of De-Social-Democratization

The postwar social-democratic project was fuelled by a considerable working-class presence (electoral, trade-union, organizational, cultural), and the high economic growth which, thanks to the Keynesian equation, made possible a conjuncture between working-class interests and the general interest. These have been eclipsed. The transformation of social democracy in progress is the effect of sociocultural and economic changes that go to the *heart of its development*, not the effect of some political and ideological assault at the margins.

In fact, today, two of the most essential links in the formation of social democracy's identity and *modus operandi* have been shattered or greatly weakened: (a) the *differentia specifica* of the social-democratic programmatic and ideological appeal; (b) the constitution of the social-democratic parties as uncontested representatives of the working class.

Among the changes itemized in this work, the most significant are the 'breakdown' of the Keynesian equation, with which a whole social-democratic practice and culture were identified; and the 'attenuation' – in some cases even the loss – of the sociological specificity of the contemporary social democracies. *With this dual development, the deep identity of postwar social democracy, its innermost memory and history, is called into question.* The whole edifice is destabilized. The organization is in the process of losing its working-class and popular reference points, and the trade unions' willingness to participate in the neo-corporatist process – like the process itself – is in doubt. The result is a marked reduction in the impact of the inherited social-democratic model, and a consequent imprecision in its contours.

In fact, at the heart of this socio-electoral, competitive and organizational disruption is the programmatic exhaustion of the social democracies, due to their inability to 'steer' the socioeconomic system. With the end of the Keynesian model as the privileged mode of regulation of the economic and the social, it is as if 'the social-democratic or socialist idea . . . found itself questioned in its very foundations'.[1] The exhaustion of the Keynesian solution means the end of the Croslandite conception of social democracy. In and of itself, it certainly does not entail the end of the social-democratic construct and *modus operandi* described throughout this study. But it contributes significantly to their profound – and irreversible? – destabilization.

The long history of social democracy has, of course, demonstrated on many occasions that 'social-democratic originality consisted less in a specific policy [e.g. Keynesianism] than in an organizational and cultural tradition rendering several policies possible over time'.[2] However, the economic

crisis of the last twenty-five years has proved that the *political effectiveness* –
not the originality – of social democracy largely revolved around a 'specific
policy', that is, Keynesianism; and that its abandonment has contributed
fundamentally to this 'organizational and cultural tradition' being called
into question.

Moreover, the tendential transformation of the social-democratic parties,
in their social structure and membership base, into 'parties of the salariat'
(notably non-working-class wage-earners) presages a general mutation of
parties of a social-democratic type. Given the cultural ascendancy of the
salaried middle strata, we are witnessing a loss of working-class influence
that is a good deal more significant than the sociological arithmetic *stricto
sensu* suggests. The working class becomes a *supporting class*, which not only
does not control the levers of endo-organizational power, but has lost much
of its influence over them. The salaried middle strata's massive entry into
the organization makes them – particularly the fraction with sizeable
cultural and educational capital – the *ruling social category* within the social-
democratic bloc.

However, the persistence of the union link – albeit sadly weakened – and
union involvement in political decision-making and the general operation
of tripartite bargaining systems – likewise in crisis – somewhat reduces
middle-class dominance within the social-democratic apparatus. Despite
their lesser legitimacy, trade unions remain a powerful mechanism for the
organization of the working masses. And they still tend – this is their most
elementary role – to *reintroduce the salience of class* into political conflict
through their discourse, activity and institutional weight. The electoral
importance of the working class, and its constitution as a 'class-for-itself'
through the unions, will always differentiate 'typical' social-democratic
parties from those socialist parties whose social base was, and remains, the
middle classes. Nevertheless, the position of social democracy in the world
of labour has been weakened. This old working-class formation has lost its
self-assurance and balance there. Its current social trajectory perfectly
expresses its *awkward position with the modern proletariat*: as a political force it
retains a sufficiently close relationship with its reference group to remain
its principal interlocutor, in the absence of a better one, but is no longer
connected to it by that fundamental bond of trust that its historical origins
promised and permitted it. As an organization and a vehicle of public
policies, social democracy remains linked to this world, but belongs less
and less to it. Thus the relationship becomes increasingly *instrumental*.
Many indices (reduced participation in the organization, protest voting or
abstention by a not insignificant percentage of the party's 'natural' social
base, working-class voting for the new extreme right) show that working-
class control over its own political representatives is increasingly exercised
over the party, and less and less *through* it. Social-democratic capacity for the
mobilization, orientation and representation of the working-class group
and disadvantaged strata has diminished significantly.

Interclassist formations with a strong working-class influence, but culturally and organizationally focused on the new middle classes and the elites,

today's parties of a social-democratic type differ substantially from the great popular formations of the 1950s and 1960s, when working-class and popular representation was massive and influential. *A fortiori* they differ from the working-class parties of the beginning of the century.[3]

In reality, social democracy is faced with the vicious circle of its contradictions and weaknesses. Changes in social stratification prompt it to broaden out to segments of the population other than the workers – without, obviously, alienating their support. Implemented in various forms since at least the revisionist crisis of the 1920s, strategies of expansion 'erode exactly that ideology which is the source of their strength among workers'.[4] The link attaching the working class to social democracy begins to loosen as a result. Nevertheless, while the Keynesian equation proved effective, the subsidence of working-class politics at the level of electoral strategies did not lead to working-class disaffection. But the social deficit of current social-democratic policies functions as cause and trigger of workers' reduced propensity to vote social democrat, and their reduced participation in membership activity. Workers are less susceptible than previously to the social-democratic appeal (programmatic, organizational, political), in part because it is less sensitive to working-class demands. It is a question of political rationality. 'As Socialists become parties like other parties, workers turn into voters like other voters,' Przeworski and Sprague have written. In this sense, social democracy reaps the fruits of its own politics. *If the left does not want to, and cannot, identify with popular strata, the popular strata cease to identify with the left.* Moreover, working-class defection cumulatively strengthens the predominance of the middle classes within the organization – a predominance which, in turn, exacerbates working-class defection.

Moderately neoliberal economic policies; a certain working-class electoral defection; the loosening of the link with the unions; the middle-class entry into the organization; class images diluted in favour of catch-all strategies; the continuous expansion of the middle strata – all these developments are interlinked as the symptoms and effects of an identical flux, a wave that slowly but structurally erodes the class specificity of the social-democratic parties. In this context, the strong presence in current social-democratic discourse of the 'social', that eternal favourite, barely withstands the test of the facts: behaviour in government. The new social-democratic construct – marked by the strong presence of the neoliberal component on the ideological and programmatic level, and by the middle classes on the organizational level – is buckling under its own weight: *a very resilient historical line of ideological and sociological continuity is in the process of snapping.*

Notes

1. Pierre Rosanvallon, *La Crise de l'État-Providence*, Seuil, Paris 1981, p. 134.
2. Alain Bergounioux and Bernard Manin, *Le Régime social-démocrate*, Presses Universitaires de France, Paris 1989, p. 184.

3. The link between a party and a social class typically includes 'a connotation of interaction' such that the one exercises its influence over the other. According to Kay Lawson, the link is a 'connexion . . . with reciprocal impact'. The link between social-democratic party and working class is certainly not broken from the latter's point of view – far from it – but it has been loosened. The link is conceived here in the dual and complementary sense of the term: in the sense of *participation* (in fact, the working class participates less and less actively within the social-democratic organization); and in the sense of *representation* (the working class identifies less and less with social democracy, as indicated by the workers' reduced propensity to vote social democrat). Considered from the viewpoint of the party, the link has also loosened. Having opted for an interclassist appeal addressed to the widest possible 'public', social democracy has a diminishing desire to be, or present itself as, the body that represents the working class. Now, the manner in which a party-organization opts to 'establish itself in representation' influences the participation the party can anticipate in exchange, for participation in an organization is more induced than spontaneous. The participation of individuals is determined largely by encouragements, the incentives offered by the organization – material incentives (tangible rewards and benefits), incentives of solidarity (adherence to the group and identification with it), or programmatic incentives. (See Peter Lange, 'La théorie des stimulants et l'analyse des partis politiques', in J.-L. Seurin, *La Démocratie pluraliste*, Economica, Paris 1981, p. 249.) In the event, ideological and programmatic options, governmental performance and organizational choices, as well as the increasingly conspicuous preponderance of the middle classes within the party, do not excite the enthusiasm of popular strata.
4. Adam Przeworski and John Sprague, *Paper Stones: A History of Electoral Socialism*, University of Chicago Press, Chicago 1986, p. 55.

13

The New Social Democracy

Social Democracy Old and New:
'While the snake is shedding its skin, it is blind'

I would like to formulate, in the clearest possible terms, the questions that are implied throughout this analysis. Is the progressive adoption of a moderate neoliberalism, or the greater priority accorded to 'new politics' themes, essential to the political approach of contemporary social democracy, or secondary? Are the marked shift in the sociological and cultural centre of gravity of social-democratic organizations and electorates towards the middle classes, and the redistribution of endo-organizational power in favour of the leader and 'technocrats', important or secondary for social-democratic identity? Or, once again, are the loosening of the link with the trade unions, and the crisis of tripartite structures of national negotiation, important or secondary for the social-democratic *modus operandi*? Is the inability of countries with a social-democratic tradition and structure to institute a new and durable model of regulation that takes account of globalization, the interconnection of financial markets, the expansion of the service sector, and the feminization of their labour force,[1] important or not for the constitution of the social-democratic parties? The answer to all these questions is clear: these political options and developments are central!

Now, these transformations, product of a long and gradual process of evolution, predate the 'new' social democracy *à la* Blair, Schröder, or D'Alema. A number of the reforms and revisions vaunted by the new social democracy, from managerial competence or practical acceptance of the anti-interventionist macroeconomic consensus, to openness to the middle classes, were – in large part – set in train, or established, before the 'new' social democrats came to power in the socialist parties. The 'third way' proposed by Anthony Giddens is certainly presented as 'an attempt to transcend both old-style social democracy and neoliberalism'.[2] But in which unknown, fabled country is this 'old-style social democracy' to be found? Where was it practised? After 1982 (failure of French Keynesianism) and 1984 (abandonment by the Greek socialists of their expansionary economic policy), which country, which government, adopted the recipes of 'old-style social democracy'? In the last twenty years, which social-democratic party has not jettisoned its ideology and traditional policy-making? In reality, the 'third way', conceived as a route 'different' from, or 'intermediate' between, two actual opposed extremes, does not exist, because this 'old-style social democracy' does not exist or, when it does, involves only small minority currents. Contrariwise, conceived as a political and/or theoretical initiative for refounding social democracy, the 'third way' not only fully exists, but is prospering and becoming progressively dominant.[3] In a sense, since the beginning of the 1980s European socialism in its entirety has been largely pointed, according to different rhythms and in different forms, in the ideological-programmatic direction described in part by political enthusiasts for the 'third way', often *ex post*.

In addition, the opposition between supporters of the 'old' and 'new' social democracy, whatever the content attributed to either term, crystal-lized within parties that were *already* in the process of transformation. They confronted one another in parties that were in fact becoming 'new' – in part regardless of the deliberate intentions of the competing elites, in part because of them and thanks to their actions. Obviously, here it is almost impossible to disentangle 'external' constraint and inescapable situation from conjunctural option; profoundly reluctant choice from deliberate strategic preference. But in any event, social democracy in the 1980s, in full de- and recomposition, was in the process of changing before its 'great transformation'.

'While the snake is shedding its skin, it is blind.' Ernst Jünger's naturalist image partly fits the social-democratic mutation of the last thirty years, when the transformation had yet to discover its theorization, or a clearly defined and consistently adopted ideological-programmatic expression.[4] But the 'new' social democracy has definitely not sprung up like some jack-in-the-box. It largely predated its concept. In a sense, the 'third way' was already present as well, prior to its adoption by New Labour and theoretical formulation by Giddens. The new social democracy of the 1990s is the worthy, direct *heir* of 1980s social democracy. The continuity between them is manifest, and manifestly strong.

The major innovation made by the partisans of the *new* social democracy consisted in the explicit, conscious, deliberate, and – above all – aggressive assumption of this new identity. The concepts of the 'radical centre' or the 'new centre' have audaciously pushed back the 'limits of what can be said', transgressing inherited programmatic and ideological proprieties. They have brought a new coherence, an unimpaired visibility, an impressive clarity to the trajectory of change. The elaborations and slogans of the 'new' social democrats have made it possible to go straight into the new universe of social democracy, to which – in large part – it was *already* inclining. What had been a fragile intellectual construct, a taste for ambivalence, a lukewarm affiliation, a gentle change, was at a stroke accelerated, magnified, transformed into a forceful adherence, even into a symbolic rupture, a message of renaissance. Thus were born British New Labour, with its 'radical centre', the SPD of the 'new centre', the PDS and the 'Olive Tree', the 'modernist' and European PASOK of Costas Simitis. Towards the second half of the 1990s, with and thanks to the new generation of social-democratic elites, the moderately neoliberal turn begun in silence, the opening to the middle classes that had in fact started some time before, the progressive loosening of the link with the unions, the slow redistribution of intra-organizational power, the gradual abandonment of the language of class – all these developments were accelerated and began *converging*, cumulatively intensifying their effects. The image became unique, complete, and was wholeheartedly adopted. Thus, with the appearance of the 'new' social democracy, the question of social-democratic identity received a novel response, and enables us to pinpoint a new consciousness.

Obviously, not all social-democratic forms and fabrics are identical – far from it. Some verge on neoliberalism; others candidly yield to it; yet others are more distant from it.

As I have already stressed, the neoliberalization of options has been more inventive, eccentric, advanced, and deliberate in Great Britain than elsewhere (see Chapter 9). Labour's whole programme was inventive (e.g. the policy of devolution, promotion of the theme of 'community', initiation of a debate on the sacrosanct British electoral system). In addition, the discourse of New Labour has sometimes assumed a very 'traditionalist' complexion, references to 'Middle England' – 'the repository of English traditionalism'[5] – being an exemplary expression of this. 'Like the new right,' Colin Hay and Mathew Watson have written, 'the "Third Way" represents a flexible synthesis of (a generally understated) neoliberal economics and a (loudly-proclaimed) legitimating normative philosophy – in this case neocommunitarianism for Thatcher's neoconservatism.'[6] This situation is explained largely by the dominance of the opposition's ideas ('Social democracy had never captured the conservative nation,' Gregory Elliott has written),[7] the severe defeat of the trade unions, the absence of a competitor on Labour's left, as well as the strong liberal tradition in Great Britain. The ideas that have historically been the strength and pride of British society – the high value placed on the individual and individual responsibility – reappear at regular intervals, and find a much more sympathetic audience there than elsewhere.[8] In this light, the neoliberalization of British Labourism is not simply more conspicuous, more advanced and more audacious: it is also more profound.[9] Thus, while the symbolism of the centre – 'beyond left and right' – was crucial in Great Britain, in France a return to the symbolism of the left, a *moderate* reactivation of the left/right divide, a combination of the neoliberal option with elements of a 'soft' neo-Keynesianism, were the distinguishing signs that marked the programmatic renewal undertaken by the PS after 1995. In Germany, spurred on by the Blairite example and the SPD's long spell in opposition, Gerhard Schröder adopted an approach (the 'new centre') that at first sight seems closer to the British pattern. Nevertheless, the German case is more composite. The 'social market economy' remains an inescapable reference in a country where, unlike in England, there is no classical liberal tradition.[10]

In Scandinavia (particularly Sweden) and Austria, too, the more classically social-democratic legacy remains relatively strong even today. The SAP and the SPÖ continue to represent a version of social democracy that is more working-class and popular, although their long spell in power has contributed substantially to the dilution of their programmatic originality and a challenge to their former influence.

These differences indicate that there is not one, but several 'third ways'. But beyond these differences, it is clear that the extraordinary diversity (ideological, programmatic, organizational/institutional, sociological) of the socialist cultures and structures of the nineteenth and twentieth centuries is in the process of shrinking.[11] The transformation is profound, because it is not merely ideological. On the contrary, in a single dynamic it encompasses actors and structures that are 'external' to the social-democratic enterprise (electorate, unions), those that are 'internal' (cadres and membership base, leadership, organizational structure), as well as the ideological and programmatic elaborations of the social-democratic elites.

It also embraces the 'policy style' – that is, 'the standard operating procedures for handling issues which arrive on the political agenda'.[12] *Social democracy's overall cartography* is altering (and everywhere in the same direction) – that is the essential change. Whether this is dubbed the 'third way' or something else is a simple matter of terminology. To identify a *global* change with its most articulate, bold and aggressive version – Blair's 'third way' – is to restrict its scope and import.

The 'Triple' Coherence of an Incoherent Identity

In effect, after much groping and hesitation, social democrats have adopted a distinctly aggressive programmatic posture, particularly during the second half of the 1990s. The adoption of a moderate neoliberal discourse, supplemented in some cases by a moderately expressed post-materialist sensibility,[13] as well as a more classically social-democratic discourse, has created a rather 'social-liberal' programmatic profile. The new social democracy is a more moderate force programmatically and ideologically than ever: moderately neoliberal, moderately non-liberal, moderately ecological and 'post-materialist', and sometimes moderately 'law-and-order'. 'Modernity', 'responsibility', 'competence', 'across-the-board appeals to the whole electorate' – these have become the hallmarks of its 'natural party of government' strategy (see Chapter 9). By means of this strategy, the loss in social identity and left-wing identity has been immediately counterbalanced by a gain in 'modernity', and managerial and economic competence.

This new posture – an updated, extended and accentuated formulation of the semi-catch-all strategy of the 1950s and 1960s – represents the most striking and emphatic ideological opening to the middle classes and the enterprise culture in social-democratic history. It thus combines the most advanced 'ideological depolarization' with the boldest interclassist semantics in the entire history of European socialism. We should remember that this interclassist semantics finds a real – not rhetorical – support in the interclassist composition of social-democratic organizations and electorates, which is likewise historically unprecedented. Ideologically and sociologically, social democracy is a political force with a 'trans-border' identity; or, more traditionally, with a 'catch-all' identity.

Yet one way of aggregating ideas and interests is substituted for another only when the latter has disappeared. The working-class format and the catch-all format do not mix. They cannot be juxtaposed or combined. When one is centre-stage, the other is off-stage. These two formats – or strategies – are separate, and cannot be superimposed. Now, what the majority of political commentators meant by the social-democratic 'catch-all' strategy of the 1950s and 1960s was, in reality, neither a catch-all strategy nor a working-class strategy, nor even a 'dual' strategy (which is, by definition, impossible). Instead, it was a 'semi-working-class' and a 'semi-catch-all' strategy (see Chapter 3). The reality constituted by two 'half-realities' – products of two 'half-strategies' – was the social-democratic reality of the 1950s, and especially the 1960s.

In definitively abandoning its working-class strategy of yesteryear – but also its 'semi-working-class' and 'semi-catch-all' strategy of the 1960s – in favour of an aggressively and resolutely trans-border strategy, today's social democracy has opted not simply for another strategy, but for another identity.

It is an identity that contains three 'factors of coherence':

(a) In presenting itself so clearly as a 'moderate' and 'responsible' force, social democracy has hit upon a pragmatic balance – or rather, a coherence – between its discourse in opposition (which traditionally tended to be left-wing) and its practice in government (traditionally right-wing).

(b) In effecting its historically most emphatic opening to the middle classes, and foregrounding an 'interclassist' semantics so explicitly and systematically, social democracy effectively combines – for the first time since the Second World War – the interclassist logic of its rhetoric with the interclassist logic of its electoral and organizational penetration (likewise historically unprecedented). It thus establishes a balance and coherence – a correspondence – between the trans-border programmatic/ideological profile of the new social democracy and the sociology of its organization and electorate (which is equally trans-border).

(c) At the same time, changes in the contemporary social-democratic universe have 'resolved' the sociological contradiction of the social democracy of the 1960s and 1970s. Social democracy no longer runs the risk of becoming a political force torn between cadres and members increasingly derived from the middle classes (which was the case in the 1960s), and an electorate that has remained popular in its basic structure. In the final analysis, the organization's break towards the middle classes and the 'catch-all' format was not an evasion. Instead, it was an anticipation, the portent of a sociological groundswell to which social-democracy-in-the-electorate was to yield, with a significant time lag and on a reduced scale. This made possible a certain sociological *rebalancing* – and homogenization – between the different spaces (organization, electorate, associations) of the social-democratic edifice. There is no doubt that social democracy is more interclassist than ever. But this interclassism – which, by definition, is a source of contradictions, even tensions – currently penetrates all the spaces (all the 'stages', to recall Christine Buci-Glucksmann and Göran Therborn's imagery) of the social-democratic edifice. Compared with the 1960s and 1970s, contemporary social democracy is socially much more diverse, but it is noticeably more homogeneous in its diversity.

So in terms of its ideological priorities, and the class structure of its organization and electorate, the new social democracy is partially 'liberated' from its traditional 'bugbears', particularly left-wing rhetoric and the working-class 'bogy'. As of now, and for the foreseeable future (the medium term, as they say), social democracy has found a certain equilibrium: it is coherent in its social-liberal moderation; it has hit upon a balance between its programmatic-ideological profile and the social profile of its organization and electorate; it is homogeneous in its marked sociological heterogeneity. In a way, there is consistency between the men and women who *are* the new social democracy and the ideas that *make up* the new social democracy. Thus if we locate the trans-border identity (sociological, ideological) in this perspective, a hypothesis suggests itself: because it is sustained by this 'triple' coherence, in all probability the new social-democratic identity *is not circumstantial or ephemeral.*

Fundamentally, contemporary social democracy, which is consciously and deliberately constructing its identity on diversity and on the basis of diversity, is not searching for an 'old-style' cohesion. On the contrary, it is building its cohesion *on the absence of strong attachments* (ideological, sociological, cultural) and *strong commitments* (programmatic). The cohesion of contemporary social democracy is, in a way, 'postmodern': the ties that bind (ideological, cultural, sociological or programmatic) are weak. But it draws its strength from its weakness, from lowered expectations, from its minor relevance as a link. In effect, this weak link draws its strength from the fact that the only legitimate, acceptable and conceivable link is one that does not commit or tie it too much. In political parties, and particularly mass parties (organizational model of the left), great diversity and heterogeneity (ideological, programmatic, cultural, sociological) have always been 'disruptive' factors. But in structures like current social-democratic structures, which base their cohesion on *minimal* cohesion, that might not be the case. Political and ideological minimalism can make do with minimal cohesion.[14]

The most important factor that could cause social democracy to lose its balance is an 'old bogy': the working class and those consigned to the scrapheap. The latter, together with their interests and expectations, participate neither on an equal footing, nor according to the rule of the 'just measure', in the novel organizational and ideological-programmatic synthesis of the new social democrats. It is clear that the working class and the ideas developed in its name are no longer highly rated, either in the organization or in the dazzling shop window of social-democratic ideology. This impairs the balance – which is in any case unstable – of the new social democracy, even though recent electoral growth contributes to masking it for the time being. In the medium term this could prove to be a time bomb ticking away under the foundations of the impressive edifice of contemporary social democracy.

Obviously, we should not think that the heterogeneous, even heteroclite, elements that go to make up the programmatic and social identity of social democracy today could be combined in any manner whatsover and in all circumstances. Hybrid combinations – in Ancient Greek, *hubris* means 'immoderation', and in the modern language it means 'insult' – derived from the crossing of heterogeneous priorities cannot survive unaltered – or not for long, at any rate – because of the great difficulty they experience in adapting to the exigencies of government. They have proved possible in opposition; they have even exercised a certain fascination, as the initiatives of Blair and Schröder attest. They turn out to be a lot more difficult – even impossible – in government, as the recent governmental experience of the Swedish and Norwegian social democrats indicates, even though they (and especially the former) are renowned for their capacity for programmatic renovation and firm social anchorage. The disastrous electoral perform-ance of the SAP at the 1998 elections, the bad performance of the DNA in 1997, or the poor result of socialists in the 1999 European elections, certainly do not prove anything about the future of the social-democratic governmental experiences now under way. But they suggest that scepticism is not unfounded.

No doubt social-democratic leaderships have to manage – and confront – an identity that is hard to handle. But everything indicates that *they are not faced with a choice of identity*. That choice has been made. The main lines of the new social-democratic physiognomy are already delineated. *Alea jacta est*? In all probability, yes. Naturally, were the governmental experiments now under way to fail, social democracy might again be destabilized. It could thus become less neoliberal or more neoliberal, more 'new politics' or less 'new politics', more bourgeois or less bourgeois, more left-wing or less left-wing. Everything will depend on the intra- and extra-organizational context of such a failure. But it could adopt this 'more or less' without really repudiating itself fundamentally, either ideologically and program-matically, or organizationally. After much trial and error, hesitation, and all sorts of incidents, social democracy has successfully negotiated a cross-roads: far from being like a ferret forever on the run and escaping, its contemporary identity is finally beginning to take a 'finished' shape. For socialist and social-democratic high commands, the most difficult task is *behind* them.

A Weak Identity: Entrepreneurial Identity, Strategic Flexibility and Electoral Instability

'Trees with deep roots are the ones that grow tall,' Frédéric Mistral wrote. Firmly rooted in the working class, the great social-democratic parties of the pre- and interwar periods were formations with a strong social, ideological and political identity; and in attenuated fashion, this remained the case in the initial postwar period. Simultaneously structures for 'organizing the masses' and structures 'organized by the masses', they possessed a remarkable capacity for mobilization and orientation of their social base. The three traditional branches of the social-democratic constellation – party, trade unions, associational network – have now been weakened (and have been for some time) through a cultural and organizational process that is analogous to the secularization of religious institutions. But they have also been profoundly transformed.

Pursued as well as imposed, diversification in the membership and electoral base of social democracy, which resulted from changes in social stratification and catch-all strategies, has dealt a heavy blow to the social and cultural cohesion of social-democratic organizations. The party-community no longer exists, just as the political – and especially social – terrain conducive to its development no longer exists. In addition, the social-democratic parties have gradually lost their aura in intellectual circles. What Perry Anderson has written of the SPD is in large measure valid for the majority of the new century's social-democratic parties:

> Social Democracy has come to power without much depth of support in intellectual opinion. The trend – first with the radicalisation to the left of the sixties, then with the opposite swing of recent years – has gone against it. By the end, the Kohl regime had few sympathisers, but Schröder cannot count on any prior groundswell in his favour.[15]

In effect, what the modern social-democratic edifice lacks is the stabilizing principle afforded by profound organizational, social and cultural anchorage. It lacks a strong (albeit summary), and strongly shared, ideology. It is an edifice – and an identity – constructed predominantly on the political and programmatic level. Social-democratic 'self-identity' is currently more political, and considerably less ideological (in the sense of subscribing to an ideological 'grand system'), sociological or cultural. Compared with the social-democratic identity of the past, it lacks depth, social and cultural density. It is less composite, less compact, less robust.[16]

The biggest challenge its environment could present to any party concerns the attributes that make it what it is, and among them *its class* and *its space* (political and ideological). The stability of a party depends less on its electoral capacity than on its ability to defend its 'identitarian' territory. When the 'privileged' electorate of the party is not well protected, it is not so much the party's electoral performance as its identity that is called into question.[17] Now, once their 'identitarian' territory has diminished, along with their ability to defend it, the electoral capacity of contemporary socialist parties largely depends on a *specifically political* trade-off. With its weak social, ideological and cultural identity, social democracy today finds itself more bound up with the mechanism of competition than in the past. Its fate is more linked to the political context specific to each conjuncture. The 'political venture' dimension of its identity is reinforced. It becomes more significant, conspicuous, vigorous, present. Today more than ever, social democracy as a political enterprise depends on the quality of its *political appeal* (leadership, candidates, tactical coups, programme, governmental record, etc.); and that, obviously, is a direct function of competing appeals. However, the quality of this appeal derives from a conjunction of favourable circumstances, intra- and extra-organizational, which, by definition, is *uncertain and aleatory*. Its sociological and cultural protective screen having partially disintegrated, social democracy must assert and impose itself in the political and electoral arena without the whole arsenal and 'reserves' of yesteryear at its disposal.

This has some important consequences.

The new social democracy, with its entrepreneurial culture, is certainly more 'open' and flexible ideologically, but it is also less present in the laboratory of ideas that is the social terrain. It is constructed in line with a logic that allows it to 'catch' the *moods* of public opinion, rather than *movements* of opinion, let alone *social movements*. The experience of recent years indicates that the latter become important for social democracy only retrospectively (the case of the PS after the social movement of December 1995 is exemplary here, as is that of the SPD after the strong emergence in force of the ecological and pacifist movement). The inability of socialist headquarters to anticipate the emergence of social movements and new political currents (e.g. the ecological movement, 'new politics' parties, the new extreme right) is only the most visible symptom. In a sense, social democracy has a very good grasp of opinions that have *been formed*, and a very bad one of situations in which opinion *is formed*. (These are often crisis situations or moments when historical time accelerates and, as Pierre Bourdieu has written, opinion polls – and, we should add, social democracy's experts – are 'incapable of producing the slightest reasonable forecast' about them.)[18] Postwar social democracy has frequently proved very adept at recuperating new themes and new ideas, particularly when they have become a *fact of public opinion*, but markedly less well equipped to generate a new vision of society and the future. To a rather greater extent than the 'old' social democracy, the 'new' one is constructed in order to be close to public opinion. But it is less close to the 'surprise actor' that civil society often is.

Correlatively, social democracy's *autonomy vis-à-vis* its environment, and its ability to control it, have decreased drastically. Social democracy is no longer constructed as a '*strong institution*' capable of significantly influencing the 'value systems and attitudes' of contemporary societies, and has not been for a long time. Once, socialist and social-democratic parties were not merely machines for the conquest of power, but (as Marc Lazar put it) 'major matrices of political identity and culture'.[19] Today, they no longer perform this role. The diffusion and inculcation of social values and norms (elevation of the collective and collective action, diffusion of an egalitarian culture, etc.) no longer form part of the modern social-democratic universe. Thus, not only has 'the old socialist idea of parties as agenda-setting vanguards' been largely abandoned,[20] but often the more modest role of 'spur' as well. In this respect, social democracy as a left-wing force has lost its originality. 'Politically and economically correct', it vacillates and wavers at the slightest movement of public opinion, which its experts are charged with scrutinizing attentively. More so than in the past, it thereby becomes dependent on the 'short term', the shortest short term there is: the next electoral deadline. Precisely because it is a force with a weak identity (organizational, sociological, cultural, and ideological), and precisely because it is largely constructed as an electoral machine, the new social democracy retreats – often without even doing battle – in the face of national and international economic and geopolitical constraints. Socially and ideologically weakened, followers rather than forerunners, social democrats take to observing ideological and electoral rhythms which they do not control, but which are imposed on them by electoral and ideological competition, or the international balance of forces. In the absence of strong reference points, modern social-democratic engagement lacks any sense of the *longue durée*.

The weakness of social-democratic identity is not only a source of disadvantages, for *it is not without its compensations*. 'Cantharides contains something that acts as an antidote to its own poison'; the other side – the good side of the 'bad'? – of 'entrepreneurial' social democracy is precisely its *positive capacity for adaptation*. If socialist and social-democratic organizations are currently less robust and less compact, they are by the same token less ponderous, more flexible and more 'open'. When leadership autonomy is great, bureaucracy is weak, and members are submissive and/or few in number; when the importance of ideology and social class as factors in a cohesive identity is diminished, the party is more flexible, has more rapid 'reflexes', adapts better to the unforeseen and to new issues. Thus, the 'negative' aspects of the new social-democratic identity are intimately bound up with 'positive' compensations. Indeed, adaptability makes these organizations capable of responding more quickly to the stimuli of the social environment and electoral competition.[21]

From this angle, Blair's formula of 'permanent revisionism' perfectly captures the new social democrats' propensity to renew their ideological and programmatic arsenal incessantly. This is considerably aided by the structure of endo-organizational power and the loosening of the link with the trade unions, as well as by contemporary social democracy's 'flexible', trans-border ideology. *The 'new' social democracies – whether in their left- or right-wing versions, whether 'southern' or 'northern' – are structurally 'lighter' and, from a tactical viewpoint, more 'flexible' than the social democracies of the past.* Their recent electoral successes are simply the reward for their extraordinary powers of adaptation and renovation. One of the characteristics of contemporary European socialism turns out to be precisely its ability to 'lose and gain strategic flexibility [very] readily'.[22]

Thus, adaptation to the conceptions of the surrounding environment and, in consequence, strategic adaptability, increasingly become a distinguishing characteristic of contemporary social democracy. This was much less true of the great 'activist organizations' that the socialist and social-democratic parties were historically. However, this strategic flexibility is accompanied, and complemented, by *strategic 'modesty'*. Social democracy is no longer up to the task of seeking to reverse the terms of the current strategic situation, either in economic affairs (witness its attitude towards globalization) or in international relations, without risking paying a significant electoral, ideological and organizational price. Precisely because it is a force with a weak identity, that is to say, without solid support, or the dense and dynamic consistency of the past; and precisely because it has definitively lost its 'iconoclastic' character, and the spirit of resistance and innovation that distinguishes any iconoclastic political force, social democracy today does not have the means, the will, or the *strong* support seriously to contest the established structures of power and influence, both national and international. It lacks the aggressive and obstinate mentality which, in a distant past, derived from the core of a popular movement (or at least part of this movement), which social democracy was supposed both to represent and to structure – and sometimes to betray. Today's social democrats 'tinker with the margins of the system. They potter about in its backyard. . . . They all share a panic fear of conflict.'[23] In 1999 the resignation of Oskar Lafontaine, and the participation of 'social-democratic' air forces in what was a 'centre-left' war against Serbia, were two symbolically significant expressions of the new social democracy's strategic 'modesty'. Indeed, social democracy's hands are freer than ever to play and juggle with ideas, with tactical coups, with its image and political marketing. It plays a tactical – and occasionally strategic – game of small steps, often very skilfully. But it cannot play a game of large-scale movements. It cannot play for big stakes.

Moreover, this gain in tactical flexibility and electoral effectiveness, which is attributable to increased leadership autonomy and the ideological and programmatic flexibility of a less 'integrated' structure, is accompanied by a very substantial loss in stability, or a surplus of fragility. Electoral power that is not based on the substratum of an organization well anchored in society, and possessed of a clear and distinct ideological and programmatic identity, undeniably remains genuine power. But as my data have established, it proves inconstant, and hence fragile (see Part II). It can thus rapidly be transformed into its opposite, a veritable impotence: veritable, but probably temporary, for as a result of its greater strategic flexibility, the new social democracy tends rapidly to remedy any persistent electoral weakness, through appropriate revisions.

However, given the challenge to working-class 'centrality', today's socialists have no well-targeted, well-centred, stable alternative social base. They must win over everyone, and especially the middle strata, to conserve the base required for power. Now, at present there is nothing to suggest that these strata could constitute a solid support and privileged base for left-wing parties – alongside the working class, obviously. As long as the salaried middle strata prove incapable of supporting *one* political formation in an electorally cohesive fashion – that is to say, massively and enduringly – in the same way as the working class once supported the left, it seems to me that the weakening of the working class, as well as its relative estrangement from left-wing parties, is a *loss that cannot be compensated* in terms of social democracy's electoral *stability*.

In the absence of the stability imparted by working-class entrenchment, social democracy will be condemned, like the financial markets, to a constant search for the stable floor that will permit it to bounce back electorally. Its electoral competitiveness will be enormously hampered by adverse circumstances, and probably enhanced by auspicious circumstances. Social democracy has become more vulnerable and exposed. An electorally vulnerable force can suffer considerable and rapid losses, and can then make up the lost ground – sometimes just as rapidly. But what it cannot be is consistently successful over a long period.[24] This is the other side – the 'bad side'? – of the 'entrepreneurial' structure and culture of today's triumphant modern social democracy. Whether or not it adopts the 'third way', and whatever its dreams, the new social democracy will be vulnerable, exposed to economic circumstances, the jolts of the political game, and rapid alterations in the situation.

The Politics of the Spectacle: The Marketing Left?

The overall map of the social-democratic space is in the process of changing. Yet the widespread belief that the ongoing weakening of traditional recruitment structures, the crisis of the great ideological systems, the increased personalization of electoral choice, the enhanced role of 'experts' and political marketing, lead to the politics of the spectacle, advertising and 'appearances', is rather misleading. It is an exaggeration often made by observers – and actors – on the right, but especially on the left.

Let us take the example of leadership. The personalization of electoral campaigns and the greater impact of leadership do not betoken the withering of politics – an argument in favour of spectacle-politics. Specialist studies show that 'in reality voters listen – and respond – to what the candidates say'.[25] Appraisal of leaders certainly depends on their 'personal equation' (actual or supposed competence, telegenic appearance), but it also depends on their 'responsiveness' to the electorate's concerns.[26] The 'power of the spoken word' rests on this capacity. An effective leader is not the one who best distils 'soundbites', or wields the 'aesthetic and emotional influence of words'.[27] Above all, it is the leader who is able to present a party – their own party – a policy, and especially a cleavage. 'For the

majority of voters the issues represent a choice between two "borders" . . .
and parties achieve success by clearly signalling with which border they are
identified.'[28]

This is still true even today, when the leaders of great left-wing and right-
wing parties are orientated towards the centre, which in some countries
consequently becomes the new collective obsession of the political class.
Certainly, as Alain Lancelot has rightly emphasized, 'an election is only
secondarily the choice of a programme'.[29] Certainly, too, a candidate's
superiority over his or her competitors contributes to significantly increasing a party's electoral chances. But 'brilliant victories' like those of Silvio
Berlusconi in Italy, are not, as Marc Lazar has emphasized,[30] possible all
the time. Indeed, everything suggests that in systems of 'party government'
the leader-candidate's image remains a *secondary* element in partisan
strength, even if it is markedly more important than it was in the past.[31]

So it is not 'image' in the televisual sense of the word, but image in the
sense of '*vague policy package*' referred to by Giovanni Sartori[32] that determines a leader's and party's powers of attraction. The modern leader is not
a sovereign, a sort of terrestrial deity, whose deeds command the political
contest and the activities of voters. Moreover, if today's voters are distinguished by less attachment to parties, they are better educated and
informed than previously, more attentive to the issues and the unfolding of
the political contest, and better able to 'read events'. Above all, the
judgements they make on parties, leaders, and issues 'appear more structured and more coherent'[33] – the index of a greater lucidity and political
competence. The processes of 'cognitive mobilization' produce more
'sophisticated' voters and members.[34]

Thus there is not a kind of 'black art' about leadership or professionalized campaigns and political advertising. To persist in reducing a party's
politics to the dimension of the 'spectacle' is to search for the underlying
key to it – that is, the party's ability, in the new media landscape, to
combine 'content' with 'form', what is expressed with its expression. And
the professionalization of political communication is based above all on
marketing, but also on the public spoken word – on the 'public use of
reason', as Kant called it.[35] As a consequence, the political options of a
party and its leader continue to influence the affiliation and loyalty of
citizens significantly, particularly in countries with a parliamentary regime
where 'collective' actors (institutions, parties) count for more than 'individual' actors.[36]

Let us resume the argument developed above. Within today's social
democracies, a 'managerial' culture – I am tempted to say: a managerial
pensée unique – is solidly entrenched. The leader's autonomy has increased.
Tacticism gains ground. Tactical manoeuvres with an eye to gaining
or retaining power (the 'enterprise project' in terms of micro-economy)
have a stronger endo-organizational impact. More so than in the past,
politics is increasingly about nothing more than politics. 'Politics
has been reduced to the language of politics,' writes Antonio Polito.[37]
This corresponds (in part) to the new reality of contemporary social

democracy. For all sorts of reasons, the 'war of appearances' has become more important.

In this respect, Stuart Hall is right when he asserts of the 'style' of the Labour government in Great Britain: 'this is not a superficial "style" . . . but something that goes to the heart of the Blair project'.[38] Social democracy no longer has at its disposal the organizational, sociological, cultural, and ideological arsenal of the past, which was defensive but also offensive. It is less well anchored in the social fabric. In this sense – and in this sense only – it is 'superficial'. The current socialist and social-democratic space has indeed lost its profundity. To employ a terminology alien to political punditry, we might say that the *surface* structure of contemporary social democracy is strengthened at the expense of its *deep* structure; or, better, that the deep structure is becoming more and more surface.

Even so, Hall is wrong to think that New Labour is trying to govern 'by spin, through the management of appearances alone'.[39] One does not win elections – and above all, one does not govern – 'through the management of appearances alone'. The new social democracy has ideas. And it seeks to 'sell' them like any good firm, utilizing the best available methods of political marketing. This is something that is not in and of itself reprehensible; it is also something that is not in and of itself effective.

The new social democrats employ the new methods of doing politics systematically. Let me put it clearly and crudely: they do it well, and they do well. But to reduce the ideas of the new social democracy – the 'marketing-left', as Claude Demelenne has it – to the 'spectacle' and the 'professionalization of communication' is to ignore the profundity of its change in identity.[40] If contemporary social democracy is 'superficial', it is so for much more important reasons. Moreover, to consider the use of new communication technologies and the professionalization of election campaigns as a 'crisis' or a 'debasement' seems to me to be out of step, virtually *archaic*. We do not know whether it is possible to restore the passion, excitement and collective ethos of the 'old' party organization. But were it to prove possible, it would not occur in defiance of the technological, institutional and sociohistorical gravity of advanced modernity.

Certainly, by virtue of wanting to win over everyone and the whole of society to conserve the requisite power base, it is a 'modest' socialism, promoter of a species of political and ideological 'minimalism', that presents itself to voters. This creates the illusion of 'a gravity-defying victory of style over substance', as Boris Johnson wrote in the *Daily Telegraph*.[41] But ideological attenuation, as well as the growing importance of television, of the leadership, and 'spin doctors', does not signify that triumphs of staging and 'special effects' are taking control. To believe that is to ignore not only the composite character of contemporary social democracy, but also the 'sophisticated' nature of electorates in advanced modernity. The 'entrepreneurial' culture in the new social democracy has been substantially strengthened. But it is not the only culture in town.

In the societies of advanced modernity, 'propaganda via the image' tends to replace 'propaganda via print' (Ostrogorski), and the 'theatricalization' of politics has been professionalized. But the need to 'stage' oneself, in some fashion or other (and the fashion certainly counts), is a practice 'of extraordinary antiquity'.[42] No political appeal or 'leadership appeal' can do without it. Was it not Alcibiades who severed his dog's 'beautiful' tail to attract the Athenians' attention? But who today remembers Alcibiades for his 'dog's tail'? Social democracy has not changed because of the 'spin doctors', and its alteration is not reducible to them. That is why this alteration is historically significant.

Social Democracies, Southern European Socialism, and the Term 'Social Democracy'

In countries without a profound social-democratic tradition, like France, Italy or Greece, the 'modernization' of the socialist parties, or even communist parties – I am thinking of the PCI in the second half of the 1970s and the 1980s – became synonymous with their social-democratization for a period; and this is still partly true today. Resort to the notion of 'modernization' was a kind of convenient cliché to explain the 'lag' of these parties, and outline the path they should follow in future. 'According to an intellectual mode,' Angelo Bolaffi wrote in 1983, 'which has so to speak a naive and linear image of modernization, everything in political phenomenology that diverged from the social-democratic model was liquidated as politically and culturally backward or as the resurgence of irrationalism.'[43]

To regard social democracy as a way of structuring the left that is superior to any other, as 'a substantive *summum bonum*',[44] is to discount other political configurations which are equally based on the working class, and have flourished thanks to it. It is to erase from the political and social map national historical paths of undeniable political effectiveness (e.g. in Italy or France). The merit of this argument is not affected by the fact that, having once inveighed against anything that presented itself as social-democratic, entire wings of the French or Italian left have since discovered the advantages of the social-democratic path and *modus operandi*.

Let us take the example of bi- and tripartite national bargaining, and the phenomenon known as 'social corporatism'. The system of institutionalized and centralized collective bargaining (whether at national or branch level) has often been regarded as the expression of 'modernity' or 'maturity' in industrial relations.

The inability of the united left in France in the 1980s, or of the Greek and Portuguese socialists once in power (certainly in an unpropitious conjuncture), to lay the foundations of a French, Greek or Portuguese 'social-democratic compromise' is eloquent. For countries without a unified and centralized trade-unionism and without a deep social-democratic tradition, like France, Spain, Italy, Portugal, or Greece, enduring and sustained institutionalization of social conflict is either difficult or impossible. The same is true, for different reasons, of Great Britain. This does not mean that the PS, PASOK, PSOE, PSP or, in another register, British Labour are a variety of 'failed' social democracy, an 'ontological flaw', a 'mistake' within a family – the social-democratic family – that is implicitly, or even explicitly, regarded as 'normal'. These parties are not *abnormal*; they are not 'atypical'. No political Darwinism obliges the non-classically social-democratic socialist parties to adapt to the exigencies of the social-democratic model (whose specificity is itself being diluted today) – assuming, obviously, that we do not reduce social democracy solely to 'reformism' and 'moderation', but attribute to it a more 'intensive' political, social and institutional content.

In reality, political parties are in some sense condemned to 'store their previous states in their memory', and despite their demonstrable capacity for evolution, they cannot readily, at will, transcend – and escape – their distinguishing qualities and characteristics. Each party is the bearer of its own tradition, and these traditions, sometimes strongly institutionalized, are 'embedded in the parties' identities and self-conceptions'.[45] The weight of the past, the national historical, economic and social determinants that presided over the birth and original development of the working-class movement (political and trade-union), the structure and strength of that movement, social stratification, the power and culture of the 'adversary', the national electoral market – these substantially condition the current evolution of the European left, as well as the forms taken by social conflict. To expect otherwise is to get entrapped in a 'social-democratico-centric' conception of social and political conflict. The trade-union and political left of each country 'speaks' the specific language of its basic structure and institutions, and – for better or worse – can speak only that language.

That said, what we discover when we leave the universe of the better-delineated social democracy of the 1950s and 1960s, and examine the ongoing mutation of this political force, is not a universe of 'pure' difference between it and the socialisms of southern Europe. An interplay of convergences – mutual or unilateral, depending on the domain – releases us from describing the relationship in terms of substantially different models or 'binary oppositions'.

In the 1980s and 1990s, the distance that traditionally separated the southern socialist parties from those of a social-democratic type, and which (according to some) made southern European socialism a 'deviant' case in the European socialist/social-democratic universe, narrowed significantly. In fact, despite a marked convergence, the most striking gap is evident in terms of the relationship with the trade unions and tripartite central bargaining;[46] and it is precisely on the level of competitive status, doctrine and programmes that we can detect the most spectacular convergence. As for the sociology of the electorate and membership, convergence is only moderate. Although comparison is more difficult on those counts, the contrasts between the relevant forces remain significant.

If the – relative – fading of the lines of difference licenses the thesis of a partial 'social-democratization' of the southern European socialist parties, this 'social-democratization' is considerably more conspicuous in the light of the ongoing mutation of European social democracy than that of the social-democratic paradigm of the 1950s and 1960s. In reality, the southern socialisms are converging *only* with the new social democracy *in statu nascendi*, which is itself in the process of '*de-social-democratization*'. The narrowing of the distance is the direct product of a dual dynamic of convergence, which is complementary and mutual.

Hence the trend is towards convergence. On both sides this is the effect of a pragmatic, defensive adaptation to the new economic, social and cultural situation of advanced capitalism, rather than an offensive option for the institution of a new social-democratic model. The convergence flows from the *dilution* of the relatively strong 'models' that structured the postwar socialist family. It is in large part the product of the 'banalization' of the left in Europe (e.g. the end of the very striking specificity of the Scandinavian model, whose prototype was the SAP; the Austrian model; the British model – Labour is becoming a party like all the others, while it remains a party different from the rest; and, given the context of our analysis, the Greek 'national-popular' model of the 1970s and 1980s; or, in another register, the PCI).

Certainly, the social-democratic continent is not a single entity. But nor, *a fortiori*, is the socialist continent in its entirety. And despite the convergence of policies, the plural character of European socialism is asserted – and confirmed – every day. Yet convergence is the prevalent trend. This leads the content of the concept 'social democracy' either to vanish, or to be defined in unduly extensive fashion. It thereby loses much of its distinctive capacity.

With the calling into question of 'old' models and the old coherence, the meaning of the term 'social democracy' shifts. In its practical usage it increasingly becomes – in a sense, *it once more becomes* – a *generic* term, designating the set of parties of 'moderate' socialism, whether social-democratic or not. What is more, the sharp delegitimation of the word 'socialism', following the collapse of the regimes of 'real socialism', tends in the same direction. It is scarcely surprising, then, if the term 'social democracy' has largely lost its often pejorative edge, particularly in southern Europe – countries with a strong communist tradition – but also beyond, in the intellectual or popular milieux of the European left. For terminological convenience, in this book I myself have often switched from the *narrow* to the *generic* usage of the term, and vice versa, without warning the reader in advance. This generic usage is currently – albeit incorrectly – the most common, prevailing over all others. The present reduction in the distance that morphologically separates social democracy from southern socialism – or, more accurately, the *social democracies* from the *southern socialisms* – obviously favours the generic use of the term. But reduction does not signify total abolition of the borders that separate different types of constitution and action on the socialist/social-democratic left. The generic acceptation of the term 'social democracy' is based on different principles from the narrow sense. Current developments are weakening the impact of the social-democratic model (and the national social-democratic models), and significantly restricting the scope of this narrow sense. But for all that, they do not render it pointless.

Notes

1. Élie Cohen, 'La gauche et l'économie dans les expériences de pouvoir', in Marc Lazar, ed., *La Gauche en Europe depuis 1945*, Presses Universitaires de France, Paris 1996, pp. 657–8.
2. Anthony Giddens, *The Third Way*, Polity Press, Cambridge 1998, p. 26.
3. We must distinguish between theoretical reflection on the renewal of contemporary social democracy and the 'real' third way of Tony Blair. Giddens's book is significantly influenced by the British context. Its themes and proposals are nevertheless of more general value.
4. Quoted in Monique Chemiller-Gendreau, Anicet Le Pors, Marcel Rigoux and Gilbert Wasserman, 'Gauche: pendant la mue le serpent est aveugle', *Le Monde*, 15 July 1993.
5. Stuart Hall, 'The Great Moving Nowhere Show', *Marxism Today*, November/December 1998, p. 13.
6. Colin Hay and Mathew Watson, 'Neither Here Nor There? New Labour's Third Way Adventism', in Lothar Funk, ed., *The Economics and Politics of the Third Way*, LIT, Hamburg 1999, p. 174.
7. Gregory Elliott, *Labourism and the English Genius*, Verso, London 1993, p. 93.
8. Albert O. Hirschman, *The Rhetoric of Reaction*, Belknap Press, Cambridge, MA and London 1991, pp. 131–2
9. According to Hirschman (ibid., p. 132): 'the more recent rhetorical assault against the Welfare State in the West has not been nearly as vigorous and sustained in Continental Western Europe as in England and the United States. None of this implies that in countries with a strong *liberal* tradition it is impossible to establish a comprehensive set of social welfare policies. But it is here that their introduction appears to require the concurrence of exceptional circumstances, such as the pressures created by depression or war, as well as special feats of social, political and ideological engineering. Moreover, once introduced, Welfare State provisions will again come under attack at the first opportunity.'
10. Jacques-Pierre Gougeon, 'Une nouvelle étape pour la social-démocratie allemande', *La Revue Socialiste*, no. 1, 1999, pp. 98, 103. Under the influence of the party and unions, his partner and rival Oskar Lafontaine, but also the swing of the ideological pendulum, Schröder's approach was subsequently 'corrected' in a left-wing direction. And everything indicates that it is in the process of being recorrected in a more neoliberal direction (Lafontaine's resignation contributing substantially) without, for all that, being abandoned.
11. See Pascal Perrineau, in Gérard Grunberg, *Vers un socialisme européen?*, Hachette, Paris 1997, p. 120.
12. Jeremy John Richardson, quoted in David Arter, 'Sweden: A Mild Case of "Electoral Instability Syndrome"?', in David Broughton and Mark Donovan, eds, *Changing Party Systems in Western Europe*, Pinter, London and New York 1999, p. 169.
13. This was more pronounced in Scandinavia, Germany and the Netherlands, less so in Austria, and rather weak in Great Britain, Belgium or Greece.

14. We might add that the strengthening and – paradoxically – the weakening of the leadership is something that makes the management of centrifugal tendencies in the different social-democratic spaces (organization, electorate, associational network) easier. In organizations with minimal cohesion leadership is a factor of stability and weak leadership is a factor of flexibility.

15. Perry Anderson, 'The German Question', *London Review of Books*, 7 January 1999, p. 15.

16. It is symptomatic of this evolution that the elitist dimension of the social-democratic configuration – the structure of leaders and elected officials surrounded by professionals and experts, a kind of modern variant of the oligarchy dear to Michels – is reinforced at the expense of its 'societal' dimension. This trend is clearly reflected in political debate by an 'individualization' of political conflict, in the sense that the individual politician and intra-elite debate occupy an increasing role in it. On these aspects of public debate, see the very interesting conclusions of Lauri Katvonen and Axel Rappe, 'Social Structure and Campaign Style: Finland 1954–1987', *Scandinavian Political Studies*, vol. 14, no. 3, 1991, pp. 241–59.

17. Angelo Panebianco, *Political Parties, Organization and Power*, Cambridge University Press, Cambridge 1988, pp. 211, 218.

18. Pierre Bourdieu, *Questions de sociologie*, Minuit, Paris 1984, pp. 231–3.

19. Marc Lazar, in Alain Bergounioux and Lazar, *La Social-démocratie dans l'Union européenne*, Les Notes de la Fondation Jean-Jaurès, Paris 1997, pp. 16–19.

20. Donald Sassoon, *One Hundred Years of Socialism*, I.B. Tauris, London 1996, p. 673.

21. Let us take the example of 'southern Europe socialism'. Engaging 'belatedly', having lived (with the exception of the French and Italian parties) under dictatorial regimes, and benefiting considerably from their position of opposition, the socialist parties of Spain, Greece and, to a lesser extent, Portugal have established themselves not only as the principal formations on the left, but also as one of the two principal formations in their respective countries, with a governmental vocation. And this at a time (second half of the 1970s and the 1980s) when northern social democrats, affected by an often 'traumatic' governmental experience, seemed to be ideologically and electorally exhausted. In effect, the parties of southern Europe, with few links to a political subculture, a more interclassist character, and a very strong and autonomous leadership, have exhibited a greater strategic flexibility – and less programmatic coherence – than most of the more classically social-democratic parties. This largely explains their ability in the 1990s to preserve their main electoral gains of the 1980s, despite a natural weakening attendant upon the corrosive effect of being in power. But after a certain initial immobilism the social-democratic parties of northern Europe have likewise demonstrated their strategic flexibility – this is clearly signalled by their ambitious programmatic renovation and their return to power in the course of the 1990s.

22. Jonas Pontusson, review of Herbert Kitschelt, *The Transformation of European Social Democracy*, *Comparative Political Studies*, vol. 28, no. 3, 1995, p. 472.

23. Claude Demelenne, 'Pour une gauche debout', *Politique*, nos 9–10, 1996, p. 76.

24. Something the results of the 1999 European elections proved in spectacular fashion.

25. Peter R. Schrott and David J. Lanque, 'How to Win a Televised Debate: Candidate Strategies and Voter Response in Germany, 1972–87', *British Journal of Political Science*, no. 22, July 1992, p. 467.

26. On these two components of the leader's image, see, *inter alia*, Marianne Stewart

and Harold Clarke, 'The (Un)Importance of Party Leaders: Leader Images and Party Choice in the 1987 British Election', *The Journal of Politics*, vol. 54, no. 2, May 1992, pp. 447–67.

27. Robert Michels, *Political Parties*, trans. Eden and Cedar Paul, Jarrold, London 1915, p. 75.

28. Ola Listhaug, Elaine Macdonald Stuart and George Rabinowitz, 'Ideology and Party Support in Comparative Perspective', *European Journal of Political Research*, no. 25, 1994, pp. 112, 144. This explains the weakness of centre parties, as well as the weakness of the 'ideology of the centre', assuming such an ideology exists (ibid., p. 144). On the importance of divisions as determinants of electoral choice, see also Stefano Bartolini and Peter Mair, *Identity, Competition and Electoral Availability*, Cambridge University Press, Cambridge 1990.

29. Alain Lancelot, ed., *1981: les élections de l'alternance*, Presses de la Fondation Nationale des Sciences Politiques, Paris 1986, p. 21.

30. Lazar, in Bergounioux and Lazar, *La Social-démocratie dans l'Union européenne*, p. 16.

31. By contrast, in systems where the president of the republic represents the keystone of the institutions, and the presidential election is the centrepiece of the system, largely structuring political life, the leader a party has at its disposal is – or can be – a 'critical' factor in the balance of forces.

32. Giovanni Sartori, *Parties and Party Systems*, Cambridge University Press, Cambridge 1976, p. 329.

33. Nonna Mayer and Pascal Perrineau, *Les Comportements politiques*, Armand Colin, Paris 1992, p. 64.

34. Ronald Inglehart, *La Transition culturelle*, Economica, Paris 1993, pp. 419, 431.

35. Jean-Marc Ferry, 'Pour une justice politique dans l'État social', in *L'action politique aujourd'hui*, Éditions de l'Association freudienne internationale, Paris 1994, p. 71.

36. In this respect, the case of Germany is exemplary. See Max Kaase, 'Is there Personalization in Politics? Candidates and Voting Behavior', *International Political Science Review*, vol. 15, no. 3, 1994, pp. 211–30. For the presidential systems, see the very comprehensive analysis of Thanassis Diamantopoulos, *Electoral Systems*, Patakis, Athens, 2001 (in Greek).

37. Quoted in Eric Hobsbawm, 'The Death of Neo-Liberalism', *Marxism Today*, November/December 1998, p. 6.

38. Hall, 'The Great Moving Nowhere Show', p. 13.

39. Ibid.

40. Demelenne, 'Pour une gauche debout', p. 76. Demelenne, a very perceptive representative of this line of thought, writes: 'Underneath a few gadgets, most of the stars of the new left are hollow, desperately hollow' (ibid.).

41. Quoted in the *International Herald Tribune*, 3 February 1999.

42. At the beginning of the century, when, for the Independent Labour Party, 'the spoken word in the open air still remain[ed] its main weapon . . . orators [were] trained in special courses where they practice[d] exposition and controversy' (Moisei Ostrogorski, *La Démocratie et les partis politiques*, Fayard, Paris 1993, p. 312).

43. Angelo Bolaffi, 'Au centre, les socialistes allemands', *Politique aujourd'hui*, no. 3, December 1983–January 1984, p. 65.

44. Colin Crouch, 'The Fate of Articulated Industrial Relations Systems: A Stock-Taking after the "Neo-liberal" Decade', in Marino Regini, ed., *The Future of Labour Movements*, Sage, London 1992, p. 167.

45. Sheri Berman, *The Social Democratic Moment: Ideas and Politics in the Making of Interwar Europe*, Harvard University Press, Cambridge, MA and London 1998, pp. 211–12.
46. The relationship to the trade-union movement remains a sizeable difference between certain of the parties of southern Europe and 'typical' social democracies. But it constitutes a less important difference than it did in the past. If the role of the union connection is fading, the difference that is 'constructed' starting from, and in relation to, this connection necessarily becomes less significant.

Part IV

Social Democracy in Context

Europe will need to respond effectively to the continuing challenges of globalization.

(Party of European Socialists [Manifesto for the 1999 European Elections])

14

The Unions and Left Oppositions

If social democracy in government (contemporary social democracy is a governmental force even when it is not in government) shelters behind the constraints, both national and international, on economic and social administration, what can we expect of the 'other left'? In the first instance, the 'social' left represented by the trade unions, long-time partners in the social-democratic enterprise? Then the 'radical' left (communist, post-communist, Red-Green, or ecological)? Or even of Europe and the Party of European Socialists (PES)? What could contribute to establishing a political alternative to neoliberalism? To what extent, and how? And in what conceivable framework? For this alternative – or its impossibility – forms part, even in its absence, of contemporary social democracy. Paraphrasing Jacques Attali, we might say that to 'identify the place' of social democracy is not only to 'confer a meaning on the place it occupies', but also – and possibly primarily – to divine the meaning of the 'place' it does not occupy.

The Low Horizons of the Trade Unions

The trade unions have been weakened, but they are not moribund – far from it. 'The weakening of the trade-union movement in the 1980s and 1990s', Göran Therborn has written, 'has not transformed West European unions into mere clones of their American or Japanese cousins.'[1] And with the exception of the United States and Great Britain, where we see 'broad and conclusive evidence of a dramatic decline in the influence of unions', in the majority of countries 'unions have retained most of the *institutionally based* capacities for the defense of worker interests that they had prior to the 1980s', despite a reduction (which is not, however, general) in union density.[2] Thus, if unions are not as weak as is commonly argued, it remains true that the sphere of trade-union influence (and I am not referring to *institutional* influence here) is dwindling even where union numbers remain significant, or are even on the increase. Trade-unionism is no longer – or rather, to avoid idealizing the past and minimizing the effects of the present, is less of – an influential and self-confident force than it was in the past. Trade-unionism has become weaker. Increasingly, it is an institutional interest group, a 'service' organization – and less and less of a movement.[3] Not that this in any way prevents 'micro-conflictuality' at enterprise level, or 'incessant guerrilla warfare opposing union forces and management'.[4]

This 'guerrilla warfare' must not, however, be allowed to mask the decline in the strength and role of unions, particularly within the individual firm. The weakening of the 'voice mechanisms'[5] represented by workers' collectives at the workplace (works councils and trade-union groups) is something that affects the daily life of working-class wage-earners. The emergence and consolidation of capitalist sectors that are non-unionized, or barely unionized – the diffusion, in a sense, of a *tradition of non-trade-unionism* – is a far from negligible economic, social and cultural reality, even in the economies of institutionalized-organized capitalism. The 'trade-union deserts' (Bernard Thibault) are difficult to repopulate at a time when workers are sceptical, mistrustful or disheartened, and employers are arrogant and aggressive. As Jelle Visser has stressed: 'some unions may even grow larger and stronger than ever before. However, we can be less confident that *encompassing* union movements – as we have known them for much of the past century in the democratic part of Europe – will make it into the next century.'[6] This development is already creating an uncontrolled and uncontrollable process of micro-deregulation, analogous to that of the United States or a large number of firms in southern Europe; in future, it could encourage it further.

Faced with this danger, unions have more to gain than lose from a 'political' strategy, a strategy of intervention at the central-national level, even at the European level. In a defensive period they even have an interest in using the 'ideology of the national interest', which can be articulated only at the central political level (see Chapter 5), against the ideology of the market favoured by 'sectional' capitalist interests today. And this is all the more true in that the traditional strike weapon, while it is very effective in a phase of expansion (considerably more so in corporatist than non-corporatist countries), is much less so in periods of crisis.[7] Thus, in the current environment the unions' abandonment of a 'national' strategy in favour of a 'decentralized' or 'local' strategy could turn out to be a miscalculation. As Paul Boreham and Richard Hall have written:

> To advocate such a strategy is to misread the nature of the power relations between labour and capital at the level of the enterprise and the economy as a whole. It is to consign the union movement to the conflict with capital at the weakest point – the workplace itself – where workers are subject to the power of a jealously guarded managerial prerogative and are susceptible to the appeal of the possibility of a sheltered, core-status job.[8]

To implement a *political-national* strategy, the unions need – today possibly more than ever – a fairly well-disposed 'third party', which involves preserving (in some way, at least) the *link with the social-democratic parties*. Obviously, the neoliberal policies implemented by social-democratic governments demonstrate that unions cannot passively await salvation from the election of friendly governments. They thus have an interest in not identifying too closely with their traditional partner. The socialist parties, for their part, have an even greater interest in not identifying too closely with the world of trade-unionism, and in freeing themselves from the overly close embrace of a burdensome ally. And this is what they have done virtually throughout Europe. In a social context in which trade-union and working-class centrality have been put in question, the importance to the social-democratic parties of the 'organic' link with the trade-union world has diminished dramatically. No 'catch-all entrepreneurial organization' would build its strategy and political future on the privileged, exclusive base of the working-class group. This explains why an ongoing relaxation of former attachments is the rule, with each actor encroaching minimally on the territory of the other in the framework of a co-operation that is now fluctuating, unstable, and often conflictual.

But socialists/social-democrats know full well that they cannot govern effectively for long *against* the trade unions. They also know that preservation of their union influence is a factor of electoral stabilization, particularly in countries where populist poles of the right or the extreme right threaten to entrench themselves enduringly among some sections of popular strata. In reality, parties and unions have an interest in a greater freedom of action, but at the same time both have an interest in *renewing*, on condition of a redefinition, *the terms of a political contract that is more than a century old*. This is why the umbilical cord has not been severed, even if it does not possess the content, the strength and vitality of yesteryear.

Thus, despite their weakening, unions wield power, and that power is not insignificant. If they were able to attenuate the new neoliberal orientation of social-democratic programmatic documents in the 1980s (see Part II), they are still inclined to 'push' social democracy in a less neoliberal direction. The unions constitute an 'external' and, in part, an 'internal' *buffer* which, although it is much more peripheral than in the past, *restricts* the social democrats freedom to pursue their strategy and vocation. After all, unions are often the last refuge of a social-democratic ideology abandoned by social democracy itself. And in particular, they are always capable of bouncing back and asserting themselves as central actors on the social scene, as was demonstrated by the impressive French trade-union movement of December 1995,[9] or the major mobilization of the Danish union base in April–May 1998. The capacity for action of the 'organized wage-earning masses' is thus not a hollow concept.[10] Unions will always be inclined to push social democracy in a less pro-capitalist direction, making it more 'open' and more 'sensitive' to the interests of waged labour.

But will this influence be such as to encourage a radical reorientation of current social-democratic politics? Will it be of a kind to rekindle the passion for 'that part of liberty which we call equality', as Heine termed it?[11]

Profound economic and social changes in advanced capitalism have not only weakened trade-unionism, but have also challenged a historically important aspect of union presence and activity: unions are much less potential sites and arenas for criticism of, and opposition to, capitalism than they were in the past (though trade-union anti-capitalism was a very complex and ambiguous phenomenon). The unions' present goal is largely defensive: to inflect the economic and social policies of incumbent governments. The objective of social transformation has been renounced, despite the resurgence here and there of 'centres' with an alternative culture. The unions are no longer tempted or obliged to articulate 'a language of principles and solutions' transcending the horizon of capitalist society, if only on the rhetorical level.[12] Abandonment of anti-capitalism, whether rhetorical or real, definitely does not mean renunciation of a whole culture of social critique, of which trade-unionism was historically a vehicle. But potential trade-union influence on social-democratic parties is not deployed, and will not be deployed (at least in the near future), in a radically anti-capitalist or 'socialist' direction, whatever content we attribute to the latter term. Worse still: trade unions' 'programmatic appeal' does not even outline an attractive socioeconomic prospect in the framework of capitalism, one that might have a good chance of attracting the attention of social-democratic strategists. In reality, the trade-union world is less capable than it once was of inspiring original ideas and new practices on the political level.

In addition, profound changes in the productive fabric and the current of ambient individualism have largely swept away not only the anti-capitalist vocation, but also the traditional and often 'communitarian' collectivism, of trade-union institutions. Trade-union action today is only in the second instance a means of asserting identity and global rejection of the enemy. Contemporary solidarities – 'social struggles', as they are called – derive less from any homogeneity of interests and tradition (based on communal existence) than from a concrete, temporary convergence around certain mobilizing themes. More so than in the past, the new solidarities are *specialized* in character and objective, and frequently *ad hoc*. Their character is somewhat makeshift and transient.[13] The enormous difficulty involved in maintaining the new networks of solidarity and action created during the impressive strikes by British miners (1984–85) and French workers (December 1995) is indicative of this. This does not mean that the influence of 'social struggles' on the left's programmatic options is negligible. The impact of the December 1995 mobilization on the French left, and even beyond, is tangible proof. But it could mean – and this is a hypothesis awaiting confirmation – that their impact can be momentarily strong, but not really profound: incapable of informing socialists' programmatic posture and governmental practice in anything other than circumstantial or electoral fashion.

Having preserved most of their 'institutionally based capacities', but losing momentum and more divided than ever, unions remain the *principal* representatives – and interlocutors – created by the world of wage-labour. This world is certainly very heterogeneous, but in its majority it remains orientated towards egalitarian values and the state. This cannot be ignored by any party of the left, be it socialist, communist, post-communist, or whatever. If it ignores it, it does so at its political and electoral peril. But the trade unions do not have the ideas, the cohesion, the will, nor, in the end, the strength to push social democracy towards a *fundamentally different* politics.

The Pink, the Red and the Green: 'Disaffected' Liberals and 'Disaffected' Social Democrats

With the onset of the 1950s, a period of routinization set in for socialists and social democrats, marked by an absence of new, mobilizing projects and an impoverishment of thought and internal debates. Only with the 1960s, in a new international context and with the arrival of new generations and ideas, did European socialism rediscover some of its internal intellectual vitality.[14] Even then, as Donald Sassoon has stressed:

> socialist parties were doomed to be taken by surprise by all the changes which modernity thrust upon them over the following thirty years: the permissive society, pop culture, feminism, black consciousness, homosexual rights, the plight of the Third World, ecology, the end of ideology, European integration, the revival of ideology, the crisis of the family, the end of communism in Eastern Europe, the growth of nationalist separatism. *Not one novelty worth writing or thinking about had been envisioned or predicted by the European socialist movement.*[15]

Indeed, social-democratic renewal was the product of pragmatic adaptation to social, economic and cultural evolution. Moreover, it came, for the most part, from outside: social movements, old and new, the new left, ecological networks and parties, the new right. Social democracy 'pirated' ideas that were developed outside it, and often against it.

But could the 'creative radicalism' (to use Geoff Eley's phrase)[16] of the new social movements and the 'new politics' oppositions, the more traditional radicalism of *some* (not all) communist parties or parties of a communist origin, as well as the trade unions' natural vocation to defend an economic policy favourable to the world of wage-labour – could these become the vectors (or rather, the joint vectors) of a 'new vitalizing vision', either in co-operation with social democracy (where the electoral arithmetic permits or prescribes it), or against it?[17] Might they, perhaps, contribute *involuntarily* to making it possible to 'safeguard' (to use Mario Telo's term) the identity of the social-democratic actor once again? For such a safeguard, bound up with the 'coherence' between the currently proclaimed identity of social democracy and its past economic and social options – a coherence that is today on the verge of rupture – is the issue that implicitly confronts the new social democracy.

Today, it is beyond dispute that in the majority of cases the presence of 'radical' poles, old and new, is conducive to a more audacious, more imaginative, and sometimes less pro-capitalist politics in several spheres (economic policy, unemployment, the environment, the construction of the EU, relations between the sexes, minority rights, cultural liberalism in general). It simultaneously constitutes a kind of 'external' *obstacle* and ideological-political *stimulus*. The function of these poles is on the one hand to 'correct' and 'moderate' the revisionist ardour of social-democratic leaders, and on the other to act as a laboratory of ideas.[18]

More specifically, the new social movements 'have put new issues on the political agenda [and] provided the recruiting ground for a new political elite, in particular for a new elite on the left'.[19] Together with the 'old' poles and the trade unions, the 'new' poles, which derive from the arena of 'movement politics', have contributed to a certain 'ventilation' of the social-democratic project and its governmental practice. We have seen tangible signs of this in the experiences of the *gauche plurielle* in France and the SPD–Green coalition in Germany. In a seeming paradox, rivals to the left of social democracy contribute to the promotion of a politics that is closer to specifically social-democratic declarations and objectives.

But be careful! The parties that occupy either the space to the left of social democracy, or the space of the 'new politics', or both at once, are profoundly different from the former communist oppositions. As a general rule, formations to the left of social democracy lack strong organizational structure, a compact class 'infrastructure', and coherent programmes. This is true in particular of the 'green' parties. Often built as the political expression of the new social movements, the Green parties, although they often claim to be a party-movement, do not possess a solidity equivalent to that conferred on the old social-democratic and communist parties by the communitarian and 'solidaristic' fabric of the working-class movement. Despite some far from convincing assertions, they are not constructed as 'parties of identity'. Moreover, the socially and culturally very heteroclite strata they represent, which are often very individualist, are not distinguished by a common mode of life based on collective – and collectively shared – values. It is scarcely surprising, then, if their 'anti-systemic' tendency has proved fragile, and if the rhythm of their 'absorption' into the system is exceptionally rapid. In fact, today everything suggests that the ethic of compromise, which coexists with an ethic of rupture in the Green parties, is prevailing.[20] The discourse of Green dissidence (or 'desubordination', to employ Ralph Miliband's term) has not had the depth of the communist anti-systemic discourse of the past – a discourse which Michel Hastings has characterized as a 'discourse of scission'. In addition, the ecological parties lack a stable electorate. A large share of Green electoral support comes from urban and middle-class categories. These voters are 'volatile', often register a 'protest' vote, and are very sensitive to electoral appeals and the circumstances of party competition. All of this weakens the position of the ecological formations, limiting their potential for electoral expansion as well as their potential for political pressure.

And the communists? Communists are 'disaffected social democrats'![21] This thesis of the Belgian socialist Henri de Man was profoundly unjust to the communist movement in the 1930s and its radical struggle for an egalitarian socialist society. Today, it is not very far from the truth. Robert

Hue, PCF leader, could still declare, during the 1999 Fête de l'Humanité: 'I challenge any party to assemble so many people. The Communist Party is alive and well!'[22] But notwithstanding the message delivered by the national secretary of the French communists, the PCF, like the other communist or post-communist parties, is no longer a guide and model – either as regards structure and organizational coherence, or when it comes to the representation of popular classes. In reality, the field of divergences within the traditional left has diminished significantly. According to Donald Sassoon, 'less than a decade after the collapse of the communist system, the European left ... has adopted a language and tone that possesses a cohesion it has never before achieved in its history'.[23] The combined effects of the fall of the Berlin Wall and globalization, real or perceived, have contributed to delegitimating the radical anti-capitalist politics – or systematic oppositional stance – of the communist parties, the extreme left, or some left-wing fringes within social democracy or close to it.[24] In fact, a large number of communist parties (not all), and all the small or medium-sized post-communist parties, have gradually inflected their discourse in a less 'anti-systemic' direction, and are progressively donning (as Alain Duhamel would have it) the new clothes of 'social reformism'.[25]

To summarize (and generalize), we are witnessing a *dual convergence* in the spaces of national competition:

(i) Organizationally and ideologically more polymorphous and diverse than ever, the forces to the left of social democracy are converging. The communists and post-communists are abandoning their radical anti-capitalist project, and becoming a shade more 'new politics'; while the properly 'new politics' formations are, in their turn, becoming much less 'anti-systemic' and a little more 'left-wing' (in the sense that they accord greater importance to socioeconomic themes).
(ii) Having in their great majority renounced, or being in the process of renouncing, their anti-systemic vocation, these peripheral oppositions are converging with social democracy, which for its part, in adopting a more 'new politics' profile, feels closer to them.[26]

Thus, without always openly acknowledging it, the Red, Red–Green, or Green oppositions are metamorphosing. Far removed from certain 'hard' communist parties of the past, the majority of these parties convey the reassuring impression of a force of peaceful protest, *flexibly assimilated into the 'system' and flexibly opposed to it.* After the fashion of the German and French Greens, they are, in addition, becoming 'national players'.[27] To generalize Alain Duhamel's observation about the PCF, this is 'the hidden metamorphosis'.[28]

With this dual convergence and metamorphosis, a new dialectic of competition and reconciliation is set in train on the left and centre-left of the party-political spectrum. Socialists and 'oppositional reformists' are *ideologically more complementary than competitive*, while remaining *electorally more competitive than complementary*. A displacement of roles is under way in most of Europe's party systems: to stick with Henri de Man's language, the majority of communists, post-communists and Greens currently act like 'disaffected social democrats', while social democrats act like 'disaffected neoliberals'. And paradoxically, both draw some of their strength precisely from the fact that they are opposed to policies they in part adopt! Hence these 'discontents' are not wholly antagonistic. They even turn out to be complementary, as the experiences of the *gauche plurielle* in France and the SPD–Green coalition in Germany tend to indicate. Now, the deradicalization of most left-wing forces creates a strategic situation that is propitious to the specifically social-democratic dynamic of de-radicalization. If the left-wing forces are likewise following a *centripetal* motion, the price of moderation becomes less high (occasionally even nil) for the social-democratic parties, moderate parties *par excellence*. In consequence, they can desert their traditional ideological and political zone at reduced risk.

The socialist parties and their left (or 'neither left nor right') rivals have become forces of pressure *vis-à-vis* one another and, simultaneously, forces under pressure. Faced with the socialists who are solidly entrenched in the institutions, and know how to recuperate the new and old themes expressed on the margins of the system, these parties do not find life easy. They are certainly 'different' enough, and powerful enough, to leave their mark on ideological competition and social-democratic policy. But at the same time, they are rather 'similar', powerless to influence this competition decisively, and seriously reorientate social-democratic policy options. Thus, their influence is not negligible, but it is not strong either. Consequently, while the dialectic of competition on the left and centre-left of politics can supply a corrective to social-democratic politics towards the left (as well as in a more 'new politics' direction), this 'corrective' would not appear to be such as to change the political orientation of contemporary social democracy fundamentally – at least for the time being.

Notes

1. Göran Therborn, 'Europe in the Twenty-first Century: The World's Scandinavia?', in Peter Gowan and Perry Anderson, eds, *The Question of Europe*, Verso, London and New York, 1997, p. 365.
2. Miriam Golden, Michael Wallerstein and Peter Lange, 'Postwar Trade-Union Organization and Industrial Relations in Twelve Countries', in Herbert Kitschelt *et al.*, eds, *Continuity and Change in Contemporary Capitalism*, Cambridge University Press, Cambridge 1999, pp. 223–4.
3. John Scott, *Stratification and Power: Structures of Class, Status and Command*, Polity Press, Cambridge 1996, p. 241.
4. Michel Vakaloulis, 'Antagonisme social et action collective', in Vakaloulis, ed., *Travail salarié et conflit social*, Presses Universitaires de France, Paris 1999, p. 245.
5. Colin Crouch, 'Exit or Voice: Two Paradigms for European Industrial Relations after the Keynesian Welfare State', *European Journal of Industrial Relations*, vol. 1, no. 1, 1995, p. 77.
6. Jelle Visser, 'The Strength of Union Movements in Advanced Capitalist

Democracies: Social and Organizational Variations', in Marino Regini, ed., *The Future of Labour Movements*, Sage, London 1992, pp. 42–3.

7. Philip O'Connell, 'National Variation in the Fortunes of Labor: A Pooled and Cross-Sectional Analysis of the Impact of Economic Crisis in the Advanced Capitalist Nations', in Thomas Janoski and Alexander Hicks, eds, *The Comparative Political Economy of the Welfare State*, Cambridge University Press, Cambridge 1994, pp. 234–6.

8. Paul Boreham and Richard Hall, 'Trade Union Strategy in Contemporary Capitalism: The Microeconomic and Macroeconomic Implications of Political Unionism', *Economic and Industrial Democracy*, vol. 15, Sage, London 1994, p. 344.

9. See Sophie Béroux, René Mouriaux and Michel Vakaloulis, *Le Mouvement social en France. Essai de sociologie politique*, La Dispute, Paris 1998. See also the very comprehensive analysis of Michel Vakaloulis, "Mouvement social et analyse politique", in Claude Leueveu et Michel Vakaloulis, *Faite mouvement*, PUF, Paris, 1998.

10. Jan Michels, 'La gauche sans la lutte des classes', *Politique*, nos 9–10, 1999, p. 98.

11. Quoted in Eustache Kouvélakis, *Philosophie et révolution de Kant à Marx*, doctoral thesis, University of Paris VIII, 1998, p. 64; forthcoming, Presses Universitaires de France, Paris 2001.

12. Andrew Richards, *Down But Not Out: Labour Movements in Late Industrial Societies*, Instituto Juan March, Madrid 1995.

13. Ibid.

14. Gérard Grunberg, *Vers un socialisme européen?*, Hachette, Paris 1997, pp. 38–43.

15. Donald Sasson, *One Hundred Years of Socialism*, I.B. Tauris, London 1996, p. 197; emphasis added.

16. Geoff Eley, 'Socialism by Any Other Name? Illusions and Renewal in the History of the Western European Left', *New Left Review*, no. 227, 1998, p. 115.

17. Ibid.

18. The same role of 'corrective' has often been performed in the past by the communist parties (where they were strong), and the trade unions (where they were closely linked to the social-democratic party), or by both at once. As social democracy's entire historical trajectory has demonstrated, the influence of parties to the left of social democracy, and the pressure they exert over it, has a far from negligible impact on its identity and its ideological and programmatic development.

19. Hanspeter Kriesi, 'Movements of the Left, Movements of the Right: Putting the Mobilization of Two New Types of Social Movements into Political Context', in Kitschelt *et al.*, eds, *Continuity and Change in Contemporary Capitalism*, p. 421.

20. The case of the German Greens, a formation in the vanguard of the ecological movement, is exemplary. In government the Greens abandoned their traditional pacifism and anti-NATO stance (supporting the NATO intervention in Kosovo), as well as their commitments on the cancellation of nuclear energy. In addition, they have made a major compromise on the question of the 'dual nationality' of immigrants living in Germany.

21. Quoted in Mario Telo, *Le New Deal européen: la pensée et la politique sociales-démocrates face à la crise des années trente*, Université de Bruxelles, Brussels 1988, p. 109.

22. Robert Hue, quoted in *Le Monde*, 14 September 1999.

23. Donald Sassoon, 'Socialisme fin-de-siècle. Quelques réflexions historiques', *Actuel Marx*, no. 23, 1998, p. 144.

24. Ibid., pp. 144–6.

25. *Libération*, 10 July 1998.
26. As for the Green parties, the reorientation of the social democrats in a more 'new politics' direction has prevented the specifically 'new politics' parties from differentiating themselves sufficiently and occupying their initial privileged, and electorally profitable, niche unhindered. At the same time, and symmetrically, these parties, electoral spokespersons of 'post-materialist' strata, have been pushed by the persistent centrality of the social question, and by social-democratic repositioning towards a more pro-capitalist posture, to adopt a programmatic profile that is rather more 'traditionally left-wing'. They have thus been prompted to accord greater importance to the social question and socio-economic themes, in order to compete with the social democrats on their own terrain and to take advantage of the social shortcomings of economic adminis-tration by socialist governments. Indeed, the weakness of social democracy on its own privileged terrain – equality and the welfare state – has created a veritable *political and programmatic vacuum*, which the left-wing oppositions (in the first place, post-communist or communist in origin, but also in part those that are more classically 'new politics') have sought to fill.
27. German social democrat Erhard Eppler *à propos* of the German Greens, Erhard Eppler, 'Some programmatic remarks about the German SDP', in Cuperus and Kandel, eds, *European Social Democracy: Transformation in Progress*, Friedrich Ebert Stiftung, Amsterdam 1998, p. 244.
28. *Libération*, 10 July 1998.

15

The European Union, Globalization
and 'No Alternative'

Europe and Globalization

'Contemporary globalization', David Held *et al.* have written:

> is not reducible to a single causal process but involves a complex configura-
> tion of causal logics. These . . . embrace the expansionary tendencies of
> political, military, economic, migratory, cultural and ecological systems. But
> each is mediated by the late-twentieth-century communications and transport
> revolution which has facilitated globalization across every domain of social
> activity and dramatically expanded . . . global interaction capacity.[1]

Combined with 'a wave of neoliberal deregulation, initially among core
Western economies', these trends 'encouraged an explosion of global
trade, investment and financial flows'.[2]

Today, however, it seems to be taken for granted that economic, and
particularly financial, globalization was – in the last analysis – 'the result of
explicit or implicit *political* decisions, and not of some implacable economic
determinism'.[3] Above all, globalization is the product of *strategic* action,
even if this action was not always conceived as such, particularly by minor
states. In fact, 'states, and above all the world's most powerful states, have
actually played a very active and crucial role in making globalization
happen, and they are increasingly encumbered with the responsibility for
keeping it going'.[4]

Globalization has increased the cost of traditional left-wing policies, and
encouraged their abandonment in favour of the neoliberal option. Globalization puts the left in an extremely difficult position: any action that is
necessary and effective within national borders is, by definition, of limited
impact. And passive integration into the 'globalized' world primarily represents more impotence for states, particularly minor states with a traditionally strong social democracy; and also more impotence for the left in
government.

Thus, the left will not be capable of sustaining the development of a
relatively egalitarian economy, with low unemployment and high wages,
without 'voluntarist' action at the inter- and supranational level (first of all,
the level of the European Union, a 'global-regional' body of power and

authority that is at once relatively strong and sufficiently *close* to be open to direct social-democratic influence). Inaction at the European level, and more generally at the international level, could translate into the definitive disappearance of specifically social-democratic economic policies.

In this context, can we anticipate a *European* left-wing macroeconomic policy from social democrats? Can we expect the implementation of a 'voluntarist' economic strategy, the converse equivalent of the voluntarist-elitist strategy for the construction of monetary Europe? Can we, at the very least, expect a policy of neo-Keynesian inspiration on a European scale? Or will it always be postponed, deferred?

The challenge facing social democrats is sizeable. For the first time in postwar Europe, socialists are in power simultaneously in the three major European countries (Germany, France, United Kingdom). For the first time, too, socialists are no longer 'lagging behind integration'. Having in part (but only in part) surmounted their traditionally strong divisions over the construction of Europe, they now pose as the 'party of Europe' within the European Union. Schröder's statement – 'I am a European not "by necessity" . . . but by inclination'[5] – perfectly describes the mindset of the overwhelming majority of socialist parties in Europe. Moreover, having largely lost the capacity for socioeconomic 'steering' at the national level, the majority of socialists are, for the first time, profoundly convinced that their economic and social effectiveness presupposes national and European co-ordinated action. The political and intellectual upgrading of the European level, considered more 'pertinent' (the 'large area approach', as Larry Elliott and Dan Atkinson would say), is the instinctive social-democratic response to the very real downgrading of the national level, which is increasingly regarded as 'non-pertinent' or 'insufficiently' pertinent. Thus a number of social democrats are timidly searching for a new balance between *politics and markets*, and perhaps – at least in some cases – a new, *moderate* version of 'politics against markets'. A number of social democrats would indeed like to re-establish the 'Keynesian capacity' of the nation-state, profoundly challenged by globalization (at least 'European-level globalisation'), and transpose it to the European level.[6] If the challenge is great, the opportunity is less 'historical' than it appears.

The Weighty Actuality of the Past

A policy is not conceived and realized in a vacuum. Policies previously implemented either at the national level, or at the European level, are not without their consequences for today's policies.

For example, the signing of GATT, 'one of the first post-Maastricht acts of the European Union',[7] and then the policy of the World Trade Organization (WTO), have accelerated and strengthened policies entailing the 'systematic dispossession of the state'.[8] They have also, we should add, strengthened policies that mean 'dispossession' (a precautionary dispossession!) of the European Union. A European Union constructed on the basis of the Maastricht Treaty signifies not 'a super-state . . . but less state', Perry Anderson has written.[9] Granting autonomy to the central banks and the European Central Bank – conservative, 'inflation averse' institutions[10] – at the national and European levels respectively constitutes an institutional constraint which significantly limits social-democratic freedom of manoeuvre. Privatizations have significantly reduced the ability of national governments to pursue an active industrial policy. The crisis of the national systems of bi- and tripartite bargaining has diminished the social-democratic movement's capacity for intervention. The EU in particular, having denied itself most of the traditional instruments of an effective macro-economic policy (with the exception of monetary policy), will not easily be able to circumvent the 'trap' that it has inspired and set. Given this set of economic choices at national and community levels, which have subsequently become *constraints* (in part put in place by social democrats themselves), the *radical* reorientation of social-democratic economic policies becomes very difficult in the short, and possibly the medium, term. These constraints are all the more constraining in that they weigh on a social democracy with diminished resources at its disposal. To an extent that seems to us today politically incomprehensible and electorally 'irrational', *social democracy has voluntarily destroyed many of its own instruments of economic intervention*. Hence it is not at liberty to choose a 'new future'. That is why it restricts itself to a 'minimalist' administration of the economic and social question which is coherent, and in perfect conformity with its 'minimalist' ideological/programmatic profile. As its policies in recent years demonstrate, social democracy tries modestly to 'mitigate' the present – and not always even that.

Even ideas – and sometimes initiatives – of 'modest correction' clash with the very 'orthodox' orientations of the European economic establishment, European bankers, and international economic organizations. At the level of the EU, they also run up against the fact that the differences between member states are considerably greater than the common ground. The left is not a 'European political subject'; hence – at least in the medium term – it cannot be a 'global political subject'.[11] But even if we accepted the hypothesis that such policy proposals could be implemented, their impact would be somewhat limited. Without supervision of the freedom of international markets and capital mobility (and not only financial capital mobility), a change of paradigm in economic policy is virtually impossible. In the medium term, any politics which wants to defend the social state and public services, and reduce economic and class inequalities, but abstains from posing the issue of neoliberal globalization, will be irrational and ineffective. To put it simply and pragmatically (partially borrowing Torben Iversen's terms): if social democracy does not attempt to influence the process of globalization, and if

> the principle of economic efficiency is going to be a cornerstone in the social democratic strategy, as it has in the past, then monetarism and sector- or industry-based wage bargaining *must be accepted* as the institutional

foundations for the economy, despite their antithetical relationship to traditional socialist commitments to wage solidarity and full employment.[12]

Accordingly, there will be no social-democratic politics worthy of the name without a re-regulation of 'globalized' flows at continental and global levels – without 'throwing a grain of sand into the well-oiled cogs'[13] of capital mobility (and not only financial capital and financial speculation, which are merely its most conspicuous aspects). What is involved is not a return to the state and its regulatory activity (globalization has *favoured state activity*, and multiplied the legal and institutional 'nets' that 'regulate deregulation'),[14] but the *content* and *objectives* of that activity. Faced with neoliberal modernizaton and globalization, the political and social forces that aspire to more justice must employ 'modern', 'global' weapons. Globalization is not an obstacle to growth, yet it sets in train a profoundly inegalitarian dynamic.[15] Hence it is not possible to redistribute the inegalitarian results of globalization without acting on it.

Social Democracy, a Force for Macroeconomic Destabilization?

If it is governments (including social-democratic governments) that have (actively or passively) decided to deregulate international financial markets, and introduce the institutions characteristic of market capitalism into national economic spaces, reasserting control over these markets and institutions is a plausible *political* move (just as the move to deregulation was *politically* plausible), but difficult to achieve. In fact, all those who aspire to change the international economic and financial architecture confront 'a formidable problem of action and collective co-ordination: if it was easy to abolish national regulations, it is *a lot more difficult* to agree on an international re-regulation acceptable to all parties concerned'.[16]

Such a change in economic and financial policy presupposes challenging too many vested interests at international and national levels, too many of the certitudes of contemporary economics, too many ideological verities. It also involves the possibility, which should not be underestimated, of an economic – and consequently a political – confrontation with the United States. The USA occupies a very important place in the world economy and a hegemonic position over 'the apparatus of production of economic norms' (i.e. the bloc of international financial institutions plus the 'set of expert institutions that elaborate the criteria of economic credibility of states').[17]

Notwithstanding the theoretical controversies it provokes, globalization is a reality. And this reality, like every reality, has its own logic, produces results, and generates constraints. Once set in motion, globalization, real or perceived, has become part of the established economic order and, in consequence, is viewed as a *factor of economic stability*.[18] Thus – at least to a certain extent – globalization creates globalization, and tends to be self-reinforcing. This disadvantages and discourages, demoralizes – even mortifies – all those who aspire to check it, since simply by virtue of their ambition they are aligned with the 'camp of destabilization'. They are on the 'bad' side of history. They become supporters of a 'leap in the dark'.

A 'different' politics (the famous *autre politique*, to use the French political term) thus involves ruptures and, as a result, electoral risks that are too significant to be envisaged by leaders and organizations preoccupied with, and haunted by, immediate electoral returns. Social democracy is a moderate political force – moderately neoliberal and moderately non-liberal. It is a prudent and electoralist force of reform, without strong convictions – a force for which governmental vocation has become a kind of 'second nature'. It is as such, and *because it is as such*, that it currently dominates Europe.

Were social democracy to take another road, adopt a different economic and social policy, that would doubtless be intellectually highly stimulating and socially subversive, but social democracy – this social democracy – would not then be social democracy. Such a social democracy would unquestionably have to renounce 'the politics of *preference-accommodation* (whether directed at capital or the electorate), in favour of *preference-shaping*'.[19] In at least some cases (e.g. Great Britain, Italy), it would equally have to give up its 'almost pathological preoccupation with respectability'.[20] This would involve too many electoral risks for an 'electoralist', catch-all political force; too many organizational risks for an organization that is internally far from compact and close to the electoral-professional model; and too many intellectual risks for a force with a trans-border ideological profile.[21] Thus social democracy would not be faithful to its 'responsible' and 'pragmatic' nature, and its 'minimalist' identity ('a-programmatic', in Mario Telo's phrase). Which means: it would no longer be itself.

Fundamentally, social democracy's freedom of manoeuvre today is seriously restricted. Its desire, whether rhetorical or real, to correct neoliberal logic is constrained by its past neoliberal options (of which 'deflationary psychosis' is only one aspect); by its strategy of prudence and moderation to appease the fears of capital (which did, after all, prove successful and was the condition of its accession to power); and by an organizational and sociological cartography that is scarcely conducive to policies involving a radical return to the 'social'.

'Governments must satisfy two electorates today: their national electorate and the international capital market,' Colin Crouch and Wolfgang Streeck have written.[22] Social democracy is a force for macroeconomic stability, and the logic of 'destabilizing reforms' ('structural reforms', to use a now-outmoded language) is not *its* logic. The adoption of such a logic would cause the impressive 'modernist' construction of contemporary social democracy to disintegrate. It would affect the sinews of war: the *confidence of its 'two' electorates*, the confidence of capital and the 'markets', national and international, and hence the confidence of the moderate electorate. Social democracy would thus align itself with the camp of economic 'destabilization', even its *own political and organizational destabilization*. Avoiding a major policy reorientation is the *ransom to be paid for maintaining its ideological, organizational and electoral stability.* The logic of 'no major alternative' – and even, in cases like New Labour or PASOK, 'no alternative' at all – is a central constitutive element in the new social-democratic identity, consciously and positively adopted as such.

Let us summarize. A radical reorientation of social-democratic policy runs up against the following factors, which 'rule' the universe of contemporary social democracy as well as the economic space of advanced capitalism, endowing them with their stability:

  (i) the deficit in trade-union power and ideological and cultural influence;
 (ii) the blunted radicalism of the 'oppositional' left-wing forces;
(iii) the new sociology of the social-democratic organizations, which confirms the hegemony of the middle classes;
 (iv) the interclassist format of the social-democratic electorates, by far the most interclassist in the history of social democracy, which drastically diminishes the social democrats' capacity to adopt coherent policies benefiting popular strata, since it raises the potential electoral cost of such policies considerably;
  (v) the very 'orthodox' orientations of the European and global economic establishment, as well as the United States, the world's greatest power;
 (vi) the absence of a European political system with strong public power;
(vii) the differences in economic and social philosophy between the member states (the 'clash of national interests'), which are often significantly greater than the common ground;
(viii) the extreme heterogeneity of the various national welfare states, which precludes the construction of a European welfare state;[23]
 (ix) the constraints resulting from past economic options (liberalization of markets, stability pact, autonomy of central banks at the national level and of the European Central Bank at continental level, etc.).

A radical – which does not mean 'anti-capitalist' – reorientation of social-democratic politics comes up against all these factors, which are linked either with the deep identity of social democracy or with its environment, itself partly fashioned by its previous policies.

It is therefore hardly surprising if social democracy, whose economic policy is not identified with neoliberal conservatism, has opted for the politics of 'small steps' – something that is confirmed by its current economic policy. And if socialists and social democrats (or at least some of them) want a powerful, 'neo-Keynesian' Europe, they do not possess, and have not armed themselves with, the requisite institutional and political means. Consequently, as far as the wider horizon of major political alternatives goes, we are obliged to observe that social democracy is not – and does not propose – a *major* alternative to globalization of the neoliberal variety.

Victims, accomplices and instruments of the globalization and neoliberalization of economic priorities, the social democrats suffer from a *deficit of alternatives*. It is a deficit that neither the trade unions, traditional partners of the social democrats, nor the new and old protest poles have the power or ideas to make good. In the wrestling match that has opposed the logic of the market and the logic of solidarity for at least three 'half-centuries', the former is prevailing today – comfortably. A specifically social-democratic logic – not rhetoric – is *virtually absent* from the European political and social scene at present. The institution of a 'social-democratic model of globalization' – in Pervenche Berès's terms, 'social democratic globalization' versus 'liberal globalization'[24] – does not seem to be on the agenda in the short or medium term.[25] The absence of any major alternative is the major phenomenon of the past three decades.

Notes

1. David Held, Anthony McGrew, David Goldblatt and Jonathan Perraton, *Global Transformations*, Polity Press, Cambridge 1999, pp. 136–7.
2. Ibid., p. 426.
3. Robert Boyer, 'La politique à l'ère de la mondialisation et de la finance: le point sur quelques recherches régulationnistes', *Recherches, L'année de la régulation*, vol. 3, La Découverte, Paris 1999, p. 14.
4. Leo Panitch, 'Globalization in Crisis: Bringing the (Imperial) State Back In', paper presented to the 'Politics Today' conference in memory of Nicos Poulantzas, Athens 1999.
5. Gerhard Schröder, *Le Monde*, 16 September 1998.
6. Frank Vandenbroucke, *Globalisation, Inequality and Social Democracy*, Institute for Public Policy Research, London 1998, p. 18. The debate within the European Union, and a list of some of the policy proposals advanced, is eloquent: a less strict interpretation of the stability pact; co-ordinated reduction of interest rates; strengthening of European investment policies in trans-European networks (transport, infrastructure, energy, information technology), whose financing could in part come (following Jacques Delors's proposal) from a major European loan; reorientation of fiscal policy in favour of popular strata, who have borne the burden of increased taxation within the current EU since the 1980s; harmonization of tax policy so as to avoid intra-European competition to attract capital; co-ordinated support for demand, etc. These proposals – which are not radical, and are far from having been agreed or applied – indicate the mindset of a number of European socialists, who are seeking timidly to correct the excesses of current orthodox policies. Needless to say, they do not really fit with the 'spirit' of the British approach.
7. Larry Elliott and Dan Atkinson, *The Age of Insecurity*, Verso, London and New York 1999, p. 172.
8. Ricardo Petrella, *Le Monde Diplomatique*, August 1999.
9. Perry Anderson, 'The Europe to Come', in Peter Gowan and Perry Anderson, eds, *The Question of Europe*, Verso, London and New York 1997, p. 130.
10. Torben Iversen, *Contested Economic Institutions: The Politics of Macroeconomics and Wage Bargaining in Advanced Democracies*, Cambridge University Press, Cambridge 1999, p. 57.
11. The phrase is Massimo D'Alema's.

12. Iversen, *Contested Economic Institutions*, p. 175; emphasis added.
13. Howard Wachtel, *Le Monde Diplomatique*, October 1998, p. 20.
14. 'What is distinctive about contemporary globalization is the magnitude and institutionalization of its political regulation', David Held *et al.* have written (*Global Transformations*, p. 437).
15. Jean-Paul Fitoussi and Pierre Rosanvallon, *Le nouvel âge des inégalités*, Seuil, Paris 1996, p. 133.
16. Boyer, 'La politique à l'ère de la mondialisation et de la finance', p. 43.
17. Bruno Jobert, 'Des États en interactions', *Recherches, L'année de la régulation*, vol. 3, pp. 81, 83, 86.
18. Never mind the potential for destabilization contained in the new order, as attested, for example, by the most recent crises in Asia, Russia and Brazil.
19. Colin Hay, *The Political Economy of New Labour: Labouring under False Pretences?*, Manchester University Press, Manchester 1999, p. 158.
20. Leo Panitch and Colin Leys, *The End of Parliamentary Socialism: From the New Left to New Labour*, Verso, London and New York 1997, p. 19.
21. The resignation of Oskar Lafontaine, whose policy proposals, while not radical, ran counter to the suggestions of the economic establishment, was a moment of great symbolic import. This 'forced' resignation demonstrates the fear of socialist and social-democratic leaderships faced with a change of course in economic policy. In this sense, the 'Lafontaine affair' is a moment of assertion and confirmation of the identity of the new social democracy: Oskar Lafontaine was a potential destabilizing factor in a political family that has made macro-economic stability its standard-bearer.
22. Colin Crouch and Wolfgang Streeck, 'L'avenir du capitalisme diversifié', in Crouch and Streeck, eds, *Les Capitalismes en Europe*, La Découverte, Paris 1996, p. 19.
23. Jobert, 'Des États en interactions', p. 89; Giandomenico Majone, *La Communauté européenne: un État régulateur*, Montchrestien, Paris 1996.
24. Pervenche Berès, 'The Social Democratic Response to Globalization', in René Cuperus and Johannes Kandel, eds, *European Social Democracy: Transformation in Progress*, Friedrich Ebert Stiftung, Amsterdam 1998, p. 157.
25. Social democracy is not a force that will accept the risks. It will not really behave as a force of economic 'destabilization' – unless the destabilization comes from elsewhere. The crises in Asia, Russia and Brazil have shown the extent to which the credibility – and legitimacy – of the neoliberal paradigm of globalization can be undermined from within, by the financial and economic disorder it generates. Contemporary social democracy is a political force that is ideo-logically and programmatically highly composite. Now, the peculiarity of ideological/programmatic amalgams and patchworks is invariably to produce ambiguities and contradictions, but also to leave open or half-open different – and often contradictory – possibilities. Or to induce paralysis. In the event of a major financial crisis – and this is merely hypothetical – the regulatory interven-tion of states, and the EU in particular, would emerge as a solution to resort to, a credible, innovative and, above all, necessary solution to the impossibility of self-regulation of market forces by themselves. The disorder a 'crisis' would produce would be such as to reactivate the non-liberal dimension, the 'heretical core' of the 'social-democratic soul' (Hay, *The Political Economy of New Labour*, p. 183).

16

The Party of European Socialists and Socialist Co-operation in Europe

A Party in Search of an Identity and a Role

The Confederation of the Socialist Parties of the European Community (CPS), founded in 1974, succeeded the Liaison Bureau of the Socialist Parties of the EC, and was intended to be an ambitious organizational response to the relaunch of the communitarian dynamic at the time. But despite its transnational aims, the Confederation – also referred to by its French name, Union – marked a sharp decline in co-operation between European socialists. Handicapped by the arrival of new, rather Eurosceptical members (British, Dutch, Irish),[1] by the left turn of others (the French), and by the national introversion of nearly all its members (connected with the onset of the economic crisis and the 'territorial instinct' this induced), socialists were not able to direct the process of constructing the European Community. Moreover, particularly during the 1970s, they gave the impression of a deeply divided political family, with an uncertain 'European' commitment. For the Confederation of the 1970s and 1980s the supranational aim was merely rhetorical, without any real impact either on the programmatic objectives or on the life and structures of the organization. In effect, as Guillaume Devin put it: 'rather than a renewal, the creation of the Confederation instead marked a peak'.[2]

The creation of the Party of European Socialists (PES) in November 1992, on the initiative of the Socialist group in the European Parliament, represented a new step in the process of co-operation between the Community's socialists. Its promoters' clearly stated objective was to create 'a political instrument allowing socialist bodies to exercise *a decisive influence* in the European Community',[3] by moving towards the creation of a 'genuine party'.

Nearly a decade after the creation of the PES, we can draw up an initial balance sheet of European socialist co-operation.[4] This balance sheet is 'positive overall'. It suffers, however, from significant weaknesses that are very revealing about the limits of any transnational party activity at the European level.

A Mixed Balance Sheet

1. Compared with the stagnation of the preceding period, the PES has contributed to the rejuvenation, reorganization and deepening of co-operation within European socialism. A more homogeneous party than the Confederation, today it is more than a simple framework for co-operation, more than a liaison structure, more than a round-table organization. The PES has established itself, and has gradually been recognized, as the *undisputed organizational centre* of socialist co-ordination at EU level, imparting a new dynamic to social-democratic regional 'integration'.

2. The political influence of the PES has increased (notably through the Leaders' Conference), and its authority is more clearly asserted and consolidated at the European level (see below). Today, the PES is more coherent and better equipped than the European People's Party (EPP), its eternal partner-opponent, to conduct 'effective' action within European institutions. The new strategy of 'numerical preponderance' adopted by the EPP (the desire to encompass the maximum number of national parties in order to optimize its influence) has put a question mark against its traditional coherence and 'federalist' capacity.[5] Faced with this development, the socialists pride themselves today on being – after their failure at the 1999 European elections – the 'premier group' (!) in the European Parliament, stressing that their numerical inferiority is largely compensated by their greater political homogeneity. Contemporary socialists no longer 'lag behind integration'.[6]

3. However, the organizational and logistical infrastructure of the PES was and remains very slight, which is an index of the party's weak institutionalization. The size of its 'professional' staff is fairly stagnant, despite a small reinforcement since 1992, the year the party was founded.[7] The secretariat is limited and overly dependent on the parliamentary group, both in financial terms and as regards recruitment of personnel.

4. The Bureau, political organ *par excellence*, which – according to the statutes – is supposed to implement Congress decisions and decide on political orientations in the intervals between Congress meetings, in reality performs this role only very partially. Its activity is largely devoted to administrative questions and co-ordination (despite an increased 'politicization' in the last two or three years); and it is not greatly concerned with questions of general policy. It is rare for the Bureau, responsible for the political line, to make declarations of general import. It is also rare for it to intervene in the everyday political life of the EU. This patent lack of political energy and dynamism reveals the uncertain situation of the PES – and of all the Europarties – and assumes an eminently political significance: exactly like the party, the Bureau is a body without a clearly defined role. If its activity does not follow European political life, this is because the PES does not form part – except in a marginal or interim manner – of this political life, which is

itself weakly structured. There is no *political demand*, either from the institutional system of the Union or European populations, to elicit a *supply*, prompting the Bureau – that is, the party – continually to assert itself as an influential, decision-making body. From this viewpoint, the largely 'administrative' activity of the Bureau is eminently political, and should be treated as such.

5. In the Congress – the party's highest assembly, convened every two years according to the constitution – everything – or nearly everything – is settled in advance; everything – or nearly everything – is played out in advance. The culture of majorities and oppositions, constitutive of traditional modes of representation, is practically absent from this great media circus. Basically, what is missing is a principle of European, and potentially supranational, legitimation superior to the national principle, which is commonly accepted and currently dominant.[8] In this sense the operation of the congresses is indicative of the contradictory character – and all the ambiguity – of the PES, which is constructed on a transnational ambition whose legitimation nevertheless appears problematic even in the eyes of the agents promoting it. In the PES, conflict ('vexed questions') is almost systematically repressed or deferred; this is the sign of an 'immature' transnational construct.[9]

6. The party exerts only a marginal influence on the elites of the national parties, as it does on the national delegations within its parliamentary group. The PES has not contributed to the creation of a 'European space of socialist activism' either. Ordinary members of the national parties do not feel that they belong to an organizational arena extending beyond national borders. Symmetrically, contacts in the PES occur in the intimacy of a narrow circle, often restricted to the 'international affairs' specialists of the national parties (the 'internationalism of the functionaries', in the words of the Catalan socialist Raimon Obiols).[10] Thus, the PES remains an 'elite exercise';[11] closed in on itself, it has not found the 'openings' to associate socialist activists *extra muros* in its proceedings. In practice, the quasi-totality of adherents of the member parties (national elites included) do not form part of its life, and it does not form part of their universe. Like the other transnational parties, the PES acts largely in isolation: it has no *direct* organizational contact with European societies.[12]

7. The PES is barely capable of supervising its parliamentary group (which, according to the statutes, is a fully fledged member of the PES), and of genuinely guiding its daily political options. Like the other groups, the socialist group, assured of the 'structuring support' of the parliamentary institution (Guillaume Devin), represents the most 'integrated' element within the European socialist family. In addition, it is equipped – and obliged – to handle a much higher volume of business than the party can deal with. Thanks to its position in the European Parliament, it is distinguished by its functional superiority relative to the party.[13] Moreover, within the Parliament dilution of the 'partisan treatment of certain questions',[14] and operation by the conjunction of centres, favours the

group's independence. That said, the trend is towards better co-ordination and a strengthening of exchanges. On the 'major questions' and political options, the PES seems currently better placed to influence the positions adopted by socialist parliamentarians, notably through increased contact and collaboration between the president of the group and the leading party organizations.[15] In addition, 'party spirit' – the sense of belonging to the same transnational organization – is growing ever stronger.[16]

The Apex of the Contradictions: Socialist Summit Meetings

Within the EU's 'institutional triangle', the Council of Ministers is simultaneously the principal component of the 'community legislator' and one of the constitutive elements of its 'executive'.[17] Thus, despite the recent strengthening of the Parliament, endowed with joint decision-making power in some spheres, the Council remains the focal institutional site and privileged locus of decision-making. It is therefore not surprising if the European parties tend to concentrate their efforts on influencing this privileged instance of the exercise of power. 'Parties will go where the power is,' Simon Hix has written, 'and in the EU, decisional power rests with the European Council and not the European Parliament.'[18]

As a result, socialist summit meetings, in the form either of the party leaders' conference, or especially the summit of socialist heads of state and government (pre-Council meetings), assume a particular importance. In fact, summit conferences are becoming a galvanizing element in the revitalization of the Europarties, and particularly the PES, which takes considerable advantage of the fact that the majority of government leaders in Europe are socialists.

Meetings between socialist leaders date back to the 1970s, but the Party Leaders' Conference became an organ of the party, recognized as such in the statutes, only in 1992. The figures indicate that the meeting of these 'conclaves', which was irregular, episodic and occasional in the 1970s and 1980s, became regular and sustained in the 1990s.[19] The uninterrupted functioning of these summits is indicative of the path followed in relation to the Confederation, and clearly indicates the trend towards increased co-operation in European socialism. Occasions for negotiating, elaborating points of view, and resolving conflicts, they contribute to the creation of an 'ethos' of co-operation at the highest level, as well as to a certain 'Europeanization' of the left/right divide. This generates an undoubted 'integrationist effect'. In addition, these meetings (prepared by groups of experts including representatives of the PES) are usually followed by a press conference, which – thanks to the presence of prominent personalities – enhances the party's visibility among the European publics.

But the most important contribution of these summits, particularly the summit of the heads of state and government, is the influence they exert on the Council's agenda, and thus on decision-taking within the EU.[20] The

PES can now say, as claimed by the SPD's slogan for the 1979 European elections, 'Our word counts in Europe'.[21] The party – finally! – is acquiring the status of a community-wide political interlocutor. In visible – though scarcely institutional – fashion, it is becoming a *back-door partner* in the process of integration. This is a development whose significance should not be underestimated, even if the 'back-door' character of the partnership (consisting in initiatives that do not always leave a written trace) resists systematic analysis.

Nevertheless, the importance and integrationist effects of this 'functioning by summits' must be qualified. The heads of national parties and governments act solely in their capacity as *national* leaders (their legitimation deriving exclusively from their position on the national political scene), not as 'bearers' or 'vehicles' of a European socialist identity. No doubt the participation of representatives of the PES, particularly the presidents of the PES and the parliamentary group (as well as, by invitation, socialist commissioners), adds a *European and supranational touch* to these conclaves of an intergovernmental type. But it cannot offset the 'superiority' possessed by the national heads in terms of authority and legitimacy. Thus it cannot be the spearhead of a supranational logic. Without lingering too long over personal destinies that we know to be very different, we are obliged to observe that the balance of influence, bound up with the role of personalities, operates to the detriment of the presidents of the PES and the parliamentary group. Since they face leaders with high celebrity status, personal capital and 'delegated' capital (attributable to the weight of the country represented by a premier), the capacity of the PES's representatives to convert their arguments at socialist summits into decisions and deeds is not very strong.[22]

In reality, the summit meetings have nothing very supranational about them, because when it comes to their composition and operation (equal representation of parties, practice of unanimity, and hence reduced decisional autonomy), they inevitably tend to push national parties (and leaders) to the forefront, accentuating their primacy in the PES. This yields the following paradoxical result. Summit meetings highlight the PES and enhance its visibility as a Europarty; at the same time they doubly devalue it: as a structure with a supranational design (by reinforcing intergovernmental logic within it), and as a structure *tout court*. In the latter respect, it is interesting to note that the leaders' authority, and the legitimation of this authority, is totally independent of their participation in the organizational life of the PES (which is *nonexistent*). The importance assumed by summit conferences confirms the preponderance of a body that is largely 'external' to the organization of the PES. This quasi-superimposed body acts in the name of the party – and nominally forms part of the party – but in reality, in the absence of an organizational foundation, it possesses very considerable autonomy in relation to it. Armed with a collective authorization linked to their national pedigree, the leaders supervise the edifice called the 'PES' from on high and – virtually – from without, largely substituting themselves for the collective organization.[23]

In sum, if meetings between leaders represent an important step forward in socialist co-operation, and an accelerator indicating increased co-operation, they are also a step backward, since they indicate growing 'intergovernmentalism', as well as a certain depreciation of the PES as a system of *collective* action. With the plethora of summits, the party is in reality adopting a presidential style with 'several heads'.[24] Contrary to the view of some analysts, I do not believe that summit meetings can assume the role of an *engine of integration*, breaking through the institutional weakness of the Europarties and their weak identity.

The Network Operation of a Weak Integrationist Institution

That said, it remains the case that the influence of the PES has grown since 1992, thanks to the leaders' meeting. This is a real advance in co-operation between European socialists, an advance also for the PES's self-assertion within – or rather, alongside – the EU's decision-making instances. However, this 'tangential' and 'back-door' aspect makes the PES less an authentic party, even *sui generis*, and more of a 'proto-party', this term indicating a limited, even elliptical and highly incomplete, partisan profile.[25] Unable to perform the traditional functions of a genuine political party, this proto-party – provisionally? – performs various functions of co-ordination, advice and pressure.

Basically, the PES operates in large part as a *political network*, whose influence is bound up with the set of connections and contacts it is in a position to make.[26] The PES is unintelligible outside the relations that are formed, on the one hand, between the party's instances and elites and, on the other, between the men and women who occupy positions of power and influence within the EU and national parties. These relations are either interpersonal[27] or institutional and semi-institutional relations,[28] or – most frequently – a combination of the two. The links thus established, whether institutionalized or not, are channels of influence and pressure that enhance the party's European capacity (i.e. its ability to influence decisions about European construction), whether direct or back-door. Operating via networks is, in addition, considerably encouraged by the fact that the boundaries delimiting the prerogatives of the three components of the European institutional triangle do not correspond to the classical model of the separation of powers. Thus, an important aspect of the PES's consolidation derives from the fact that the links it can make have tightened significantly over the last few years. The PES is a structure that is progressively and discreetly strengthening its penetration of the institutional fabric of the EU through its active *presence*.

The PES and the 1999 European Elections[29]

While the PES has made its presence felt more among the EU's institutional elites, acquiring a certain 'obviousness' and 'visibility' (if only via the ambiguous path of the socialist summits), the threshold of visibility has not as yet been crossed within European societies — far from it. The presence of the PES (as of all the Europarties) in the national media is marginal (albeit markedly stronger than in the past), and its influence on the political life of EU countries virtually nonexistent. The PES does not as yet possess the image and recognition of a real actor in European public opinion. It is thus virtually incapable of attracting media attention and *mobilizing support* ('identitative' or 'systemic') on European questions.[30] Its visibility remains too low even during campaigns for the European elections. The elections of 1999 largely confirmed this.

The Manifesto

The PES manifesto for the June 1999 elections was prepared – a 'reassuring' enterprise or strange irony of fate? – under the responsibility of the Briton Robin Cook and the Frenchman Henri Nallet. Adopted by the Milan Congress (1 March 1999), this manifesto was structured around four major themes ('a Europe of jobs and growth, a Europe that puts citizens first, a strong Europe, a democratic Union that works better'), and offered '21 commitments'. The manifesto's ideological orientation (fruit of a laborious compromise) reflects the ideological and programmatic orientations of contemporary social democracy. It is, however, closer to 'continental' social democracy, and themes dear to the left (creating employment, striving for growth, promoting social Europe) are prioritized in the PES's objectives. An attachment to some classically social-democratic values and, above all, its tone distinguish this manifesto both from various British formulations and from the EPP's manifesto which, while invoking Christian 'personalism', was much closer to the logic of the market.

The text directly takes its place in the long tradition of Europarties (of every political complexion) producing documents 'which are . . . bland, offering little more than platitudes . . . [and] little in the way of hard policy proposals'.[31] Written in very general terms that blur its European message, the socialist programme in reality contains *no* concrete commitments. Any issues that might give rise to disagreement (e.g. concrete measures to promote employment, reform of the European budget, reform of European institutions, enlargement) are either evaded, or invariably dealt with in extremely vague terms.

Thus, in the consensual logic that governed its composition, this document is no different from other manifestos adopted in the past either by the PES, or by the Union. Gilbert Germain has written:

The fact that the procedure for finalizing such programmes obliges the representatives of the member parties, in the framework of the programme commissions initiated by the Federations, to compare viewpoints, to understand each other's positions on certain specific issues better, and to search for a consensual basis acceptable to all (even if it is a lowest common denominator), already seems to us to be a determining factor in the evolution of political families towards greater cohesion at a European level, in both conceptual and practical terms.[32]

Certainly, compared with the Confederation's failure to present a joint manifesto for the 1979 elections (it confined itself to a simple 'Appeal to Voters'), the production of the manifesto for the 1999 elections indicates that a considerable 'consensual basis' exists in today's PES. It is even growing continuously. But this basis is weak. And it will remain so as long as the process of finalizing programmes is marked by the same profound contradiction. As Germain has rightly emphasized, the programme is the quintessential medium of debate among socialists, and a way of developing greater cohesion. Yet at the same time, it is the quintessential instrument for 'fudged consensus' and, consequently, for restricting debate. This inevitably produces superficial cohesion. The persistent production of programmatic documents based on the lowest common denominator demonstrates the great distance that remains to be covered before any real cohesion exists within socialism in Europe.

Moreover, minimalist programmes cannot be transformed into instruments of action. Given the overly general character of the commitments made, it seems to me natural that the last PES manifesto, just like previous ones, did not become the political instrument, if only verbally, of an authentically European campaign. Programmatic formulations with weak doctrinal and practical impact are not the kind of thing that genuinely encourages the electoral activity of the member parties – something that was demonstrated once again in June 1999.[33]

Basically, the national socialist parties, and with them the PES, find themselves in a doubly impossible situation: bound by a programme with strong commitments, they are equally bound by a programme whose commitments are too feeble. In addition, they cannot escape this dual impossibility (which in reality is a problem of identity) by defining a halfway position. Despite the growing ideological convergence in European socialism, identifying a middle way between an 'extensive' programme (which alone provides a basis for consensus) and an 'intensive' programme (which renders that consensus difficult to achieve) is a procedure that has yet to find adequate modes of elaboration.

'With regard to future electoral statements,' wrote Axel Hanisch, former PES general secretary, in 1995, 'the PES might pose the following questions: how far should we push the pursuit of joint statements and thus often the lowest common denominator? Wouldn't setting the views of certain isolated parties to one side lead to the expression of firmer political electoral objectives?'[34] These questions, posed after the 1994 elections, retain all their topicality in the wake of those of 1999. They demonstrate that the process of achieving 'integrated' programmes is slow – slower than some optimistic observers envisaged. There are two reasons for this. First of all, the absence of 'integrated' programmes directly corresponds to the PES's weak internal 'integration': we are dealing with a game of mirrors. Next, it is based on 'institutional' freedom. As long as the Europarties do not have to direct a governmental system, they can allow themselves to privilege the unity of their organization, and hence to be imprecise, incoherent, and flexible in formulating their policies, and 'permissive' as regards the 'commitments' they make. Since the 'logic of influence', which presupposes effective transnational construction, is weak, the 'logic of membership' prevails.[35] Thus, for want of institutional power and significant influence, consensus is privileged. Decision-making based on consensus is of very limited 'integrationist' value and impact.

The Network Europe Group

Created in 1998, the Network Europe group responded to the PES's wish to rejuvenate its ideas and experiment with new, more inventive forms of joint work. Network Europe assigned itself the objective of bringing a new dynamism to the communications activities, internal and external, of the PES and its group in the European Parliament. The clearly stated ambition of this communications network, probably inspired by the effectiveness of the British Labour Party's communications structure, was 'to be the best'.[36] 'We, Network Europe,' they declared,

> will be a dynamic and innovative team. . . . It is our task to add value to the information and communication activities within the European socialist family. Therefore we want to:
> – Make the group more visible
> – Make the members more visible
> – Turn the discussions on European issues from a top and bureaucratic phenomenon to a relevant issue among the citizens of Europe. . . .[37]

Network Europe proceeded to create three working groups: Polling Network, Media Network, and Issues Network, with a specialist named to take charge of each. These working groups at the European level have multiplied contacts (including face-to-face contacts by trips to most European capitals) with the press offices and opinion research and communications officials of the member parties of the PES.

A European survey, the so-called 'Pan-European Poll', was conducted under the auspices of Network Europe in December 1998 by Gallup International. Focused on the issue priorities and attitudes to Europe of public opinion in the member countries, the survey also tested the attractiveness (and unattractiveness) of different 'messages' about European construction. The aim of the research, which was not narrowly pre-electoral (no question on party choice, voting intentions, or rating of parties was asked), was to assemble the requisite body of information to facilitate communication with the citizens of Europe by the PES and parliamentary group. The results have served as the guide that has largely 'structured' Network Europe's work in internal and external information.

Certain conclusions follow from the work done by Network Europe.

The Internet websites of the group and the PES have been manifestly improved and modernized, as have internal information systems (by the development of the 'European Socialist Information Space' [ESIS] on the Intranet). All this has aided better 'structuration' and diffusion of information.

Network Europe has organized and encouraged joint work between the PES's officials and experts on one side, and those of the member parties (and national delegations to the Parliament) on the other. It has thus contributed to establishing an initial European socialist 'nucleus' in the spheres of public opinion research, the media, and electoral management.

However, this attempt at co-operation, unknown on such a scale before the creation of Network Europe, has remained confined to a very restricted personnel, a largely isolated micro-collective; and, after a flamboyant start, it is increasingly losing momentum and influence. Over and above the difficulties inherent in this kind of joint work, it appears that the primarily national character of the 1999 European elections was a 'structural' obstacle that contributed significantly to the group's loss of momentum and influence. Moreover, the prominence given to Network Europe circumvented the communications structures that already existed in the party and parliamentary group. This created significant tensions, particularly with the communications officials of the group, who (by Network Europe's own admission) were much better acquainted with 'the corridors of the European Parliament'.[38] These tensions impaired the whole communications effort and influence of Network Europe. Finally, on reading the manifesto, it is interesting to note that Network Europe's policy proposals have not really been 'incorporated' into the official programmatic document of the PES. An implicit disavowal of the work done by the group, this does not bode well for its future.

An overview of the 1999 elections indicates that the PES did not embark on a genuinely European campaign which, extending beyond the national dimension, could have highlighted the party and the transnational themes of which it is the vehicle. The 1999 campaign was not an authentically transnational experience. Notwithstanding worthy efforts by the PES leadership to multiply contacts and strengthen joint work, the campaign did not really engage the PES on a more ambitious course, or allow the co-ordination of important joint activities. Certainly, the party tested new, resolutely 'modern' forms of communication and publicity. However, the impact of these innovations was rather disappointing; after the initial commotion, it waned. In addition, the failure to adopt a common acronym and logo (e.g. PES–SPD, PES–PASOK) – something that was always deferred[39] – is an index of the weakness of the European dimension of the last PES electoral campaign, even at the level of symbolic semantics. The party was unable to surmount the barrier of 'non-visibility' and achieve the objective agreed at the Malmo Congress (1995): 'to pass from the role of internal coordination to external representation, promoting the public role of the PES'.[40]

The experience of the 1999 elections proved that what the social democrats have to offer in terms of European identity is still too weak really to contribute to the formation of a 'European consciousness' as defined by Article 138A of the Maastricht Treaty. At the same time, the weakness of any 'European consciousness' – regarded not as a substitute for national consciousness, but (in Dimitris Tsatsos's terms) as a 'second level' of politics and politicization directly bound up with the existence of a *European common good* – damages any appeal in terms of identity that does not employ national idioms and is not directed to national clienteles.[41] The nation remains the centre of partisan identifications, and this handicaps transnational party regroupment. The 1999 European election campaign confirmed this yet again.

Conclusions: Between the National and the Supranational

1. Appreciably more than in the past, the PES is assuming the function of framework and instrument – in short, organizer – of socialist co-operation. The PES is now located at the heart of social-democratic networks at the EU's 'systemic' level (socialist group in the European Parliament, member parties, heads of socialist governments, commissioners from the socialist family); and it occupies a significant (though not central) position in the set of social-democratic networks in Europe. Moreover, its activity, which largely depends on rhythms and developments within the EU's institutional system, is establishing it as a structure with strong political and operational autonomy, not as a mere regional organization (the 'European' section) of the Socialist International. It is equally obvious that the party enjoys greater operational capacity in its dealings with the other actors in the European game. It exercises a certain influence – and pressure – on the community's decision-making bodies, particularly through summit meetings and the socialist group in a European Parliament with greater powers. This influence, however, is exercised through structures (the socialist heads of state summit, the parliamentary group) that are largely 'autonomous' *vis-à-vis* the party, while theoretically belonging to it. These structures are stronger and more visible than the PES. In consequence, the latter's influence (which in some instances is more nominal than real) is without solid institutional and political foundation. In addition, it does not pursue (or not sufficiently) a supranational approach to the European phenomenon (and in some ways signals the reintroduction and

reassertion of an intergovernmental type of logic). Thus, the areas resistant to an authentically supranational logic are numerous, and they decisively mark the contours of the PES and the European partisan landscape in general.

2. The structure and operational logic of the PES – which are primarily confederal and partly federal, but intended to be supranational – attest to the complexity of the situation. Despite being strengthened, the PES remains a 'party of parties' whose authority is drastically restricted by the national units composing it. Neither a centralized party, nor a polycentric party (in the sense that the authority of member parties is strong, but ultimately confined to the space defined by the party), the PES is, instead, a party with a weak centre and overly autonomous 'territorial' structures. For want of a strong link between the central decision-making system and the member parties, real authority, which derives from the national parties, is thus often transferred *outside* the PES.[42] In sum, the PES is traversed by contrary trends that complement, and are superimposed upon, one another; and while it is no longer 'bereft of a role', it remains a party in search of a European role, structure and vision. In terms of Panayotis Soldatos's classification, we might say that the PES, even in its strengthened form, remains a 'weak integrationist institution'.[43]

3. As such, the PES is incapable of imposing itself as a source of power and constraint, and hence as a political force in the literal sense of the term. In effect, in politics a logic of *exclusion* operates in the constitution of any political group, in its production as a group. The dialectic of exclusion/inclusion renders a group cohesive, and hence aggressive towards the 'exterior' and repressive towards the 'interior'. Whether we are talking about international organizations, social movements, secret societies or political parties, this 'particularistic logic' is universal, and fundamental to the political.[44] Each political group 'creates' its own adversaries, presents itself as their adversary/challenger, and thus defines and asserts itself as a distinct group, with a distinct identity and distinct interests. Now, the PES seems incapable of being 'aggressive', of 'creating' its own 'enemies' – external and internal – and endowing itself with a genuine identity, a strong and strongly shared identity. The largely consensual functioning of the EU's institutions (the rule of the grand coalition in part determines the process of decision-making), and the programmatic affinity between socialists and centre-right forces (grouped around the EPP), contribute to this. However, in politics, those who cannot establish themselves as a structure of division and adversity are in fact basically incapable of presenting and imposing themselves as a political force in the literal sense of the term. This inability to conform to the logic of the most commonplace and universally known political code is indicative not of a new political 'ethic', but of the *extreme vulnerability* of the identity of European socialists. Like the other Europarties, the PES remains to this day a proto-structure – and this is not conducive to its operating as an authentic political force.

4. The Confederation, wrote Guillaume Devin in 1989, basically remains 'the instrument of national socialist politics, less for the purpose of transcending them, than to legitimate them through joint formulas'.[45] Heir to the Confederation, today's PES, while it is not the 'instrument of national politics', is a structure that has yet to find its place and role in the persistent toing-and-froing between the 'national' and the 'supra-national'. Certainly, this toing-and-froing is a matter of the balance to be struck – not a sharp division – between pro-integrationists and Euro-sceptics. Consolidated and strengthened as it unquestionably is, the current PES is still seeking to cut a path through difficult terrain dominated by the question of boundaries: the boundary between the national and the supranational; the boundary between the nations that compose Europe and the Europe that is more than the nations that compose it; and the boundary between the 'nationalist' dimension and the internationalist dimension in the innermost tradition of European socialism. On this terrain, where contradictory interests, fragile loyalties and heterodox logics coincide, the PES – like all the Europarties – is seeking its bearings. Accordingly, we should not be amazed if it is groping about, hesitating, making slow progress, and if it often 'advances masked'. The 'boundary' is internal; it runs through the party, its executives, and its member parties. But it does not constitute a 'frontline': it is mobile, fluid, undecided, inconstant, imperceptible but real. Traversed by contra-dictory tendencies and aspirations, the PES – like European socialism in its entirety – finds itself in what, in terms of identity, is a no-man's-land. The 1999 elections only served to confirm this state, which is a state of mind, but also a strategic state. They demonstrated that a 'Common Market of political parties' has yet to emerge in Europe.[46]

5. Socialist efforts to strengthen their co-operation and presence at the European level can be interpreted as a contribution to European political integration. Nevertheless, political and partisan conflict in Europe remains primarily and profoundly 'national-territorial'.[47] And the socialist parties have neither defined a *social-democratic road* to European construction, nor hit upon the means to 'insert their com-bined weight in the variety of policy openings within the [European] Union'.[48] For its part, the PES, despite reinforcement, remains at the 'project' stage – a project which, to this day, is vague, modest, and uncertain in its contours; a project that lacks radicalism either for Europe, or for socialism. European socialism in its entirety still lacks an effective transnational structure capable of co-ordinating the activities of the national socialist parties in hegemonic fashion. The 'European internationalism' of the PES is too respectful of liberal logic and national interests; its organizational structure, directed from above, is too asthenic, and its implantation in the European societies virtually non-existent.

The PES does not – or not yet – constitute the requisite political matrix to initiate effective collective action at a European level. There is no doubt that its weakness mirrors, in large part, that of European socialism in general, as well as the weakness of the system called the 'European Union'. Social democracy, this modern, pro-European social democracy, possesses a hegemonic project neither for Europe, nor for the societies of Europe. The social democrats' greatest failure at the dawn of a new century possibly consists in their inability to put forward a *social-democratic project for Europe.*

Notes

1. With the affiliation of the British Labour Party, and to a lesser extent the Danish SD and Irish Labour Party, what was gained in representativeness was lost in cohesion. Even the name of the party became subject to different national locutions. Characteristically, British Labour retained the term 'Confederation' (the Italians, 'Confederazione' and the Danes, 'Samenslutingen'); while at the other extreme the Dutch, one of the most pro-integrationist parties, used the term 'Federation' (*Federatie*). Most other parties positioned themselves midway, employing the term 'Union' (the Germans, *Bund*). See Guillaume Devin, *L'Internationale Socialiste,* Presses de la FNSP, 1993, p. 273.

2. Guillaume Devin, 'L'union des partis socialistes de la Communauté européenne. Le socialisme communautaire en quête d'identité', in *Socialismo Storia,* Franco Angeli, Milan 1989, p. 268. During the 1970s the Confederation found itself far removed from the pro-European declarations of the socialists in 1966, when they stated their 'objective and unceasing struggle for the achievement of a Federal Europe' (Seventh Congress, 1966). It also found itself far removed from the 1971 statement, when socialists restated their conviction that European construction must lead to the creation of a 'United States of Europe in the form of a federal state' (Eighth Congress, 1971).

3. Guy Spitaels, *Rapport d'activité de l'Union, 1990–1992,* The Hague.

4. To do this, I will rely on numerous interviews on the subject conducted by the author with PES executives and socialist Euro-MPs. These interviews, done since 1992 in successive stages, would not have been possible without the support of the University of Paris-II (in the framework of the constitutional laboratory directed by Pierre Avril).

5. The affiliation of Silvio Berlusconi's Forza Italia to the EPP, and the opening to the British Conservatives, are two eloquent symptoms of the contradictions contained in this strategy.

6. Mario Telo, 'La social-démocratie entre nation et Europe', in Telo, ed., *De la nation à l'Europe,* Bruylant, Brussels 1993, p. 52.

7. According to Ton Beymer, general secretary of the PES, seventeen people (fifteen of them full-timers) currently work for the party (interview with the author, Brussels, November 1999). By way of comparison, the PES had thirteen paid collaborators in 1994 (as reported by Luciano Bardi, 'Transnational Party Federations, European Parliamentary Groups and the Building of Europarties', in Richard Katz and Peter Mair, eds, *How Parties Organize: Change and Adaptation in Party Organizations in Western Democracies,* Sage, London 1994, p. 362); and the Confederation had eight in 1985–87 (figure reported by Gilbert Germain, *Approche socio-politique des profils et réseaux relationnels des socialistes, libéraux et démocrates-chrétiens allemands et français du Parlement Européen,* doctoral thesis, Institut d'Études Politiques de Paris, 1995, p. 288).

8. In a traditional party a political tendency or current can, without too much

difficulty, be placed in a minority. But in a 'transnational' party a national party cannot be placed in a minority, because a nation cannot readily be placed in a minority, i.e. a position of subordination.

9. According to Andy Smith, institutional systems in which conflict on the plane of values is systematically repressed are immature systems ('L'Union européenne, un régime politique impossible?', oral communication, Montpellier, 1999).

10. Raimon Obiols, 'La nécessaire dimension transnationale du socialisme européen', *Nouvelle Revue Socialiste*, no. 11, 1990, p. 140.

11. Geoffrey Pridham and Pippa Pridham, *Transnational Party Co-operation and European Integration*, George Allen & Unwin, London 1981, p. 163.

12. Bardi, 'Transnational Party Federations', p. 362.

13. See Devin, 'L'union des partis socialistes de la Communauté européenne', p. 275; Bardi, 'Transnational Party Federations', p. 360.

14. Robert Ladrech, 'La coopération transnationale des partis socialistes européens', in Telo, ed., *De la nation à l'Europe*, p. 126.

15. Interview with Ton Beymer (Brussels, November 1999).

16. The assertion by PES officials that the 'osmosis between the Party and its Parliamentary Group is such that outside observers sometimes have difficulty distinguishing between the two' is a patent exaggeration (see *Activities Report of the PES, from Malmo to Milan*, PES, Brussels 1999).

17. Jean-Louis Quermonne, *Le Système politique européen*, Montchrestien, Paris 1993, p. 41.

18. Simon Hix, 'Political Parties in the European Union: A "Comparative Politics Approach" to the Organisational Development of the European Party Federations', paper, Manchester 1995, p. 15.

19. The figures are unambiguous: from one meeting per annum on average for the period 1970–84 (1970–74: 3 meetings; 1975–79: 4; 1980–84: 5), we pass to around two per annum for 1985–89 (8 meetings), to more than 3 per annum for 1990–94 (17 meetings), and around 4 a year in the second half of the 1990s (17 meetings). The figures for 1970–94 derive from Hix, 'Political Parties in the European Union', p. 17, and thereafter from the PES secretariat, as communicated to the author. These figures involve both meetings of leaders and meetings of participants in the Council.

20. On the influence exercised by meetings between the leaders of the Europarties, see the examples cited by Simon Hix and Christopher Lord, *Political Parties in the European Union*, Macmillan, London 1997, pp. 189–95.

21. Quoted in Pridham and Pridham, *Transnational Party Co-operation and European Integration*, p. 238.

22. Faced with such leaders as Blair, Jospin or Schröder, the creditworthiness and weight of Rudolf Scharping (who is also a minister in Schröder's government) are not, and cannot be, of equivalent impact. The increased importance of summit meetings within the Europarties means that the personal impact of their president is greater today than in the past. Thus, given the specific demands of this new situation, the human capital possessed by the Europarties, and especially the political celebrity of the president, will in large part determine their dynamic and their future.

23. 'In fact,' Luciano Bardi was already writing in 1994, 'by enhancing the role of national party leaders, the continuing importance of intergovernmental decision-making is probably more of a hindrance than an incentive for the development of Europarties' ('Transnational Party Federations', p. 361).

24. In the initial phase of the Scharping presidency, a marked decline occurred

in the democratic functioning (and functioning *tout court*) of the party's organization. The downgrading of the Bureau, whose meetings became less regular, was the most evident consequence of this reduction in joint work, which was bound up with the priority accorded by Scharping to the leaders' conference.

25. Panayotis Soldatos, *Le Système institutionnel et politique des communautés européennes dans un monde en mutation*, Bruylant, Brussels 1989, p. 231.

26. See Robert Ladzeck, 'Party Networks, Issue Agendas and European Union Governance', in *Transnational Parties in the European Union*, Aldershot, Ashgate 1998, pp. 51–85.

27. Germain, *Approche socio-politique des profils et réseaux relationnels*, p. 297.

28. Examples: the link between the general secretary of the PES and the president of the parliamentary group, or between the Bureau and socialist commissioners. Depending on their sphere of responsibility, the latter are invited to participate in Bureau meetings, and in practice either participate directly, or send a representative.

29. This subsection, focused on the activity of the PES in the 1999 European elections, summarizes the conclusions reached by Gérard Grunberg and Gerassimos Moschonas in 'Socialistes: les illusions perdues', in Pascal Perrineau and Gérard Grunberg, *Le Vote des Quinze*, Presses de la Fondation Nationale des Sciences Politiques, Paris 2000.

30. On L.N. Lindberg and S.A. Scheingold's distinction between 'identitative' and 'systemic' support, see Soldatos, *Le Système institutionnel and politique des communautés européennes*, p. 241.

31. Julie Smith, *Europe's Elected Parliament*, Sheffield Academic Press, Sheffield 1999, pp. 93, 96.

32. Germain, *Approche socio-politique des profils et réseaux relationnels*, pp. 309–10.

33. The appearance of the Blair–Schröder manifesto a few days before the June elections spectacularly demonstrated the extent to which the programmatic documents of the PES scarcely 'constrain' and 'commit' their signatories. This manifesto – a differentiating document within European socialism, not a unifying one – was badly received, and produced friction (and French irritation) within the PES.

34. Axel Hanisch, *Rapport d'activités*, Brussels, 1995.

35. The terms 'logic of influence' and 'logic of membership' come from Jon Erik Dolvik, as cited in Richard Hyman, 'National Industrial Relations Systems and Transnational Challenges', *European Journal of Industrial Relations*, vol. 5, no. 1, 1999, p. 103.

36. The 'quality of excellence', in the words of Network Europe, was the principle on which the group wished to base its action: 'To have the best management systems (internal communication networks, Intranet, information management and outreach strategy), the best European political website, the best political story adaptable to national circumstances, the best European polling programme, the best media management' (Network Europe, *Final Report*, internal document, Brussels, 30 June 1999, pp. 2–3).

37. Ibid., pp. 2, 6.

38. Ibid., p. 47.

39. Some PES executive officers seem to be convinced that socialists will be in a position to present themselves under a common acronym at the next European elections.

40. *Activities Report of the PES, from Malmo to Milan*, Brussels 1999.

41. See Dimitis Tsatsos, 'Des partis politiques européens? Premières réflexions sur l'interprétation de l'article 138a du traité des Maastricht sur les partis', Brussels (no date), p. 5.
42. In the absence of centralization and cohesion, no instance of the PES can prevent or punish dissidence.
43. Soldatos, *Le Système institutionnel et politique des communautés européennes*, p. 186.
44. Danilo Zolo, *Democracy and Complexity*, Polity Press, Cambridge 1992, pp. 41–2.
45. Devin, 'L'union des partis socialistes de la Communauté européenne', p. 282.
46. The words of Henk Vredeling, quoted by Hix, 'Political Parties in the European Union', p. 2.
47. Ibid., p. 3.
48. Robert Ladrech, 'Postscript: Social Democratic Parties and the European Union', in Ladrech and Philippe Marlière, eds, *Social-Democratic Parties in the European Union*, Macmillan, London 1999, p. 222.

Part V

Social Democracy in Historical Perspective

In the scenario of strong and weak, social democracy will always support the weak.

> (Quoted in René Cuperus and Johannes Kandel, 'The Magical Return of Social Democracy')

17

On the Verge of an Identity Change

The Last Deep Root

Social democracy has not been able to curb the development of capitalism; like a social chameleon it has, in a sense, embraced its logic and its contradictions. However, it has established various state, social and institutional safeguards, and modified the capitalist dynamic by inflecting it towards the framing of a different civilization. Today, social democrats more or less (and the 'more' or 'less' counts) adopt the logic – and ethics – of the market. They have made their latest great historical compromise with the 'structural power' of capital. This compromise – which, like the postwar compromise, assumes in part the form of 'modernization' – is the most painful and agonizing of all.

A *democratic compromise* – or 'social-liberal' compromise, in Mario Telo's terms – underlay the wave of democratization that swept Europe at the beginning of the twentieth century and immediately after the First World War. Sometimes through alliances with liberal currents in particular, the 'democracy-first strategy'[1] had as its objective 'to win political liberties and recognition of basic rights for workers'. For tactical reasons, this led socialists to accept a residual social policy, without much active engagement by the state.[2] The politics of democratization assumed very different forms and was integrated into distinct – even conflicting – strategic designs.[3] In addition, implementation of the 'strategy of political equality' often occurred in a diffuse climate of elite hostility and reaction against the 'tyranny of the masses' and democratic forms of government. However, this 'democratic' strategy changed the nature of parliamentary government; whatever the desire of the other parties, it transformed the content of public debate, 'projecting class difference and conflict – something denied by liberal parliamentarism – directly on to the political stage'.[4] Moreover, and above all, it did not prevent social-democratic forces of the time remaining true to their ideological arsenal, which was more or less anti-capitalist and frequently of Marxist inspiration or coloration.

The central aspect of social-democratic programmatic reorientation in the 1930s consisted in expansion of the state's economic engagement (deficit spending, employment, welfare, etc.), and rejection of the automatic functioning of the market. 'The specificity of the social-democratic compromises that were sought or implemented from the crisis of 1929

onwards consists . . . in the search for a post-liberal solution,' Mario Telo
has written.[5] The intellectual framework and ideological prop of this post-
liberal solution was 'anti-capitalist reformism'. In theory, interwar social-
democratic reformism (not identified with 'revisionism') was conceived as
a gradual, step-by-step strategy which, with the state playing a key role,
would cumulatively lead to a profound transformation of the capitalist
system.

Following the Second World War (and particularly from the second half
of the 1950s), social democrats one after another progressively and definitively abandoned their anti-capitalist credo. The state was regarded less and
less as an instrument of transition to socialism (and increasingly as an
instrument for the regulation of capitalism and 'social protectionism');
private initiative was promoted more and more, particularly in the framework of the mixed economy. The reconciliation with the 'social market
economy' undertaken by the SPD's Bad Godesberg conference (1959) was
the most important step symbolically in a strategy that began to spread, in
various forms, to the majority of European countries.[6] However, the promotion – and institution (once in government) – of a fairly powerful public
apparatus of *regulation* (administration), *production* (public sector and services), and *protection-redistribution* (welfare state) formed part of the 'social-
democratic idea'.[7] The bi- and tripartite postwar compromise, which was at
the base of the construction of the modern social state, the mixed economy,
and greater attention to the interests of the subaltern classes, was *post-liberal*
– and partly anti-liberal – in character, contesting the omnipotence of the
markets.

Notwithstanding significant ideological revisions and renunciations, and
despite social democracy's paralysis in the 1920s (when it had difficulty
asserting its specificity, and remained the prisoner of the liberal orthodoxy
of the epoch), none of these previous 'turns' called into question the role
of state intervention – or even some state planning – ideologically (before
the Great War), or practically (the 1930s and immediate postwar years).
The question of the state has always been at the heart of social democracy's
identity. Social democracy was also able to promote the political and trade-
union rights, the economic and symbolic interests, of the working-class and
popular strata, and often to advance them in practice. As Gérard Grunberg
has indicated:

> the evolution of the relationship between socialism and economic liberalism
> that took place from the thirties to the seventies was possible because the
> socialist parties were able to interpret this relationship in the light of their
> own values, goals and identity. They did not only conform to economic
> liberalism, but also transformed it. This transformation involved five main
> areas: the process of class compromise, the welfare state, Keynesian policies,
> nationalisation and economic planning.[8]

Now, with the exception of the welfare state – where, despite cuts, 'paradoxically, most social democratic pledges in favour of market solutions are not

signs of irreversible neo-liberalism, but merely attempts to assure the economic viability of welfare statism'[9] – social-democratic policy has been jettisoned in all these 'areas'. Not only has the role of the state in steering the economy been minimized, but this has been accompanied by a conscious strategy of *deregulatory interventionism* aimed at promoting the market. Planning, already scarcely practised in the majority of cases, has been totally abandoned. The policy of public property in some major enterprises has been replaced by a policy of outright or partial privatization. The strategy of moderate redistribution of wealth towards popular strata in the context of a major social compromise has been renounced in practice. Social democracy has ceased to be an effective force for even the moderate promotion of equality and working-class influence, particularly trade-union influence.

In any revision and compromise, the implicit but crucial question is this: is there a 'possible coherence' between the new ideological/programmatic profile and the historically defined identity of the actor engaged in the revision? Basically, the issue is 'safeguarding' identity in the new historical phase.[10] In previous compromises, such preservation – or rather, a certain preservation – was possible, despite some important costs in terms of social-democratic identity. While social democracy emerged transformed, and sometimes sorely tested, following each turn and revision, it was not denatured and altered in its essentials.

Thus, throughout all previous formulations and versions of historical social democracy – which, at national level, splinter into an indefinite series of particular cases – an immutable, central, common core went *unquestioned*: the attribution of an important role to the state, and the preservation and affirmation of the privileged representative link between social democracy and working-class/popular strata. *The state and the promotion – a certain promotion – of the interests of disadvantaged groups are the two points of contact – and continuity – between the different stages of social-democratic history.*

Indeed, the active role assigned to the state by social democrats (in the form either of the radical-revolutionary state, or of the reformist-redistributive state, or a combination of the two) is a near-constant element in the long social-democratic tradition. Similarly, the attribution of centrality, real and/or symbolic (and varying with the times), to the promotion of working-class interests is also a quasi-constant in this tradition. It assumed highly diverse forms depending on the epoch, and varied from country to country in the same epoch. Let me give a few examples. It took the form of promoting the *democratic* rights of worker-citizens, which fell well short of the objective of redistribution (social democracy at the end of the nineteenth and beginning of the twentieth century). Or it took the form of promoting a sort of *radical equality*, which went well beyond the 'modest' objective of redistribution, and had as its precondition the overthrow of capitalism (historical social-democratic parties belonging to an anti-capitalist, revolutionary tradition). Or it could involve advancing '*immediate*' *working-class interests*, which was bound up with the necessity of improving the hard daily lot of the 'have-nots' (this involved both explicitly and openly anti-capitalist parties, and the more moderate parties); or promoting redistribution *stricto sensu* (this extended to all parties after the Second World War and, to a certain extent, in the interwar period). In short, this dual 'core' forms part of the political heritage (in Seraphim Seferiades' terms) of both the 'revolutionary-rational' model of continental social democracy up to World War I (especially before 1910), and the 'reformist-rational' model of subsequent phases.[11] The presence of this 'dual core' was also confirmed in England: Labourism's 'pure path to reformism',[12] which the left-wing turbulence of 1918–26 destabilized only temporarily, is no exception. In consequence, this core was constitutive of the social-democratic revolutionary project, which *in practice* frequently amounted to simply a '*transforming*' *reformism*.[13] In other countries (or the same countries somewhat later), it was also constitutive of '*classical*' *reformism*, which (as in Belgium up to the beginning of the 1930s) operated from without, being as a general rule an oppositional reformism – or only exceptionally a governmental reformism.[14] It was equally constitutive of the 'administrative' reformism (*réformisme gestionnaire*) which, particularly from the 1930s to the end of the 1970s, characterized the governmental practice of social democrats in different ways at different times.[15]

Thus, over the very long historical term these two elements have constituted the hard core, the enduring and crucial node which, regardless of the historically highly variable content and forms of the link, connected the anti-capitalist social democracy of the original Second International to the 'force for *social capitalism*' represented by postwar Keynesian social democracy. They are the 'core tenets' of a long tradition marked by more breaks than continuities.[16]

Today, this historical dual core has been largely removed by the neo-liberal upsurge in social-democratic ranks. Bergounioux and Grunberg, two perceptive analysts of the social-democratic phenomenon, are certainly correct when they claim that 'European socialism has gone through successive definitions ... [and] this invalidates critiques of a teleological kind, which diagnose the end of socialism at each historical stage that differs from the previous one'.[17] Moreover, Bergounioux is likewise right when he asserts that 'socialism was historically constructed at the intersection of two dynamics, that of the market and that of democracy'; and that 'we are still witnessing the clash of these two logics'.[18] But to maintain – as he proceeds to – that 'the fundamental matrix constitutive of European socialism persists', because 'the social-democratic parties still find themselves on the same side – the side of those who believe it is possible to exercise collective control and to oppose another legitimacy to that of the market',[19] is a claim that must be qualified. For a start, the range of 'those who believe that it is possible to oppose another legitimacy to that of the market' is immense. A large number of liberals, Christian democrats, and even conservatives have adopted a clear position against 'unbridled' liberalism, without thereby becoming 'social democrats'. Next, the pursuit of policies of deregulation and competitive rigour by social democracy has, *for the first time in its history*, directly challenged what was most dear, hallowed and enduring in its ideological and political tradition: the socially and economically active role of the state, and the interests of the most disadvantaged groups in the population.

In effect, in its conscious and explicit adhesion to a moderately but clearly neoliberal mode of regulation, social democracy has made the decisive ideological leap: for the first time so openly and systematically, it has elevated the market and devalued the utility of the economically active state.[20] Thus, it has not endorsed – or rather, has only marginally endorsed – the 'clash of two logics' to which Bergounioux refers. In reality, 1980s social democracy was (in Claude Demelenne's strong words):

> complicit with one of the most gigantic *coups d'état* of the postwar period: that which hoisted the financial markets into power. The left has been on the wrong side in all the battles: total liberalization of capital movements, signature of the GATT accords, creation of the World Trade Organization (WTO), installation of an unbridled free-trade regime, construction of a market and fortress Europe . . . deregulation, privatization and the undoing of public power.[21]

Furthermore, in the race for competitive disinflation and rigour, the governmental left has, despite its social discourse, departed in practice from defence of the interests of wage-earners, and particularly the 'poorest of the poor'. Social democracy has thus been transformed from a political force for the moderate promotion of equality within a socioeconomic system that is by definition inegalitarian, into a force for the *moderate promotion of inequality* in the face of forces that are even more inegalitarian.

In other words, it has been transformed from a force that has long since renounced its anti-capitalist vocation into a force that today is even abandoning its moderately *anti-plutocratic* vocation (as Vilfredo Pareto termed it). So it is scarcely surprising if social democracy 'does not succeed so readily in inflecting economic demands to the left ideologically'.[22] Nor is it surprising if left-wing leaders act 'in ways that reinforce their structural dependence on capital . . . and render labor increasingly peripheral as a political actor'.[23]

Now, what is involved here is an *extra-ordinary* development (in the etymological sense of the term) – and an extraordinary default – which probably extends to the '*last*' *deep root*, the last distinctive foundation of the social-democratic edifice, such as we have known it for three half-centuries.

Over the long term, social-democratic history is doubtless the history of its modernizations and 'adaptations'. But the latest 'adaptation' constitutes a 'break' (and it is irrelevant whether all the previous 'adaptations' have equally been perceived and experienced as 'breaks'). In effect, by calling into question the essentials of its basic culture and former governmental practice, social democracy is verging on a rupture in its identity. The distance between its past and its present, what it claims to be and what it does, 'what it wants to be and what it has been', is such as definitively to problematize the 'possible coherence' to which Telo refers. If it has not already expired, a 'pact' that has lasted more than a century seems, since the second half of the 1970s, to be on the point of being broken. Hence the crisis in the *partisan imaginary* of social democracy, which persists even in parties that are currently victorious; hence the deficit of self-conception, which reflects, expresses and reveals profound doubts about the ethical objective of contemporary socialist action. Basically, as Marc Lazar has clearly shown, the content of social-democratic 'reformism' is more than ever under the spotlight: 'it is conspicuous by its imprecision and is scarcely distinct from the reformism to which other political currents (centrists, social-liberals, Christian democrats, even some ecologists) adhere'.[24] The reforms promulgated and implemented by today's social democrats are not integrated into a coherent, specifically social-democratic project. To adopt Ilvo Diamanti's formula, what we are dealing with is 'reforms without reformism'.[25] In reality, the new social-democratic 'reformism' is a *reformism of resignation*. To start with, social redistribution, traditionally the first plank in social-democratic reformist action, is practically abandoned. In the second place, 'structural reforms', the other traditional plank in social-democratic reformist action,[26] are either utterly anaemic and sparse, or are not integrated into any overall left-wing strategy (despite the implementation of left reforms). Moreover, some of these reforms – 'structural reforms' still exist! – derive from the *conservative* arsenal. Many of the most important reforms implemented by contemporary social democracy (NB: not all) are clearly integrated – and not always with a 'guilty conscience' – *into the enemy's reformist project* (privatization, market liberalization, independence of central banks, etc.). A reformist 'spiral' is definitely at work. Just as in the past, socialist reformism entailed the formation of non- and anti-socialist reform movements,[27] so today right-reformism drags socialists along in its wake. 'Democracy in Europe was often expanded and consolidated by its enemies,' Stathis Kalyvas has written.[28] In some countries the social state has likewise been 'expanded and consolidated by its enemies'. Today, the same applies to neoliberal reform.

Certainly, from a macro-historical point of view, the neoliberal compromise is ultimately a change of limited impact compared with the postwar compromise (of which a less developed, but more composite and often more radical, version emerged on a large scale in the 1930s). The great break in historical continuity is located elsewhere: in social democracy's renunciation of its anti-capitalist vocation and assertion of its 'reformist' identity. Visible in the attitude of some currents and leaders in the working-class movement from the 1880s and 1890s, reformism began to dominate social-democratic *practice* somewhat shamefacedly in the first decade of the twentieth century,[29] was clearly asserted in 1914, and consolidated as a central attribute of social-democratic identity in the 1920s and 1930s. But the peculiarity of the neoliberal compromise is that it is a *borderline-compromise*, which consists in barring – certainly in practice, partially in ideology – the paths not of any continuity whatsoever with the past, but of *the most basic continuity conceivable*. Thus, the latest revisionist undertaking, and the latest wave of policies implemented in the name of social democracy, go considerably beyond *anything* called 'social democracy' up to the 1970s. In effect, social democrats have ended up accepting – certainly in practice, partially in rhetoric – that state intervention, as well as some aspects of the welfare state, threaten not liberty and democracy, as the most extreme supporters of liberalism assert, but economic growth and competitiveness. While it is not total, the switch is fundamental. In an ironic sense, compared with the most classical and celebrated revisionism – that of Bernstein, promoting the gradual socialization of the means of production – the new revisionism (based on the market and the gradual privatization of state property) makes it possible to appreciate the spectacular gulf between the current enterprise and past revisionism.[30] The evolution of social democracy thus fully confirms Albert Hirschman's analysis. Curiously, according to Hirschman, it was the third great 'reactionary' wave, criticizing the welfare state and welfare capitalism (whereas the first was ferociously opposed to the French Revolution and the second to universal suffrage and political equality), the one 'least consciously intent on reversing the ongoing trends or reforms', which had 'the most destructive impact'.[31]

'Destructive impact' is the right way of putting it. Social democracy embodied 'a social experiment of enormous proportions': the politics of solidarity.[32] But its ongoing modernization is such as to demolish the foundations of social-democratic 'modernization' in the initial postwar period – especially if the new social democrats continue further along the path that has been marked out, which is not a foregone conclusion. Social democracy is on the verge of a change in its identity because it is no longer capable of embodying that 'social experiment of enormous proportions'; and because it is not capable of definitively turning its back on the logic – and politics – of solidarity either. It thus finds itself in a strategic 'in-between' because its identity is intermediate. Perry Anderson gives us a superbly accurate portrait of contemporary social democracy's *borderline-state*:

> once, in the founding years of the Second International, it was dedicated to the general overthrow of capitalism. Then it pursued partial reforms as gradual steps towards socialism. Finally it settled for welfare and full employment within capitalism. If it now accepts a scaling down of the one and the giving up of the other, what kind of a movement will it change into?[33]

The Popular Space: A Historical Crisis of Representation

The unprecedented character of the new social-democratic modernization is confirmed, reinforced, and finds its 'sociological' base in the loosening of the ties that used to bind the social-democratic elites to the social-democratic 'people'.

The Subaltern Classes on the Margins of the
Social-Democratic System

Two new intermediaries have gradually entered and interposed themselves between social democracy and popular strata, between the political 'representatives' and the politically 'represented', blurring the historical relation of representation: an ideological/theoretical element – the economic philosophy of neoliberalism – and a sociological element – the dominant and domineering middle-class presence in social-democratic organizations. Without being directly linked (each in part acts independently of the other), the effects of these two new intermediaries reinforce and complement one another. With neoliberalism, which ceases to be an isolated enclave on enemy ideological territory, social democracy's ideological/ programmatic horizon alters, without undergoing wholesale neoliberalization. With this change, disadvantaged strata – those who work in uncompetitive or low-wage services industries, who find themselves unemployed or socially marginalized – cease to be at the heart of the *practical* ideology and activity of socialist governments. In addition, with new middle strata increasingly controlling the vital organizational and cultural levers of the social-democratic system, workers and the disadvantaged cease to be at its 'institutional' centre. They are displaced to the margins. Thus, through these two new intermediaries, which have rapidly become extremely conspicuous and influential, the system of 'social democracy' ceases predominantly to echo the material and symbolic preoccupations of the subaltern classes.

Social-democratic rhetoric traditionally concerned the 'weight of the world', and still does. The social democrats' desire to promote the interests of low-income wage-earners, as well as those members of the population who are 'drawn from the dregs of society, the out-of-work, the social wrecks' – as Moisei Ostrogorski would say – is clearly indicated. But the 'attenuation', even loss, of the sociological specificity of social-democratic organizations (which in some cases has completely disappeared) could complicate programmatic renewal by a 'return to the social'. A sociological absence is not easily remedied, or remedied by proxy. And even where this 'return to the social' might occur, the new sociology of the organizations would probably defy and thwart its implementation. Political experience attests to the frequent disparity between 'saying' and 'doing', programme and performance. Seconded by the familiar constraints of power, the new sociology of social-democratic organizations possesses (or could acquire) a dynamic that leads to what we might call a programmatic 'crash'. This involves imposing, in a period of financial crisis of the state and globalization, a political and social course other than that set out in the programmatic texts. But the course defined by the act of governing is, and always has been, the only one that counts. Accordingly – as Gerrit Voerman has written – if the 'express desire' to promote the interests of the poorest 'is not backed by the adhesion of some of those concerned, the legitimacy [of the social-democratic parties] risks being rocked'.[34] This has not yet come to pass. But control of the organizations by the 'contented majority' could prove a sizeable obstacle to any attempt at renewal or modernization by a radical 'return to the social'. A sociological absence – let me repeat this – is not remedied easily, or remedied by proxy.

Social democrats have definitely not abandoned the platform of equality and social justice. These ideals still form part of their armoury. However, given the neoliberalization of their economic philosophy, the infiltration of their organizations by the middle classes, and the electoral priority accorded to the latter,[35] this rhetoric functions as what a diver would call a 'decompression stage': a border-zone, a zone of contact that is indispensable to the transition from one state to another, from one social democracy to another, without abolishing loyalties and filiations, and without 'smashing' the machine. In this context the 'social' discourse, the discourse on 'social justice', becomes incoherent, and tails off. It is without momentum or bite. It is an inoffensive discourse.

The Social-Democratic Subsystem and the Elite/Popular Divide

The crisis of the major ideologies contributes substantially to reinforcing the 'marginalization', both real and symbolic, of popular strata. In the past the existence of great collective belief systems had the effect of providing individuals with a framework, making them feel secure, and establishing 'systematic links between the top and bottom of society'.[36] As Emmanuel Todd has stressed, each of the great ideologies united individuals from different social and professional milieux in one and the same belief. Thus, each ideological subsystem 'had its people and its elite, who felt solidarity with one another'.[37] Now, the crisis of the major ideological systems has important sociological consequences. In France, for example, according to Todd, the demise of Catholicism also meant the end of the links between Catholic bourgeois and peasants. The death of communism also betokened 'the end of the solidarity between workers and teachers, and the advent of innumerable individuals restored to their minuscule human scale'. The shattering of the great ideologies that divided society into hostile 'vertical blocs' – rivalling one another, but internally relatively 'solidaristic' – has helped to widen the distance between the 'people' and the 'elites'.

Moreover, the association between the middle classes and 'modernity', which (I must repeat) finds exemplary political expression in the ideological formulations of the 'new' social democracy, contributes to a divide between the categories of people who participate in the new 'modernity' and those who have missed the boat. The contrast with the past is all the greater when we think of the representation of the working class as the class 'of the future', which was once widespread but is now increasingly outmoded. The supremacy of the salaried middle strata (particularly their higher echelons) within the organizational space of social democracy, which gradually emerged over recent decades and is now irrevocably established, helps cumulatively to reinforce the sense of a gulf between 'elites' and 'masses'.

On the basis of this perception and dividing line, the higher sociocultural categories of the population, with their significant economic, cultural or educational capital (inherited or acquired), appear to form a 'world apart'. Politicians, 'sophisticated' union leaders, 'spin doctors', highly rated journalists, politically influential businessmen, university professors, communications and political marketing professionals, senior executives in the public and private sectors, executives in EU institutions, 'politicized' artists – these constitute a relatively homogeneous milieu, notwithstanding different partisan loyalties. Because of the crisis or dilution of strong ideological subsystems, this politically fragmented milieu has largely lost the sense of 'solidarity' with the base of society. In the absence of strong, opposed ideologies, intellectual, sociological and mental affinities prevail over division and adversity within it. The segments composing it are in some sense 'de-social-democratized', 'de-Christianized', or 'de-communized'. With this development, contemporary politics risks unwittingly leaving a large proportion of society outside the political picture, becoming, as it were – if only partially – a quasi-private space specializing in public affairs. A new sociological and symbolic border, internal to the social-democratic subsystem, is thus established. Within *le tout Paris* – to recall and use Anne Martin-Fugier's expression – or the smart sets of London, Athens or Brussels – semi-enclosed, luxury milieux – there is a social-democratic component.

This component is no longer equipped to represent – or even imagine – the 'grandeur and misery' of the most modest milieux. It is cloistered in its certitudes and its mental fortresses. Its social discourse is increasingly reduced to the *bien-pensant* ethics of smart districts, moralistic and focused on interclassist values ('human dignity', 'rights', anti-racism, etc.). This is the 'consensus of fine sentiments', developed on the ruins of traditional economic and social politics.[38] It is not surprising that the losers from globalization – the 'dark continent' of social exclusion – often feel betrayed by this left, which was once 'their' left. Their expectations and problems are 'politically inexpressible'.[39] In effect, part of the contemporary social-democratic elites is in the process of distancing itself from 'its' people. The Roman emperors, wrote Étienne de La Boétie, were fond of taking the title 'Tribune of the People', an office considered holy and sacred, in order to assure themselves of the people's confidence, and erase all memory of the adverse effects of their actual policies.[40] Intent – via the politics of the 'new centre' or 'radical centre' – on rallying the most 'in' sections of the population – those who combine economic dynamism with the weapons of culture and upward social mobility[41] – the elites of the new social democracy dispense even with that ambition.

In addition, in some countries the consolidation of the popular bases of the new extreme right, its breakthrough in urban working-class districts hit by the crisis, further weakens the bond of representation between the left (socialist or communist) and working-class/popular strata. Especially as a result of its 'failure' in social policy, the left no longer succeeds in drawing the mass of workers and subaltern classes in its cultural wake (see Part II). The populist extreme right tends in part to take over the *tribunitial* function of articulating the demands of a plebs that feels increasingly excluded from the 'system'. Indeed, populism has no fear of the people, that 'great body of unknowns':[42] 'the ideas I defend? Yours', claims Jean-Marie Le Pen, in classic fashion.[43] Thus, a new cleavage is superimposed on the left/right divide, opposing the 'elites' to the 'people', separating those 'above' from those 'below'. And this division weakens the popular entrenchment of the social-democratic parties.

This being so, today, perhaps for the first time since the beginning of the twentieth century, popular strata are *deprived of a political representation that is at once uncontested and more or less effective*. Indeed, 'parties of the poor' no longer exist (despite the fact that the world of the poor – and, consequently, that of the rich – has grown). *A fortiori*, 'parties of the excluded' no longer exist (despite the fact that the 'world of the excluded' – and, consequently, that of the 'excluders' – has likewise expanded). In other words, there are no longer parties equivalent to those of the 'Red belts', to speak of a period that is not so remote after all.[44] Constructed as representative bodies *par excellence* of disadvantaged social milieux – or, in the specialist language of political science, as 'parties of social integration' – such parties have disappeared from the modern political landscape. That, indeed, is the story of the modern left. While it is not identical to neoliberal or populist conservatism, its political platform no longer corresponds to popular 'demand'. Tested by twenty-five years of austerity policies and catch-all appeals, the social and psychological contract that bound popular strata to social democracy and the left has become looser organizationally as well as electorally. Worse still: the famous *fracture sociale* is in part installed within socialist and social-democratic organizational space (see Part II).

Working-class/popular distance from social democracy – which is a sign of deterioration, not rupture, in the link of representation – indicates the incapacity of a structure to perform not any old function, but a central function that formed part of its *raison d'être* and innermost history: defence of the interests of the subaltern classes, historical – and contemporary – source of any left-wing initiative with a majority vocation. In a sense, this defence became coterminous with social democracy, a factor of both political identity and electoral vitality. From this perspective, the crisis in the relationship between social democracy and the subaltern classes is the weightiest consequence historically of the new social-democratic compromise. Especially were it to persist, this constitutes the defining, crucial weakness – the Achilles heel – of social democracy's latest, ongoing transformation and modernization; and distinguishes it from all previous modernizations. It is the critical crisis. Because of it, contemporary social-democratic culture is characterized by a 'major blurring of ideology and identity', in Marc Lazar's words. And because of it, the social-democratic parties, 'regarded not as plain agents of political competition, but as producers of meaning', are in crisis.[45]

Social-Democratic Parties without Social Democracy?

Let me take up, and reformulate, the question posed by Perry Anderson. What is left of social democracy after these successive waves of de-radicalization, especially the latest of them? Does a specifically social-democratic political logic persist, as Alain Bergounioux maintains?

Even if this might appear paradoxical, the structure remains, but without the function. Although it is significantly modified and weakened, the social-democratic organizational-institutional apparatus is still there, and ensures a certain basic continuity. The social-democratic structure described throughout this study has not exploded, even if its centre has largely fissured and its contours have altered. Social democracy has not evaporated; nor has it gone over to the 'enemy camp'. And it cannot. It cannot become another political force (liberal, Christian democrat, etc.), even if it is significantly different *by comparison with itself.* There also remains a social-democratic inclination (in Bergounioux's terminology, a 'social-democratic political logic'), which is suspicious of 'any market', and takes the route of legislation and social negotiation.[46]

In reality, while the change in social democracy is significant, it has not created a new structure of political-social polarities, as happened during the transition from the 'Whig Left' to the working-class/socialist left.[47] We are not witnessing the demise of the left/right divide, the world turned upside down. The contradictory identity of contemporary social democrats, who face the dual impossibility of both breaking with and adopting the logic of solidarity (by implementing policies in the interests of disadvantaged social strata), is at root an 'impossible' identity. Precisely because it is such, for all its aggressive overtones and novel revisionist concepts, this 'impossible' identity does not – and will not be able to – obliterate the divide of the Industrial Revolution, or the compromise bound up with that divide.[48] Moreover, 'the institutions of industrial class society are still in place in Europe, and they are not likely to evaporate in the foreseeable future', even if 'they are less significant as rallying-points of collective identity and behaviour'.[49] So contemporary socialists are thus not proposing a 'refoundation' of the democratic game and the capital–labour compromise, or a new 'narrative of origins', to borrow François Furet's term. Instead, in and through their actual policies, they 'propose' a significant *rearrangement* of the terms of that compromise, to the advantage of capital and middle strata. Social democracy has changed – it has even changed profoundly. But the change is not comparable to that of the nineteenth century: it does not mark – to quote Michele Salvati – 'a profound, epoch-making shift, similar to the divide between the liberal democratic left of the post-French Revolution period and the distinctly socialist left that came after'.[50]

So what is left of social democracy at the beginning of the new century? A social-democratic structure and sensibility remain operative (to talk, as

Bergounioux does, about a social-democratic 'logic' seems to me excessive). But this 'structure' (which has itself changed considerably), and this 'sensibility', are not such as to fix a distinctively social-democratic stamp, a left-wing hallmark, on the social and political system, except in a very feeble way. In other words, there is a social-democratic pole in the European party systems, which is often strong; and a social-democratic political sensibility not identified with 'unbridled' liberalism, which is hesitantly seeking the path to a more socially orientated national and European politics. However, what does not exist – at least not now, or not yet – is a *clearly defined* social-democratic social and economic 'role', which is *perceived as such*. Nor is there a logic that is liable to shatter the legitimacy of market logic, ready and able to ground a different legitimacy, which is clearly antagonistic to neoliberal orthodoxy. What the 'social-liberalism' of contemporary social democracy is, and what it proposes, is an *attenuated version of liberalism*, supplemented with important 'new politics' ingredients (and certainly retaining some 'old' social-democratic ingredients, especially in the domain of social policy), rather than an attenuated version of classical social democracy. In short, a left-wing alternation exists – and any alternation is such only because it preserves a certain specific identity that is more than merely rhetorical. So there is an alternation, the functional prerequisite of competitive democracy and the conflict between majority and opposition. But what does not exist is a left-wing alternative, even a moderate left-wing alternative. Now, in the past, a sort of 'social democracy without a social-democratic party' emerged. Today, it is perhaps neither exaggerated nor out of order to pose the question, which runs implicitly throughout this work, of whether a sort of '*non-social-democracy with a social-democratic party*' – or, more simply, *social-democratic parties without social democracy* – are in the process of emerging.

Notes

1. Sheri Berman, *The Social Democratic Moment: Ideas and Politics in the Making of Interwar Europe*, Harvard University Press, Cambridge, MA and London 1998, p. 207.
2. Mario Telo, *Le New Deal européen: la pensée et la politique sociales-démocrates face à la crise des années trente*, Université de Bruxelles, Brussels 1988, pp. 41, 51.
3. For the 'conflicting' cases of the SAP and SPD, see Berman, *The Social Democratic Moment, passim.*
4. Alain Bergounioux and Gérard Grunberg, *L'utopie à l'épreuve. Le socialisme européen au XXᵉ siècle*, Éditions de Fallois, Paris 1996, pp. 34–5.
5. Telo, *Le New Deal européen*, p. 41.
6. The British Labour Party, with its celebrated Clause 4, did not follow this trend to programmatic revision (remaining attached to a more 'statist' approach), like the French and Italian socialists. In practice, however, the governmental dispensation of the three parties diverged considerably from their ideological and programmatic options.
7. Jean-Paul Fitoussi and Pierre Rosanvallon, *Le nouvel âge des inégalités*, Seuil, Paris 1996, p. 164.

8. Gérard Grunberg 'Socialism and Liberalism', in René Cuperus and Johannes Kandel, eds, *European Social Democracy: Transformation in Progress*, Friedrich Ebert Stiftung, Amsterdam 1998, p. 61.
9. P. Pennings, quoted in Cuperus and Kandel, *European Social Democracy*, pp. 14–15.
10. See Telo, *Le New Deal européen*, p. 42.
11. Seraphim Seferiades, *Working-Class Movements (1780s–1930s). A European Macro-Historical Analytical Framework and a Greek Case Study*, PhD dissertation, Columbia University 1998, pp. 71–3.
12. Ibid., p. 99.
13. Pascal Delwit and Jean Puissant, 'Les origines et les limites. Les débuts du réformisme socialisme en Belgique', in Hugues de la Paige and Pascal Delwit, eds, *Les Socialistes et le pouvoir*, Labor Brussels 1998, p. 255.
14. Guy Vanthemsche, 'Les mots et les actes: 100 ans de pratique réformiste en Belgique', in Hugue de Le Paige and Pascal Delwit, eds, *Les Socialistes et le pouvoir*, Labor, Brussels 1998, pp. 62–74.
15. Ibid., p. 81.
16. It will be obvious that my analysis differs from that of Colin Hay, for whom the 'transhistorical' elements that make up the 'ethical tradition (or imperative)' and the 'political practice' of social democracy are as follows:

   (i) a commitment to *redistribution* – to the principle that the distribution of social advantage within any capitalist society at any time can never be equitable and must be addressed through a constant imperative to redistribute;

   (ii) a commitment to *democratic economic governance* – to the principle that the market, left to its own devices, can only generate outcomes which are inefficient, inequitable and unacceptable and that, accordingly, the state must take responsibility for market outcomes and for the degree of intervention required to ameliorate their excesses;

   (iii) a commitment to *social protectionism* – to the principle that it is the primary responsibility of the state to ensure that its citizens are provided for in terms of health, education and welfare in its broadest sense and across the life span. (*The Political Economy of New Labour: Labouring under False Pretences?*, Manchester University Press, Manchester 1999, pp. 56–7)

   This analysis is penetrating, but inaccurate. It is penetrating because it not does not commit the double error of defining social democracy either by reformism and 'gradualism', or by 'what social-democratic parties do' ('According to such a view, social democracy will persist almost indefinitely – indeed, by definition – regardless of the context in which it is expressed': ibid., p. 56). Nevertheless, the drawback of this approach, focused on the three commitments in question, is that it is not genuinely historical. In reality, it describes only the 'core set of ethical tenets' (p. 56) of postwar social democracy, in part of interwar social democracy. Thus it defines social democracy in the habitual sense of the term (see Chapter 1), without really taking account of the orientations of historical social democracy at the end of the nineteenth century and the beginning of the twentieth – i.e. revolutionary social democracy (as least as regards some parties in the European socialist/social-democratic family). This social democracy – the social democracy of the first period – integrated the state and working-class interests in a quite different perspective from 'redistribution', 'democratic economic governance' and 'social protectionism'. Specific to social democracy in subsequent phases, the three commitments defined by Hay are insufficiently *inclusive* to account for the whole of a historical evolution that is distinguished by its extraordinary richness and complexity. That said, the social-democratic tradition, like any tradition, must be considered as 'a space, a constellation of points in movement', not as a fixed, immobile reference point. From this angle, Hay's approach is heuristically very useful, because it facilitates evaluation of contemporary social democracy in the light of its *recent* tradition, particularly that of the postwar period. It also enables us not to fall into the trap of regarding every adaptation or renovation as 'a departure from and betrayal of that tradition' (p. 56).

17. Bergounioux and Grunberg, *L'utopie à l'épreuve*, p. 363.
18. Alain Bergounioux, in Bergounioux and Marc Lazar, *La Social-démocratie dans l'Union européenne*, Les Notes de la Fondation Jean-Jaurès, Paris 1996, p. 21.
19. Ibid.
20. It is superfluous to add that, given the individualism it involves, promotion of the market sacrifices the last remaining traces of the 'collectivist' spirit of historical social democracy. It is, however, worth adding that the most important function of the neo-communitarianism of New Labour is to reconstruct a sense of the collectivity, the latter being irrevocably undermined by the dominion of commercial logic and the neoliberal turn of contemporary social democracy. From this angle, New Labour is doubly distinguished from continental socialism: it is further down the neoliberal road, and more advanced in its attempt to propose a 'doctrine' designed to remedy the inhumanities of individualism. However, this 'doctrine' exhibits strong affinities with Thatcherite neoconservatism.
21. Claude Demelenne, 'Pour une gauche debout', *Politique*, nos 9–10, 1996, p. 76.
22. Gérard Grunberg and Étienne Schweisguth, 'Recompositions idéologiques', in Daniel Boy and Nonna Mayer, eds, *L'électeur a ses raisons*, Presses de Sciences Politiques, Paris 1997, p. 148.
23. Rand W. Smith, *The Left's Dirty Job: The Politics of Industrial Restructuring in France and Spain*, University of Pittsburgh Press, Pittsburgh, PA 1998, p. 224.
24. Marc Lazar, 'La social-démocratie à l'épreuve de la réforme', *Esprit*, no. 251, 1999, p. 133.
25. Ilvo Diamanti, 'Des réformes sans réformistes en Italie', *Esprit*, no. 251, 1999, p. 101.
26. Structural reforms are measures *redefining* the framework of economic and social life (strengthening of collective actors like trade unions, nationalization, decentralization, etc.). On the content of 'classical' reformism, see Fitoussi and Rosanvallon, *Le nouvel âge des inégalités*, pp. 188–9.
27. Vanthemsche, 'Les mots et les actes', p. 70.
28. Stathis Kalyvas, *The Rise of Christian Democracy in Europe*, Cornell University Press, Ithaca, and London 1996, p. 264.
29. Parties constructed according to the 'revolutionary-rational' model were 'revolutionary in rhetoric, but increasingly reformist in conviction and, more importantly, in practice' (Seferiades, *Working-Class Movements*, p. 73).
30. Seraphim Seferiades, 'Social Democratic Strategies in the Twentieth Century', in Ilias Katsoulis, ed., *The 'New' Social Democracy at the Turn of the Century*, Sideris, Athens 2000 (in Greek).
31. Albert O. Hirschman, *The Rhetoric of Reaction*, Belknap Press, Cambridge, MA and London 1991, p. 6.
32. See Douglas Hibbs, *Solidarity or Egoism?*, Aarhus University Press, Aarhus (Denmark) 1993, p. 66.

33. Perry Anderson, Introduction, in Anderson and Patrick Camiller, eds, *Mapping the West European Left*, Verso, London and New York 1994, pp. 15–16.

34. Gerrit Voerman, 'Le paradis perdu. Les adhérents des partis sociaux-démocrates d'Europe occidentale 1945–1995', in Marc Lazar, ed., *La Gauche en Europe depuis 1945*, Presses Universitaires de France, Paris 1996, p. 578.

35. What Mathias Greffrath has written of the CDU and SPD, the major German parties, is valid for all the social-democratic parties of Europe: 'no one yet dares – especially not at election time – to defy the majority middle class, which defends its standard of living and prefers to drag behind it a growing number of excluded, rather than agreeing to share work, income and opportunity' (*Le Monde Diplomatique*, June 1998, p. 13).

36. Emmanuel Todd, *L'illusion économique. Essai sur la stagnation des sociétés développées*, Gallimard, Paris 1998, p. 264.

37. Ibid.

38. Fitoussi and Rosanvallon, *Le nouvel âge des inégalités*, p. 21.

39. Philippe Marlière, 'Sociology of Poverty or Poverty of Sociology? Pierre Bourdieu's *La Misère du monde*', *Journal of the Institute of Romance Studies*, no. 4, 1996, p. 316.

40. See Étienne de La Boétie, *Le Discours de la servitude volontaire*, Payot, Paris 1993.

41. Jacques Bauduin *et al.*, 'Vaste chantier . . .', *Politique*, nos 9–19, 1999, p. 7.

42. Stuart Hall, 'The Great Moving Nowhere Show', *Marxism Today*, November/December 1998, p. 14.

43. Quoted in Pascal Perrineau, *Le Symptôme Le Pen*, Fayard, Paris 1997, p. 231.

44. Gerassimos Moschonas, '*Quo vadis* social-démocratie?', in Michel Vakaloulis and Jean-Marie Vincent, eds, *Marx après les marxismes II: Marx au futur*, L'Harmattan, Paris 1997, p. 310.

45. Marc Lazar, 'Invariants et mutations du socialisme en Europe', in Lazar, ed., *La Gauche en Europe depuis 1945*, p. 42.

46. Bergounioux, in *La Social-démocratie dans l'Union européenne*, p. 22.

47. See Michele Salvati, 'A View from Italy', *Dissent*, Spring 1999, p. 83. And this despite the fact that the accumulated corroborating evidence – which is, however, difficult to quantify – indicates that a section of the higher middle classes and big capital is increasingly converging on contemporary social democracy. This phenomenon is very apparent in Great Britain and Greece.

48. An expression of this compromise, which has not been altogether demolished, is the still very strong legitimation of the social state, despite a certain weakening of its capacity for action. The latter is the jewel in the crown of the capital–labour compromise, and 'probably, the most lasting heritage of the organized labour movements of which Europe was the original home' (Eric Hobsbawm, 'The Death of Neo-Liberalism', *Marxism Today*, November/December 1998, p. 7).

49. Göran Therborn, 'Europe in the Twenty-first Century: The World's Scandinavia?', in Peter Gowan and Perry Anderson, eds, *The Question of Europe*, Verso, London and New York 1997, p. 366.

50. Salvati, 'A View from Italy', p. 81.

18

A Moment of Strategic Pessimism?

The Long Downturn

The twentieth century was the century of the historically unprecedented and unparalleled presence, assertion (dynamic or passive), and institutionalization of a large *popular space*, which was powerfully structured and highly robust. This space was simultaneously popular 'movement', popular 'public opinion', and popular 'political organization'. Its organization (political and associative) conferred on workers and disadvantaged groups a *power to define their own identity* and a *strategic capacity* rarely attained in the history of subaltern classes. The working class was more involved in politics – a *novel* politics – and became more visible than any previous dominated class, with the possible exception of the Enlightenment bourgeoisie, which preceded it in the Revolution.[1] The twentieth century was the 'moment' – but was it only a moment? – of the assertion and institutionalization of the *common people* (versus the 'people-as-ethnic group' or the 'people-as-nation') as the central actor of modernity (see Chapter 1). The working class not only 'devised' its own political autonomy – 'a case already rare in the history of oppressed classes' – but was able 'to propose – and this really was a first in that history – to translate it into a hegemonic political position'.[2]

Today, what was won politically and ideologically at the end of the nineteenth century, and especially during the twentieth – *autonomous* working-class representation – is in the process of disappearing – in large measure, at least. We are witnessing a slow and progressive increase in the distance, almost the dissociation, or what Leo Panitch calls a 'disarticulation' – organizational, sociological, cultural, and in part electoral – between left-wing parties (especially the social-democratic parties) and popular milieux. As for the autonomous political organization and representation of the working class and disadvantaged groups, the last twenty years have been those of the 'long downturn'. This is a development no one envisaged in the aftermath of the Second World War. The political link between the left and the 'people' has certainly not been broken. But conceived as a 'connection with mutual impact' (see Chapters 7 and 10), it has been doubly loosened: on the part of the 'representatives' (social democracy conceives and presents itself less and less as an instance of working-class and popular representation); and on the part of the 'represented' (the working class and disadvantaged groups identify less and less with social democracy, while they do not recognize any other political force as their privileged representative – which would offer a *solution* to the problem of representation). Given the constitution of the new social democracy (in most cases) as an extremely and aggressively *inclusive* force, claiming to represent the demands of the whole of society, the result is a *representative deficit* coupled with a deficit of *political autonomy* for the 'common' people. In reality, what is at issue is the end of the political form of the 'working-class party', in both its moderate, social-democratic version and its radical, communist version. A major political issue at the beginning of the last century, working-class political autonomy is again in question.

This deficit is, among other things, the combined result of two complementary and convergent developments.

Rather than exercising, as in the past, a *positive formative influence* on the construction of working-class people's identity, social democracy exerts an adverse influence through the 'catch-all' strategy, and the 'minimalist' ideology underpinning it: it dis-organizes the working class, contributing to the construction of a fragmented identity – in short, a non-identity. This minimalist attitude is not peculiar to the 'new' social democracy, as Adam Przeworski and John Sprague have shown so well.[3] What is new is the degree of 'minimalism' harboured and conveyed by the current 'minimalist' ideology. With the new social democracy, we have graduated from the semi-working-class, semi-catch-all strategy of the 1950s, and particularly the 1960s and 1970s, to the *aggressively* and *directly* trans-border strategy of the 1990s. Thus, contemporary social democracy seeks to accommodate in its broad church highly diverse social groups, with opposed interests and values: capitalists and workers, 'excluded' and 'excluders', smart, snobbish districts and council estates; but also left-wing intellectuals with a 'universalist' culture, the traditional middle classes, and popular strata prey to xenophobia and 'law-and-order' appeals. In this variegated scenario, the working class and the 'common' people are no longer the 'subject' that social democracy is principally supposed to represent; and the bourgeoisie is no longer the 'adversary' social democracy is supposed to combat. The image of friend/enemy is dimming, inevitably aggravating the problem of representation. We pass from a strategy that included – albeit partially – a popular dynamic in its calculations and objectives to a strategy confined to the much more modest goal of 'not losing contact' (i.e. electoral contact) with disadvantaged groups and the organized working class. Thus, subaltern classes, 'popular' strata, 'ordinary people' – in short, the 'people' – are not only no longer invited to conceive themselves as a 'subject' and act as a historical 'subject' – there is nothing really new about that – but their specificity is more than ever diluted in the interclassist, all-encompassing discourse of contemporary social democracy.

Eustache Kouvélakis has written that since the French Revolution, 'reform' has followed 'revolution' like its shadow, and is to be understood as an internal moment of its accomplishment.[4] Since the emergence – and especially the consolidation – of the working-class movement, the 'reformist' road and the 'revolutionary' or 'radical' road have tracked one another, each the shadow of the other – each defined, in a complex game of enmity and reconciliation, by opposition and reference to the other. We should perhaps note here that the historical crisis of communism – the century's most ambitious project – has contributed substantially to putting a question mark against the 'project of politicization' which sprang from working-class and popular culture. The fact that the two political poles derived from the working-class matrix – social-democratic and communist – entered into crisis almost *simultaneously* has widely precipitated the end of what remained of a political form: the 'working-class party'.[5] In this simultaneous crisis, what has actually been discredited is not so much one of the two poles to the advantage of the other as the 'working-class' alternative both represented in rival forms. In particular, the historical defeat of the communist pole, and the working-class alternative embodied by it, has not only not favoured the social-democratic, reformist road; it has 'liberated' social democracy from its *own* working-class and popular commitment, and its own 'interventionist' engagement. The 'Red Atlantis' has thus been doubly lost. The defeat of communism has legitimated and encouraged both the neoliberal option and the 'interclassist' option in social democracy, while reducing the ideological and electoral cost of both. In a sense, therefore, in this historical game 'for two players' dating back at least to the October Revolution, the 'complementary enemies' of the twentieth century remained complementary to the very end.

However, the belief that the deficit in political autonomy of popular strata results exclusively from the 'turn' – why not betrayal? – of the new (and old) social-democratic elites, or the failure of 'real socialism', requires qualification.

According to Robert Castel, the constitution of a force of protest and social transformation:

> requires at least three conditions to be met: an organization structured around a common condition; preparation of an alternative project for society; and a sense of being indispensable to the operation of the social machinery. If social history gravitated around the question of the working class for more than a century, it is because the working-class movement achieved the synthesis of these three conditions.[6]

Today, the various components of the popular space do not constitute a sociologically, psychologically and organizationally 'cohesive' whole.[7] They are not characterized by the 'common condition' to which Castel refers and they are not organized around it. More particularly, working-class confidence is – as Michel Verret put it so eloquently – 'triply impaired': in its numerical confidence, its productive confidence, and lastly, its solidaristic confidence.[8] In the first instance it was 'overtaken' within the wage-earning classes by the promotion of more up-market categories; then it was struck head-on by technological development, unemployment and job insecurity, encouraging a certain de-collectivization of the working-class condition.[9]

Today's workers (internally divided and socially weakened), junior employees, insecure labourers, the unemployed, young people in search of their first job, people who have taken early retirement, single-parent families, the inhabitants of deprived neighbourhoods, minorities of every sort (principally immigrant workers), the 'have-nots' more generally – these people represent a *heterogeneous set of situations*, not a more or less 'compact', self-confident social force.[10]

The working class unquestionably retains a significant 'capacity for anti-capitalist nuisance'.[11] And as Hout *et al.* have written: 'moving to more complex, multidimensional models of class does not imply that classes are dying'.[12] Even so, the working-class movement 'has lost the sociological and symbolic centrality of the Fordist epoch'.[13] And classical, bipolar class conflict – with two highly inclusive collective actors – has receded, leaving behind it a battlefield of greater complexity and fragmentation. There the economic condition of the subaltern classes, at least in their most peripheral echelons, has clearly deteriorated. But at the same time, everything suggests that their *political* condition – their impact as a social force, their capacity for collective mobilization and action – has deteriorated *even more sharply*. Hence the loss of the 'proud and jealous sense' of working-class and popular independence. In reality, for all their numerical importance, popular groups and categories do not 'add up' politically and culturally, or exert sufficient influence on social-democratic policy, or the policy of any party with a majority and a governmental vocation. The popular space has waned. Labour movements are 'down but not out', Andrew Richards has written.[14] Hence the deficit in political autonomy is a largely *indirect* effect (neither automatic nor inevitable) of that waning.

The 'crisis' in the representation of the popular classes is thus a two-edged phenomenon. Moreover, it would be incoherent to attribute an electoralist character to social democracy, and a capacity for 'recuperating' themes from below ('civil society' or the margins of the 'official' system), and at the same time argue – or rather, give it to be understood – that this social democracy is 'oblivious' of any popular dynamic! Any force with an 'entrepreneurial' culture – and certainly social democracy (which has frequently demonstrated its capacity for adaptation) – almost never ignores (at least, not completely) a social dynamic that could 'benefit' it – that is, bring in some votes. If social democracy has 'abandoned' '*its*' people, this is because the trends affecting these people are significant enough to reduce their importance as a 'collective actor' and as a reservoir of reliable left-wing voters that cannot be ignored.

From a rather more macro-historical vantage point, the elaborations of contemporary social democracy are merely the expression of a profound strategic pessimism. At the sophisticated level of partisan strategies, they register recognition of the significant social and political waning of the popular space. At the same time, they further this process.

Thus, the revisions inspired by neoliberalism are the latest in a long process distancing social democrats from the plebeian people and popular cultures. In conscious, aggressive fashion – sometimes even with the euphoria and zeal of the neophyte – contemporary, 'post-pessimist' social democracy draws *extreme* ideological, programmatic and organizational consequences from a 'pessimistic' strategic situation – a situation it considers adverse to any political force that is too closely identified with the working class and disadvantaged groups. The 'new' social democracy encourages, accelerates and furthers – but certainly does not trigger – a political (and simultaneously sociological and cultural) process which, in the last quarter of the twentieth century, gradually called into question the *autonomous* political representation of the working class and popular strata. With the new social democracy, the 'project of politicization' spawned by working-class culture is actually, as well as rhetorically, being exhausted.

An Epoch-Making Shift?

Politics always involves an interpretation of social existence. It also foregrounds a concrete conception of the 'public interest'. The challenge to the political autonomy of the popular arena, indissociable from the new social-democratic identity, confirms – and creates – a novel 'interpretative order'. In this new order – the 'interpretative' order of the new century – the weight, presence, interests, expectations, and ideas (however confused, vague, or underdeveloped) of popular strata are only marginally represented in the political system. The predictable result is that popular strata are gradually deserting the public arena, and the public arena is distancing itself from popular spaces and milieux. This desertion is an important, often underestimated, aspect of the phenomenon of 'depoliticization': the crisis of the political bond as one of the principal social bonds.

Obviously, 'pure' working-class or popular representation has never been the rule. While social democracy was constituted as a *pole of attraction* for the popular classes, as well as a *pole attracted* by them, it has also – at least since Bernstein – always been attracted by the middle classes. Social democracy has always sought to combine social groups that are very different, and have distinct – even opposed – interests and values. Moreover, the social history of the twentieth century demonstrates that 'reform can best be made effective and durable, when tactics are able to link the interests and fate of the poor with the fortunes of the better-off'. And as Peter Baldwin has likewise explained: 'not ethics, but politics explains it'.[15]

If 'pure' class strategies were not realistic in the past, they are still less so today. But in posing so clearly, openly and aggressively as an *inclusive* political force for the first time, contemporary social democracy has made more than a stylistic innovation. And it has undergone more than a refit, in line with current tastes, of its working-class/popular profile at the beginning of the twentieth century, or its semi-catch-all/semi-working-class profile in the immediate postwar period. With any highly developed catch-all strategy, the real question concerns 'how': *how* to combine contradictory, even opposed, interests today? *How* to link 'the interests and fate of the poor with the fortunes of the better-off'? And, consequently, *how* to represent, and *whom* to represent?

Now, despite some worthy but inadequate efforts, current economic and social conditions confirm social democrats' incapacity to implement policies of 'positive discrimination'[16] in favour of workers and disadvantaged sections of the population. This necessarily leads to the subordination of their interests to the 'fortunes of the better-off'. And today – exactly as in the past – 'not ethics, but politics explains it'.

So, thanks to the convergent developments described above (waning of the 'working-class people' as a collective actor, abandonment by social democracy of its role as organizer and representative of popular milieux, renunciation of its redistributive policies), it is as if the 'short twentieth century' was, from the viewpoint of the political organization – and representation – of the lower classes, only an exceptional 'moment', merely the *great parenthesis*, in the history of human society.

A parenthesis? Obviously, it is too soon and too easy to say that. But the trends of recent years are undoubtedly a new and important step in a regressive process. If this process deepens and expands, the great historical window that was spectacularly opened with the twentieth century will begin to be closed.

In politics, one can see the world through another's eyes, but one cannot become this 'other'. Social democracy can play, cheat, juggle with neoliberal ideas, but it is not – and cannot become – neoliberal. If only for electoral reasons, contemporary social democracy, whose anchorage points in the popular space are noticeably less affirmed and solid, remains a *pole attracted* by the popular classes. It has not lost this vocation (at least, not completely). And the more poverty and inequalities spread, the more the resistance of society and the trade-union movement to the effects of current policies grows, the greater are the chances that the socialist parties will pursue a social course. This is certainly a matter of electoral calculation, and may become more so in the future. But it is also a question of sensibility and culture. At a time when the neoliberal project is proving incapable of keeping its promises, the self-assertion and mobilization (social, trade-union, electoral) of the popular classes – with, outside, or against social democracy – could reactivate a whole 'egalitarian' cultural core that exists somewhere in the soul of social democracy. For even in those socialist parties that are the most ardent defenders of the 'economically correct', a working-class/popular memory and egalitarian culture 'inhabits some refuge of shadow and pride', to borrow a phrase from Aimé Césaire. There is no need to point out that reactivating this culture will be easier if it rests on electoral calculation. Or – to put it better – if the electoral-entrepreneurial culture of contemporary social democracy 'goes through' an *egalitarian calculation* in order to be 'vote-maximizing'.

Social democracy thus remains a force attracted by the popular classes. But today it is significantly more attracted by the middle classes and, in part, by the world of enterprise. If this trend grows in the future, it will mark 'a profound, epoch-making shift'. It will represent the 'closing' of that window: the end of an epoch. We are not there yet, but we are not far off either. In this context, the real question (at once both political and scientific), the question of questions people often want to avoid, is this: what is the power of attraction exerted by the popular classes today, and what will it be tomorrow? The answer, which exceeds the scope of this book, will largely determine future social-democratic identity. For it will determine the 'how' of the 'link' – productive or fatal, but in any event necessary – between the 'poor' and the 'better-off'.

In addition, it will determine whether the 'short twentieth century' was the great parenthesis in the history of human society or, alternatively, whether the 'third way' is the great parenthesis in the history of social democracies.

Notes

1. Michel Verret, 'Classe ouvrière et politique', in Guy-Patrick Azémar, ed. *Ouvriers, ouvrières: un continent morcelé et silencieux*, Éditions Autrement, série Mutations, no. 126, Paris 1992, p. 198.
2. Ibid., p. 200.
3. See Adam Przeworski and John Sprague, *Paper Stones: A History of Electoral Socialism*, University of Chicago Press, Chicago 1986.
4. Eustache Kouvélakis, *Philosophie et révolution de Kant à Marx*, doctoral thesis, University of Paris VIII, 1998, p. 6; Presses Universitaires de France, Paris 2001.
5. The crisis of Keynesian social democracy, which became evident in the second half of the 1970s, roughly speaking coincided with the retreat of communism, and in particular Eurocommunism, which was apparent from the beginning of the 1980s, and in any event well before the fall of the Berlin Wall. A few years later, the historical defeat of the October Revolution, or what remained of it, did not open the way for the reformist left but, rather, for the cultural 'counter-revolution' of neoliberal reformism.
6. Robert Castel, *Les Métamorphoses de la question sociale. Un chronique du salariat*, Fayard, Paris 1995, p. 441.
7. Cohesion is conceived here only in the *relative* sense of the term. In reality, no social group is 'cohesive'. One cannot treat the working class or, *a fortiori*, the multi-class popular space or, for that matter, any social class, 'as if they were themselves unified rational subjects' (Colin Hay, *The Political Economy of New Labour: Labouring under False Pretences?*, Manchester University Press, Manchester 1999, p. 79). A social 'entity' is cohesive only in a relation of comparison (relative to another entity or its own past).
8. Verret, 'Classe ouvrière et politique', p. 203.
9. Robert Castel, 'Pourquoi la class ouvrière a-t-elle perdu la partie?', *Actuel Marx*, no. 26, 1999, pp. 16–22.
10. One of the foremost historical contributions of the 'old Marxism' was that it imparted an unprecedented historical confidence to the 'labouring classes'. Today, such a 'Marxism' (whether Marxist or not), able to unify the heteroclite categories where economic and social insecurity is concentrated, is dramatically lacking.
11. Michel Vakaloulis, 'Antagonisme social et action collective', in Vakaloulis, ed., *Travail salarié et conflit social*, Presses Universitaires de France, Paris 1999, p. 245.
12. Mike Hout, Clem Brooks and Jeff Manza, 'The Persistence of Classes in Post-Industrial Societies', *International Sociology*, vol. 8, no. 3, 1993, p. 270.
13. Vakaloulis, 'Antagonisme social et action collective', p. 245.

14. Andrew Richards, *Down But Not Out: Labour Movements in Late Industrial Societies*, Instituto Juan March, Madrid 1995.
15. Peter Baldwin, *The Politics of Social Solidarity*, Cambridge University Press, Cambridge 1990, pp. 229, 299.
16. Castel, *Les Métamorphoses de la question sociale*, p. 375.

Conclusions

In the course of this work, I have sought to examine the evolution of the force and form represented by the 'social-democratic party' in its main dimensions, before proceeding to an overview of that evolution.

At the obvious risk of tiring the reader, the following points must once again be emphasized.

Social democracy was a specific and original 'structuration' of the left. On bases that were not wholly foreign to some major communist parties, or even Christian democratic parties, an institutional-political configuration gradually took shape, whose component parts, rather commonplace when taken separately, formed an original and unprecedented whole as a result of their precise combination and weighting. In particular, social democracy in the initial postwar period was a *'distinctive set of institutions and policies'*, a relatively distinctive *'system of action'*. As a rather well-defined species, social democracy is not reducible to left-wing reformism, or simply identifiable with the 'progressivist pole' in political systems. For in a sense, there is a specifically social-democratic reformist *savoir-faire*, sustained and adopted by political formations issuing from the great working-class and popular tradition of West European capitalism. The case of southern European socialism – or, in a quite different context, the American Democratic Party – demonstrates that the social-democratic 'mode' is not some 'natural state' of the non-communist left, or of the anti-/non-right-wing space.[1]

Over the last twenty-five years, *all* the parameters that defined the social-democratic partisan space, and accounted for its specificity in the initial postwar period, have been in mutation to a greater or lesser extent. This involves all levels of social-democratic life. It simultaneously affects the power structure and class character of the organizations, the membership culture, the leadership, the link with the trade unions, the size and social composition of the electorate, location in the arena of partisan competition, ideas, economic and social policies, political style, image – everything that goes to make up an identity. *The transformation is profound, because it is not exclusively ideological-programmatic,* even though the latter is the most pronounced, conspicuous and discussed dimension of the transformation. It encompasses every dimension of social democracy in a single dynamic. This mutation is the result of several small or large changes, which are complementary and convergent.

According to Alain Bergounioux and Bernard Manin, the long history of social democracy has frequently demonstrated that 'social-democratic originality consisted less in a determinate policy [e.g. Keynesianism] than in an *organizational and cultural tradition*, making several policies possible over the course of time'.[2] Today, what is in question is not simply the effectiveness of the structuration of social democracy, but also its originality. If all the parameters that defined the social-democratic partisan space in the postwar period are more or less in the process of changing, it is precisely its 'organizational and cultural tradition' that is impaired. The progressive weakening or transformation of historical social democracy's 'supporting institutions' (partisan organizations, party/trade-union link, party/associational network link, bi- and tripartite national bargaining systems), and 'supporting social base' (traditional working class) have gradually led not to a decline (a 'crisis' or 'crash') of the system of 'social democracy', but to its redefinition. The distinctive attributes that made social democracy a more or less *co-ordinated* whole are under challenge everywhere to varying degrees. Social democracy is no longer – or rather, is no longer *sufficiently* – 'a distinctive set of institutions',[3] a unique implement capable of generating and maintaining a specifically social-democratic *modus operandi*.

As a result, the 'originality' of social democracy has been put in question. Rather than the establishment of a new mode of constitution, a new 'originality', we are witnessing a dilution of any originality whatsoever. Social democracy is less and less presented and experienced as a 'different' force, a 'separate' structuration. It certainly remains a political family distinct from conservatism; and this it will continue to be. It retains some of its historical character traits, and cannot at present readily elude its *genetic code*, its *institutional memory*, its *organizational know-how*; it will probably not be able to do so in the future either. But it has become – or is increasingly becoming – an 'ordinary' political force and form. Hence social democracy as a 'distinctive set of institutions and policies' is having a hard time of it. The 'internal institutional space' of social democracy – to adopt Seraphim Seferiades' term[4] – has been significantly redefined, or is in the process of redefinition. This only serves to highlight the break with the past. A wind of change is blowing through the social-democratic continent, and shaking what Léon Blum (one of the historic leaders of French socialism) called *la vieille maison*. The 'typical' social-democratic trademark has become blurred. Social democracy is undergoing 'de-social-democratization'.

In the internal space of contemporary social democracy, the organic links with the working-class movement are looser; the structures (party, union, associative) are unravelling, and guard their autonomy with jealousy and pride; the *old coherence* (party of the working class, organization with a strong working-class presence, strong link with the trade unions, bi- and tripartite negotiation, semi-working-class/semi-catch-all ideological profile, etc.) is breaking up. All this enhances the *importance of the elites and the leader*. This evolution – one aspect of which is 'the development of a new plebiscitarian type of party'[5] – is particularly important for an understanding of the mechanism through which the contemporary social-democratic movement establishes and formulates its ideology. The leadership becomes the *exclusive proprietor* of the vital space that is the *internal institutional space*, and assumes a well-nigh crucial role 'in formulating the mainstream movement discourse'.[6] The definition of identity has become the quasi-exclusive privilege of the party elites and the leader, and not, as in the past, a 'system with several components' of which the leadership was a part, even if it doubtless occupied a central position. Although party organizations operate more democratically than they did in the past, the leadership is becoming *autonomous vis-à-vis* the whole 'social-democratic' system (which, moreover, is less and less of a 'system'). It thus secures extraordinary power, which is isolated and isolating. And fragile. The leader (and the group surrounding him or her) is the *isolated manager of isolated ideologies* (in the sense that these ideologies are less the product of 'collective' elaboration than in the past).[7] In this respect social democracy today is more appropriately defined in ideological/programmatic terms (whose content is largely specified by the leader and his modern *custodes novellarum*) than in terms of 'organizational and cultural tradition'.

Obviously, we can define social democracy 'extensively, not comprehensively'. This is what Steven Lukes has done in another context – and legitimately so. According to Lukes, what ultimately defines the left is the commitment to the principle of rectifying inequalities, or the 'project of rectification'.[8] 'What has distinguished the Left in all its historical forms over the last two centuries', Norberto Bobbio has written, 'is what I am inclined to define as the "ethos" (which is also "pathos") of equality.'[9] Today, this commitment – albeit if only rhetorical – to the principle of rectifying inequalities has changed only partially. No doubt the new social-democratic elites have partly renounced 'classical' postwar values and cultural codes, and it is also beyond dispute that the definition of 'the social' and 'equality' is significantly conditioned by endorsement of the neoliberal option. But notwithstanding this redefinition, social democrats have not abandoned their preferred weapon, which they have used for more than a century with unfailing consistency. This weapon is sizeable: 'we represent the interests of the popular classes'. We social democrats of the early twenty-first century, who no longer represent a single class (and no longer wish to), who speak in the name of the people and the nation, in the name of competitiveness and markets, even enterprise, who have endorsed 'sound' management of the public finances, monetary stability as well as the discourse of 'sacrifice' – despite everything, we remain the best representatives of the disadvantaged sections of the population, and best placed to reduce inequalities. In this political genus, which is neither intellectually nor electorally extinct, social democrats possess and exploit their historical pedigree.

Now, in the light of the current social-democratic system of 'normative beliefs' (thus, in adopting and applying social-democratic criteria for evaluating social-democratic politics), the social-democratic performance of the last twenty-five years is disappointing. According to this system, prioritizing employment, arresting the current trend towards redistribution of wealth to the rich, defending (and rationalizing) the social state, and inventing novel, complementary social institutions to combat the new zones of poverty and insecurity – these ought to be the first task of the left and social democracy in office. Yet this is not the case or, when it is, only very inadequately. This is the major, clear lesson of the second half of the 1980s and the 1990s.

After twenty-five years of crises, renewals, and ideological and programmatic abrogation; after twenty-five years of groping, hesitation, and broken social promises; but equally, after twenty-five years of worthy efforts and new projects of a left-wing or 'solidaristic' nature, things are now clear: nothing shattering is to be expected from social democracy's corner. Hence we should not surrender what we have for some fanciful alternative. Through its 'unprecedented accommodation with capitalism',[10] social democracy has in practice abandoned its 'rectifying project'. For a political family that constructed its profile and physiognomy (its revolutionary historical physiognomy and its postwar reformist, managerial physiognomy) around the social question, this is an *extraordinary* development. 'With what measure ye mete, it shall be measured to you again,' says the Sermon on the Mount. Social democracy is a force that no longer respects its own 'measure' (i.e. the 'rectifying' project). It no longer performs 'its role'. Social democracy today, modernized social democracy, appears to be incapable of an effective response to a supremely central question of advanced modernity: the social question.

The transformation of social democracy is profound for another reason. It is the result of a prolonged political evolution, a dynamic of *de-re-composition* which, while it is not linear (far from it), dates back at least to the 1960s.

Depending on the country concerned, different actors and factors have advertently or inadvertently contributed to this: the student movements of the 1960s; the resurgence of industrial conflict towards the end of the same decade and the crisis of mass trade-unionism; feminism; changes in the audiovisual landscape; the economic crisis; European integration; globalization; the influence of neoliberalism; the emergence of the ecological movement; the self-assertion of the 'new cultural class'; the expansion of the middle classes and transformation of the 'labouring classes'; and, obviously, the collapse of communism. These influences have exercised contradictory attractions. Consequently, the movement of *de-re-composition* has not been unidirectional. The new social-democratic elites typically derive from the student movement, and have left-wing origins. As Donald Sassoon has written: 'Neo-revisionists often originated from the first "New Left", and had been deeply influenced by the new individualist politics of the 1960s and 1970s.'[11] Contrariwise, it is also characteristic that another section of the social-democratic elites, notably those who occupy key positions in the economic administration of current left-wing governments, derives from the very conservative economic establishment. All these contradictory origins and influences have figured in the subtle and complex mechanism of social-democratic redefinition and, ultimately, overhaul. But they operated on a terrain – in reality, a common denominator – which was not simply ideological: the progressive weakening of the 'supporting institutions' and 'supporting social base' of historical social democracy. The revisionist ardour of the contemporary social-democratic elites was not slow to latch on to the electoral downturn of the 1980s – and legitimate itself.[12]

The recasting of social democracy was thus a slow, pragmatic process. It unfolded in the absence of a *hegemonic model* to act as an exemplum and possibly a locomotive (like the SPD at the beginning of the twentieth century, the SAP in the 1930s, the British Labour Party in the late 1940s or, in its own way, the French Union of the Left or the SAP again in the 1970s). It was conducted in disorderly fashion, marked by perplexity, doubt, sometimes even euphoria. Retrospectively, the change certainly seems coherent, systematic, inevitable. But from day to day, as the real actors made decisions, ambivalence, double language, internal conflict, and stop–go prevailed.

The overhaul of social democracy in the absence of a hegemonic model was the product of a largely *defensive* adaptation to the new economic, social and cultural situation of advanced capitalism (although that adaptation subsequently assumed an offensive form, as with supporters of the 'third way'). Reduction of the diversity in European socialism since the 1980s – Pascal Perrincau has spoken in this context of a socialist 'monoculture'[13] – was likewise the result of a defensive adaptation. Today's *convergence* is, in large part, the product of the '*banalization*' of the left (e.g. the end of the striking specificity of the Scandinavian model, whose prototype was the SAP; of the Austrian model; of the British model – Labour is becoming a party like all the rest, while remaining different from them; of the Greek 'populist' model of the 1970s or 1980s; or, in another register, of the PCI). The recasting – and convergence – derives more from the dilution of the strong 'models' that structured the postwar socialist/social-democratic family than from a general, aggressively reformist philosophy for the establishment of a new social-democratic model.

Given this framework of gradual, pragmatic reform, the social democracy of the 1980s, already in full de-re-composition, was changing before the supporters of the 'third way', or 'social-democratic monetarism',[14] took over the helm. A number of the reforms and revisions bruited by the new social democracy had been largely set in train, or completed, before the 'new' social democrats came to power in the socialist parties (managerial competence, practical adherence to the anti-interventionist macro-economic consensus, highlighting of the theme of 'modernity', openness to the middle classes, progressive loosening of the link with the trade unions, slow redistribution of intra-organizational power, abandonment of the language of class).

Towards the second half of the 1990s, all these developments accelerated and started to *converge*, compounding their effects. The major innovation made by supporters of the new social democracy consisted in the deepening and acceleration of reform and revision. Taking an aggressive and often iconoclastic turn, this was the particular contribution of the 'modernizers'.

The 'post-pessimistic', new social democracy of the late 1990s is the direct, worthy heir of the 'pessimistic' social democracy of the 1980s.

Formalized by Anthony Giddens, Blair's 'third way' is the most audacious (and eccentric) formulation of the new social-democratic spirit. Because of the radicalism of his initiative, Blair holds centre-stage in the drama of this long revision. He is, however, neither the originator nor the designer. Before him came Kinnock, Smith, and also Mitterrand, Rocard, Gonzales, Carlsson, Vranitsky. As Colin Hay and Mathew Wilson have emphasized, the British 'third way' is mainly 'a *post hoc* rationalisation for a reform trajectory established long before'. At the same time it represents 'a flexible repertoire of legitimating rhetoric'.[15] But it is more than that. Conferring coherence and perspective on the new social-democratic reformism, this '*post hoc* rationalisation' has greatly contributed to the emergence and consolidation of the new definition – and new self-consciousness – of European social democracy. The 'third way' forcefully captured the new social-democratic spirit, theorized from the outset as a necessary, dazzling irruption of 'modernism' faced with a 'past' regarded as anachronistic and well-nigh provincial. The 'third way' did not, however, unleash the great movement of revision (and modernization), which had been begun in Britain and Europe long before.

The *overall* social-democratic cartography is changing (and everywhere in the same direction): that is the essential change. Whether we want to call it the 'third way' or something else is merely a matter of terminology. But to identify this *global* change with its most 'right-wing' and possibly most formulated and aggressive version – Blair's 'third way' – is to reduce its import and impact. To identify this change with the 'third way', a variant of the social-democratic dynamic of modernization that universalizes British specificity, is to underestimate a political groundswell to which social democracy in western Europe has ceded in very different forms.

Overestimating the import of the British road within European socialism also renders the diversity of the latter unintelligible. Gérard Grunberg has written:

> Despite the undeniable convergence, the national peculiarities of the differ-
> ent European socialist parties have not disappeared. The cultures of the
> French, German and British parties, to take these three examples, remain
> distinct in numerous respects. Whether in relation to economic liberalism,
> the role of the state, public services, the political construction of Europe, the
> relation with left-wing forces – the Communist Party in France – or to
> institutions. Each party remains primarily a national party . . . the public
> spaces are national . . . as are the electorates.[16]

Essentially, the tension between diversity and convergence – the second widely prevailing over the first, if we consider the extraordinary richness of the socialist cultures and structures of the nineteenth and twentieth centuries – indicates that there is not one, but several 'third ways', which share a common matrix while differing significantly from one another.

Thus, if the dynamic of transformation is universal (and doubly so, embracing all aspects of social-democratic identity and all countries); if it began well before the 'new' social democrats' arrival in power, then the new profile of contemporary social democracy is not an episode, some dazzling tactical feat or pyrotechnics. This profile has been developed patiently, by a slow and continuous apprenticeship. It thus possesses continuity, or at least a certain continuity. It is endowed with 'historicity' because it recapitulates, clarifies, highlights and, above all, *reformulates* the results of previous experience. This imparts a certain political depth to it.

Moreover, and above all, this new profile is balanced and, in the last analysis, coherent. The new physiognomy of social democracy is supported by a triple coherence: between its discourse in opposition (now 'moderate' compared with the traditionally left-leaning discourse of the past) and practice in government (similarly, and traditionally, moderate); between its resolutely catch-all programmatic/ideological profile (the most catch-all format in the entire history of social democracy) and the interclassist structure of its organization and electorate (likewise, by far the most interclassist in social-democratic history); and finally, between programmatic minimalism and 'electoral maximalism'.[17] Contemporary social democracy is a force in equilibrium. And in all likelihood, because it is based on this 'triple' coherence, the new social-democratic identity is not merely conjunctural in character.

Obviously, following a governmental failure or depending on the context of intra- and inter-party competition, social democracy could once again be destabilized. It could thus become, as I have stressed above, less or more liberal, less or more 'new politics', less or more bourgeois, less or more left-wing: it all depends on the intra- and extra-organizational context of partisan competition. But it could adopt this 'more or less' without really disowning – without fundamentally changing – the current framework of its ideological, programmatic, organizational or social references.

Contrariwise, to change fundamentally would now be to imperil its whole equilibrium, acquired in the course of a painful journey. It would be to call into question a multilevel structure that has been established slowly, and to challenge not a particular leadership group or ideology (which, after all, is not so difficult), but an entire mode of partisan construction (and reconstruction). Any retreat would appear far from easy. Social democracy is no longer a political force 'in transition'.

Social democracy has, to a certain extent, broken the 'organic' links that united it with certain social groups (workers, left-wing intellectuals and, later, a section of public-sector employees). Contemporary social democracy is largely constructed as a *minimal regroupment*, essentially restricted to the electoral sphere, and incapable of eliciting and organizing *intensive* support from the groups in question. Social-democratic self-identity is currently more political, and a good deal less ideological (in the sense of adhesion to a 'major' or 'minor' ideological system), sociological or cultural. It is a weak identity. Correlatively, the *autonomy* of social democracy with respect to its environment, and its capacity to control it, has declined

dramatically. Social democracy is no longer constructed as a 'strong institution' (Angelo Panebianco), or as a 'great matrix of political identity and
culture' (Marc Lazar), and has not been for a long time. Its cohesion –
which, in a sense, is 'postmodern', since it is based on weak integrating
links – stabilizes the new social-democratic edifice downwards, on the basis
of the *minimum minimorum*.

In that the 'reserved' territory (social, ideological, organizational, cultural) of social democracy has diminished, the *political enterprise* aspect of
its identity is strengthened significantly. Today more than ever, social
democracy depends on the quality of its *political appeal* (leadership, candidates, tactical coups, programme, record in government, etc.), and on the
conjuncture of partisan competition. This has electoral consequences. The
gain in tactical flexibility (a weapon in electoral competition), which is
attributable to enhanced leadership autonomy ('innovation from above')
and the ideological and programmatic flexibility of a less 'integrated'
structure, is accompanied by a very substantial *loss in stability*. An electorally
unstable force can suffer significant and rapid losses and sometimes, just as
rapidly, regain the lost ground. It is thus incapable of being relatively
consistently successful over a long period. The new social democracy is
electorally vulnerable. However, thanks to its greater 'adaptability', it is
capable of flexible strategic responses to counteract this vulnerability, by
taking advantage of its setbacks. Flexibility is a pronounced characteristic
of contemporary socialist parties (both 'left-wing' and 'right-wing'). The
most important aspect of the new social-democratic programmatic profile
is possibly not the profile itself, but the fact that it has been aggressively
(and fairly rapidly) adopted. This explains why the 'new' social democracy
displays greater openness to new sensibilities, whether left, right, or 'neither
left nor right' (e.g. feminist ideas, minority rights, ecology, neoliberal
ideas).

Contemporary social democracy is 'slight' and far from compact (ideologically and organizationally), flexible, adaptable and modest (program-
matically and strategically), unstable and scarcely cohesive (electorally). It
therefore lacks the ambition, the vision, and the *solid bases* seriously to
challenge established structures of power and influence, national or international. Hence its quasi-general resignation to the ongoing neoliberal
globalization; its passivity about the direction of European unification; and,
finally, its active participation in the cultural 'counter-revolution' of the
market – apart from certain aspects – as necessary, useful and inevitable.
Social democracy today is not capable of political and ideological
hegemony. Yet this 'slight', flexible and modest social democracy is *coherent*
in its 'slightness', flexibility and modesty. It will therefore find it very
difficult to depart from the organizational, sociological and political orbit
defined by its current identity, which tends towards the 'entrepreneurial'.
To regard the new social-democratic identity as circumstantial and ephemeral is to misjudge the whole logic of a transformation of which this identity
is simply the crystallization.

The mutation of the social-democratic/socialist family signals the beginning of a new stage of social-democratic history. The active role of the state, and the attribution of a real and/or symbolic centrality to the promotion of working-class interests – core tenets of a long heritage – have been largely abandoned by contemporary social democracy. This dual core, which ensured a basic continuity in a long tradition marked by more breaks than continuities, has been largely removed by conscious, explicit adherence to a moderately, but manifestly, neoliberal mode of regulation. Social democracy certainly still seeks to ally in one project the celebrated 'invisible hand' of liberalism with the 'visible hand' of the state. But the balance between the two has changed. Moreover, judging from the governmental experiences of social democracy today, the content of state interventionism (which remains operative, but is mainly *deregulatory* interventionism) is only partially integrated into the postwar tradition of the reformist-redistributive state   when it is not breaking with it completely.

The modernization and revisions in progress are neither the most spectacular, nor the most significant, in the long history of social democracy. But the waning of these core tenets of the social democratic legacy threatens to breach the last line of resistance, the last line of continuity. This serves to distinguish the current revisionism from all previous initiatives *en bloc.* This decisive ideological and political leap is encouraged and strengthened by the trend towards marginalization of the working-class and popular element in social democracy's institutional and ideological subsystem. By contrast, it is discouraged by the maintenance, albeit obviously considerably weakened, of the trade-union link; by the – still! – significant working-class presence in social-democratic electorates, and by social democracy's electoral anchorage in the public sector: factors that preclude adoption of a 'pure' neoliberal approach.

However, the extent of social-democratic 'revision' and transformation (the two are not identical, revision being a crucial dimension of the more general dynamic of transformation) does not result in a new structure of political-social polarities, as was the case during the transition from the liberal 'left' to the socialist left. The social-democratic mutation does not involve a radical 'refoundation' of the social-political struggle issuing from the Industrial Revolution and the capital–labour compromise, rather, it involves an important *rearrangement* of the terms of the latter to the advantage of the market, the middle classes and enterprise. Hence it is not the world turned upside down, the collapse of a world, or some clear and sharp transition to a new order.

This is why the new social democracy has not succeeded in equipping itself with strong symbolic resources, in appealing to a 'reformist imaginary',[18] whatever its content. This is also why the labour of ideological and theoretical innovation hitherto undertaken by what is called the 'new' social democracy, however iconoclastic, only partially challenges the priority of the theme of equality. The new social-democratic 'reformism' is, in the end, a *reformism of resignation*: either it is not integrated into an overall strategy, or it is integrated (albeit only partially) into the opponent's reformist project. It does not 'make sense' of social-democratic action; it does not generate a sense of the left.

Nevertheless, social democracy, tacitly or explicitly 'freed' from its own working-class and popular commitments, and its own reformist project, has once again ruptured its own historical continuity, just as it did in the first decade of the twentieth century and in 1914, in the interwar period, and the 1950s. To borrow something Eustache Kouvélakis said in a different context, it has thus contributed to the 'irruption of a new temporality'.[19] The 'imperative of rectification' has certainly not been completely abandoned, and the more mixed cases of the *gauche plurielle* in France or the Scandinavian social democrats (particularly the Swedes, who are less unfaithful to their popular lineage) oblige us to qualify this assertion. Obviously, too, we can find in contemporary social democracy tendencies that have remained true to the working-class and reformist vocation of this great political force. But none of this challenges the 'preponderant' trend. With the social democrats' neoliberal turn, with their catch-all roaming, with the new contacts they have established with the world of enterprise, and with the collapse of communist legitimacy, the greatest project of the twentieth century – the 'project of politicization' derived from working-class and popular culture – has been defeated, in both its reformist and its revolutionary variants. The *political* class conflict on which the left – and social democracy – constructed its formidable historical (and electoral) dynamic has thus been repressed. And this despite the fact, confirmed by this work, that social class continues to structure electoral choice, albeit less strongly and securely than in the past.

'The twentieth century is likely to be known as the century of the worker,' John Dunlop, US Labor Secretary, said in 1978.[20] Everything suggests that this will not be true of the twenty-first century. Politically speaking, as a result of the social-democratic defection and the formidable defeat of communism, the working-class and popular universe, socially fragmented and weakened, is becoming largely 'privatized'. For the first time in at least a century, the zone of poverty and social insecurity has ceased to be something that is assumed to have its own party representation (or representations). It is no longer represented effectively, or is represented solely via trade-unionism. The social-democratic (and communist) retreat creates within class society a zone that is *politically* (not socially) a *class zone of quasi-non-classes*, and within the political system a *zone of quasi-non-representation*. The 'minimalist' discourse of contemporary social democracy, and its 'minimalist' administration of the social question – analysed throughout this study – precisely help to shape this zone into a zone of non-representation. The absence of a clearly defined left-wing *differentia specifica* in economic and social affairs cumulatively strips the right/left divide, which encapsulates political adversity in west European capitalism, of part of its force and impact, for it creates within this divide a *major zone of non-division*. Thus, the marked deterioration in the bond of representation between the left and popular strata is the most weighty historical consequence of the new social-democratic profile and 'compromise'; and its most important 'window of vulnerability', its Achilles heel.

If the working-class movement has lost the centrality it had in the Fordist epoch, this is not simply the result of social democracy's neo-capitalist turn and the communist shipwreck. To a great extent, the political formulations and strategic options of contemporary social democrats merely 'theorize' and 'politicize' the diminution – whether passing or enduring, only history will decide – of the *political potential* of the popular classes, and particularly of the working class. This class, the 'subjective agency' of socialism, has not been conquered in a *direct* political confrontation – as the Parisian proletariat was in 1848, for example. Nor has it been 'betrayed' by leaders disloyal to the cause of the working class (as in a sense with MacDonald, who deserted Labour in 1931). On the contrary, it has (as Robert Castel stresses) been undermined, circumvented, outflanked, and finally weakened in its potential for collective mobilization by a profound sociological transformation in the structure of the wage-earning class and working conditions.[21] That said, the formulations and options of the new social democracy have, in turn, contributed to structuring, accelerating, and finally 'producing' the political *peripheralization* of the popular classes. Nevertheless, this peripheralization is not a simple party matter. Moreover, it is independent of the fact that the working-class movement 'seeks to restructure its own resources so that it can survive as a contender on an increasingly forbidding terrain'.[22]

So is the new social democracy the other face of the right, a right that dare not speak its name? Various aspects of contemporary social democracy are more than a mere 'left-wing tint' (social measures, a more consultative approach to economic policy, some consideration of trade-union interests and, in other spheres, a more environmentally friendly policy, a greater openness to cultural liberalism). Moreover, the *social* counterpart to liberal macroeconomic policies would be less easy to conceive and apply without social democracy's popular and reformist tradition (and the expectations aroused by it), and without its rootedness (albeit considerably weakened) in the popular classes and trade unions. Contemporary social democracy, a widely neoliberalized social democracy, seeks modestly to mitigate the most extreme effects of neoliberalism.

I therefore find it difficult to accept, as it has been said of New Labour, that the new social democracy 'has no substance and represents nothing but submission to the right'.[23] Certainly, to use Rand Smith's classification once again, social democracy has graduated from a 'market-modifying' to a 'market-adapting' strategy (with New Labour positioned closer to a 'market-embracing' than a 'market-adapting' strategy). But if such a strategy 'accepts the market as the final arbiter ... [it] allows more time for adjustment and is certainly more labor friendly than the *market-embracing* approach'.[24] With his theorem that 'the only full employment policy is austerity', Hayek has not become the social democrats' favourite prophet. And the shade of Keynes continues to haunt several of them (though certainly not the British), even if the Keynesian dream has been abandoned. Contemporary social democracy is not identified with the right (even if it subscribes to the economic paradigm of the right) – just as the forces of the right and centre were not identified with, or 'subject' to, social democracy during the *trente glorieuses*, years of the social-democratic consensus.

To argue, however, that 'it is absurd to suggest that the parties of the centre-left have rejected the social democratic tradition',[25] is profoundly to misjudge the extent of the change in social-democratic policies. There cannot be social-democratic policies ('new' or 'old') that do not reduce inequalities (even moderately), and promote the interests of disadvantaged groups and social rights (even modestly). Now, whatever the rhetoric, articulated in schizophrenic fashion between two registers; whatever the success of the tightrope act to which contemporary social democrats daily and systematically devote themselves, they are nevertheless confronted with a problem that is intellectually, socially and economically insoluble: the acceptance of market regulation and the *practical* promotion of left-wing social and economic objectives are fundamentally incompatible. And here the analogy with centre-right politics during the *trente glorieuses* loses all relevance. For in largely adopting Keynesian policy and the social state, the postwar right did not abandon or 'betray' the interests of its natural social base (big capital and the middle classes). At the time, the world of enterprise benefited from the social-democratic consensus as much as – if not more than – the world of labour. By contrast, in taking for its precept 'outside the liberal club, no salvation!',[26] and not wanting to touch the middle classes, contemporary social democracy has largely abandoned the objective of equality and the interests of popular strata. Social democracy has 'converted executive alternation into "un jeu à risque nul" for capital'.[27] Widespread political cynicism among the European electorates, the distancing from the working-class and popular electorate, the extreme right's penetration into the new plebeian arenas, conflicts with the trade unions – these are not portents, but signs confirming this abandonment and this *jeu à risque nul*. And that is a real break in the social-democratic tradition.

Obviously, whoever says modernization says break. Modernization is, by definition, a break in a political and ideological trajectory. This break can signify 'correction' of the trajectory; or take the form of a *global re-examination* of it. In the first case, modernization is a significant adjustment *within* a tradition; in the second, the modernization is *outside the tradition*. Obviously, the boundary between the two possibilities – and alternatives – is never as straight as a die, and establishing the 'critical threshold' is difficult. But the trend of the last quarter-century permits of little doubt. Everything indicates that at least since the beginning of the 1980s, social democracy has entered into a crucial phase of global re-examination (not adaptation and adjustments). Rather than being an attenuated version of traditional social democracy, what the 'social-liberalism' of contemporary social democracy is, and what it proposes, is an attenuated version of liberalism, supplemented by some important 'new politics' ingredients (and sometimes some very 'old politics', 'law-and-order' ingredients). Moreover, the electoral, organizational and sociological mechanics that precede, accompany, or follow this revisionist dynamic lead progressively – but not inexorably – to a global redefinition of social democracy's innermost physiognomy. Given this context of general transformation, any deepening of the renovation in progress will – conclusively – render it a modernization *outside the tradition*, in *a clear break* with the social-democratic tradition.

Notes

1. Gerassimos Moschonas, *La Gauche française (1972–1988) à la lumière du paradigme social-démocrate. Partis de coalition et coalitions de partis dans la compétition électorale*, doctoral thesis, University of Paris II, 1990; *La Social-démocratie de 1945 à nos jours*, Montchrestien, Paris 1994.
2. Alain Bergounioux and Bernard Manin, *Le Régime social-démocrate*, Presses Universitaires de France, Paris 1989, p. 184.
3. Karl Ove Moene and Michael Wallerstein, 'How Social Democracy Worked: Labor-Market Institutions', *Politics and Society*, vol. 23, no. , 1995, p. 186.
4. Seraphim Seferiades, *Working-Class Movements (1780s–1930s). A European Macro-Historical Analytical Framework and a Greek Case Study*, PhD dissertation, Columbia University 1998, p. 66.
5. Patrick Seyd, 'New Parties/New Politics? A Case Study of the British Labour Party', *Party Politics*, vol. 5, no. 3, 1999, p. 401.
6. Seferiades, *Working-Class Movements*, p. 67.
7. In the past, structures and actors with a different rationality from that of the party leadership (trade unions, associations, sections of the party membership) were in a position to contribute – if only by exerting contrary pressures – to the formulation of the 'mainstream movement discourse'. Its final formulation was thus more 'collective' than it is today.
8. Steven Lukes, 'What is Left? Essential Socialism and the Urge to Rectify', *Times Literary Supplement*, 27 March 1992.
9. Norberto Bobbio, 'At the Beginning of History', *New Left Review*, no. 231, 1998, p. 84.
10. Gregory Elliott, *Labourism and the English Genius*, Verso, London and New York 1993, p. x.
11. Donald Sassoon, *One Hundred Years of Socialism*, I.B. Tauris, London 1996, p. 736.
12. The 'weightiest' argument in the arsenal of the new social democrats is electoral: in fact, in the majority of cases the electoral downturn preceded the aggressive ideological and programmatic turn to the 'third way' and neo-capitalism, and the return to power precisely followed this shift. Thus political time, the sequence of electoral highs and lows, fuels and strengthens the argument in favour of the positions of the new social democracy – something that is readily forgotten by left-wing critics. Similarly, the left turn of the French PS was largely encouraged and legitimated by the severe electoral failures of 'monetarist socialism' (as well as by the great social mobilization of December 1995).
13. Pascal Perrineau, in Gérard Grunberg, *Vers un socialisme européen?*, Hachette, Paris 1997, p. 120.
14. The term derives from Seraphim Seferiades, 'Social Democratic Strategies in the Twentieth Century', in Katsoulis Ilias, ed., *The 'New' Social Democracy at the Turn of the Century*, Sideris, Athens 2001 (in Greek).

15. Colin Hay and Mathew Wilson, 'Neither Here Nor There? New Labour's Third Way Adventism', in Lothar Funk, ed., *The Economics and Politics of the Third Way*, LIT, Hamburg 1999, p. 178.

16. Grunberg, *Vers un socialisme européen?*, p. 123.

17. Elliott, *Labourism and the English Genius*, p. 197.

18. Zaki Laïdi, 'Qu'est-ce que la troisième voie?', *Esprit*, no. 251, 1999, p. 46.

19. Eustache Kouvélakis, *Philosophie et révolution de Kant à Marx*, doctoral thesis, University of Paris II, 1998, p. 2; Presses Universitaires de France, Paris 2001.

20. Quoted in Ethan Kapstein, *Sharing the Wealth: Workers and the World Economy*, Norton and Company, New York and London 1999, p. 66.

21. Robert Castel, 'Pourquoi la classe ouvrière a-t-elle perdu la partie?', *Actuel Marx*, no. 26, 1999, pp. 16, 23.

22. Rand W. Smith, *The Left's Dirty Job: The Politics of Industrial Restructuring in France and Spain*, University of Pittsburgh Press, Pittsburgh, PA 1998, p. 225.

23. Quoted in Geoff Mulgan, 'Whinge and a Prayer', *Marxism Today*, November/ December 1998, p. 15.

24. Smith, *The Left's Dirty Job*, pp. 11, 211.

25. Mulgan, 'Whinge and a Prayer', p. 15.

26. Viviane Forrester, *L'horreur économique*, Fayard, Paris 1996, p. 56.

27. Serge Halimi, quoted in Gregory Elliott, 'Velocities of Change', *Historical Materialism*, no. 2, 1998, p. 52.

Epilogue

'We Social Democrats', Ernst Wigfors, leader of the Swedish social demo-crats, proclaimed in 1930, 'cannot accept a system where during all times, even the best, up to 10 per cent of the workers must be unemployed, and during worse times, even more. We refuse to admit that this is necessary and natural despite how much people come armed with theories stating that this must be so.'[1] Today, a whole century's social gains have certainly not been swept away. Eroded as they are, capacities for economic and social regulation of the crisis are a lot more significant than they were in the 1920s and 1930s, precisely because of the social model largely inspired by social-democratic *savoir-faire*. And in all probability, as Karl Ove Moene and Michael Wallerstein have written, 'in spite of the recent retreat, the legacy of social democracy in terms of a relatively egalitarian income distribution may be long lasting, at least in comparison to other societies'.[2] The same applies to the social state, 'the most lasting heritage of the organised labour movements of which Europe was the original home'.[3] The social state is 'quite simply central'.[4]

Nevertheless, we can no longer interpret social democracy, following Douglas Hibbs, 'as quite dramatic evidence of the politics of solidarity'.[5] This is patently no longer true. What is true is that the majority of social democrats have accepted 'a system where during all times, even the best, up to 10 per cent of the workers must be unemployed, and during worse times, even more'.

Social democracy was – and is – a great historical, political and social current. It is therefore hardy. In a little over one hundred years its cartography has been subject to numerous changes in its various aspects, while retaining part – a part that diminished at each step, but nevertheless remained substantial – of its 'essence'. But like the identity of any social actor and any collectivity, partisan identities are not 'essences'. Innumer-able social identities once thought to be eternal have disappeared, are on the way to disappearing, or have been profoundly disrupted and altered.

Social democracy is in the process of metamorphosing. That is the argument of this book. This metamorphosis is not a mere disguise to win over the electorate. Social democracy is not some modern Zeus, king of the Greek gods, who disguised himself as a bull or a swan to seduce the object of his desire, while retaining his divine identity. The social-demo-cratic metamorphosis is profound. And it is profound because it is not simply ideological/programmatic, but encompasses every dimension of the

system of 'social democracy'. Thus, concealed under the same nomencla-
ture, and sometimes the same behaviour, are realities that are no longer
the same. Most of the time, what is done today *in the name* of social
democracy is not 'social-democratic', in either the classical or the habitual
sense of the term. It is not altogether 'non-social-democratic', either.

The 'name is our soul', wrote Odisseas Elitis, a great poet of modern
Greece. But our soul is never indivisible. Social democracy is a hybrid
political entity. It has been since at least 1914, when Émile Vandervelde,
one of the major figures in Belgian socialism and newly appointed minister
of state, having voted war credits, went to the front to buck up the troops.
He was welcomed by soldiers singing the *Internationale!*[6] Social democracy
is a hybrid political entity. As we know, the existence of the hybrid beings
of mythology – those famous 'half-men, half-beasts' – contravenes the
laws of nature; it is a virtual ontological and biological scandal. But the
existence of hybrid political entities like social democracy contravenes no
law, either natural or political. Today more than ever, the term 'social
democracy' accommodates distinct realities, a unique mix of two currents
that historically are enemies.

The 'secret' of this book entitled *In the Name of Social Democracy* is a 'non-
secret': the destiny of social democracy pertains to a historical contest
between two versions of modernism, liberalism and socialism, or – in more
current terms – between the logic of the market and the logic of solidarity.
The 'unfinished' character of this conflict – which is without a definitive
solution and is at least a century-and-a-half old, but still contemporary – is
perhaps its most important feature. The struggle continues; it is still
present, and always lurking in the background are its innumerable historical possibilities. Today – as in the past, but much more so than in the past
– this social and intellectual contest has been transferred into the *very heart
of the social-democratic ranks*. Social democracy is a political force that is torn
between two versions of modernity: at the same time it has chosen *largely to
renounce its own version in the name of its opponent's*.

So is contemporary social democracy the 'moderate wing' of liberalism,
just as it was once accused of being the 'moderate wing' of fascism? Can we
talk about 'politics without a left', as Perry Anderson has written?[7] Faced
with this type of question, which directly confronts the redoubtable – and
mysterious – problem of the survival and disappearance of collective
identities – in this case, an identity that is more than a century old – any
academic work trembles. It would have been easy to say, like Plato in *The
Republic*, that 'these things . . . equivocate, and it is impossible to conceive
firmly any one of them to be or not to be or both or neither'.[8] However,
the *trend* of the last twenty-five years does not leave much room for doubt.
The ideological/programmatic, organizational, cultural, and sociological
apparatuses of contemporary social democracy represent the *transcendence
in actuality* of the legacy of a whole historical trajectory. The latest modernization is outside the social-democratic tradition, and breaks sharply with it.
In fact, 'the only Left that is left'[9] is on the verge of a rupture in its identity.
It is on the point of crossing the 'critical threshold'. To believe the contrary

is simply to perpetuate a misunderstanding that persists in defying the logic of nearly three half-centuries of political and social history.

To conclude, however, that social democracy is 'dead', which would seem to be consistent with the analysis above, would likewise be to defy the logic of almost three half-centuries of political and social history. The social question, Eustache Kouvélakis has written, is inscribed 'in the *longue durée* of modernity'.[10] This *longue durée* establishes boundaries that are difficult to cross – but not impassable – in the action of political actors, particularly those, like social democracy, which were born and matured with the social question, a question that is at once both 'archaic' and yet dangerously modern. Perhaps, then, from a macro-historical viewpoint it is still too soon to respond to the intractable and crucial question of identity. If the ubiquity of the social question, that 'young–old' problem lodged at the heart of a triumphant capitalism, proves that social democrats have not fulfilled their own 'egalitarian' ambitions, it nevertheless has this paradoxical virtue: it creates and re-creates an electoral and ideological space for the left, which the latter has an interest in filling sooner or later. This does not mean that it will do so. Like those soldiers at the front who were attracted by the *Internationale*, social democracy remains a force attracted by the popular classes, the state, and redistributive policies. But it is noticeably more attracted by the middle classes, the market, and the logic of capital.

Social democracy is ready to 'exit' from its own history. It is playing out the epilogue. But who is not afraid of the 'end', and who can predict and foresee it? Given the fascination exercised both by the prospect of the 'exit' and by the 'pull of the past', the road ahead promises to be difficult. All the more so since the 'pull of the past' is surprisingly modern, and cannot simply be written off – as is so often done, in desperately simplistic fashion – as 'antiquated'. It is therefore better to be prudent. Only time will tell if social democracy, which has hitherto withstood the test of time (and not by chance), will continue to be inscribed 'in the *longue durée* of modernity'. And on the side of which modernity.

In questions of politics (and social history), it is good to recall that 'the worst is not always sure (to happen)'.[11] The future often has amazing surprises in store: 'The book of life is the supreme book.'[12]

Notes

1. Quoted in Sheri Berman, *The Social Democratic Moment: Ideas and Politics in the Making of Interwar Europe*, Harvard University Press, Cambridge, MA and London 1998, p. 150.
2. Karl Ove Moene and Michael Wallerstein, 'Social Democratic Labor Market Institutions: A Retrospective Analysis', in Herbert Kitschelt *et al.*, eds, *Continuity and Change in Contemporary Capitalism*, Cambridge University Press, Cambridge 1999, p. 207.
3. Eric Hobsbawm, 'The Death of Neo-Liberalism', *Marxism Today*, November/December 1998, p. 7.

 4. Jean-Paul Fitoussi and Pierre Rosanvallon, *Le nouvel âge des inégalités*, Seuil, Paris 1996, p. 148.
 5. Douglas Hibbs, *Solidarity or Egoism?*, Aarhus University Press, Aarhus (Denmark) 1993, p. 66.
 6. The episode is related in Mateo Alaluf, 'Le compromis et le renoncement: les impasses de la social-démocratie', in Hugues de Le Paige and Pascal Delwit, eds, *Les Socialistes et le pouvoir*, Labor, Brussels 1998, p. 302.
 7. Perry Anderson, 'A Sense of the Left', *New Left Review*, no. 231, 1998, p. 79.
 8. Plato, *The Republic*, Books 1–V, trans. Paul Shorey, Loeb Classical Library, Harvard University Press, Cambridge, MA 1994, 479C.
 9. Donald Sassoon, *One Hundred Years of Socialism*, I.B. Tauris, London 1996, p. 777.
10. Eustache Kouvélakis, *Philosophie et révolution de Kant à Marx*, doctoral thesis, University of Paris VIII, 1998, p. 1; Presses Universitaires de France, Paris 2001.
11. Albert O. Hirschman, *The Rhetoric of Reaction*, The Belknap Press, Cambridge, MA and London 1991, p. 154.
12. Pascal Quignard, *Petits Traités*, I, Maeght, Paris 1990.

Select Bibliography

Ahn, Jae-Hung, 'Ideology and Interest: The Case of Swedish Social Democracy, 1886–1911', *Politics and Society*, vol. 24, no. 2, 1996.

Alaluf, Mateo, 'Le compromis et le renoncement: les impasses de la social-démocratie', in Hugues de Le Paige and Pascal Delwit, eds, *Les Socialistes et le pouvoir*, Labor, Brussels 1998.

Andersen, Jorgen Goul, 'Denmark: Environmental Conflict and the "Greening" of the Labour Movement', *Scandinavian Political Studies*, vol. 13, no. 2, 1990.

—— and Bjorklund, Tom, 'Structural Changes and New Cleavages: The Progress Parties in Denmark and Norway', *Acta Sociologica*, vol. 33, no. 3, 1990.

Anderson, Christopher, 'Economics, Politics and Foreigners: Populist Party Support in Denmark and Norway', *Electoral Studies*, vol. 15, no. 1, 1996.

Anderson, Perry, 'Introduction', in Anderson and Patrick Camiller, eds, *Mapping the West European Left*, Verso, London and New York 1994.

—— 'The Europe to Come', in Peter Gowan and Perry Anderson, eds, *The Question of Europe*, Verso, London and New York 1997.

—— 'A Sense of the Left', *New Left Review*, no. 231, 1998.

—— 'The German Question', *London Review of Books*, 7 January 1999.

—— 'Renewals', *New Left Review* (second series), no. 1, 2000.

Andeweg, Rudy, 'Elite–Mass Linkages in Europe: Legitimacy Crisis or Party Crisis?', in Jack Hayward, ed., *Elitism, Populism and European Politics*, Clarendon Press, Oxford 1996.

Arter, David, 'Sweden: A Mild Case of "Electoral Instability Syndrome"?', in David Broughton and Mark Donovan, eds, *Changing Party Systems in Western Europe*, Pinter, London and New York 1999.

—— *Scandinavian Politics Today*, Manchester University Press, Manchester 1999.

Avril, Pierre, *Essai sur les partis*, Payot, Paris 1990.

Aylott, Nicholas, 'The Swedish Social-Democratic Party', in Robert Ladrech and Philippe Marlière, eds, *Social-Democratic Parties in the European Union*, Macmillan, London 1999.

Baldwin, Peter, *The Politics of Social Solidarity*, Cambridge University Press, Cambridge 1990.

Bardi, Luciano, 'Transnational Party Federations, European Parliamentary Party Groups and the Building of Europarties', in Richard Katz and Peter Mair, eds, *How Parties Organize*, Sage, London 1994.

Bartolini, Stefano, 'The European Left since World War I: Size, Composition and Patterns of Electoral Development', in Hans Daalder and Peter Mair, eds, *Western European Party Systems*, Sage, London 1985.

—— *Electoral, Partisan and Corporate Socialism. Organisational Consolidation and Membership Mobilisation in Early Socialist Movements*, Estudio/Working Paper 83, Juan March Institute, Madrid 1996.

—— and Mair, Peter, *Identity: Competition and Electoral Availability*, Cambridge University Press, Cambridge 1990.

Bauduin, Jacques, Goldman, Henri, Le Paige, Hugues and Maissin, Gabriel, 'Vaste chantier . . .', *Politique*, nos 9–10, 1999.

Beck, Ulrich, *The Reinvention of Politics: Rethinking Modernity in the Global Social Order*, Polity Press, Cambridge 1997.

Becker, Frans and Cuperus, René, 'Dutch Social Democracy between Blair and Jospin', in Cuperus and Johannes Kandel, eds, *European Social Democracy: Transformation in Progress*, Friedrich Ebert Stiftung, Amsterdam 1998.

Beilharz, Peter, 'The Life and Times of Social Democracy', *Thesis Eleven*, no. 26, 1990.

Bell, Daniel, 'Socialism', *International Encyclopaedia of Social Sciences*, pp. 506–32.

Bensaïd, Daniel, *Lionel, qu'as-tu fait de notre victoire?*, Albin Michel, Paris 1998.

Berès, Pervenche, 'The Social Democratic Response to Globalization', in René Cuperus and Johannes Kandel, eds, *European Social Democracy: Transformation in Progress*, Friedrich Ebert Stiftung, Amsterdam 1998.

Bergounioux, Alain and Manin, Bernard, *La Social-démocratie ou le compromis*, Presses Universitaires de France, Paris 1979.

—— and Grunberg, Gérard, *L'utopie à l'épreuve. Le socialisme européen au XXᵉ siècle*, Éditions de Fallois, Paris 1996.

—— and Lazar, Marc, *La Social-démocratie dans l'Union européenne*, debate in Les Notes de la Fondation Jean-Jaurès no. 6, Paris 1997.

—— and Manin, Bernard, *Le Régime social-démocrate*, Presses Universitaires de France, Paris 1989.

Berman, Sheri, *The Social Democratic Moment: Ideas and Politics in the Making of Interwar Europe*, Harvard University Press, Cambridge, MA and London 1998.

Bernstein, Eduard, *The Preconditions of Socialism*, trans. Henry Tudor, Cambridge University Press, Cambridge 1993.

Béroux, Sophie, Mouriaux, René and Vakaloulis, Michel, *Le Mouvement social en France. Essai de sociologie politique*, La Dispute, Paris 1998.

Bille, Lars, 'Danemark', in Guy Hermet, Julian Thomas Hottinger and Daniel-Louis Seiler, eds, *Les Partis politiques en Europe de l'Ouest*, Economica, Paris 1998.

—— 'The Danish Social-Democratic Party', in Robert Ladrech and Philippe Marlière, eds, *Social-Democratic Parties in the European Union*, Macmillan, London 1999.

Bobbio, Norberto, 'At the Beginning of History', *New Left Review*, no. 231, 1998.

Bolaffi, Angelo, 'Au centre, les socialistes allemands', *Politique aujourd'hui*, no. 3, 1983–84.

Boreham, Paul and Hall, Richard, 'Trade Union Strategy in Contemporary Capitalism: The Microeconomic and Macroeconomic Implications of Political Unionism', *Economic and Industrial Democracy*, vol. 15, Sage, London 1994.

Botopoulos, Costas, *Les Socialistes à l'épreuve du pouvoir*, Bruylant, Brussels 1993.

Bouvet, Laurent, 'Le blairisme est-il un socialisme?', *La Revue socialiste*, no. 1, 1999.

Bowler, Shaun and Farrell, David, *Electoral Strategies and Political Marketing*, St. Martin's Press, New York 1992.

Boy, Daniel and Mayer, Nonna, 'Que reste t il des variables lourdes?', in Boy and Mayer, eds, *L'électeur a ses raisons*, Presses de Sciences Politiques, Paris 1997.

—— 'Secteur public contre secteur privé: un nouveau conflit de classe?', in Mayer, ed., *Les Modèles explicatifs du vote*, L'Harmattan, Paris 1997.

Boyer, Robert, 'La politique à l'ère de la mondialisation et de la finance: le point sur quelques recherches régulationnistes', *Recherches, L'année de la régulation*, vol. 3, La Découverte, Paris 1000.

Braunthal, Gerard, *The West German Social Democrats, 1969–1982: Profile of a Party in Power*, Westview Press, Boulder, CO 1983.

Brossard, Olivier, 'L'emploi et le chömage', in OFCE, *L'économie française 2000*, La Découverte, Paris 2000.

Buci-Glucksmann, Christine and Therborn, Göran, *Le Défi social-démocrate*, François Maspero, Paris 1981.

Bull, Martin, 'The Great Failure? The Democratic Party of the Left in Italy's Transition', in Stefen Gundle and Simon Parker, eds, *The New Italian Republic*, Routledge, London and New York 1996.

Butler, David and Stokes, Donald, *Political Change in Britain*, Macmillan, London 1970.

Camiller, Patrick, 'Spain: The Survival of Socialism?', in Perry Anderson and Patrick Camiller, eds, *Mapping the West European Left*, Verso, London and New York 1994.

Capdevielle, Jacques, *Les Opinions et les comportements politiques des ouvriers: une évolution inévitable? Irréversible?*, Les Cahiers du CEVIPOF, Presses de la Fondation Nationale des Sciences Politiques/CEVIPOF, Paris 1999.

Caravale, Giulia, 'Leader e sistema di partito in Gran Bretagne' *Politico*, vol. LXIII, no. 4, 1993.

Castel, Robert, *Les Métamorphoses de la question sociale. Une chronique du salariat*, Fayard, Paris 1995.

—— 'Pourquoi la classe ouvrière a-t-elle perdu la partie?', *Actuel Marx*, no. 26, 1999.

Castles, Francis G., *The Social Democratic Image of Society*, Routledge & Kegan Paul, London and Boston, MA 1978.

Cautrès, Bruno and Heath, Anthony, 'Déclin du "vote de classe"? Une analyse comparative en France et en Grande-Bretagne', *Revue Internationale de Politique Comparée*, vol. 3, no. 3, 1996.

Cayrol, Ronald, 'L'électeur face aux enjeux économiques, sociaux et européens', in Pascal Perrineau and Colette Ysmal, eds, *Le Vote surprise: les élections législatives des 25 mai et 1er juin 1997*, Presses de Sciences Politiques, Paris 1998.

—— *Le Parti travailliste*, Montchrestien, Paris 1992.

Charlot, Monica, ed., *Élections de crise en Grande-Bretagne*, Presses de la Fondation Nationale des Sciences Politiques, Paris 1978.

Clement, Wallace, 'Exploring the Limits of Social Democracy: Regime Change in Sweden', *Studies in Political Economy*, no. 44, 1994.

Cohen, Élie, 'La gauche et l'économie dans les expériences de pouvoir', in Marc Lazar, ed., *La Gauche en Europe depuis 1945*, Presses Universitaires de France, Paris 1996.

Cole, Alistair, 'Studying Leadership: The Case of François Mitterrand', *Political Studies*, XLII, 1994.

Coleman, John, 'Party Organizational Strength and Public Support for Parties', *American Journal of Political Science*, vol. 40, no. 3, 1996.

Cours-Salies, Pierre and Vincent, Jean-Marie, 'Présentation' in Robert Michels, *Critique de Socialisme*, Kimé, Paris 1992.

Courtois, Stéphane and Lazar, Marc, *Histoire du Parti communiste français*, Presses Universitaires de France, Paris 1995.

Crewe, Ivor, 'On the Death and Resurrection of Class Voting: Some Comments on *How Britain Votes*', *Political Studies*, vol. XXXIV, no. 4, 1986.

—— 'Labor Force Changes, Working Class Decline and the Labour Vote: Social and Electoral Trends in Postwar Britain', in Frances Fox Piven, ed., *Labor Parties in Postindustrial Societies*, Oxford University Press, New York 1992.

Crouch, Colin, 'The Fate of Articulated Industrial Relations Systems: A Stock-Taking after the "Neo-liberal" Decade', in Marino Regini, ed., *The Future of Labour Movements*, Sage, London 1992.

—— 'Exit or Voice: Two Paradigms for European Industrial Relations after the Keynesian Welfare State', *European Journal of Industrial Relations*, vol. 1, no. 1, 1995.

—— and Streeck, Wolfgang, 'L'avenir du capitalisme diversifié', in Crouch and Streeck, eds, *Les Capitalismes en Europe*, La Découverte, Paris 1996.

Crowley, John, 'Tony Blair: un modèle politique pour la gauche?', *L'économie politique*, no. 3, 1999.

Cuperus, René and Kandel, Johannes, 'The Magical Return of Social Democracy', in Cuperus and Kandel, eds, *European Social Democracy: Transformation in Progress*, Friedrich Ebert Stiftung, Amsterdam 1998.

Dalton, Russell and Bürklin, Wilhelm, 'The German Party System and the Future', in Dalton, ed., *The New Germany Votes*, Berg, Providence, RI and Oxford 1993.

—— 'The Two German Electorates', in Dalton ed., *Germans Divided*, Berg, Oxford 1996.

Dangeville, Roger, trans., *La Social-démocratie allemande par Engels et Marx*, Union Générale d'Éditions, Paris 1975.

Dauzier, Pierre and Lombard, Paul, *Anthologie de l'éloquence française*, Éditions Table Ronde, Paris 1995.

De Deken, Johan Jeroen, 'The German Social-Democratic Party', in Robert Ladrech and Philippe Marlière, eds, *Social-Democratic Parties in the European Union*, Macmillan, London 1999.

de la Boétie, Étienne, *Le Discours de la servitude volontaire*, Payot, Paris 1993.

Delwit, Pascal, 'Le Parti socialiste', in Delwit and Jean-Michel De Waele, *Les Partis politiques en Belgique*, Éditions de l'Université de Bruxelles, Brussels 1996.

—— 'The Belgian Socialist Party' in Robert Ladrech and Philippe Marlière, eds, *Social Democratic Parties in the European Union*, Macmillan, London 1999.

—— and Puissant, Jean, 'Les origines et les limites. Les débuts du réformisme socialiste en Belgique', in Hugues de Le Paige and Pascal Delwit, eds, *Les Socialistes et le pouvoir*, Labor, Brussels 1998.

Demelenne, Claude, 'Pour une gauche debout', *Politique*, nos 9–10, 1999.

Denver, David, *Elections and Voting Behaviour in Britain*, second edition, Harvester Wheatsheaf, London and New York 1994.

Desportes, Gérard and Mauduit, Laurent, *La Gauche imaginaire et le nouveau capitalisme*, Grasset, Paris 1999.

Devin, Guillaume, 'L'union des partis socialistes de la Communauté européenne. Le socialisme communautaire en quête d'identité', *Socialismo Storia*, Franco Angeli, Milan 1989.

—— *L'Internationale Socialiste*, Presses de la FNSP, Paris 1993.

de Voogd, Christophe, 'Pays-Bas: victoire et doutes de la coalition violette', in Alfred Grosser, ed., *Les Pays d'Europe occidentale*, Documentation Française, Paris 1999.

de Winter, Lieven, 'The Selection of Party Presidents in Belgium', *European Journal of Political Research*, vol. 24, no. 3, 1993.

Diamanti, Ilvo 'Des réformes sans réformistes en Italie', *Esprit*, no. 251, 1999.

—— and Lazar, Marc, eds, *Politique à l'italienne*, Presses Universitaires de France, Paris 1997.

Diamantopoulos, Thanassis, *Electoral Systems*, Patakis, Athens, 2001 (in Greek).

Dittrich, Karl, 'Testing the Catch-all Thesis: Some Difficulties and Possibilities', in Hans Daalder and Peter Mair, eds, *Western European Party Systems*, Sage, London 1985.

Dixon, Keith, *Un digne héritier: Blair et le thatchérisme*, Raisons d'Agir, Paris 2000.

Dogan, Matei, 'Political Cleavages and Social Stratification in France and Italy', in Seymour Martin Lipset and Stein Rokkan, eds, *Party Systems and Voter Alignments*, The Free Press, New York 1967.

—— 'Classe, religion, parti: triple déclin dans les clivages électoraux en Europe', *Revue Internationale de Politique Comparée*, vol. 3, no. 3, 1996.

—— and Rose, Richard, *European Politics*, Macmillan, London 1971.

Dorey, Peter, 'The Blairite Betrayal: New Labour and the Trade Unions', in Gerard Taylor, ed., *The Impact of New Labour*, Macmillan, London 1999.

Dormagen, Jean-Yves, *I comunisti, dal PCI alla nascita di Rifondazione comunista*, Editori Koinè, Rome 1996.

Droz, Jacques, *Le Socialisme démocratique (1884–1960)*, Armand Colin, Paris 1968.

Dunleavy, Patrick, 'Class Dealignment in Britain Revisited', *West European Politics*, vol. 10, no. 3, 1987.

Duverger, Maurice, *Political Parties*, trans. Barbara and Robert North, Methuen, London 1964.

Eisenberg, Christiane, 'The Comparative View in Labour History: Old and New Interpretations of the English and German Labour Movements before 1914', *International Review of Social History*, vol. XXXIV, 1989.

Eley, Geoff, 'Socialism by Any Other Name? Illusions and Renewal in the History of the Western European Left', *New Left Review*, no. 227, 1998.

Elliott, Gregory, *Labourism and the English Genius*, Verso, London and New York 1993.

—— 'Velocities of Change', *Historical Materialism*, no. 2, 1998.

Elliott, Larry and Atkinson, Dan, *The Age of Insecurity*, Verso, London and New York 1999.

Eppler, Erhard, 'Some Programmatic Remarks about the German SPD', in René Cuperus and Johannes Kandel, eds, *European Social Democracy: Transformation in Progress*, Friedrich Ebert Stiftung, Amsterdam 1998.

Esaisson, Peter, '120 Years of Swedish Election Campaigning', *Scandinavian Political Studies*, vol. 14, 1991.

Esping-Andersen, Gøsta, *Politics against Markets: The Social Democratic Road to Power*, Princeton University Press, Princeton, NJ 1985.

—— *The Three Worlds of Welfare Capitalism*, Polity Press, Cambridge 1990.

—— 'Politics without Class: Postindustrial Cleavages in Europe and America', in Herbert Kitschelt *et al.*, eds, *Continuity and Change in Contemporary Capitalism*, Cambridge University Press, Cambridge 1999.

Farge, Arlette and Kouvélakis, Eustache, 'Y a-t-il un espace public populaire?', interview in *Futur Antérieur*, nos 39–40, 1997.

Faux, Jeff, 'Lost on the Third Way', *Dissent*, Spring 1999.

Fedele, Marcello, *Classi e partiti negli anni 70*, Editori Riuniti, Rome 1979.

Ferry, Jean-Marc, 'Pour une justice politique dans l'État social' in *L'action politique aujourd'hui*, Éditions de l'Association freudienne internationale, Paris 1994.

Fitoussi, Jean-Paul and Pierre Rosanvallon, *Le nouvel âge des inégalités*, Seuil, Paris 1996.

Fondation Saint-Simon (collective), *Pour une nouvelle république sociale*, Calmann-Lévy, Paris 1997.

Forrester, Viviane, *L'horreur économique*, Fayard, Paris 1996.

French, Steve, 'A "Third Way" through Social Pacts? Trade Union Weakness and the Limits of German Corporatism', in Lothar Funk, ed., *The Economics and Politics of the Third Way*, LIT, Hamburg 1999.

Fröschl, Erich and Duffek, Karl, 'The Austrian Experience: Debates on the Austrian Social Democratic Platform', in René Cuperus and Johannes Kandel, eds, *European Social Democracy: Transformation in Progress*, Friedrich Ebert Stiftung, Amsterdam 1998.

Garrigou, Alain, 'Conjoncture politique et vote', in Daniel Gaxie, ed., *Explication du vote*, Presses de la Fondation Nationale des Sciences Politiques, Paris 1989.

Germain, Gilbert, *Approche socio-politique des profils et réseaux relationnels des socialistes, libéraux et démocrates-chrétiens allemands et français du Parlement Européen*, doctoral thesis, Institut d'Études Politiques de Paris, 1995.

German, Lindsey, 'The Blair Project Cracks', *International Socialism*, no. 82, 1999.

Giddens, Anthony, *The Third Way: The Renewal of Social Democracy*, Polity Press, Cambridge 1998.

Gillespie, Richard, '"Programma 2000": The Appearance and Reality of Socialist Renewal in Spain', in Gillespie and William Paterson, eds, *Rethinking Social Democracy in Western Europe*, Frank Cass, London 1993.

—— 'The Resurgence of Factionalism in the Spanish Socialist Workers' Party', in David Bell and Eric Shaw, eds, *Conflict and Cohesion in Western European Social Democratic Parties*, Pinter, London and New York 1994.

Glyn, Andrew, 'The Assessment: Economic Policy and Social Democracy', *Oxford Review of Economic Policy*, vol. 14, no. 1, 1998.

Glyn, Andrew and Wood, Stewart, 'New Labour's Economic Policy' in Andrew Glyn, ed., *Social Democracy in Neoliberal Times*, Oxford University Press, Oxford, New York 2001.

Golden, Miriam, Wallerstein, Michael and Lange, Peter, 'Postwar Trade-Union Organization and Industrial Relations in Twelve Countries', in Herbert Kitschelt *et al.*, eds, *Continuity and Change in Contemporary Capitalism*, Cambridge University Press, Cambridge 1999.

Goldthorpe, John, *Order and Conflict in Contemporary Capitalism*, Clarendon Press, Oxford 1984.

Gougeon, Jacques-Pierre, 'Une nouvelle étape pour la social-démocratie allemande', *La Revue Socialiste*, no. 1, 1999.

Grahl, John, 'Le gouvernement Blair et le modèle social britannique', *L'économie politique*, no. 3, 1999.

Grunberg, Gérard, 'Existe-t-il un socialisme de l'Europe du Sud?', in Marc Lazar, ed., *La Gauche en Europe depuis 1945*, Presses Universitaires de France, Paris 1996.

—— *Vers un socialisme européen?*, Hachette, Paris 1997.

—— 'La victoire logique du Parti socialiste', in Pascal Perrineau and Ysmal Colette, eds, *Le Vote surprise. Les élections législatives des 25 mai et 1er juin 1997*, Presses de Sciences Politiques, Paris 1998.

—— 'Socialism and Liberalism', in René Cuperus and Johannes Kandel, eds, *European Social Democracy: Transformation in Progress*, Friedrich Ebert Stiftung, Amsterdam 1998.

—— and Moschonas, Gerassimos, 'Socialistes: les illusions perdues', in Pascal Perrineau and Gérard Grunberg, eds, *Le Vote des quinze*, Presses de la Fondation Nationale des Sciences Politiques, Paris 2000.

—— and Schweisguth, Étienne, 'Recompositions idéologiques', in Daniel Boy and Nonna Mayer, eds, *L'électeur a ses raisons*, Presses de Sciences Politiques, Paris 1997.

—— and Schweisguth, Étienne, 'Vers une tripartition de l'espace politique', in Boy and Mayer, eds, *L'électeur a ses raisons*.

Guger, Alois, 'Economic Policy and Social Democracy: The Austrian Experience', *Oxford Review of Economic Policy*, vol. 14, no. 1, 1998.

Habermas, Jürgen, *The Structural Transformation of the Public Sphere*, trans. Thomas Burger, Polity Press, Cambridge 1989.

Hall, Stuart, 'The Great Moving Nowhere Show', *Marxism Today*, November/ December 1998.

Hassard, John and Parker, Martin, *Postmodernism and Organizations*, Sage, London 1993.

Hassenteufel, Patrick, 'Partis socialistes et syndicats: l'autonomisation réciproque', in Marc Lazar, ed., *La Gauche en Europe depuis 1945*, Presses Universitaires de France, Paris 1996.

Haupt, Georges, *Aspects of International Socialism 1871–1914*, Cambridge University Press, Cambridge 1986.

Hay, Colin, *The Political Economy of New Labour: Labouring under False Pretences?*, Manchester University Press, Manchester 1999.

—— and Watson, Mathew, 'Labour's Economic Policy: Studiously Courting Competence', in Gerard Taylor, ed., *The Impact of New Labour*, Macmillan, London 1999.

—— and Watson, Mathew, 'Neither Here Nor There? New Labour's Third Way Adventism', in Lothar Funk, ed., *The Economics and Politics of the Third Way*, LIT, Hamburg 1999.

Heath, Anthony, Jowell, Roger and Curtice, John, *How Britain Votes*, Pergamon Press, London 1985.

——Jowell, Roger and Curtice, John, 'Trendless Fluctutation: A Reply to Crewe', *Political Studies*, vol. XXXV, no. 2, 1987.

——, Jowell, Roger and Curtice, John, 'Can Labour Win?', in Anthony Heath *et al.*, eds, *Labour's Last Chance?*, Dartmouth, Aldershot 1994.

——, Jowell, Roger, Curtice, John, Evans, Geoff, Field, Julia and Witherspoon, Sharon, *Understanding Political Change: The British Voter, 1964–1987*, Pergamon Press, London 1991.

—— and Savage, Mike, 'Middle-class Politics', in Roger Jowell *et al.*, *British Social Attitudes: The 11ᵗʰ Report*, Dartmouth, Aldershot 1994.

Heidar, Knut, 'The Norwegian Labour Party: "En attendant l'Europe"', in Richard Gillespie and William Paterson, eds, *Rethinking Social Democracy in Western Europe*, Frank Cass, London 1993.

—— 'The Polymorphic Nature of Party Membership', *European Journal of Political Research*, no. 25, 1994.

—— 'Towards Party Irrelevance? The Decline of Both Conflict and Cohesion in the Norwegian Labour Party', in David Bell and Eric Shaw, eds, *Conflict and Cohesion in Western European Social Democratic Parties*, Pinter, London and New York 1994.

Held, David, McGrew, Anthony, Goldblatt, David and Perraton, Jonathan, *Global Transformations*, Polity Press, Cambridge 1999.

Hemerijck, Anton and Visser, Jelle, 'Quel "modèle hollandais"?', *La Revue Socialiste*, no. 1, 1999.

Hermet, Guy, Hottinger, Julian Thomas and Seiler, Daniel-Louis, eds, *Les Partis politiques en Europe de l'Ouest*, Economica, Paris 1998.

Hernes, Gudmund, 'The Dilemmas of Social Democracies: The Case of Norway and Sweden', *Acta Sociologica*, no. 34, 1991.

Hewitt, Martin, 'New Labour and Social Security', in Martin Powell, ed., *New Labour, New Welfare State?*, The Policy Press, Bristol 1999.

Hibbs, Douglas, *Solidarity or Egoism?*, Aarhus University Press, Aarhus (Denmark) 1993.

Higgins, Winton, 'Social Democracy and the Labour Movement', *South African Labour Bulletin*, vol. 17, no. 6, 1993.

Hirschman, Albert O., *The Rhetoric of Reaction*, Belknap Press, Cambridge, MA and London 1991.

Hix, Simon, 'Political Parties in the European Union: A "Comparative Politics Approach" to the Organisational Development of the European Party Federations', paper, Manchester 1995.

—— and Lord, Christopher, *Political Parties in the European Union*, Macmillan, London 1997.

Hobsbawm, Eric, 'The Death of Neo-Liberalism', *Marxism Today*, November/December 1998.

Hodgson, Geoff, *Labour at the Crossroads*, Martin Robertson, Oxford 1981.

Hoel, Marit and Knutsen, Oddbjorn, 'Social Class, Gender, and Sector Employment as Political Cleavages in Scandinavia', *Acta Sociologica*, vol. 32, no. 2, 1989.

Hout, Mike, Brooks, Clem and Manza, Jeff, 'The Persistence of Classes in Post-Industrial Societies', *International Sociology*, vol. 8, no. 3, 1993.

Hyman, Richard, 'National Industrial Relations Systems and Transnational Challenges: An Essay in Review', *European Journal of Industrial Relations*, vol. 5, no. 1, 1999.

Inglehart, Ronald, *The Silent Revolution*, Princeton University Press, Princeton, NJ 1977.

—— *La Transition culturelle*, Economica, Paris 1993.

Ion, Jacques, 'L'évolution des formes de l'engagement public', in Pascal Perrineau, ed., *L'engagement politique. Déclin ou mutation?*, Presses de la Fondation Nationale des Sciences Politiques, Paris 1994.

Iversen, Torben, 'Power, Flexibility and the Breakdown of Centralized Wage Bargaining', *Comparative Politics*, vol. 28, no. 4, 1996.

—— 'The Choices for Scandinavian Social Democracy in Comparative Perspective', *Oxford Review of Economic Policy*, vol. 14, no. 1, 1998.

—— 'Wage Bargaining, Hard Money and Economic Performance. Theory and Evidence for Organized Market Economies', *British Journal of Political Science*, no. 28, 1998.

—— *Contested Economic Institutions: The Politics of Macroeconomics and Wage Bargaining in Advanced Democracies*, Cambridge University Press, Cambridge 1999.

Janoski, Thomas, 'Direct State Intervention in the Labor Market: The Explanation of Active Labor Market Policy from 1950 to 1988 in Social Democratic, Conservative and Liberal Regimes', in Janoski and Alexander Hicks, eds, *The Comparative Political Economy of the Welfare State*, Cambridge University Press, Cambridge 1994.

—— *Citizenship and Civil Society*, Cambridge University Press, Cambridge 1998.

Jary, David, 'A New Significance for the Middle Class Left? Some Hypotheses and an Appraisal of the Evidence of Electoral Sociology', in J. Garrard *et al.*, eds, *The Middle Class in Politics*, Saxon House, London 1978.

Jobert, Bruno, 'Des États en interactions', *Recherches, L'année de la régulation*, vol. 3, La Découverte, Paris 1999.

Kaase, Max, 'Is there Personalization in Politics? Candidates and Voting Behaviour', *International Political Science Review*, vol. 15, no. 3, 1994.

Kalyvas, Stathis, *The Rise of Christian Democracy in Europe*, Cornell University Press, Ithaca, NY and London 1996.

Kapstein, Ethan, *Sharing the Wealth: Workers and the World Economy*, Norton, New York and London 1999.

Karlhofer, Ferdinand, 'The Present and Future State of Social Partnership', in Gunter Bischof and Anton Pelinka, eds, *Austro-Corporatism, Contemporary Austrian Studies*, vol. 4, 1996.

Karvonen, Lauri and Sundberg, Jan, eds, *Social Democracy in Transition*, Dartmouth, Aldershot, 1991.

—— and Rappe, Axel, 'Social Structure and Campaign Style: Finland 1954–1987', *Scandinavian Political Studies*, vol. 14, no. 3, 1991.

Katsoulis, Ilias, 'La nouvelle vision "de classe" de la social-démocratie', in Helga Grebing, ed., *L'histoire du mouvement ouvrier allemand*, Papazissi, Athens 1982 (in Greek).

Katz, Richard and Mair, Peter, eds, *How Parties Organize: Change and Adaptation in Party Organizations in Western Democracies*, Sage, London 1994.

—— and Mair, Peter, 'Changing Models of Party Organization and Party Democracy: The Emergence of the Cartel Party', *Party Politics*, no. 1, January 1995.

Kavanagh, Dennis, 'The Labour Campaign', *Parliamentary Affairs*, vol. 50, no. 4, 1997.

Kellner, Peter, 'Why the Tories were Trounced', *Parliamentary Affairs*, vol. 50, no. 4, 1997.

Kelly, John, *Trade Unions and Socialist Politics*, Verso, London and New York 1988.

Kemp, Peter, 'Housing Policy under New Labour', in Martin Powell, ed., *New Labour, New Welfare State?*, The Policy Press, Bristol 1999.

Kern, Horst and Sabel, Charles, 'Trade Unions and Decentralized Production: A Sketch of Strategic Problems in the German Labour Movement', in Marino Regini, ed., *The Future of Labour Movements*, Sage, London 1992.

Kersbergen, Kees van, 'The Dutch Labour Party', in Robert Ladrech and Philippe Marlière, eds, *Social-Democratic Parties in the European Union*, Macmillan, London 1999.

Kertzer, David, *Politics and Symbols: The Italian Communist Party and the Fall of Communism*, Yale University Press, New Haven, CT 1996.

Kirchheimer, Otto, 'The Transformation of the Western European Party System', in Joseph La Palombara and Myron Weiner, eds, *Political Parties and Political Development*, Princeton University Press, Princeton, NJ 1966.

Kitschelt, Herbert, 'Left-Libertarian Parties: Explaining Innovation in Competitive Party Systems', *World Politics*, vol. xl, no. 2, 1988.

—— *The Transformation of European Social Democracy*, Cambridge University Press, Cambridge 1994.

—— 'Austrian and Swedish Social Democrats in Crisis: Party Strategy and Organization in Corporatist Regimes', *Comparative Political Studies*, vol. 27, no. 1, 1994.

—— *The Radical Right in Western Europe*, University of Michigan Press, Ann Arbor 1995.

—— 'European Social Democracy between Political Economy and Electoral Competition', in Herbert Kitschelt, Peter Lange, Gary Marks and John Stephens, eds, *Continuity and Change in Contemporary Capitalism*, Cambridge University Press, Cambridge 1999.

Koelble, Thomas, *The Left Unraveled: Social Democracy and the New Left Challenge in Britain and West Germany*, Duke University Press, Durham, NC 1991.

—— 'Recasting Social Democracy in Europe: A Nested Games Explanation of Strategic Adjustment in Political Parties', *Politics and Society*, vol. 20, no. 1, 1992.

—— 'Intra-party Coalitions and Electoral Strategies: European Social Democracy in Search of Votes', *Southeastern Political Review*, vol. 23, no. 1, 1995.

Koole, Ruud, 'The Dutch Labour Party: Towards a Modern Cadre Party?', in Wolfgang Merkel *et al.*, *Socialist Parties in Europe II: Class, Popular, Catch-all?*, ICPS, Barcelona 1992.

—— 'Cadre, Catch-all or Cartel? A Comment on the Notion of the Cartel Party', *Party Politics*, vol. 2, no. 4, 1996.

Korpi, Walter, *The Working Class in Welfare Capitalism*, Routledge & Kegan Paul, London and Boston, MA 1978.

—— *The Democratic Class Struggle*, Routledge & Kegan Paul, London 1983.

Kouvélakis, Eustache and Vakaloulis, Michel, 'Le retour d'une affaire classée', *L'Homme et la Société*, nos 117–18, 1995.

—— *Philosophie et révolution de Kant à Marx*, doctoral thesis, University of Paris VIII, 1998; Presses Universitaires de France, Paris 2001 and (in English translation) Verso, London and New York 2001.

Kriesi, Hanspeter, 'Movements of the Left, Movements of the Right: Putting the Mobilization of Two New Types of Social Movements into Political Context', in Herbert Kitschelt *et al.*, eds, *Continuity and Change in Contemporary Capitalism*, Cambridge University Press, Cambridge 1999.

Kunkel, Christoph and Pontusson, Jonas, 'Corporatism versus Social Democracy: Divergent Fortunes of the Austrian and Swedish Labour Movements', *West European Politics*, vol. 21, no. 2, 1998.

Ladrech, Robert, 'La coopération transnationale des partis socialistes européens', in Mario Telo, ed., *De la nation à l'Europe*, Bruylant, Brussels 1993.

—— 'Party Networks, Issue Agendas and European Union Governance', in David Bell and Christopher Lord, eds, *Transnational Parties in the European Union*, Aldershot, Ashgate, 1998.

—— 'Postscript: Social-Democratic Parties and the European Union', in Ladrech and Philippe Marlière, eds, *Social-Democratic Parties in the European Union*, Macmillan, London 1999.

Laïdi, Zaki, 'Qu'est-ce que la troisième voie?', *Esprit*, no. 251, 1999.

Lange, Peter, 'La théorie des stimulants et l'analyse des partis poltiques', in J.-L. Seurin, ed., *La Démocratie pluraliste*, Economica, Paris 1981.

La Palombara, Joseph and Myron, Weiner, eds, *Political Parties and Political Development*, Princeton University Press, Princeton, NJ 1966.

Lavau, Georges, 'Partis et systèmes: interactions et functions', *Canadian Journal of Political Science*, II, vol. 1, 1969.

—— *À quoi sert le Parti communiste français?*, Fayard, Paris 1981.

Lawson, Kay and Merkl, Peter, eds, *When Parties Fail*, Princeton University Press, Princeton, NJ 1988.

Lazar, Marc, 'Invariants et mutations du socialisme en Europe', in Lazar, ed., *La Gauche en Europe depuis 1945*, Presses Universitaires de France, Paris 1996.

—— 'La social-démocratie à l'épreuve de la réforme', *Esprit*, no. 251, 1999.

Le Gall, Gérard, 'Mars 1986: des élections de transition?', *Revue Politique et Parlementaire*, no. 922, 1986.

Leruez, Jacques, 'Royaume-Uni: un "état de grâce" persistant', in Alfred Grosser, ed., *Les Pays d'Europe occidentale*, Documentation Francaise, Paris 1999.

Leys, Colin, 'The British Labour Party since 1989', in Donald Sassoon, ed., *Looking Left*, I.B. Tauris, London and New York 1997.

Lindblom, Charles, *Politics and Markets*, Basic Books, New York 1977.

Lipset, Seymour Martin and Rokkan, Stein, eds, *Party Systems and Voter Alignments: Cross-National Perspectives*, Free Press, New York and Collier-Macmillan, London 1967.

Listhaug, Ola, 'The Decline of Class Voting', in Kaare Strom and Lars Svasand, eds, *Challenges to Political Parties: The Case of Norway*, University of Michigan Press, Michigan 1997.

—— Macdonald Stuart, Elaine and Rabinowitz, George, 'Ideology and Party Support in Comparative Perspective', *European Journal of Political Research*, no. 25, 1994.

Luebbert, Gregory, *Liberalism, Fascism, or Social Democracy: Social Classes and the Political Origins of Regimes in Interwar Europe*, Oxford University Press, New York and Oxford 1991.

Lukes, Steven, 'What is Left? Essential Socialism and the Urge to Rectify', *Times Literary Supplement*, 27 March 1992.

Luther, Kurt Richard, 'Austria: From Moderate to Polarized Pluralism?', in David Broughton and Mark Donovan, eds, *Changing Party Systems in Western Europe*, Pinter, London and New York 1999.

—— 'The Social-Democratic Party of Austria', in Robert Ladrech and Philippe Marlière, eds, *Social-Democratic Parties in the European Union*, Macmillan, London 1999.

Majone, Giandomenico, *La Communauté européenne: un État régulateur*, Montchrestien, Paris 1996.

Malefakis, Edward, 'A Comparative Analysis of the Workers' Movement in Spain and Italy', in Richard Gunther, ed., *Politics, Society and Democracy: The Case of Spain*, Westview Press, Boulder, CO and Oxford 1993.

Marlière, Philippe, 'Sociology of Poverty or Poverty of Sociology? Pierre Bourdieu's *La Misère du monde*', *Journal of the Institute of Romance Studies*, no. 4, 1996.

—— 'Le "London consensus": à propos d'Anthony Giddens et de la "Troisième voie"', *Mouvements*, no. 3, 1998.

—— 'Le blairisme, un thatchérisme à visage humain?', *Les Temps Modernes*, no. 601, 1998.

Martin, Pierre, *Comprendre les évolutions électorales. La théorie des réalignements revisitée*, Presses de Sciences Politiques, Paris 2000.

Mayer, Nonna and Perrineau, Pascal, *Les Comportements politiques*, Armand Colin, Paris 1992.

Menudier, Henri, *Les Élections allemandes, 1969–1982*, Centre d'Information et de Recherche sur l'Allemagne Contemporaine, Paris 1982.

Meny, Yves, *Politique comparée. Les démocraties: États-Unis, France, Grande-Bretagne, Italie, RFA*, Montchrestien, Paris 1988.

Merkel, Wolfgang, 'After the Golden Age: Is Social Democracy Doomed to Decline?' in José Maravall *et al.*, *Socialist Parties in Europe*, ICPS, Barcelona 1991.

—— 'Between Class and Catch-all: Is There an Electoral Dilemma for Social Democratic Parties in Western Europe?', in Merkel *et al.*, *Socialist Parties in Europe II: Class, Popular, Catch-all?*, ICPS, Barcelona 1992.

—— 'The Third Ways of Social Democracy', in René Cuperus, Karl Duffet and Johannes Kandel, *Multiple Third Ways*, Friedrich–Ebert–Stiftung, Amsterdam, 2001.

Michels, Robert, *Political Parties*, trans. Eden and Cedar Paul, Jarrold, London 1915.

—— 'Les dangers du Parti socialiste allemand', in Michels, *Critique du socialisme*, ed. Pierre Cours-Salies and Jean-Marie Vincent, Éditions Kimé, Paris 1992.

Michiels, Jan, 'La gauche sans la lutte des classes?', *Politique*, nos 9–10, 1999.

Milewski, Françoise, 'La croissance', in OFCE, *L'économie française 2000*, La Découverte, Paris 2000.

Miliband, Ralph, *The State in Capitalist Society*, Weidenfeld & Nicolson, London 1969.

Misgeld, Klaus, Molin, Karl and Amark, Klas, *Creating Social Democracy: A Century of the Social Democratic Labor Party in Sweden*, Pennsylvania State University Press, Pittsburgh 1992.

Mjoset, Lars *et al.*, 'Norway: Changing the Model', in Perry Anderson and Patrick Camiller, eds, *Mapping the West European Left*, Verso, London and New York 1994.

Moene, Karl Ove and Wallerstein, Michael, 'How Social Democracy Worked: Labor-Market Institutions', *Politics and Society*, vol. 23, no. 2, 1995.

—— and Wallerstein, Michael, 'Social Democratic Labor Market Institutions: A Retrospective Analysis', in Herbert Kitschelt, Peter Lange, Gary Marks and John Stephens, *Continuity and Change in Contemporary Capitalism*, Cambridge University Press, Cambridge 1999.

Moschonas, Gerassimos, *La Gauche française (1972–1988) à la lumière du paradigme social-démocrate. Partis de coalition et coalitions de partis dans la compétition électorale*, doctoral thesis, University of Paris II, 1990.

—— *La Social-démocratie de 1945 à nos jours*, Montchrestien, Paris 1994.

—— 'L'éclat d'un pouvoir fragilisé. Force et faiblesses du leadership socialiste', in Marc Lazar, ed., *La Gauche en Europe depuis 1945*, Presses Universitaires de France, Paris 1996.

—— '*Quo vadis* social-démocratie?', in Michel Vakaloulis and Jean-Marie Vincent, eds, *Marx après les marxismes II: Marx au futur*, L'Harmattan, Paris 1997.

—— 'The Panhellenic Socialist Movement', in Robert Ladrech and Philippe Marlière, eds, *Social-Democratic Parties in the European Union*, Macmillan, London 1999.

—— 'PASOK: From the "Non-Privileged" to the Society of Contents', *Epochi*, 21 May 2000 (in Greek).

Mulgan, Geoff, 'Whinge and a Prayer', *Marxism Today*, November/December 1998.

Muller, Wolfgang and D. Meth-Cohn, 'The Selection of Party Chairmen in Austria: A Study in Intra-Party Decision-Making', *European Journal of Political Research*, vol. 20, no. 1, 1991.

—— and Ulram, Peter, 'The Social and Demographic Structure of Austrian Parties, 1945–93', *Party Politics*, vol. 1, no. 1, 1995.

Nieuwbeerta, Paul, 'The Democratic Class Struggle in Postwar Societies: Class Voting in Twenty Countries, 1945–1990', *Acta Sociologica*, vol. 39, no. 4, 1996.

Norris, Pippa, 'Political Communications', in Patrick Dunleavy *et al.*, eds, *Developments in British Politics 5*, Macmillan, London 1997.

O'Connell, Philip, 'National Variation in the Fortunes of Labor: A Pooled and Cross-Sectional Analysis of the Impact of Economic Crisis in the Advanced Capitalist Nations', in Thomas Janoski and Alexander Hicks, eds, *The Comparative Political Economy of the Welfare State*, Cambridge University Press, Cambridge 1994.

Offerlé, Michel, *Les Partis politiques*, Presses Universitaires de France, Paris 1987.

Ostrogorski, Moisei, *La Démocratie et les partis politiques*, Fayard, Paris 1993.

Padgett, Stephen, 'The German Social Democrats: A Redefinition of Social Democracy or Bad Godesberg Mark II?', in Richard Gillespie and William Paterson, eds, *Rethinking Social Democracy in Western Europe*, Frank Cass, London 1993.

—— and Paterson, William, *A History of Social Democracy in Post-War Europe*, Longman, London and New York 1991.

—— and Paterson, William, 'Germany: Stagnation of the Left', in Perry Anderson and Patrick Camiller, eds, *Mapping the West European Left*, Verso, London and New York 1994.

Panebianco, Angelo, *Political Parties, Organization and Power*, Cambridge University Press, Cambridge 1988.

Panitch, Leo, 'Profits and Politics: Labour and the Crisis of British Capitalism', *Politics and Society*, vol. 7, no. 4, 1977.

—— 'Globalization in Crisis: Bringing the (Imperial) State Back In', paper presented to the 'Politics Today' conference in memory of Nicos Poulantzas, Athens 1999.

—— and Leys, Colin, *The End of Parliamentary Socialism: From New Left to New Labour*, Verso, London and New York 1997.

Parkin, Frank, *Middle Class Radicalism*, Manchester University Press, Manchester 1968.

Paterson, William and Thomas, Alastair, eds, *Social-democratic Parties in Western Europe*, Croom Helm, London 1977.

—— *The Future of Social-Democracy*, Clarendon Press, Oxford 1986.

Pattie, Charles, Whiteley, Paul, Johnston, Ron and Seyd, Patrick, 'Measuring Local Campaign Effects: Labour Party Constituency Campaigning at the 1987 General Election', *Political Studies*, no. XLII, 1994.

Pélassy, Dominique, *Sans foi ni loi? Essai sur le bouleversement des valeurs*, Fayard, Paris 1995.

Pelinka, Anton, *Social Democratic Parties in Europe*, Praeger, New York 1983.

—— and Plasser, Fritz, *The Austrian Party System*, Westview Press, Boulder, CO 1989.

Perrineau, Pascal, 'Introduction', in Perrineau, ed., *L'engagement politique: déclin ou mutation?*, Presses de la Fondation Nationale des Sciences Politiques, Paris 1994.

—— *Le Symptôme Le Pen*, Fayard, Paris 1997.

Philip, André, 'La pensée politique des partis ouvriers', in Léo Hamon, ed., *Les nouveaux comportements politiques de la classe ouvrière*, Presses Universitaires de France, Paris 1959.

Poguntke, Thomas, 'Parties in a Legalistic Culture: The Case of Germany', in Richard Katz and Peter Mair, eds, *How Parties Organize: Change and Adaptation in Party Organizations in Western Democracies*, Sage, London 1994.

Pontusson, Jonas, 'Sweden: After the Golden Age', in Perry Anderson and Patrick Camiller, eds, *Mapping the West European Left*, Verso, London and New York 1994.

—— Review of Herbert Kitschelt's *The Transformation of European Social Democracy*, *Comparative Political Studies*, vol. 28, no. 3, 1995.

—— 'Le modèle suédois en mutation: vers le néoliberalisme ou le modèle allemand?', in Colin Crouch and Wolfgang Streeck, eds, *Les Capitalismes en Europe*, La Découverte, Paris 1996.

Portelli, Hugues, *Le Parti Socialiste*, Mont-Chrestien, Paris 1992.

Powell, Martin, ed., *New Labour, New Welfare State?*, The Policy Press, Bristol 1999.

Pridham, Geoffrey and Pridham, Pippa, *Transnational Party Co-operation and European Integration*, George Allen & Unwin, London 1981.

Przeworski, Adam, 'Proletariat into a Class: The Process of Class Formation from Karl Kautsky's *The Class Struggle* to Recent Controversies', *Politics and Society*, vol. 7, no. 4, 1977.

—— 'Social Democracy as a Historical Phenomenon', *New Left Review*, no. 122, 1980.

—— and Sprague, John, *Paper Stones: A History of Electoral Socialism*, University of Chicago Press, Chicago 1986.

Quermonne, Jean-Louis, *Le Système politique européen*, Montchrestien, Paris 1993.

Rallings, Colin, 'Two Types of Middle Class Labour Voter?', *British Journal of Political Science*, vol. 5, 1975.

—— 'Political Behaviour and Attitudes among the Contemporary Lower Middle Class', in J. Garrard *et al.*, eds, *The Middle Class in Politics*, Saxon House, London 1978.

—— and Thrasher, Michael, 'Old Election Certainties Buried in the Avalanche', *The Sunday Times*, 4 May 1997.

Regini, Marino, 'Introduction: The Past and Future of Social Studies of Labour Movements', in Regini, ed., *The Future of Labour Movements*, Sage, London 1992.

Rey, Henri and Subileau, Françoise, *Les Militants socialistes à l'épreuve du pouvoir*, Presses de la Fondation Nationale des Sciences Politiques, Paris 1991.

Reynaud, Philippe, *Max Weber et les dilemmes de la raison moderne*, Presses Universitaires de France, Paris 1987.

Richards, Andrew, *Down But Not Out: Labour Movements in Late Industrial Societies*, Insituto Juan March, Madrid 1995.

Rohrschneider, Robert, 'How Iron is the Iron Law of Oligarchy? Robert Michels and National Party Delegates in Eleven West European Democracies', *European Journal of Political Research*, no. 25, 1994.

Rosanvallon, Pierre, *La Crise de l'État-Providence*, Seuil, Paris 1981.

Rose, Richard, *Class and Party Divisions: Britain as a Test Case*, University of Strathclyde, Glasgow 1969.

Ross, George, 'The Perils of Politics: French Unions and the Crisis of the 1970s', in Peter Lange *et al.*, eds, *Unions, Change and Crisis: French and Italian Union Strategy and the Political Economy, 1945–1980*, George Allen & Unwin, London 1982.

—— 'The Changing Face of Popular Power in France', in Frances Fox Piven, *Labor Parties in Postindustrial Societies*, Oxford University Press, New York 1992.

—— 'Saying No to Capitalism at the Millennium', in Leo Panitch *et al.*, eds, *Socialist Register 1995*, Merlin Press, London 1995.

—— and Daley, Tony, 'The Wilting of the Rose: The French Socialist Experiment', *Socialist Review*, vol. 16, nos 87–8, 1986.

Rothstein, Bo, *The Social Democratic State: The Swedish Model and the Bureaucratic Problem of Social Reforms*, University of Pittsburgh Press, Pittsburgh, PA and London 1996.

Rovan, Joseph, *Histoire de la social-démocratie allemande*, Seuil, Paris 1978.

Sainsbury, Diane, 'The Swedish Social Democrats and the Legacy of Continuous Reform: Asset or Dilemma?', in Richard Gillespie and William Paterson, eds, *Rethinking Social Democracy in Western Europe*, Frank Cass, London 1993.

Salvati, Michele, 'A View from Italy', *Dissent*, Spring 1999.

Salvik, Bo and Crewe, Ivor, *Decade of Dealignment*, Cambridge University Press, Cambridge 1983.

Sanders, David, 'Voting and the Electorate', in Patrick Dunleavy *et al.*, eds, *Developments in British Politics 5*, Macmillan, London 1997.

Sartori, Giovanni, *Parties and Party Systems*, Cambridge University Press, Cambridge 1976.

Sassoon, Donald, *One Hundred Years of Socialism*, I.B. Tauris, London 1996.
—— 'Socialisme fin-de-siècle. Quelques réflexions historiques', *Actuel Marx*, no. 23, 1998.
—— 'Le nouveau Labour, exemple ou contre-exemple?', *Esprit*, no. 251, 1999.
Scarrow, Susan, 'The "Paradox of Enrolment": Assessing the Costs and Benefits of Party Memberships', *European Journal of Political Research*, no. 25, 1994.
—— *Parties and their Members: Organizing for Victory in Britain and Germany*, Oxford University Press, Oxford 1996.
Scharpf, Fritz W., *Crisis and Choice in European Social Democracy*, trans. Ruth Crowley and Fred Thompson, Cornell University Press, Ithaca, NY and London 1991.
Schuller, Bernd-Joachim, 'The Swedish Third Way: Macroeconomic Policy and Performance', in Lothar Funk, ed., *The Economics and Politics of the Third Way*, LIT, Hamburg 1999.
Scott, John, *Stratification and Power: Structures of Class, Status and Command*, Polity Press, Cambridge 1996.
Seferiades, Seraphim, *Working-Class Movements (1780s–1930s). A European Macro-Historical Analytical Framework and a Greek Case Study*, PhD thesis, Columbia University 1999.
—— 'Social Democratic Strategies in the Twentieth Century', in Ilias Katsoulis, ed., *The 'New' Social Democracy at the Turn of the Century*, Sideris, Athens 2001 (in Greek).
Seidel, Hans, 'Social Partnership and Austro-Keynesianism', in Gunter Bischof and Anton Pelinka, eds, *Austro-Corporatism, Contemporary Austrian Studies*, vol. 4, 1996.
Seiler, Daniel-Louis, *De la comparaison des partis politiques*, Economica, Paris 1986.
—— and Meltz, Romain, 'Autriche', in Guy Hermet *et al.*, eds, *Les Partis politiques en Europe de l'Ouest*, Economica, Paris 1998.
Seyd, Patrick, 'New Parties/New Politics? A Case Study of the British Labour Party', *Party Politics*, vol. 5, no. 3, 1999.
—— and Whiteley, Paul, *Labour's Grass Roots: The Politics of Party Membership*, Clarendon Press, Oxford 1992.
Shaw, Eric, 'Conflict and Cohesion in the British Labour Party', in David Bell and Eric Shaw, eds, *Conflict and Cohesion in Western European Social Democratic Parties*, Pinter, London and New York 1994.
—— *The Labour Party since 1945: Old Labour, New Labour*, Blackwell, Oxford 1996.
Simon-Ekovich, Francine, 'La gauche et l'écologie. Quelle adaptation possible?', in Marc Lazar, ed., *La Gauche en Europe depuis 1945*, Presses Universitaires de France, Paris 1996.
Skrinis, Stavros, 'Electoral Performance and Governmental Power of the European Socialist Parties (1990–1999)', in Stavros Skrinis, George Giannopoulos and Yannis Feleris, *Elections in the European Union 1977–1998*, unpublished paper, Department of Political Science and History, Panteion University, Athens (in Greek), 1999.
Smith, Julie, *Europe's Elected Parliament*, Sheffield Academic Press, Sheffield 1999.
Smith, Rand W., *The Left's Dirty Job: The Politics of Industrial Restructuring in France and Spain*, University of Pittsburgh Press, Pittsburgh, PA 1998.

Soldatos, Panayotis, *Le Système institutionnel et politique des communautés européennes dans un monde en mutation*, Bruylant, Brussels 1989.

Strom, Kaare and Svasand, Lars, 'Political Parties in Norway: Facing the Challenges of a New Society', in Strom and Svasand, eds, *Challenges to Political Parties: The Case of Norway*, University of Michigan Press, Michigan 1997.

Sundberg, Jan, 'Finland: Nationalized Parties, Professionized Organizations' in Richard Katz and Peter Mair, eds., *How Parties Organize*, Sage, London 1994.

Taylor, Andrew, 'Trade Unions and the Politics of Social Democratic Renewal', in Richard Gillespie and William Paterson, eds, *Rethinking Social Democracy in Western Europe*, Frank Cass, London 1993.

Telo, Mario, *Le New Deal européen: la pensée et la politique sociales-démocrates face à la crise des années trente*, Université de Bruxelles, Brussels 1988.

—— 'Les représentations de l'adversaire et compromis social dans la politique de la social-démocratie allemande', AFSP, Fourth Congress, Paris 1992.

—— 'La social-démocratie entre nation et Europe', in Telo, ed., *De la nation à l'Europe*, Bruylant, Brussels 1993.

—— 'Europe et globalisation. Les nouvelles frontières de la social-démocratie européenne', *La Revue Socialiste*, no. 1, 1999.

Therborn, Göran, 'A Unique Chapter in the History of Democracy: The Social Democrats in Sweden', in Klaus Misgeld *et al.*, *Creating Social Democracy: A Century of the Social Democratic Labor Party in Sweden*, Pennsylvania State University Press, Pennsylvania 1992.

—— 'Europe in the Twenty-first Century: The World's Scandinavia?', in Peter Gowan and Perry Anderson, eds, *The Question of Europe*, Verso, London and New York 1997.

Thomas, John Clayton, *The Decline of Ideology in Western Political Parties: A Study of Changing Policy Orientations*, Sage, London 1975.

Thornqvist, Christer, 'The Decentralization of Industrial Relations: The Swedish Case in Comparative Perspective', *European Journal of Industrial Relations*, vol. 5, no. 1, 1999.

Todd, Emmanuel, *L'illusion économique. Essai sur la stagnation des sociétés développées*, Gallimard, Paris 1998.

Tsatsos, Dimitris, 'Des partis politiques européens? Premières réflexions sur l'interprétation de l'article 138a du traité des Maastricht sur les partis', Brussels (no date).

Vakaloulis, Michel, 'Antagonisme social et action collective', in Vakaloulis, ed., *Travail salarié et conflit social*, Presses Universitaires de France, Paris 1999.

—— 'Mouvement social et analyse politique' in Claude Leueveu and Michel Vakaloulis, eds., *Faire mouvement*, PUF, Paris 1998.

Vandenbroucke, Frank, *Globalisation, Inequality and Social Democracy*, Institute for Public Policy Research, London 1998.

Van Praag, Philip, 'Conflict and Cohesion in the Dutch Labour Party', in David Bell and Eric Shaw, eds, *Conflict and Cohesion in Western European Social Democratic Parties*, Pinter, London and New York 1994.

Vanthemsche, Guy, 'Les mots et les actes: 100 ans de pratique réformiste en

Belgique', in Hugue de Le Paige and Pascal Delwit, eds, *Les Socialistes et le pouvoir*, Labor, Brussels 1998.

Vartiainen, Juhana, 'Understanding Swedish Social Democracy: Victims of Success?', *Oxford Review of Economic Policy*, vol. 14, no. 1, 1998.

Verret, Michel, 'Culture ouvrière et politique', in Guy-Patrick Azémar, ed., *Ouvriers, ouvrières: un continent morcelé et silencieux*, Éditions Autrement, série Mutations, no. 126, Paris 1992.

—— *Chevilles ouvrières*, Éditions de l'Atelier, Paris 1995.

Visser, Jelle, 'The Strength of Union Movements in Advanced Capitalist Democracies: Social and Organizational Variations', in Marino Regini, ed., *The Future of Labour Movements*, Sage, London 1992.

Voerman, Gerrit, 'De la confiance à la crise. La gauche aux Pays-Bas depuis les années soixante-dix', in Pascal Delwit and Jean-Michel De Waele, eds, *La Gauche face aux mutations en Europe*, Éditions de l'Université de Bruxelles, Brussels 1993.

—— 'Le Paradis perdu. Les adhérents des partis sociaux-démocrates d'Europe occidentale 1945–1995', in Marc Lazar, ed., *La Gauche en Europe depuis 1945*, Presses Universitaires de France, Paris 1996.

Vogel, Jean, 'De la gauche imaginée à l'imaginaire de gauche', *Politique*, nos 9–10, 1999.

Volgy, Thomas, Schwarz, John and Imwalle, Lawrence, 'In Search of Economic Well-Being: Worker Power and the Effects of Productivity, Inflation, Unemployment and Global Trade on Wages in Ten Wealthy Countries', *American Journal of Political Science*, vol. 40, no. 4, 1996.

Von Beyme, Klaus, *Political Parties in Western Democracies*, Gower, London 1985.

Wallerstein, Michael, Golden, Miriam and Lange, Peter, 'Unions, Employers' Associations and Wage-Setting Institutions in Northern and Central Europe, 1950–1992', *Industrial and Labor Relations Review*, vol. 50, no. 3, 1997.

Ware, Alan, 'Activist–Leader Relations and the Structure of Political Parties: "Exchange" Models and Vote-Seeking Behaviour in Parties', *British Journal of Political Science*, vol. 22, no. 1, 1992.

Weber, Henri, 'Parti socialiste français et *New Labour* britannique: convergences et divergences', *La Revue Socialiste*, no. 1, 1999.

Western, Bruce, 'A Comparative Study of Working-Class Disorganization: Union Decline in Eighteen Advanced Capitalist Countries', *American Sociological Review*, vol. 60, 1995.

—— *Between Class and Market: Postwar Unionization in the Capitalist Democracies*, Princeton University Press, Princeton, NJ 1997.

Winock, Michel, 'Pour une histoire du socialisme en France', *Commentaire*, vol. 11, no. 41, 1988.

—— *Le Socialisme en France et en Europe*, Seuil, Paris 1992.

Wolfe, Alan, 'Has Social Democracy a Future?', *Comparative Politics*, October 1978.

Wolinetz, Steven B., 'The Transformation of Western European Party Systems Revisited', *West European Politics*, vol. 2, no. 1, 1979.

Wright, Erik Olin and Cho, Donmoon, 'State Employment, Class Location and

Ideological Orientation: A Comparative Analysis of the United States and Sweden', *Politics and Society*, vol. 20, no. 2, 1992.

Zolo, Danilo, *Democracy and Complexity*, Polity Press, Cambridge 1992.

Postscript: Social Democracy
after the Transformation

The purpose of this brief postscript is to offer some comments on the prospects for the new social democracy in the light of its most recent evolution, attending to events that occurred after the main text was written.

A Phase of Identity Consolidation?

There can be no doubt that the period of the last fifteen years marks a major turning-point in the history of postwar social democracy. Using (and abusing) the theory (and especially the terminology) of 'electoral realignments', it might be said that we have witnessed a period of social-democratic 'realignment'.[1] This 'realignment' was the compound product of several minor 'dealignments' and 'realignments', affecting the programmatic, ideological, organizational and electoral foundations of the postwar social-democratic edifice. Social-democratic realignment has not proceeded violently; it did not take the form of an earthquake. It was a gradual phenomenon, which does not mean that it was without ruptures and 'critical moments'. Nevertheless, all things considered, it was not a 'protracted' process. The comparative speed with which the new social democracy emerged is indicative of its remarkable ability to respond to new stimuli and electoral challenges: it is testimony to the formidable capacity of political organizations to adapt to new circumstances.[2]

Begun at different dates in different countries, the change gathered in intensity from the second half of the 1980s. And the temperature – particularly the ideological, programmatic and organizational temperature – rose considerably in the second half of the 1990s. During the latter years, the process became more aggressive. Following the phase of *defensive adaptation* (the 1980s), a phase of *offensive adaptation* set in, especially in the second half of the 90s (see above, Chapters 9 and 13).

Today, the new social democracy is installed and the inherited map has been redrawn. It is difficult to tell whether the period of transformation is over. In all likelihood, change will continue for a long time, albeit at a slow and discreet tempo. Possibly it will affect some programmatic or policy areas that have hitherto remained untouched.[3] These will not be identical from country to country. Even so, regardless of any subsequent evolution, everything suggests that the new social democracy has achieved a *certain degree of stability*. Social democracy seems to have discovered a new equilibrium – and a certain inertia – following the fever of the 'great' transformation. With the main ideological, programmatic, organizational and sociological characteristics of the new social-democratic profile now in place, short-term factors will henceforth have priority. Social democracy is no longer a force 'in transition'. What (in realignment theory) is called an 'ordinary' period is beginning, or rather has already begun. Thus, after a phase in which social democracy had to construct, assume and proclaim a new identity, after the gradual (and occasionally abrupt) reorganization of 'old' equilibria, consolidation of past results will be the successor tendency. The present phase is one of consolidation and 'minor adjustments'.

An Example of Consolidation: Labour's Victory in June 2001

Wolfgang Merkel has identified four social-democratic 'ways': New Labour's 'market-oriented way'; the 'consensus-oriented way to more market' pursued by the Dutch government; Sweden's '(reformed) welfare state way'; and the 'statist way' of the *gauche plurielle* in France.[4] In June 2001, British voters approved New Labour's 'market-oriented way' by a comfortable margin, returning Tony Blair to power.

According to Pierre Martin, it is invariably the case that 'when a government succeeds on a consensual issue [e.g. management of the economy], it obtains its best electoral result at the end of its first mandate'.[5] Labour's victory in June 2001 conforms to this logic perfectly.

In 1997, following the long rule of a 'strong-arm' Conservatism, the Labour Party adopted a highly centrist position. Ian Budge's analysis of Labour's 1997 election manifesto is illuminating here:

> Labour moves sharply rightwards from 1992 and for the first time in postwar history shows a preponderance of right-wing positions over left-wing ones. . . . Labour were far from whole-heartedly endorsing Thatcherite positions. A fair amount of 'clear blue water' still separated the Conservative position from their own. Nevertheless, compared with the Liberal Democrats, Labour moved rightwards and 'leapfrogged' over them for only the second time in the postwar period. In relative terms, Labour became the most centrist party.[6]

No doubt New Labour's occupation of the centre was in fact simply domination 'in a field of force created by the Conservatives' (just as the centripetal impulse of the Conservatives after the Second World War occurred 'in a field of force' created by the social-democratic agenda).[7] It remains the case that this *centripetal* position proved electorally profitable. In the context of an across-the-board advance, Labour made its greatest breakthrough among the middle classes. This was the index of a marked class realignment (see above, Chapter 7). And as Geoffrey Evans, Anthony Heath and Clive Payne have stressed, 'the dip in class voting to its lowest level in 1997 is certainly consistent with Labour's recent move to the centre'.[8]

In 2001, profiting from the Conservatives' 'rightist' turn and Europhobic profile, Labour consolidated its domination in the centre.[9] Such was its occupation of the centre that the Liberal Democrats were once again generally regarded as a centre-left party, positioning themselves (program-matically at least) to the left of New Labour. Moreover, the priority accorded 'left-wing' themes (health, education, public transport) in Labour's election campaign was highly relative: recourse to the private sector (via public-private partnerships) will introduce 'private companies into the inner sanctum of the public realm, the NHS and state schools',[10] and is even set to activate 'the second generation of British privatizations' in decidedly atypical fashion.[11] Furthermore, the new Blair government will maintain its course as regards economic policy and taxation, with Labour promising not to increase direct taxation on individuals and companies. Given this, it is not surprising that the June 2001 election confirms, and in part magnifies, the class realignment observed in 1997. Scrutiny of the results by socio-professional category indicates that New Labour advanced moderately among the middle classes and fell back markedly among manual strata, particularly the DE working-class category traditionally ranged solidly behind Labour.[12] It should be noted that the Conservative Party and the Liberal Democrats made their most important gains among the C2 and DE categories, particularly the latter, which used to be the central pillar of Labour's 'natural' electorate.[13]

Electoral developments in 2001 largely confirm tendencies that were strongly in evidence in 1997. They simultaneously confirm the novel position occupied by Tony Blair's party in the space of partisan competition and continuity in the new coalition of voters that supports this party. In this respect, the 2001 election was one of *consolidation* for New Labour. Yet this election of consolidation has created a new political axis that partly redefines the political game in Great Britain. New Labour's domination of the electoral agenda, spectacular during the campaign itself, certainly consolidates the neoliberal paradigm (hence the support given it by a large part of the British economic establishment). At the same time, however, it seals the ascendancy of a modified version of that paradigm. In future, the Conservatives will in all probability be constrained to submit to it.

More generally, the June 2001 British general election confirms three theses developed at length in this work:

1. Socialist and social-democratic parties are increasingly sustained by a vote from the middle classes, particularly the salaried middle strata. This enables them to compensate for the damage done by a certain working-class disaffection and the reduction in working-class numbers in the population.
2. Since the working class is no longer the privileged sociological marker of social-democratic electorates, the latter are now constructed on the basis of a profoundly inter-classist format, by far the most inter-classist in

the whole history of social democracy. As a consequence, the class character and *social cohesion* of these electorates have been significantly attenuated.

3. The mediation of political factors between class structure and the act of voting is currently of greater importance. Political strategy and governmental performance are central factors in explaining the electoral behaviour of social classes.[14]

Thus, the question 'are voters getting the message?',[15] must unequivocally be answered in the affirmative. The catch-all social format of social-democratic electorates is consistent with the catch-all format of social-democratic parties' ideological and programmatic discourse. Voters today are quite different from those of the 1950s and 60s. They are beginning to take party rhetoric at its word. To a considerable extent, the behaviour of social classes is explained by political factors.

The New Social-Democratic Identity: Towards an 'Adjusted' Balance?

In 1999, Ian Budge reckoned it likely that Labour, having demonstrated that the country was safe in its hands, would commence 'a cautious trek back to [its] ideological home', reverting to 'more traditional positions'.[16] Can this assessment be generalized? The extreme variety of national situations dictates the utmost caution.

Even so, certain indices point in this direction. In a still very recent past, when socialists had to fulfil the Maastricht criteria or prove their 'modernity' and 'managerial competence' (and rid themselves of the image of 'incompetence'), a posture of 'markets against politics' was adopted in a very assertive, and frequently aggressive, fashion. European governments (left and right) adopted restrictive budgetary policies and everywhere pledged to cut back the state (these policies proved all the more restrictive in that their effects were compounded by being implemented well-nigh simultaneously, in the framework fixed by the convergence criteria). In particular, social-democratic governments in the EU countries, bound as they were by an extremely powerful set of European juridical instruments (legitimized by the relevant treaties), pursued *market-making* policies (systematic suppression of national barriers to free competition), as opposed to *market-correcting* policies.[17] However, it would appear that the policy mix of a number of social-democratic governments has gradually become more composite – at once pro-enterprise and anti-exclusion.[18] We are thus witnessing a *minor* and *moderate* 'adjustment', aspects of which (notably in social policy) depart from neoliberal philosophy. This adjustment also involves a certain 'return of active government',[19] which goes beyond the logic of 'regulating deregulation'. In addition, it contains signs of a more aggressive approach to European construction – witness the proposals of Gerhard Schröder and Lionel Jospin.

It would therefore be logical for the new phase – the *consolidation* of the new social-democratic identity – to be marked by an 'adjusted' balance, social democracy's centre of gravity being situated a shade more to the left than in the previous phase, which was marked by centrist (or, as some had it, 'rightist') *drift*.[20] It is usually through a *minor* step 'backwards' that the *major* step 'forward' is legitimated and that large political formations, containing very diverse tendencies, are stabilized and strengthened. A certain reactivation of *counterbalancing cultures* (which does not necessarily betoken the reactivation or emergence of elites to challenge the currently dominant elites), is thus not unlikely. Although weakened, the 'old' social democracy remains entrenched within the shell of 'new' social democracy.[21] As a result of its options and renunciations, social democracy seems, as it were, to have reached a *border* in identity terms (see above, Chapter 17), which even the leaderships that are most 'right-wing' and most attached to the neoliberal 'rebirth' of social democracy dare not cross without providing compensation.[22] Were they to, they would imperil the very viability of the modernizing project.

A more radical move, an *isolated drift* (oriented to the left), certainly cannot be excluded in one country or another, particularly after a humiliating electoral defeat. But most probably, moves to the left, *if they occur*, will be rather *limited* in scope. Consequently, except in the case of an extreme external or internal shock, they will not be such as to call into question the essential distinguishing characteristics of the new social-democratic identity. Since social democracy is in a sense the party of 'two parallel universes',[23] it is highly likely that in the near future we shall observe *two parallel 'logics'* operating *simultaneously*: a logic 'pushing' social democracy to integrate itself further into the paradigm of economic liberalism; and another logic adjusting this paradigm by instilling into it elements derived from a largely non- or anti-liberal perspective.

The Paradox of the New Social Democracy

If the lot of political parties is change, the lot of contemporary social-democratic parties is great tactical and strategic flexibility. The new structure of social-democratic organization (characterized by enhancement and reinforcement of the leadership in tandem with its weakening, loss of influence by the party's traditional bureaucracy, loosening of the trade-union link, a managerial type of intra-organizational culture, a membership that is smaller, less oriented and less 'orienting', decline in 'identity incentives' and strong integrating links) facilitates flexibility and the policy of adjustments. This strategic and tactical flexibility is a *major identity characteristic*, on a par with the adoption of a moderate neoliberal philosophy. At the same time, the ideologically and programmatically catch-all format of social-democratic parties leaves open several possibilities, and legitimates a number of minor turns, whether to the left or the right. The decline of the 'party as a faith', in favour of the 'party as a tool',[24] and the decline of the social-democratic 'way of organizing politics' (to borrow a formula from Joel Krieger),[25] increase the potential for zigzagging between the 'two parallel universes' that make up the reality of contemporary social democracy. *But by the same token they reduce social democracy's capacity to choose between them.* Contemporary social democracy can position itself further to the left or further to the right, but it seems ill-equipped to advance a hegemonic project (capitalist, anti-capitalist, reformist or whatever), and to influence ideas, values and policies in contemporary societies *strategically.*[26]

If the objective of contemporary socialism is to promote solidarity, then the question is: Will it be in a position to promote the logic of solidarity without a policy for growth;[27] without weighing on the inegalitarian effects of globalization through co-ordinated, 'voluntarist' transnational action; without strengthening its electoral, organizational and ideological links with the popular space and its trade-union or other organizations; and without succeeding in striking a new balance between the two universes that comprise its reality today, a balance that currently clearly favours the market to the obvious detriment of the logic of solidarity?

Without an adequate response to these difficult questions, contemporary social democracy will remain trapped in the great historical paradox of partisan competition in Europe today: the old class parties – the very 'old' social democracy – successfully furthered policies of class compromise, whereas the current, profoundly inter-classist parties (oriented towards the centre and the middle ground) are incapable of conjugating the interests of the upper classes with those of the lower classes. Capitalism actually benefited considerably from the *trente glorieuses.* But even so,

> capitalist interests accepted more and more constraints: nationalisation, progressive taxation, the regulation of labour standards, the dynamic growth of a welfare state which virtually excluded such major potential consumption areas as health, education and social insurance from the reach of profit-making.[28]

Today, in contrast, the 'new' social-democratic parties are even *incapable of organizing their programmatic inter-classism into a coherent experiment.* In particular, they are incapable of imposing a compromise that genuinely has something in it for the lower classes. 'Old' social democracy, so belittled today, in large part implemented policies 'beyond Left and Right' (precisely because it was a force of the Left). Current social democracy, on the other hand, voluntarily located as it is in this ill-defined space 'beyond Left and Right', would not appear to be in a position to invent (other than in anaemic form) a genuine 'third way' (beyond Left and Right), or a 'middle way' (between Left and Right). This is indeed the great paradox of the various Third Ways, practical or theoretical. In this respect, the formulation of René Cuperus, a perspicuous analyst of social democracy, appears to be too optimistic: 'The same way as the old social democracy acted as the civilising and taming power of industrial capitalism, the new paradigm of the Third Way must be designed to be the civilising and taming power of the global info-capitalism'.[29]

Let us end this text as we began it. To stick with the terminology of electoral realignments, the cycle of a realignment begins with one realignment and ends with another.[30] As of now, the new social-democratic identity can be regarded as solid, stable and durable – that is, until a new realignment occurs. Following its great transformation (which was 'great' because it was not exclusively ideological-programmatic), contemporary social democracy is no longer a political force 'in transition'. It is here and it is here to stay – which does not preclude adjustments to the left or the right. Anthony Giddens would say, 'third way politics . . . isn't an ephemeral set of ideas'.[31] What will certainly prove to be less ephemeral is the new 'minimalist' model of social democracy.

Gerassimos Moschonas
14 June 2001

Notes

1. On the theory of electoral realignments, see Pierre Martin's recent book *Comprendre les évolutions électorales: la théorie des réalignements revisitée*, Presses de Sciences Po, Paris 2000. Some of what follows draws on this work.
2. See Thomas Rochon, 'Adaptation in the Dutch Party System: Social Change and Party Response', in Birol Yesilada, ed., *Comparative Political Parties and Party Elites*, University of Michigan Press, Ann Arbor 1999, p. 120.
3. See, by way of example, New Labour's policy for the modernization of public services, which allots an important role to the private sector.
4. Wolfgang Merkel, 'The Third Ways of Social Democracy', in René Cuperus, Karl Duffek and Johannes Kandel, eds, *Multiple Third Ways: European Social Democracy Facing the Twin Revolution of Globalisation and the Knowledge Society*, Friedrich Ebert Stiftung, Amsterdam 2001, pp. 38–56; reprinted in Anthony Giddens, *The Global Third Way Debate*, Polity Press, Cambridge 2001, pp. 50–73.
5. Martin, *Comprendre les évolutions électorales*, p. 110.
6. Ian Budge, 'Party Policy and Ideology. Reversing the 1950s?', in Geoffrey Evans and Pippa Norris, eds, *Critical Elections: British Parties and Voters in Long-Term Perspective*, Sage, London 1999, p. 6.
7. Richard Heffernan, *New Labour and Thatcherism: Political Change in Britain*, Macmillan, London 2000, pp. 159, 169.
8. Geoffrey Evans, Anthony Heath and Clive Payne, 'Class: Labour as a Catch-All Party?', in Evans and Norris, eds, *Critical Elections*, p. 100.
9. '[F]or the first time in my life', Tony Benn has written, 'the public was on the left of Labour' (*Observer*, 10 June 2001).
10. Jonathan Freedland, *Guardian*, 23 May 2001.
11. Philippe Marlière, 'Tony Blair, le "seul conservateur crédible"', *Mouvements*, no. 17, September 2001.
12. According to the ICM/*Observer* statistics (which are not wholly comparable with those used in this book), New Labour progressed within the middle classes to the tune of 2 per cent (categories AB and C1), whereas it fell back within the

358 POSTSCRIPT

C2 category by 3 per cent (especially among skilled manual workers) and even further within the DE category (minus 7 per cent). See the *Observer*, 10 June 2001.

13. The Conservative vote increased 6 per cent, and the Liberal Democrat vote 5 per cent, in the DE category (*Observer*, 10 June 2001).
14. This was dramatically demonstrated in another recent election, in Greece in April 2000. PASOK's modernization policy, constructed around Greek membership of the European Union and programmatic and political priorities inspired by the neoliberal paradigm, strengthened PASOK's influence among higher social strata and an important section of capital, as well as intellectuals traditionally distrustful of Andreas Papandreou's 'nationalist' and 'demagogic' discourse. Thus, the PASOK of Costas Simitis has gradually become the party of the 'contentment society', while retaining a significant influence among disadvantaged sections of the population, even if it is significantly reduced today. At the same time, the turn of the conservatives of New Democracy to a more 'social' policy has enabled them to strengthen their penetration of popular strata traditionally close to PASOK. Thus, the marked ideological and programmatic convergence of PASOK and New Democracy has yielded an equally marked sociological convergence of their respective electorates. As in Great Britain, only more so, politics has significantly influenced class voting. Greece in the twentieth century is an exemplary case: the behaviour of social classes closely correlates with the evolution of political rhetoric. Thus, the peculiar class dealignment that occurred there should be explained mainly on political and not sociological grounds (see Gerassimos Moschonas, 'The Path of Modernization: PASOK and European Integration', *Journal of Southern Europe and the Balkans*, vol. 3, no. 1, 2001, pp. 16–22).
15. Evans, Heath and Payne, 'Class: Labour as a Catch-All Party?', p. 96.
16. Budge, 'Party Policy and Ideology: Reversing the 1950s?', p. 7.
17. Fritz Scharpf, *Gouverner l'Europe*, Presses de Sciences Po, Paris 2000, pp. 193, 197.
18. René Cuperus, 'The New World and the Social-Democratic Response', in Cuperus *et al.*, eds, *Multiple Third Ways*, p. 163.
19. On the various 'third ways', see Merkel, 'The Third Ways of Social Democracy'.
20. The *gauche plurielle* in France must be reckoned a minor 'semi-exception' in the universe of neo-liberalized socialism. The discourse and, in part, policy of the government should not readily be classified as 'neoliberal', contrary to our analysis above (see Chapter 10), which was based on partial data. This analysis must therefore be qualified somewhat. Certainly, Lionel Jospin has not made the rupture with neoliberalism that he promised prior to coming to power. And it is also certainly the case that his policy in large part obeys the same fundamentally restrictive macroeconomic principles as the rest of Europe. Nevertheless, the policy of the 'plural Left' has yielded an important raft of social measures, strengthening (especially on the issues of working hours, youth unemployment, and extreme poverty) state intervention (while pursuing a policy of state withdrawal from the more 'classical' spheres where it traditionally intervened, as demonstrated by privatization policy). At the same time, the Jospin government has preserved the welfare state overall, and finds itself in the European and international vanguard with its proposals for regulating globalization (e.g. political steering of the International Monetary Fund and the World Bank, the proposal for European economic government). Unquestionably, there is no alternative social democracy in France. There is, however, an *alternative ideological* atmosphere, a different set of expectations both within the Jospin

government and the trade-union movement, as well as what in France is called 'the left of the left' obviously. This *alternative atmosphere* is clearly visible in the discourse of the French government and in certain aspects of its activity. There is a search for mechanisms which, within the same economic paradigm, aim to reduce the fluctuations in economic activity and mass unemployment, enhance the role of unions, and limit the social depredations of liberal policy (by means of an active social policy). To employ a technical term, the French left attributes roles of greater significance, real and symbolic, to 'secondary figures'. By comparison with the pervasive neoliberalism, every now and then it comes up with an innovatory move (35-hour week, youth employment scheme, measures for the 'excluded'). Is this so important? Possibly not. And yet this alternative current should not simply be attributed to the round of political and institutional idioms, of which each country has its own. Gropingly, the French left is searching for a different interpretative order within the European socialist and social-democratic family.

21. ' "Old" Labour remains entrenched within the shell of "New" Labour', according to Richard Heffernan, from whom we have borrowed the phrase (*New Labour and Thatcherism*, p. 172). What has been observed with respect to the British Labour Party as 'some return to the language of redistribution and fairness' (Leo Panitch, Colin Leys and David Coates, 'Epilogue', in L. Panitch and C. Leys, *The End of Parliamentary Socialism*, second edition, Verso, London 2001, p. 285) is also valid for the majority of social democratic parties.

22. Let us not forget that the conflict over redistribution remains central in political debate. On this question, see, among others, John Callaghan, *The Retreat of Social Democracy*, Manchester University Press, Manchester and New York 2000, p. 212.

23. Jonathan Freedland, *Guardian*, 23 May 2001.

24. On these terms, see Rosa Mulé, *Political Parties, Games and Redistribution*, Cambridge University Press, Cambridge 2001, p. 47.

25. 'New Labour has left behind more than politics and ideology: *it has rejected a way of organizing politics*', according to Joel Krieger in *British Politics in the Global Age: Can Social Democracy Survive?*, Polity Press, Cambridge 1999, p. 37.

26. As was the case with the Swedish SAP and the 'social-democratic image of society' it created; and as was the case with Thatcherite Conservatism and the 'conservative image' of society it generated.

27. For an excellent analysis of social-democratic economic policy and the conditions for growth, see Ton Notermans, *Money, Markets and the State: Social Democratic Politics since 1918*, Cambridge University Press, Cambridge 2000. Ton Noterman's perspective according to which '. . . the success or failure of the social democratic program depends crucially on the *institutional and political ability* to combine growth with a fair degree of price stability' (ibid., p. 3, emphasis added) reinforces many of the conclusions reached in our study.

28. Colin Crouch, 'The Parabola of Working Class Politics', in Andrew Gamble and Tony Wright, eds, *The New Social Democracy*, Blackwell, Oxford 1999, p. 75.

29. René Cuperus, 'The New World and the Social-Democratic Response', p. 168.

30. Martin, *Comprendre les évolutions électorales*, p. 61.

31. Anthony Giddens, *The Third Way and its Critics*, Polity Press, Cambridge 2000, p. vii.

References

Budge, Ian, 'Party Policy and Ideology: Reversing the 1950s?', in Geoffrey Evans and Pippa Norris, eds., *Critical Elections, British Parties and Voters in Long-Term Perspective*, Sage, London 1999.

Callaghan, John, *The Retreat of Social Democracy*, Manchester University Press, Manchester and New York 2000.

Crouch, Colin, 'The Parabola of Working Class Politics', in Andrew Gamble and Tony Wright, eds., *The New Social Democracy*, Blackwell, Oxford 1999.

Cuperus, René, 'The New World and the Social-Democratic Response', in René Cuperus, Karl Duffek and Johannes Kandel, eds., *Multiple Third Ways, European Social Democracy facing the Twin Revolution of Globalisation and the Knowledge Society*, Friedrich-Ebert-Stiftung, Amsterdam 2001.

Evans, Geoffrey, Heath, Anthony, Payne, Clive, 'Class: Labour as a Catch-All Party?', in Geoffrey Evans and Pippa Norris, eds., *Critical Elections, British Parties and Voters in Long-Term Perspective*, Sage, London 1999.

Giddens, Anthony, *The Third Way and its Critics*, Polity Press, Cambridge 2000.

Heffernan, Richard, *New Labour and Thatcherism, Political Change in Britain*, Macmillan, London 2000.

Krieger, Joel, *British Politics in the Global Age: Can Social Democracy Survive?*, Polity Press, Cambridge 1999.

Marlière, Philippe, 'Tony Blair, le "seul conservateur crédible"', in *Mouvements*, no. 17, September 2001.

Martin, Pierre, *Comprendre les évolutions électorales, La théorie des réalignements revisitée*, Presses de Sciences Po, Paris 2000.

Merkel, Wolfgang, 'The Third Ways of Social Democracy', in René Cuperus, Karl Duffek and Johannes Kandel, eds., *Multiple Third Ways, European Social Democracy facing the Twin Revolution of Globalisation and the Knowledge Society*, Friedrich-Ebert-Stiftung, Amsterdam 2001.

Moschonas, Gerassimos, 'The Path of Modernization: PASOK and European Integration', *Journal of Southern Europe and the Balkans*, vol. 3, no. 1, 2001.

Mulé, Rosa, *Political Parties, Games and Redistribution*, Cambridge University Press, Cambridge 2001.

Notermans, Ton, *Money, Markets and the State: Social Democratic Politics since 1918*, Cambridge University Press, Cambridge 2000.

Panitch, Leo, Leys, Colin and Coates, David 'Epilogue: The Dénouement', in Leo Panitch and Colin Leys, *The End of Parliamentary Socialism, From New Left to New Labour*, second edition, Verso, London 2001.

Rochon, Thomas, 'Adaptation in the Dutch Party System: Social Change and Party Response', in Birol Yesilada, ed., *Comparative Political Parties and Party Elites*, University of Michigan Press, Ann Arbor 1999.

Scharpf, Fritz, *Gouverner l'Europe*, Presses de Sciences Po, Paris, 2000.

Index